# THE C

**includes**
**LIGHT THROUGH PRISON BARS**
**and Update**

*God's*

*Blessing*

*Noel Procter*

Omnibus edition 2001
Reproduced from the original typesetting
of the single volume editions.

This reprinted edition 2003.
Reprinted 2004, 2005

ISBN 1 84291 013 2

Published for Noel Proctor by agreement with
KINGSWAY COMMUNICATIONS LTD
Lottbridge Drove, Eastbourne BN23 6NT, England.
Email: books@kingsway.co.uk

Book design and production for the publishers by
Bookprint Creative Services, P.O. Box 827, BN21 3YJ, England.
Printed in Great Britain.

# The Cross Behind Bars

**JENNY COOKE**

**KINGSWAY PUBLICATIONS**
EASTBOURNE

**THIS BOOK** is dedicated to the
glory of God, that the
Son of God may be glorified.

# Acknowledgements

I would like to thank the following people:

Archdeacon Percy Ashford—Chaplain General
Peter Marshall and Ian Porter, both of the Prison Department
(Home Office)
Norman Brown—Former Governor of Strangeways
Bill Stanton
Alison Powell and Elisabeth Pilz
My parents, John and Eunice Appleby

My thanks are due most of all to Noel and Norma Proctor for
their wonderful co-operation; and to my husband, Francis,
without whose help and support this book would not have
been written.

# *Contents*

## PART FIVE: STRANGEWAYS

## Prologue

# Belfast: December 23 1930

Tom Proctor propped up his wife Edith against the pillows in the narrow double bed. He waited a moment by the bedside in case she wanted anything, but she turned her head away. He sighed, squared his shoulders and walked stiffly out of the room. She hardly noticed he had gone. She half lay there, quite still, except for the clenching and unclenching of her hands under the sheet.

There was a banging in the parlour below and she heard someone say, 'Shhh, don't disturb our Edith.' Then the parlour curtains were drawn and she craned forward a little. They'd all be drawn now at this end of the street. All except hers upstairs.

There was a lump in her throat so big it hurt to swallow. She smoothed out the sheet over the bedspread in case anyone came up, but no one did.

The banging had started again and a shuffling as if people were tip-toeing down the passage. She heard the front door open. Suddenly she got out of bed and went to the window. She rubbed the glass and peered out. She saw them carrying the coffin. The lump lurched into her throat and made her cheeks hurt. She stuffed her fist into her mouth. 'Stanley,' she cried, but the word wouldn't come.

Oh no! There was Nanny Walker running across the street. She must have seen her at the window. Edith arranged herself back into the bed and swallowed the lump again.

There were voices on the stairs and footsteps. Then Tom was in the doorway. 'Edie, love,' he said and stood there, his body sagging against the doorpost. He crept into the room, carrying the new baby in his arms and placed him on the sheet next to her hands. Clumsily he patted her arm and then stumbled out.

The baby stirred and whimpered. Edith arranged his shawl and put her little finger in his mouth to suckle and he quietened. She made no move to pick him up and cuddle him. He lay quiet on the sheet, next to her empty hands.

After a long time they came back. The coffin had gone. Tom came upstairs and behind him a man she scarcely knew.

'This is the Rector, love,' said Tom.

'Hello, Mrs Proctor.'

Edith looked at him and then looked away. She nodded and put her hands under the bedclothes again.

'So this is your new baby,' said the Rector. He looked round for a chair and then sat on the edge of the bed.

She didn't answer.

'What are you going to call him?'

Tom leaned forward, 'We haven't quite decided yet.'

The Rector tried again, 'The service went well. Lovely showing of neighbours. I've never seen so many Catholics at a Protestant funeral.'

'They're very good,' said Tom.

There was silence in the room. Then Edith looked up at the Rector and he held her glance. He leaned forward and took her hand. It was cold. He spoke gently, 'Stanley cannot come to you now, Mrs Proctor, but one day you can go to him.'

Still she said nothing.

'Try and thank God that he's given you another baby to care for.' Edith pulled her hand away. If the new baby hadn't come when he did, she could have saved Stanley. She could have nursed him through his diphtheria. She could have...she shrugged and turned away. What was the use? The baby had come. She looked at the Rector again, nodded slightly and then looked away out of the window.

After a while the Rector got up and Tom hovered after him and showed him downstairs. When Tom came back he sat on the bed next to Edith and put his arm round her.

'It were kind of him to come.'

'Yes,' she said.

'It's not as if we go to church.'

'No.'

'Some of the lads from the Site came you know. They'll have to make up the time.'

She made no reply.

He hesitated and then said, 'Look, love, what are we going to call the new baby?'

'Stanley,' she whispered.

'No, no. Stanley's...gone, love.' He picked up the baby and rocked him. The baby's head lolled back and Tom shifted, trying to get his hand cradled round the back of the baby's neck. 'We've got to give the baby a name, love. He's our son too.'

Edith stared at the baby.

Tom leaned forward. 'I thought of a name on the way back from the cemetery. We was passing the corner shop and I noticed the Christmas tree in the window.'

Edith bit her lip. Stanley had been looking forward to Christmas so much.

Tom went on, 'We could call the baby Noel.'

She looked at the baby and pulled the shawl back from his face a little. Noel.

'Just as you like,' she said.

# PART ONE:

'Remember the hole from which you were dug'

1930 -1970

## Chapter One

# The Blurred Photograph

Noel waited in the parlour doorway. His mother was standing in the middle of the room gazing at the photo on the wall.

'Mum,' he said.

She didn't hear him. She stood, stock still, her back to Noel, staring at the photo. Noel crept in a little further until he was standing almost beside her.

'Mum,' he said and tugged at her. She put out her hand and found his, but still she didn't look at him.

'Mum!'

'Yes,' she said at last, in a voice so quiet he could hardly hear her.

'Can I go out and play?'

But she turned back to the photo and seemed not to hear him. He stared up at the photo as well.

A little boy smiled back at him. He was always smiling. Once when Noel had stuck his tongue out at the photo, the little boy still grinned back. His mum had seen him and smacked his bottom. 'Don't you pull a face at our Stanley,' she'd said.

Noel gazed up at the photo. If he screwed up his eyes the photo looked better, but usually it looked fuzzy all round the edges.

'Mum!' he said, tugging her again. 'Come on!'

'Coming,' she said and he bounced out of the parlour.

He ran down the corridor to the back room and burst in. His dad was sitting snoozing by the fire. Noel picked up a paper aeroplane, flicked it hard and watched it land right on his dad's chest. With a start, his dad woke up and flung it away.

'What yer up to now?' he shouted. 'Go and help yer mum in

the front parlour. There's Nanny Walker expected for her order.'

But at that moment his mother came into the back room and marched over to his dad. She was holding out her old purse.

'I've no housekeeping left and it's only Tuesday!' she said.

'Hum,' said Dad.

'Can't yer give me a bit more?'

'What do yer run that shop for in t'front parlour? Can't you get summat from t'till?'

'No I can't.'

'Well I've no more. That's flat.'

'You've enough for Guinness with the lads. You'll be off down to that pub in half an hour, if I know you, drinking our home away.'

Her face was red. Noel had never seen it so red before.

His dad clenched his fist. 'Aw, shut up, woman. You're warm and dry aren't you!'

'Nanny Walker's got new curtains. She told me. *We* need new ones.'

'Shut up.'

Noel looked at the curtains. They were the same as usual.

'Look, Edith, I do my best on the Site.'

'I know.'

Suddenly Noel ran forward from the safety of the doorway. 'Mum!'

'What now? What you listening for?'

Noel hopped up and down. 'Mum, you know Eddie? Well his brother sells newspapers in their street. Let me do it down here,' and his eyes glistened in the firelight.

Dad stared hard at the fire, 'He's too young, Edith. He's only seven.'

But his mum leaned forward. 'Could you? Could you do it?'

'Yes, Mum.'

'All right, son. But you'll have to give me the money.'

'Yes, Mum.'

She ruffled his hair. 'I'll be proud of you yet, son.'

Noel rushed out, whooping with delight. 'I'll go and see about it now,' he called.

When he got back Mum wasn't in the back room. Only his

dad was there, searching for his flat cap.

'Where's Mum?'

Dad sighed. 'In the parlour. At it again.'

Noel ran through and then stopped in the parlour doorway. There were a few groceries on a side table and a small cash box.

Mum was standing and gazing at the photo on the wall. Noel looked at the photo of 'Our Stanley'. The out-of-focus snap stared back at him, the golden curls for ever nodding. But today she turned to him straight away.

'Did you get the job?'

'Yes. Start next Monday.'

'Well done!' she said and turned back to gaze at her photo. Noel retreated to the passageway. He didn't quite know what to do. He flicked the paper aeroplane and it fell on the steep stairs. He wished he had golden curls.

So Noel got into the habit of getting up early before he went to school and selling newspapers in the streets of the tough end of Belfast. It was a habit that stuck.

When he was fourteen and into his last year at school he managed to get another job selling newspapers on the wards of the Royal Victoria Hospital. One evening he got home later than usual. He crept down the passage and sidled through the back room door. If he stuck his nose in his homework, maybe his dad wouldn't notice. But no sooner was he at the back room door, than he heard his dad's voice. 'That you, Noel?'

His heart sank. 'Yes, Dad.'

'Where've yer been?'

'Oh...messing about, selling papers.'

'Where?'

'With the lads. We was only on the way back from my newspaper round. You know,' and his voice trailed off.

His dad hauled himself out of the fireside chair. 'Oh yer were, were yer!' and his voice rose. 'Well let me tell you a thing or two young lad.'

As if in slow motion Noel watched his dad roll up his shirt sleeves. The tattoo on his forearm stood out blue and bulging in the firelight.

Noel shrank back against the wall. His dad was no great

height, but he seemed to tower over him, the muscles gleaming through his open shirt.

'I weren't an Army P.T. instructor in the last war for nothing!'

'No, Dad.'

His dad pulled Noel from the wall. 'Stand up. I'll make a man of you yet. Skinny little devil.'

Noel stood up as straight as he could, and fixed his eye just above the hob over the fire. If only the kettle would boil and Mum'd come in and make a cup of tea.

'Where've you been?'

'With Davey and Tommy and the others.'

'What for?'

'Messing about.'

'Messing about, eh! And what happened to Davey last week?'

Noel hung his head and his dad went on. 'Police were round at their house, weren't they?'

Noel bit his lip.

'Weren't they?'

'Yes, Dad.'

'Yes. His dad told me in the pub.'

'Yes, Dad, but Davey only pinched a bike. He weren't going to keep it.'

His dad began to shout. 'I don't care whether he meant to give it back or not, he's in trouble.' He began to unbuckle his belt. 'Don't you bring no trouble to this house.' His belt came off and he held his trousers up with the other hand.

Noel stared at the belt. 'We didn't do anything today. Honest, Dad. It were only a bit o' fun.'

His dad lowered his head and pushed it forward. He gave Noel a shake and the belt flopped at Noel's side.

'Remember the hole from which you were dug, lad! Remember it.'

'Yes, Dad.' There was a short pause.

His dad sighed. 'I'll let yer off this time,' and he put the belt on again and moved back to the fire. Suddenly he swung round and Noel jumped.

'Don't bring any trouble on this house.'

'No, Dad.'

'And don't be late tomorrow.'

After that Noel was glad to get on with his homework. They all had tea and then he began to edge away upstairs. His dad called after him, 'Where you going?'

'To get my Bible passage.'

'Yer what?'

'Mr Ewart told us to learn a passage and recite it at Sunday School next week. We copied it down.'

'Oh.' His dad turned back to the fire.

Noel sprang upstairs two at a time. He ploughed through the passage. Boring, he thought. 'John 6, verse 37.' He said the words in a soft voice, imitating the Rector. But it wasn't much fun with no one else to giggle with. He went and looked out of the window. 'He who comes to me, I will in no wise cast out.' He chanted it to the chimney pots and to the sloping roofs... '"He who comes to me...", oh, I know it now,' and he belted downstairs again. 'Dad!'

'He's gone to the pub,' said his mum, who was ironing in the corner.

Noel slouched against the big armchair. 'I think I'll leave Sunday School.'

'What?'

'Well, you don't go to church, so I'm not going....' He never finished, because his mum interrupted.

'You're going.'

'But...'

'You're *going*. That's that.'

Noel made a kicking movement at the chair. 'Well, I'm not going after the Passing-Out Parade.'

'The what?'

'Confirmation. I'm not going after.'

'We'll see about that. Anyway you're going till you leave school.'

His mum looked at him and smiled faintly. 'I suppose you could join the Boys Brigade Band instead.' She handed a pile of ironed sheets to Noel and he took them to the bottom of the stairs. 'I'd better get you some "longs" when you leave school in the summer. You can't go to work with short trousers and knobbly knees.'

'Longs!' He rushed towards the back door. 'Smashing,

Mum!' ·

'Where you going now?'

But just then they heard a knock at the front door.

'Who's that?' cried Noel, rushing back.

His mum paused in the middle of folding a pillowcase. 'I'll answer it.' She went down the hallway. 'It can't be yer dad. It's too early.' Noel bounded up behind her and put his head almost over her shoulder as she opened the door.

'Why, Mr Ewart. How do you do?'

'Hello, Mrs Proctor. And Noel.'

She looked at the tall young man on the doorstep. 'Has he been skipping Sunday School?'

'Why no.'

His mum wagged a finger at Noel. 'Have you been spending yer collection at the shop again?' She turned back to Mr Ewart.

'They will go and buy those crab apples at the corner shop, Mr Ewart. Nanny Walker's seen 'em.'

A smile flitted across the Sunday School teacher's face for a second. Then he was grown-up and serious again. He handed them a brown paper parcel. 'I've brought Noel this.'

'Thank you, sir,' said Noel, his eyes glistening. He tore off the paper. Inside was a large, black-backed Bible.

'Is this for me?'

'Yes, Noel.'

'Oh thank you, sir. It's smashing.'

His mum stared at Mr Ewart. 'But what's he done?'

'He's learned whole chapters of the Bible, Mrs Proctor, that's what he's done. And recited them to me. I'm very proud of Noel.'

Noel went pink. 'Thanks ever so much, Sir.'

'He's got a marvellous memory, Mrs Proctor.'

His mum made as if to close the door.

'See you on Sunday, Mr Ewart, sir,' said Noel.

'Yes. And don't forget this week's verse will you?'

'"He who comes to me I will in no wise cast out",' shouted Noel.

'Goodbye,' and Mr Ewart waved and was gone.

'Well,' said his mum, when they got back in the back room. 'Well.' She took the flat iron off the little hob and spat on it. It was nice and hot so she started on the shirts. 'I don't suppose you'll want to leave now.' Noel didn't answer. He sat perfectly still by the fire with the Bible on his knee and held it there, gently caressing the soft leather cover from time to time. He'd won a prize. He'd won a prize.

Later, when his mum popped her head round the back bedroom door to see if he was asleep, she saw the Bible again. He'd placed it in the very centre of the little table between the two beds. She stood there a moment, a puzzled frown creasing her forehead. Then she went out and closed the door. What would Tom say about that, then? She sighed, and dragged a straggle of hair behind its kirby grip. When he got back he'd probably be too far gone to take it in. She stood at the top of the stairs. Guinness, she thought and clenched her hands together. Guinness!

## Chapter Two

# The Thirty-Fourth Operation

That year, winter passed to summer so quickly that in no time at all Noel had left school and started work. Edith was pleased.

'He's an apprentice cloth cutter at Philips and Jones,' she told Nanny Walker. 'He'll not be doing much cutting at first, then,' said Nanny Walker tartly, 'more like brushing the floor and cleaning the boiler out!'

But Noel loved it. He'd got a job and he liked the other lads. It was true, he had to clean the place up and start that boiler and brew the tea, but often they sent him on errands in the town. And then there was the Bookies. Every week they sent Noel out to place their bets on the horses and that was fun.

The only fly in the ointment was his dad. If Noel got 'out of hand' and hung round with the other lads too much, got into 'devilment' and was late home, then his dad used his belt. 'I'll have no trouble in this house,' he would shout. Noel would hang his head. 'No, Dad.'

What on earth chance did he have to get into trouble anyway? Get up at half past five in the morning, go and collect the newspapers; cycle to The Royal Victoria; sell them, then race home, have breakfast and then off to work all day. Bike home, grab some bread and jam, back to the hospital with the evening papers, and then home again for tea. What with all that, and the Boys Brigade Band practice, playing his cornet on a Saturday afternoon at the football match, and then playing football in the street with Sammy and Davey and Jimmy and the others, life was pretty crammed. He hardly had time to breathe even thinking about it.

Early one evening Noel shot out of the house, grabbed his bike and rushed to collect the papers. He weaved in and out of the traffic, round past the Keep-Left sign at the top of Grosvenor Road, and kept on until he arrived at the hospital.

'Hello there,' called out the night porter as Noel nipped past Gate Lodge.

'Hello yourself,' called Noel over his shoulder.

Cheeky young devil, thought the night porter. Always rushing from pillar to post, that lad.

Noel set off for Ward C. He half ran down one corridor after another. They all looked the same, all painted cream and green, with shiny patches of condensation over the old pipes. Past the row of tired fire buckets, then left, left again and he was there: 'Men's Surgical' painted in red over the double doors.

'Evening, Sister.' She didn't look up from her desk, but patted her newly permed hair. 'Evening. Yes, carry on, lad.' He went in.

The ward was cream as well and the metal bars of the bed-heads were painted to match. He set off down the right hand row of beds first. The men, some young, more old, were all slumped against the pillows. They coughed. Sometimes they moaned. It was queer, he thought, how they always looked tired, even though they were in bed all day.

He slowly worked his way round the beds. 'Evening, sir. Like the *Irish News*? Thank you very much, sir. Yes, I've got *The Newsletter*.' Carefully he pocketed the ha'pennies and the farthings. Each coin was precious. He'd always worked out the change, while the patients still fumbled in their dressing-gown pockets.

At last he got to the end. There was Mac in the corner bed. Noel liked him. He was always cheerful.

'Hello, Mac.'

'Shhh,' said the Sister, who seemed to appear from nowhere. 'He's very tired.'

Mac opened his eyes. They were very blue and crinkly at the corners. Today his face was white.

'Hello there, young Noel,' he said, his voice husky.

'Are you all right sir?' asked Noel. He'd never seen Mac look so tired before.

The Sister bustled between them and took Mac's pulse. 'No, he's not,' she said.

Mac winked at Noel. 'I'm all right.'

The Sister marched round the other side of his bed and straightened the sheet. 'No more clambering into that wheelchair. No more visiting other patients.' She looked at Mac for a moment, frowned and then clattered off down the ward.

Noel put his head on one side. 'What you been up to?'

Mac waved vaguely across the ward. 'Only went and saw that old fella down there. He was going to have an operation this afternoon. I thought I'd cheer him up.'

Noel stared at Mac. 'But you said *you* were going to have another operation this morning.'

Mac sagged back against the pillows, his face dead white, but his eyes sparkling. 'Well, when I wakened up out of my anaesthetic, they'd put me back in here you see, and I thought, poor old fella down there, he's scared to death of having his operation. It were his first, you see, so I thought I'd just go and keep him company for a bit. Set his mind at rest.'

Noel shook his head and grinned. Then he sat down on the tiny chair and put the papers on his knee. 'What did you have done today?'

'Finger off this time.'

'Did it hurt?' Mac shifted slightly and gazed at nothing in particular.

Noel tried again. 'Did you...mind?'

Mac chuckled. 'No. I'm used to it now. It were bad when they took off both my legs, but I'm used to that now. You can get used to anything.'

Noel wriggled a bit closer. 'Can I see yer back?'

'Cheeky young devil!' But Mac leaned forward and let Noel lift up the faded pyjamas. His back looked like a railway line.

Noel whistled. 'Why they cut yer up so much?'

Mac smiled. 'My blood won't go round proper.'

'How many ops yer had, then?'

Mac leaned forward, his eyes twinkling. 'This'll make the thirty-fourth.'

Noel got up and began to pile up the papers and then looked suddenly at Mac.

'Mac?'

'Yes?'

'Nothing.' He gathered up the papers and edged himself

down the side of the bed.

'Mac?'

'Out with it, lad.'

Noel moved back quickly. 'Mac, why?'

'Why what?'

'Why did you go and help that other fella today?'

Mac lay back on the pillows. 'Because I wanted to.'

'But why?'

'Well...I wanted to.'

Noel heard the Sister approaching. He leaned forward urgently. 'But Mac, tell me what made you do it?'

Mac was silent for a moment. Then he said, 'Well, it's like this. I've got Jesus in my life, you see. And he's give me peace.'

Noel stared. Then the Sister was there, hustling him away.

'Thanks, Mac,' he called over his shoulder, and Mac lifted his good hand a few inches off the bedspread and waved.

As he was leaving the ward, Noel turned and looked at Mac again. He lay very still and white in his bed. Usually he was laughing and joking.

Later that night Noel couldn't sleep. He kept imagining Mac still groggy from the anaesthetic, struggling to get into that special wheelchair, arranging his dressing-gown over his stumps, and pushing himself off to see another patient. What did it mean? Why did Mac say he had Jesus in his life? Noel frowned into the darkness. 'Jesus' meant church, and reciting boring memory verses, and sitting still in cold, dark buildings, in the back row if he were lucky, and keeping his younger brother, Robert, quiet during services. But Mac wasn't like *that*. Noel turned over. He couldn't make it out at all.

A couple of weeks later, when Noel arrived at Ward C with the evening papers, the Sister on duty took him on one side. 'Mac died this morning,' she said. 'I'm sorry.' She turned back to her desk. 'There's another patient in that bed now.'

## Chapter Three

# 'You'll Last a Fortnight!'

Somehow, after Mac died, Noel couldn't work up any more interest in selling the papers at the hospital. He still grinned and chatted to the patients, but inside he felt tired. Yet he had to carry on with the job. His mum needed the money.

One morning he cycled slowly home from the hospital. The canvas bag he carried the papers in was slung empty over his shoulder and the money carefully tucked away in his breast pocket. It was Saturday so instead of going straight home for breakfast, he threaded his way through the narrow streets until he came to the river.

He got off his bike, laid it in the grass and squatted down to watch the water. It was dirty brown with creamy scum that swirled sluggishly round the banks. He found a stick and let it trail in the water. Whichever way he held the stick, the water pulled it back downstream. Noel sighed and suddenly stood up and threw the stick away. The ground was muddy and his shoes made patterns in the mud.

Why did Mac have to die? He'd asked Phil at work the same question only a few days before. Phil had laughed. 'His number were up.' Noel had turned away and pushed his fists into his pockets until he could feel his legs through the thin material. He wanted to shout, 'Mac wasn't a number. He was kind, he was...you could have a laugh with him.' But it was no good. He knew Phil wouldn't understand.

Noel bit his lip. There was his mum as well. Once he'd said to her, 'why did our Stanley die?' But she wouldn't answer, only kept banging at some pastry she was rolling out on the back room table. 'Why?' he'd persisted. 'Why?'

'It was when I had you,' was all she would say.

But what did I have to do with it? he thought. He ground his heel into the mud, until the water nearly oozed into his shoe.

It was cold, so he buttoned up his jacket and leaped on to his bike. He rode as fast as he dared down the squelchy path and flew into a skid at the end. He shot into the side road so fast he nearly knocked an old lady down who was struggling to cross the road with a heavy bag of early morning shopping. He tore past, only putting his brakes on a fraction as he shot a glance over his shoulder. Yes, she was still on her feet, waving a fist at him. Noel grinned. She didn't know his mum, so it was all right.

Later on, after dinner, his dad said, 'Where you off to this afternoon?'

'Football match.'

'Don't you get all muddy,' said his mum.

'I'm not playing football this week. I'm in the band.'

'Yer cornet's under the bed,' said his mum. She pulled the dirty plates towards her and piled them up, putting all the knives and forks on the top. 'You're to help with the dishes before you go out.'

'Oh no! It's Robert's turn.'

'It's you,' she said and marched towards the kitchen.

Robert put his tongue out at Noel and then put it in again quickly as Noel started up from his place to get him.

'Stop it,' shouted Dad. The two boys looked at each other behind his back and Robert shrugged. Noel went into the scullery and stood waiting for his mum to boil a kettle.

'Oh, go on with you,' she said. 'You'll be late. I'll do 'em.'

'Oh thanks, Mum.' He leaned forward and tried to give her a kiss on the cheek, but she swept past, intent on getting the kettle off the hob. He hung round till she got back. 'Oh, give me that teatowel,' she said and gave him a push. 'Get off with you.'

He darted past and something touched his hair. He looked back. She stood there, gazing at him. 'Don't forget yer cornet.'

'No, Mum.' He bounded upstairs and when he got to the top he touched the back of his head. Had she ruffled his hair? She was always doing it to Robert. He went into the back bedroom where he crouched down on the bit of mat between the beds and pulled out the cornet case from under the bed.

The dust flew in all directions and he blew at it hard and then took out the cornet. He rummaged in his drawer and found a clean handkerchief and gently dusted the cornet, not missing a single twirl in the brass. He raised it to his lips and blew a few notes, which echoed loud and sweet round the room. He heard his dad shouting, 'Stop that noise!' and he grinned to himself. Then he put the cornet back in its case, snapped it shut and went downstairs.

It was cold at the match and Noel was glad they had to march round the pitch playing. At least they kept warm.

During the second half there was a sudden roar from the crowd. Noel craned forward. He was at the far end and couldn't see much of the match. Was it a goal? But why were the players all bunched together. The game had stopped. Then a St John's ambulance man ran across the pitch, another man following him with a stretcher.

At last he saw someone being carried off the field. 'Who's that?' he asked Alec, next to him.

'Dunno. Must be one of our lot, though.'

'Yeah. In our colours.'

The match got under way again, but no one seemed to bother any more and soon the referee blew his whistle, declared nil-nil and everyone went home.

When Noel got back his mum and dad were standing with their coats on in the hallway. Noel stopped short, 'Where you going?'

'It's Sammy,' said his mum. 'He's been hurt.'

'Sammy!' cried Noel, 'but he was at the match this afternoon.'

'Well, he's been hurt.'

'Was it him we saw being taken off?'

'Yes.'

'I saw him being carried off.'

His mum put on her headscarf. 'I'm going round there. His mum might want some help.'

'Can I come?' asked Noel, and started to put his coat back on again.

'No. You look after our Robert.'

Noel waited and waited for his mum and dad to come back. He gave Robert some bread and jam, but when he tried to eat his own slice, it tasted of sawdust and he left it. Robert sneaked up to pinch it and Noel turned round. 'Have it,' he said. Robert stood, the bread halfway to his mouth and stared at Noel. 'It's all right,' said Robert and put it back on the plate.

At last they came back. They stood in the doorway and his dad wouldn't look at Noel.

'What happened?'

His mum came into the room and stood a few paces away from him, clenching and unclenching her hands.

'I'm afraid he's gone,' said his dad at last.

'Gone?'

'Yes. I'm afraid he died on the operating table.'

'What!'

'Yes. I'm sorry, lad.' His dad came over and tried to put his arm round him, but Noel pushed him away, and started to shout.

'Why? Why?' He banged his fist on to the table and all the plates jumped.

For a moment he caught his mum's glance. For a moment he saw a tiny woman with hurt, anger and bafflement welling up in her eyes. Then the moment passed and it was just Mum again. She shrugged and turned away.

His dad clapped a hand on Noel's shoulder and he let it rest there.

'Where's Mum?' But she'd slipped away.

His dad looked round. 'In the parlour, I expect.' Noel started for the door. 'No, lad, leave her ... she likes to be alone.'

'But why?'

'It's brought it all back to her. Stanley. You know.'

'You mean the photo?'

His dad nodded and slumped into the fireside chair. 'You'd better get our Robert to bed for us.'

Noel did as he was asked and for once Robert did as he was told and soon snuggled down in his bed.

Noel sat on the other bed in the dark. He picked up the prize Mr Ewart had given him. It didn't matter that the light was off, because he'd learned so much of it already. After a few minutes he put the prize down on the bedside table. 'Why?' he asked the darkness. Why? Why did Sammy have to die? First Stanley, then Mac and now Sammy. Noel shivered. Why did

death seem to follow him so closely? Always reaching for
others near him, but never actually getting to *him*. The bed
creaked and Noel jumped and turned round quickly. Stupid,
no one there. I don't want to die, he thought and suddenly he
could stand the dark no longer. Robert's breathing was regular, so he tip-toed out on to the tiny landing and stood under
the light bulb.

He pushed the thoughts about death as far away as he
could. Yet even while he was doing it he knew he couldn't
forget. However fast he rode his bike, however loudly he
played his cornet, however naughty he was—nearly knocking
that old lady over—or silly at the Bookie's the thought of death
kept popping up generally when he least expected it.

He wandered downstairs. His mum was still in the parlour
and his dad had gone to the pub. He stood alone by the fire and
shivered.

What happened when you died? He wished Mr Ewart
hadn't made such a thing about it last week. 'Whose side will
you be on?' Noel had been in the back row, flicking paper darts
at Davey. Davey made a baa-ing sound and Noel bleated
back. Mr Ewart had stopped in mid-sentence, 'Stop it, you big
lads. You ought to know better!'

Where was Sammy now? Mr Ewart said you met your
Maker when you died. Noel thought about Sammy. He'd only
been seventeen. Same as me, thought Noel. He tried to imagine
Sammy meeting his Maker. No giggle came to relieve the
scene. No paper dart flicked just in time to stop him thinking.
Suppose it were me? And the thought hit him hard in the face.
Suppose it were me...but I'm not ready. And he left the
thought hanging in the air.

A few nights later, before he went to bed, Noel knelt down
on the bit of mat between the two beds in the back bedroom.
He didn't quite know what to say. He'd never talked to God
before. He cleared his throat and the words stuck. At last he
got them out: 'I'd like to be a Christian like Mr Ewart said.'
The whispered words sounded strange in the darkness. But
almost at once he remembered something Mr Ewart had
made him learn: 'He who comes to me, I will in no wise cast
out.' Suddenly he clambered to his feet. He'd been heard, he
knew it. His prayer had been heard. Even though the room

was very cold and very dark, his chest felt warm.

He rushed downstairs and opened the back room door. It was late and his dad had only just got in from the pub.

'Dad?'

There was no reply.

'Dad, I want to be a Christian.'

His dad turned his head slowly and looked at him. His eyes were red and his cheeks puffy. 'You! You're like all the other hypocrites!'

Noel flinched and then stood his ground.

'You a Christian! You'll only last a fortnight!'

Noel lifted his chin up a little higher, looked his dad full in the face, then turned and steadily climbed the stairs.

## Chapter Four

# Making Something of Himself

As Noel got older things began to open up for him. He finished his apprenticeship at Philips and Jones and started to earn good money. So he was able to help at home and buy one or two bits of new furniture. Nearly every evening was taken up with meetings, at Sandy Row Methodists or at the Parish Church, or with visiting or singing in the male voice choir.

Threaded all through this busyness was something that gently hammered at him. It was hard to put his finger on it. But it had something to do with the lads and men he mixed with, amongst the maze of back streets and tiny, red brick houses, in the factory and at the church. He wanted to talk to them about Jesus, to win them, to make something of himself.

It got all mixed up inside him. Some of it was selfish, he knew that. He wanted to succeed and be praised. But some of it was genuine. His heart ached over the down-and-outs and the drunkards, who often as not ended up at the Doss House in Matilda Street, sleeping under old newspapers. And on his mind all the time were the lads at work who lost money at the Bookie's. Even though he would no longer place their bets for them, he was sorry for them. And always there were the men who slogged so hard during the week that they drank to forget on Saturday nights.

Up in his room one night Noel climbed out of bed, knelt down on the little mat and began to pray and pray that God would give him power to help these men. Ages later his mum put her head round the door. 'What you doing?'

She didn't wait for an answer. 'Praying! Get back to bed at once! Do you know what time it is? It's two in the morning!'

'I'm praying for power.'

She shook her head, turned to go and then looked back over her shoulder. 'God'll give you power if he wants you to have it.'

When she'd gone Noel crept out of bed again and lifted up the little mat. He felt the floorboards to see if his knees had worn them away at all. No, just as hard as ever! He sighed and then chuckled to himself. 'Idiot!' and he clambered back into bed. He'd bought a book at the second-hand book stall in the market the week before. It was about a Rev John Fletcher of Madeley who had worn away his floorboards with his much praying. Obviously he, Noel Proctor, wasn't in that league yet!

After a while he realized what his next step must be. And he knew he'd have to tackle his dad about it. So one evening when his dad got home early from the pub and flung himself into his armchair by the fire, Noel said, 'Where's Mum?'

'In the parlour no doubt. At it again.'

'Stanley's photo?'

'Yes.'

'Dad?'

'What?'

Noel swallowed and fixed his eyes on the hob. His words tumbled out. 'Dad, I want to go into full-time Christian work. I've thought a lot about it. I'd have to leave Philips and Jones and perhaps go to college or something. I think there's grants.' His dad sat dead still gazing at the fire. Noel moved a step nearer. The words he wanted to say kept sticking in his throat, but he took a deep breath and forced them out. 'But, Dad, I want your blessing on it.'

There! It was said now. Silence hung between them in the back room and then his dad's chair creaked as he struggled to get up. His eyes glinted in the firelight and he seemed to have difficulty in getting his words out, too. Finally he said, 'Lad, I never thought you'd come' and he wiped his eyes with the back of his hand, 'and even talk to the likes of me about a thing like that.'

Noel went pink. His dad turned away and used the back of his hand again. 'I told her', he said, 'I told yer mum. "You'll be proud of that lad one day. You'll see."'

Noel grinned. 'You wouldn't mind, then?'

'Mind? No, I would not!'

Noel grabbed his father by the hand and shook it hard and then turned and ran upstairs two at a time. He felt warm all over and in his heart he was singing as loudly as he could.

In the end the Church Army College in the Edgware Road offered Noel a place. Full of anticipation, he sailed the Irish Sea and went to London for the first time.

But he found it difficult to settle. He worked diligently and made friends yet even so some students found him hard to take.

'Sees everything in black and white.'

'He's arrogant.'

'Who does he think he is? God's gift to the Church Army!'

Sitting on his bed one morning, Noel bit his lip. It wasn't his fault if he were sure of his God and his calling. He knew now his life's work was to be an evangelist. He sighed. Arrogant, eh? The word wrapped itself round him, setting him apart. He remembered his little back bedroom in Roden Street and the shelf piled with so many books that it swayed over his bed and the dust that flew in all directions when he got a tome down. There was always someone to talk to at home. And at church. He set his shoulders as if to fight. He'd got to stick it out. He couldn't let them all down at home.

The lecture bell rang. He got up, left his room and went to the first lecture. He was first in the room, in the front row, notebook open, pen at the ready, leaning forward to catch every word the lecturer said. He pushed the words 'arrogant' and 'over-confident' to the back of his mind. There'd be time enough to worry about them later.

In June 1957 Noel passed his exams with credits and was commissioned as a Captain in the Church Army. He promised to serve as a travelling evangelist in the Durham Diocese for the next five years, living in a caravan and moving round from village to town. His mum and dad came over for the commissioning service and stayed in the college over night. Who'd have thought his old dad would come round so much? His mum had taken him on one side the evening before and said, 'He's cut right down on the drinking Noel, love. And now he's retired he takes me out somewhere every day.' She put her head on one side and smiled at Noel, straight into his eyes. 'He's even started coming to church with me on Sunday evenings.'

The next five years in the Church Army hurtled past and Noel began to wonder what to do next. He loved life with the Army. He was his own boss. But he wasn't quite satisfied and he didn't know why. 'What is it?' he wondered late one evening. He'd finished the meeting and the last few stragglers had gone home.

He put the kettle on and as he waited for it to boil he thought over his adult life. It all seemed like one long meeting, one long line of folk wanting to know more about Jesus, interspersed with himself singing a solo or playing the cornet, or standing on soap boxes or beaches or marching down windy streets. He sighed and got up to make the tea. He liked the life. Yes. And he knew in his heart of hearts what his life was all about. He was an evangelist. He rolled the word round his tongue. An evangelist.

He stared at the cup of tea and then drank slowly. He'd wanted to succeed and he had. Many had found Christ at his meetings. He'd wanted God's power for service and God had lent it to him. He'd wanted to make something of himself, to get off the big wheel that turned into a whirlpool, sucking you down—like had happened to so many of his mates when he'd been a youngster in the tough end of Belfast. Where were they now? Some in prison, he knew. A lot probably got drunk on Saturday nights, just like their old dads before them. God had helped him, even though he hadn't deserved it.

He finished off the tea and then prayed, 'What do you want me to do, Lord?' The nagging thought that had kept coming back to him over the last few months tugged at his mind again. He pushed it away hastily, knowing, even as he did so, that he was going to have to face it. 'Get ordained! In the Church of England!'

The bishop was enthusiastic when Noel went to see him. Then he looked at Noel and said, 'You must be getting on for thirty. Do you plan to get married?'

Noel grinned. 'There's a young lady back in Belfast, who I,

er, have an understanding with!'

The Bishop smiled. 'That's good. Only there is one thing.'

'What's that?'

'I do advise you not to marry until you've completed your training. A young wife can get very homesick and you'll be very busy keeping up with University trained men on the course.'

The grin faded from Noel's face. Norma had already waited for five years while he'd been in the Church Army.

'Well I'll talk it over with her and let you know.'

He walked slowly back home from seeing the bishop. He remembered the first time he saw Norma. He was cycling to a meeting at one of the Belfast churches when he heard the sound of music and singing. He rounded the street corner and saw three girls clustered round a mike. The music stopped and a tall girl with dark red hair began to talk about her faith. Her voice quavered a little over the mike. She wore a red coat and a froth of white lace showed at the hem. Several passers-by stopped to listen and one dug Noel in the ribs. 'Bet she don't know her underskirt's showing!' 'Shut up!' he shouted back, surprised by the strength of his own reaction. Later he'd discovered she was the sister of one of his friends.

After that he never wanted to look at any other woman. Some time later he proposed to her under a street lamp. He chuckled to himself as he remembered that night. He'd clung on to his bike for moral support and nearly fallen with surprise when it turned out she was very keen on him!

The day after seeing the bishop he went to phone her up. 'Er, Norma, I've been accepted at Theological College, only...'

'That's marvellous!'

'Yes, but it means we'll have to wait even longer to get married...er, Norma, I'm sorry.'

There was a tiny pause on the phone. Then she said, 'I've still got a bit to do to complete my S.R.N., so perhaps it's best. And anyway you'll be much nearer to Belfast. It's only a hop across the water from your college in Birkenhead.'

'I promise you that at the first available opportunity we'll get married.'

'I know, darling.'

So it was settled. Noel went off to college with a promise to his bishop that he'd go back and serve in the Durham diocese.

Yet it troubled him that he and Norma hadn't been able to fix a date for their wedding and he decided to do something about it. When he'd got it all arranged he rang her up.

'Hello, darling. Guess what! We can fix a date!'

'What! When!'

'Easter Tuesday any good?'

'But that's so near…after seven years…yes, yes of course! Marvellous! But how've you managed to do it?'

'I wrote to the bishop and told him we *were* getting married then. Only, er, Norma,' and his voice fell, 'I'll have to come back here to do my Finals after our honeymoon.'

But she said, 'Oh never mind. It'll only be for eight weeks and I can carry on nursing at Musgrave Park and anyway we'll be married then! Oh it'll be lovely.'

So they were married on 31st March 1964 in Belfast. The church was crowded with guests and well-wishers, a happy throng of Catholic and Protestant neighbours and friends. Noel thought he'd burst with pride when he walked down the aisle with Norma on his arm. It was a day they treasured, made all the sweeter as they'd waited so long for it to come.

When he went back to college he studied as hard as ever under Michael Hennel, the principal. He burned the midnight oil, and was the only man in his year to get a distinction in Old Testament Studies.

Noel was ordained at Michaelmas of the same year and took up his first curacy at Haughton-Le-Skerne, bringing his bride with him. During their time there, they had their first baby, a girl, and called her Susan. She was, as everyone said, a beautiful baby, but she wore them out with her crying.

Three years later Noel became vicar of Byers Green, a colliery village. While they were there the church thrived and its two Mission Churches were re-opened. They had another baby girl, Helen, with a dusting of dark red hair, like her mother. He was kept busy with three churches to run and a young family to care for. Yet often he was asked to do outside preaching engagements as well.

One evening the phone rang. Noel picked up the receiver, 'Hello?'

'This is Sidney Edmonds, chaplain at Durham jail.'

'Hello again! You'd like me to take another Sunday afternoon meeting?'

'No, not this time. We're running a mission in the prison and we wondered if you'd like to be the speaker on the Church of England night?'

'Well, yes. Thank you very much.'

He put the receiver down and stared thoughtfully at it.

'Goodness me,' he said to Norma when she came into the room. 'That was an invitation out of the blue!'

# PART TWO: WANDSWORTH

'Remember the victims'

Summer 1970

## Chapter Five

# Crime Doesn't Pay?

Noel couldn't settle down after his visit to Durham jail. He'd never seen four hundred men at a church service before and it made him feel excited and restless. At first Norma was sceptical about the numbers, 'What if they only come to get out of their cells?'

'O.K. I've thought of that. But what does it matter? Once they are *there* you can at least talk to them.'

He got up and prowled round the room, 'What an opportunity!'

He could see those rows of prisoners at the prison mission service in his mind's eye still. Some slouched in their seats, some wriggling, some pale and blank-faced. But others were alert and leaning forward, one or two with their heads in their hands. Maybe they were all dressed alike in blue, but each face was a different man, a different soul.

A few weeks later Sidney Edmonds rang him up, 'Hello there, Noel! How are you?'

'Fine, thanks.'

'Noel, it might come as a bit of a shock, but have you ever thought of becoming a prison chaplain?'

Noel stared at the receiver. 'Pardon?'

'A prison chaplain. You know, like me.'

Noel's heart gave a sudden leap as he remembered the rows and rows of prisoners in the chapel. 'Why…yes…I'm very interested.'

'Well, how would you like a day in London? At the Prison Department? They're having an interview day. There'll be about twenty there and the Department pay expenses!'

'Why not! I'm interested all right. And if it's free I can't lose!'

And so it was arranged. Noel was to go to London.

After the interview was over, Noel wondered if the Home Office would offer him a job as an Assistant Chaplain, but he had to wait five weeks before he got an official letter offering him a post at Wandsworth Prison.

'Norma!' he shouted when he'd skimmed through the letter, 'They've let me in!'

He raced upstairs and then down again, taking the stairs two at a time. He chuckled as he remembered the interview: all those dark suits and plummy voices. Perhaps they weren't such a bad lot after all! He imagined the headlines in the local paper: 'Vicar goes to jail!', 'Vicar Inside!', 'Captive Audience!' He whistled as he trotted upstairs again. Wouldn't his old mum and dad be pleased. It was a step up. No, a step forward. He sat down at his desk in the bedroom that was crammed with furniture and tried to settle. But he couldn't. A thought kept popping up at the back of his mind: God, himself and Norma. They'd succeed between them. Nothing would stop them. His hard work was always blessed and, yes, he knew he could get results in prison.

But somehow the thought didn't seem quite right if he said it aloud, if he took it out and aired it in broad daylight. It seemed...arrogant? Carefully he pushed the thought to the back of his mind and began to cover it with more acceptable thoughts. Of course if God allowed it, he'd succeed. If it were God's will and he were a channel, he'd succeed. But in his heart of hearts, he knew. The three of them together couldn't fail.

In April 1970 Jack Beisty, the Governor of Wandsworth, and the Chaplain, Joe Nicholson, invited Noel, Norma and the girls to visit the prison and see their new house. When they arrived outside the prison Norma stared open-mouthed at the enormous gates, 'You're never going in there!'

'Yes I am. Every day.'

She shivered. 'You'd best be on your way. I'll wait.'

He squeezed her arm. 'I'll try not to be too long.'

He crossed the road, lifted his hand to ring the bell at the massive gate and looked back. She was standing near a wall, her shoulders hunched against the wind and her collar up. Little Helen was in her pushchair and Susan darted about near her mother. Noel swallowed. What a lot he expected of his wife.

'Name?'

He turned quickly. A Prison Officer had opened a window in the gate.

'Oh, er, Noel Proctor.'

'The Rev.?'

'Yes.'

'Come in.' He saw the glint of a key through the glass, then heard a bolt being drawn and a key turned. A small door opened in the gate and Noel climbed in. The door clanged behind him and he jumped. The Officer locked and bolted it again, then showed him to a small room and asked him to wait for the Governor.

He couldn't sit down but paced round the room, every now and again glancing out of the window at Norma. The glass was so grimy that she didn't see him when he waved. He watched her open her carrier bag, get out a greaseproof paper parcel and try and balance it on one knee. She'd done jam sandwiches for the girls the night before.

He darted a glance at the clock on the wall. He'd only been here three minutes! He turned to the window again. A sleek car purred up to the gate. Then the car door opened and a lady gracefully extended her legs and daintily swung out. She'd wrapped herself against the wind in a pale beige fur coat and hat. The fur framed her beautiful face, and earrings glinted just below her hat. When she reached back inside the car for her handbag he noticed bracelets on her wrist, and as she turned back, pearls at her neck.

Partly obscured by the car stood Norma in her thin poplin raincoat. She'd refused to buy a winter coat that year. 'We'd better spend the money on warm coats for the girls....' Noel frowned. That thin raincoat wouldn't keep a breath of wind out, never mind a downpour. He gazed at the lady again. Well, after all, the Governor's wife did have a position to keep up, didn't she?

The door banged and another Officer came in.

'The Governor will see you now, Mr Proctor.'

He led Noel through the entrance hall and Noel heard the Officer on the gate greet the lady by name. They stood back and then followed her across the courtyard, their heavy foot-steps contrasting with the tapping of her stiletto heels. It seemed to Noel that every finger of her left hand flashed with rings. He turned to the Officer beside him and said in a whisper, 'Is that the Governor's wife?'

The Officer smirked and then grew deadpan again.

'Oh no, sir, that's the wife of one of the criminals in here.'

Noel was so astonished that he couldn't speak. As they marched down one long corridor after another he kept think-ing of Norma in the thin raincoat.

'But I'm supposed to be in here to tell men crime doesn't pay!'

The Officer shrugged. 'It's a mad world.'

Noel raised his eyebrows. 'I'm the one that's mad!'

The Officer suddenly gave him a really friendly grin and then stopped outside a door. 'In here, sir. You'll be all right.'

Later on, his head in a whirl, Noel tumbled out of the little door in the big gate and ran to meet Norma. She looked pale and the girls were squabbling. He took her arm.

'Come on. We just go down here, turn right at the bottom and we're there.' She pulled herself up to a full standing position and tried to show an interest, but her feet ached and her head hurt, so in the end instead of saying, 'How did you get on?' she said, 'Honestly I thought you were never coming out,' and then bit her lip.

But he had grabbed the pushchair with one hand and Susan with the other and was walking quickly. 'Take my arm,' he called and she hurried to catch up. Where on earth was he taking her now? He turned the corner and they were in a quiet suburban road.

'Here we come,' he said and then stopped again. Norma stood as if rooted to the pavement and gazed at a gracious double-fronted, bay-windowed semi.

'Here we are. Our new home!'

She leaned against the gatepost, a little flush in her cheeks.

'You mean we are going to live here?' Only posh people lived in houses like this in Belfast.

'Yes.'

'But....'

They ran down the path and opened the front door. Norma

stood in the doorway that opened on to a square entrance hall and then tip-toed across it. He smiled at her and then she darted from room to room. The sun had come out and the house was flooded with brightness and light. She stopped in the kitchen and stared at the back garden from the window. Her eyes took in the huge Copper Beech tree, all the leaves about to unfurl, the red showing at the tips.

'Noel, it's beautiful.'

He laughed. 'I know. The Governor told me.'

'Look at that tree.'

'The same colour as your hair.'

'You old flatterer! Oh it's lovely. Do you think the oak bookcase will fit in the hall?' And away she went, the girls prattling at her heels, to inspect the bedrooms.

He leaned against the sink and smiled. It had been a hectic day. But he felt deeply glad. And Norma was happy, too. He bowed his head. 'Thank you,' he said quietly.

## Chapter Six

## 'These Men Are Cons'

On Noel's first morning Joe Nicholson took him along with him on his rounds. 'First we've to interview every man on reception.'

Noel stared. 'Reception?'

'Yes, we get coachloads coming in every evening from the Courts. Those are the ones who don't get bail and they have to stay here until their case is heard. Can be as long as seven months sometimes. Noel watched Joe carefully as he did the interviews: 'Name? Occupation? Do your relatives know you're in here?'

A burly chap with a crew cut burst into tears at the desk. 'My mam'll die when she finds out I'm in here,' he said and he put his head in his hands. Noel leaned forward. He wanted to put his arm round the man, to say, 'I'll phone her for you,' but the presence of Joe restrained him. Joe waited till the man had been led out and then said to Noel, 'There's fifty more like him,' and he spread his hands out. 'Don't give all your sympathy out at once or you'll get exhausted. And,' he wagged a finger at Noel, 'remember. These men are cons. That big chap in here just now, he always weeps like that. The snag is, he doesn't give his old mother a second thought when he's breaking and entering!' Noel sat still.

Another man came in, protesting that his rings had been 'removed'. Joe sat unperturbed, 'You'll get them back when you leave.' The man was elderly and fussed, flicking dust off his prison trousers.

Joe sighed. 'Drunk again last night, Mr Jones. Well you'll soon be moved out of here. Probably to Pentonville.'

When he'd gone, Noel said, 'Why Pentonville?'

'All the down-and-outs and tramps go there. They're brought in on a vagrancy charge, often drunk, too. You see, Noel, this is an Allocation Prison. We get them from the Courts before their cases are heard. Then from here they are allocated to the most suitable prison for their offence. After their case has been heard that is.'

'Oh.'

'Wandsworth is also a Category B prison. You get your seasoned criminals put away here. But minor offences like maintenance and driving go to a Category C or even to a Category D, which is an Open Prison.'

By the time they'd seen about fifty remand men, Noel's head ached. Joe patted him on the shoulder. 'Go and get some coffee and then meet me in the hospital wing. It's been a busy morning.'

The days of the first week flew past until Noel felt his head was bursting. One morning he'd gone with Joe from bed to bed in the hospital, and helped to give Communion to a young man who'd tried to hang himself in his cell. It was only half way through the little service that he'd realized what the man had really tried to do. Why, he thought. Why? But the man was too ill to be questioned.

Back in the office Noel said to Joe, 'Can I visit that man?'

'Of course. But remember there's "Punishment" to do first.'

'Punishment?'

'Yes, the Punishment Block. Then when we've visited that, our statutory duties are finished for the day. Anything else, like extra hospital visits, is over and above that.'

George Jenkins, the Church Army Captain, looked up. 'Give him a rest.'

'No, I'll come to Punishment,' said Noel quickly.

It was very quiet in the Punishment Block. Joe was just unlocking the first cell door, when suddenly there was a noise like a wild cat screaming and a frenzied rattling at a cell door at the far end. Joe hardly stopped in his tracks. 'They get like that sometimes,' he said, but all the same he locked up the cell again.

Noel turned round and peered down the corridor. He saw an Officer in a blue shirt flash his keys on the end of their chain and open a cell door. The prisoner inside hurled himself out

like a stone from a catapult, beating his fists against the air,
and threw himself in a sobbing heap on the floor. He had long
brown curly hair that hid his face, and a slender young body.
Another Officer came up and the two of them tried to get him
on to a chair.

Joe gestured towards the sobbing heap, 'He knifed another
fellow in a fight.'

Noel winced. He felt so battered by the emotion in the place
that all he wanted to do was sag into a chair and sort out his
feelings. He'd come across so much misery and vice in one
week alone that he wished desperately he could go and rest
somewhere quietly, to picture to himself all the faces he'd seen
and pray for them. The emotion some of the prisoners gener-
ated was so strong he could almost touch it. Whatever had he
taken on? Would he ever be able to cope?

But Joe was pulling him into the next cell. Yet another man
to try and help. Noel squared his shoulders. He'd nothing left
to give anyone, but he'd have a try. As it turned out he didn't
have to. The prisoner in that cell turned his back on them and
deliberately walked away. 'Get lost!' he growled.

Joe shut the cell door smartly and locked it again. 'Never
stay when you're not wanted.'

At last Noel's first week was over. He staggered home.
He realized he was very hungry and as he came down the
garden path, Norma called out to him, 'Come on, eat your
dinner. It's a lovely evening. Let's go for a walk on Wandsworth Common.'

He ate, hardly tasting the food and his shoulders were so
tense that Norma noticed them.

'Tell me all about it,' she said when he'd finished. So as the
girls played on the Common, he poured it all out and as he did
so, the tension gradually slid off his shoulders and he became
happier. He linked arms with her, 'What would I do without
you?'

She laughed and tossed her hair, 'Not much, I'll bet!'

The days sped by, crowded with impressions so vivid that they
jostled round Noel's mind until he didn't know if he were
coming or going. Everything was larger than life in prison,
everybody demanded of him, and pulled at him for attention:

'Phone my wife.'

'Help me to find a job.'

'Can I join the choir?'

'My Mum's died.'

'My daughter's sick.'

'I'm fed up with this place.'

'Get lost!'

'Church! Hypocritical lot.'

'Please pray with me. I'm scared of my cell mate.'

And so it went on—the interviews with the reception men, the hospital visits later on in the morning, and the daily round of the Punishment Block. On top of all that there were Sunday services to run, counselling sessions to arrange, meetings every night: choir, Bible study, the Church of England's Men's Society, Confirmation classes.

The only thing that kept Noel going that long hot summer was Norma. Every evening she and the girls walked up the road to meet him, and then the four of them took a walk on the Common, lapping up the evening air. And he talked. And talked. And she listened, offered advice and listened again. They forged a bond between them, sharing together their inmost thoughts.

He was sure he was going to succeed. He felt it in his bones. God, Noel and Norma. 'What a trio,' he joked one night and she laughed. 'I mean it,' he said. 'When we first got married, I thought, well, a wife's the one at home and I'm the one who gets out and about, but,' he looked sideways at her, 'now I know better. I know you're my partner. And it's simple: I can't succeed without you.'

'Stopping at home in the background?' She was careful to look at her shoes.

'No—well—yes—but no, I mean *you*!'

They laughed and linked arms. 'When I'm on my own, Chaplain proper, I'll get you in to speak to the lads.'

'What me?'

'Yes, *you*!'

Some evenings they spent most of their time laughing. Norma giggled, 'Do you know what our Helen calls Mrs Cracknell from next door?'

'No?'

'Mrs Freckle!'

Noel chuckled and threw a ball for Helen and she toddled after it. 'I had a right head-case today,' he said. 'I was interviewing the reception prisoners and one comes in and slumps in a chair. Little fella with a red nose. Well I looked at his file and I says to him, "What, you in again?" He says, "Yes, I nicked a car." I says, "Not taking and driving again?" He nodded. Then I says, "Don't you want to be at home with the wife and kids?" Well he drew up his chair, leant across the desk, scratched his head and then,' Noel groaned, 'he says, "I've got a wife and two kids. I've got a common-law wife and she's got two kids, and now my girlfriend's in the family way. There's so much heat on me outside, I decided to get out of the way for a bit." The little fella waved his arm round the room and says, "Bit o' peace in here!" And he leaned back in his chair, a big grin on his face, looking as if he were in an expensive hotel!'

Norma giggled. 'What did you say?'

'What could I say? I just went through the rigmarole of the form with him.'

Some evenings they walked slowly, their heads bowed.

'That young man I met on the first week in the hospital, the one who tried to hang himself. He's being sent to a Remand Centre.' He sighed. 'But why did he do it?'

'I tried to talk to him. He was very quiet. He listened, but he never said anything at all really. His four brothers and sisters are in foster homes. He absconded once from an Approved School and his dad hid him under the roof for two years until the Police found him.'

'Under the roof?'

'Yep. They rigged up a sort of trap door in the bedroom ceiling. He never went out for a walk during the day for two years. He just looked at me, Norma, white-faced and black smudges under his eyes and said in a controlled voice, "What have I to live for, Sir?" and then he shuddered and said, "You see I can't bear being sent to prison again. I know I can't."'

'Did you tell him about Jesus?'

'Yes, but he didn't really "hear" me so I thought it was best just to listen.'

'What was his offence?'

'Oh, he began by taking and driving away, then house breaking. You know, the usual pattern.'

Noel shook his head. 'Honestly Norma, he's only in his twenties. I could weep for him. And there's so many others, I want to help them all. But how can I? There's a man in the cell across the landing from that young man. He's in television. He got so screwed and uptight with himself that he took a diamond ring from a jeweller's tray and then stood outside the shop waiting for the police to arrest him! Said he wanted to get away from it all, have some peace and quiet.'

Norma stared up at the evening sky. 'But you get peace and quiet out here.' They stood still and gazed at the immense bowl of the sky. 'I know, but there it is.' The trees were all a bright gauze of new green and the light stood in columns between the silver birch trunks. They wended their way home in a companionable silence.

'You know, Norma, that's all those lads ever see in there through their bars, the sky, the roof tops, a few birds and the stars. They never get a change, or a holiday or go to the seaside.'

Norma shuddered. 'Terrible.'

He sighed deeply, 'The trouble is some of 'em have done terrible things.'

'What's the answer?'

'Only one I know of. That's if they'll listen.'

They were quiet for a few minutes and then he said, 'There's another problem, too. Joe's warned me to be very careful about any of the prisoners who say they want to become Christians.'

'Why?'

'In case they are saying it so as they'll get a good Parole report for the "Home-Leave Board"!'

'Oh no! How can you tell if they're genuine, then?'

'Joe says you get a feel for who's telling the truth in the end, but that you've got to watch it.'

The next Sunday Noel was to preach for the first time. Joe got up to introduce him with a mischievous grin: 'Well, lads, may

I introduce you to Ireland's answer to Billy Graham! Oh and he's John McCormick as well! He'll play and sing to you.' Joe gave him a friendly slap on the back and pushed him towards the lectern.

Noel's ears burned but he got up all the same and forced his legs to walk towards the small lectern. He looked over the rows of faces. All he wanted to do was tell them they were human beings with dignity, even though they were in here, and that God loved them even though they couldn't see him and that Jesus had died to save them. As he began to speak he suddenly realized he wasn't afraid any more and he poured his heart out for fifteen minutes and then went and sat down again. He'd held them, he knew that. They'd listened and no one tittered when he played his cornet. And at the end of the service several men requested him to come and visit them in their cells.

After the service Noel looked at his watch: eleven o'clock. The men had dinner at half past eleven, so he couldn't visit until after one o'clock, when the Officers had finished their meal. So he stayed back in the chapel on his own and as he was kneeling there he thought about the men who had asked him to visit them after the service.

The evening before there'd been a film shown in here, 'Jane Eyre', and the men had soaked it up. He'd stayed, but with his back to the screen. He'd let his eyes roam over their rapt faces, pausing over each one and picturing them well, happy, straight and above all, Christian.

He sat on quietly. He could hear the bustle outside and smell the institution dinner smells, but he stayed on. If only he could get these men to understand...it wasn't just a question of being Ireland's answer to Billy Graham, even though that was a standing joke in the Chaplains' office, but if only he could get the power to change them.

The still voice he'd half heard before seemed to speak to him again. This time there were no words, only his heart growing warmer, as if it would melt right in two. A love welled up in him and swept over him, spilling out, enough for every face in that prison, Officers and all. He suddenly sat up straight. If he worked, and drove himself and pushed himself and fought, he'd be able to talk to nearly every man in that prison. And the power he'd had before wouldn't desert him. He'd give these men hope. He'd lead them to repent, he'd change them. He imagined them, a straggling crew of cloth cap chaps, all with shining faces because they'd found peace. 'Let me do it, Lord,' he whispered. 'Please. Please. Someone's got to give 'em hope.'

A door banged and Noel started. Joe Nicholson had come in. He came up to Noel and his eyes bore right into him.

'A good word you gave this morning.'

Noel flushed. 'Thank you, Joe.'

'Even George has a soft spot for you now.'

Noel grinned. George from the Church Army was all right, under the crust!

Joe stopped suddenly and stared hard at Noel.

'Don't forget the victims, man,' he said.

'Pardon me?'

'The victims. The people the cons bash up, or lie to, or steal from, or knife.'

Noel swallowed and said nothing.

Joe said, 'Don't ever forget the victims. And above all don't forget yourself and don't forget your family. The cons'll squeeze you on all sides and then try and con you.'

'They won't take me for a ride!'

'No?'

'No!'

They walked together out of the chapel.

'Coming to the Officers' Club?' asked Joe.

'Er—no thanks.'

But when Joe had gone, Noel felt unsure. Was he too sympathetic to the cons? And whose side was he on anyway? The answer slid into his mind almost at once. He was on God's side. He wasn't to be a Cons' man, nor a Staff man; no, he'd be a God's man. He bowed his shoulders. It was rather a lonely feeling being a God's man. You were left in the middle somewhere.

As he finally left the chapel, he met George. 'Coming to the Club?'

'Er, no thanks.'

'Oh, go on, have a drink. Everyone goes to the Officers' Club before Sunday lunch.'

'No thanks.'

'Have it your own way.' And George stumped off.

Noel sighed. But he wouldn't compromise over drink. He remembered his dad hiccuping up the stairs late every night, and he'd begun to realize that about three-quarters of the men inside were in prison because of drink, one way or another. So instead he wandered past the lads in the dinner queue, nodding to one or other of them here and there. He liked to show his face and to wear his dog collar like Joe did. At least the lads knew who he was then.

## Chapter Seven

# 'Dear John...'

The following Saturday Noel was off to work early, even before the girls were up. He got to the prison and was let in at the gates.

'I.D. card?' asked the duty Officer.

Noel fished out the identity card from his wallet and showed it to him. 'O.K., Chaplain. You're in.'

When he got to the office George Jenkins was already there, hopping up and down with vexation, the phone in one hand and a desk diary in the other. Finally he slammed down the phone.

'Some character on the phone wants to visit that Muslim prisoner.'

'You mean the one with three wives and ten children?'

'That's him. Some visiting Muslim priest wants to see him.'

George crashed the chair from out under his desk and sat down with a thump. Noel grinned. Then George said, 'What you doing in here so early? Neglecting that pretty wife of yours again?'

'No, I'm not!'

George glared at him. 'I saw you here on Saturday night, all Sunday morning and half the afternoon, not to mention every evening since. I don't know why she puts up with you.'

Noel opened his mouth to retaliate and then shut it again. Hopeless to explain how understanding Norma was. All the same, the remark stung him, and he tried to push it to the back of his mind.

After a bit George said, 'Joe's being made Regional Chaplain. 'He's off to some meeting or other today, so we're on our own.'

'Oh, he's got promotion has he?'

'Hummmph!'

'Shall I do Punishment, then?'

'Yes, and I'll do the hospital.'

So Noel set off for the Punishment Block. He could hear Joe's words ringing in his ears: 'If prisoners commit an offence within the prison, they are brought before the Governor for adjudication, and then he can pronounce up to twenty-eight days in solitary confinement; it's at his own discretion. And the only person who'll stop and talk to them is the Chaplain. The Governor, the Medical Officer and the Chief Officer all call and see them as well, but they're even busier than us. So it's over to the Chaplain.' Noel shuddered. It was the first time he'd ever done it alone.

But all was quiet on the block. Officer Byrom gave him a wave. 'All's quiet at the moment.'

Noel grinned. He liked John Byrom.

Noel unlocked cell door after cell door, taking care to double check he'd locked them behind him. The cons seemed pretty reasonable. But when he got to the end of the corridor he heard a growling noise. John Byrom came trotting up behind him, 'Watch out,' he said. 'It's Jimbo Green.'

Noel unlocked the door. Inside Jimbo was prowling up and down. Four paces up. Three paces down. His head was pushed forward, his chin jutted out aggressively, and his huge arms hung loose by his side, with his fists half clenched. He was unshaven and the cell smelled. 'I'll wait,' muttered John Byrom.

Noel stepped into the cell. 'Good morning, how are you today?'

Jimbo bared his teeth and made to shove him, but just pulled his fist away at the last minute.

'Is there anything I can do for you?'

Jimbo glared at him and then came and stood too close.

'You're only a little fella, aren't you?' and he sniggered.

Noel winced and then stood his ground, and stared straight into Jimbo's bloodshot eyes. 'What's it to you if I am only a little fella?'

Jimbo smashed his fist on to the bunk and Noel jumped, then he raised his fist again and said, 'If I ever see your ugly mug in here again, I'll....'

'Enough,' shouted John Byrom and marched into the cell. 'Watch out, Jimbo, or you'll get another seven days.'

Noel said, 'I'll come and see you Jimbo any time you need me,' and then nipped smartly out of the cell. It was a relief to breathe fresh air. John Byrom just got the door locked in time, before the great hands were clawing at it on the other side.

Noel wiped his brow. 'Wow! I was quite worried for a minute.' John Byrom shook his head. 'He wouldn't slop out this morning and he won't get washed.' Noel wrinkled his nose.

'He's just had a "Dear John" recently and he's been like this ever since.'

'A what?'

'"Dear John". You know, a letter from the wife: "Dear John, I'm sorry to have to tell you I won't be waiting for you when you come out. I've found a better fella than you...." or words to that effect. In his case it was "Dear Jimbo".'

'I see.' Noel sat on a minute and pondered. There was nothing he could do at the moment for Jimbo.

As he went back to the office he found himself thinking about Darwin's theory of evolution. He'd always taken such a stand against it before. Now sometimes he wasn't sure. Some of the cons were so aggressive, the animal seemed to have taken over from the human. In fact, animals didn't usually attack their own kind, unless they were overcrowded. He stopped dead in his tracks.

Only yesterday the Governor had said overcrowding in Wandsworth was going to be the big problem of the decade. He frowned. Darwin or no Darwin, the prospects didn't look rosy for the cons or for the Officers.

# PART THREE: EASTCHURCH

**'Something in me died'**

**Autumn 1970 – Spring 1974**

## Chapter Eight

# Wet Rafters

One morning in the late summer Noel got an official letter. 'Here, Norma, look at this. What a quick result to my interview. I'm being moved already!'

She groaned, 'Oh no! Not this soon! I'm only just getting straight here.'

'It's to Eastchurch Open Prison, on the Isle of Sheppey.'

'Where's that?'

'At the mouth of the Thames Estuary, really off the coast of Kent.'

'Mmmm.'

'Oh, and they're building us a brand new house on the campus.'

'Mmmm,' said Norma and her eyes strayed to the magnificent copper beech tree in the garden.

They lingered on over the breakfast table and munched an extra slice of toast. Noel idly reached across and flicked on the radio to get a time-check. They heard the announcer say: 'Last night the IRA increased their bombing campaign in West Belfast. There were also separate shooting incidents in the Falls Road and in the Grosvenor Road. British troops have now been called in to patrol the grounds of the Royal Victoria Hospital.'

He half rose to his feet and turned off the radio. She put down her toast half-eaten and they stared at each other. At last she found words, 'Why, Noel, why?'

'I don't know. Politics I suppose.'

'But people are getting murdered. On both sides.'

He shook his head and suddenly he looked old and weary. He knew if he thought about the troubles in Northern Ireland too much he'd put his head in his hands and cry, 'Those streets, those houses, those people, that are all getting bombed, are *my* streets, *my* houses, *my* people.' So instead he said, 'We must be thankful we're bringing up the girls over here.'

'Yes, of course.' And Norma got up, found a box of tissues and blew her nose. 'I hope my mum's all right. And your parents, too.'

After a pause she said, 'When do you start the Eastchurch job?'

'November 1st. All Saints Day.'

'Oh no! That means I've only got four weeks to pack in! What about measuring up for curtains?'

He looked at the letter again. 'They suggest we go down one day next week.'

So the following week they made the fifty mile journey to Eastchurch. When they finally got off the bus and walked down the road at the Campus, they looked in vain for their new house. Beyond the wire fence Noel could see nothing but rough, tussocky marsh grass. The wind came howling across those marshes bending the grey-green grass almost flat, and bringing with it the taste of salt and the memory of heavy seas. Norma shivered. 'I wouldn't like to get lost on those marshes. The bus conductor said they were treacherous.' The wind wrapped itself around them, so they linked arms for warmth. Little did they know that before they had been there four years another bitter wind would bow their spirits to the dust.

Noel noticed a workman meandering along with a wheel-barrow and went and asked him where their new house was. The builder scratched his head, bit his nails and waved vaguely over his shoulder at a small building site. 'Mr Harvey'll tell yer. He's over there.'

They trailed across the muddy road until they found Mr Harvey.

'Could you tell us where our house is?'

Mr Harvey pursed his lips and pointed to a half-built structure with no roof. 'That's the only house we're working on round here!'

'Then that must be it,' said Noel.

Norma stared at the squelching mud and wet rafters. 'How

can I measure up for curtains when there's not even a floor to walk on!' And she snapped the tape measure away in her bag. Noel groaned. This was too much.

Eventually Mr Harvey realized why they were so worried and promised to get cracking on the job.

'I hope he keeps his word,' said Norma when they got back to Magdalene Road, late that night. They'd bought fish and chips and were eating them ravenously out of the paper.

'Noel?'

'Yes?'

'Why didn't Eastchurch have huge gates and walls like Wandsworth?'

'Well, it's a Category "C" and "D" prison. "D" is completely open and "C" just has a wire fence. It's for first time offenders, or petty criminals, or driving or maintenance offences. Fines, you know. It's not for hardened criminals.'

'Oh. But if there's no big wall, what's to stop them running away?'

'Nothing. But if they abscond, they'll lose remission.'

'It'll be different from Wandsworth, then!'

'Yes. For a start it's not Victorian.'

She laughed. 'More like an army barracks!'

'Actually it is a converted RAF base from the last war. They say the boats left for Dunkirk from Sheerness.'

She groaned. 'Sheerness! My shopping metropolis on the coast! And only one bus every half hour.' She piled up the fish and chip papers and went to put the kettle on.

'It'll feel funny. Only one bridge on to the island from the mainland.'

He handed her the teapot and caddy. 'But, that's the whole point. It means there's only one *exit* from the island so it's easier to catch escapees!'

As it turned out, the house was just about ready by the time they went down there. Noel was welcomed to his new post in a special service at the prison chapel. This was a modern church built just near the wire fence and called 'The Chapel of St Peter and the Chains'. George Jenkins and the new Senior Chaplain, Albert Stevenson, came down to the service with the Proctors from Wandsworth.

After the service Noel and Norma were introduced to Tiny Townsend, the governor, Wally Clarke, the deputy governor, and Chief Officer Shute. Norma struggled to make conversation with Wally Clarke. 'Lovely service.'

'Yes, very nice.'

'That modern cross hanging over the altar is very nice.'

Wally smiled. 'Thank you. I designed it myself.'

'Did you really? It's wonderful.'

She gazed at the plain, empty cross. It was made of wood, with a metal crown of thorns made out of jagged nails at the top, and there were stakes driven into the wood where the hands and feet should have been.

She half turned to Noel who was shaking hands with as many people as he could, and said, 'Look at that cross.'

He half inclined his head to listen, but his eyes were still on the men.

'Yes, dear?'

'It's very moving isn't it?'

But he had walked after the crowd of men and didn't take in what she was saying. She lingered to look again at the cross and as she turned to leave she caught Wally's eye.

'How did you do it?' she asked.

He looked down and smiled modestly. 'I wanted to create something that spoke without words.'

'Without words?'

'Yes. The cross was to be empty...the nails were spikes... and the stakes...separated Jesus from life...there's a lot of suffering goes on in this chapel; men separated from their wives and children. From freedom.' His voice was low. 'Well, that's what I tried to do anyway.'

She gazed again at the cross and then at Wally. If only Noel could have heard what he said. She looked round for him, but he was in the middle of a cluster of inmates, jotting down names, patting one fellow on the back, grinning at another, a list in one hand and a ballpoint pen in the other. She sighed inwardly and then looked back at Wally. 'Thank you,' she said and then went to join Noel.

Soon they settled down in the modern house and the days sped into weeks and months. They had to cram as much furniture as they could into the house and even put some in store. Norma quickly made friends with other Officers' wives and Noel settled down into his new job.

He spent a lot of time puffing on his bike up the long, steep hill to 'C' block to visit the one hundred and fifty men behind wire up there and then free-wheeling downhill to 'D' block to see the four hundred men there. As it was an Open Prison and there was nothing to make the men go to church unless they really wanted to, he had to work hard to involve them. He started a 'surgery' every evening where men with problems could come and talk to him. It was exacting work. But at least be became known as a chaplain who kept his word, and put himself out to help people. And the numbers at church on a Sunday morning crept up from about the thirty mark to nearly a hundred.

## Chapter Nine

# The First Nails

The wind blew day in and day out the first winter they were at Eastchurch. It blew across the North Sea and over the bleak marshes, swirled round the five-hundred-acre prison campus and sent their front door rattling. Noel got used to battling against it as he cycled round the wooden, single-storey huts to talk to the prisoners. Sometimes its rough gusts were a relief after the regimental atmosphere on the campus.

One day the phone rang at home and Norma crossed the lounge in three paces to answer it. She had to squeeze past a joiner and his mate in the hall who were putting in a new pane of glass in the front door where the wind had shattered it the night before.

When she put the receiver down her hands were trembling.

'Noel,' she called, but he was upstairs in the tiny fourth bedroom working on his sermon at his little desk. She sat down suddenly on the settee. It couldn't be true. She'd have to go back to Belfast.

'Noel!' This time he heard and ran downstairs.

'My mother's been taken ill. She's had a stroke. She's in hospital.' She began to cry and he fumbled for a handkerchief. They sat down and made plans. 'Of course you must go,' he said.

'I'll take Helen with me, and I'll ask Mrs Shute to help you with Susie,' she answered.

Noel took her hand. 'But will *you* be all right?'

She flushed and shook her head. 'I don't even know yet if I'm pregnant again.'

'I reckon it's pretty certain.'

She began to cry again. 'Poor mum. I'll have to go. It must

be because they rehoused her after all the intimidation in Hutchinson Street. The shock of moving her has given her a stroke.'

'Ay. These troubles in Northern Ireland do even more damage than people realize.'

Next day Norma and Helen went to Belfast. On the journey Norma kept thinking of her mother and how hard she'd worked after she had been made a widow when Norma was only eight.

Once in Belfast Norma left little Helen with her Aunt Ellen and then went straight to the hospital. As she rushed down the echoing corridors she caught a whiff of disinfectant and all at once she remembered herself as she used to be before she married: Staff Nurse Long, with starched hat, and a face set into a careful mould. 'Don't worry. It'll be all right,' she'd say to worried relatives. A pat on the shoulder here, a carefully non-involved smile there.

Suddenly she was at the Women's Ward and a pretty, young nurse smiled and said, 'Can I help you?'

'Mrs Long, my mother. Is she...all right?'

The girl's face lost its bright look. 'Well, she's...you'd better see for yourself.'

Norma almost ran into the side ward and then stopped, bewildered. But surely these were all geriatric patients? The girl glanced over her shoulder and said, 'Here we are.'

Norma felt as if someone had frozen her. She crept down the ward to the end bed. Her mum didn't recognize her, but lay with staring eyes and a mouth dribbling slightly, like a little bird in the big hospital bed, with the cot sides up.

'Oh no,' whispered Norma, and then the girl was at her side again, gently pushing her on to a chair. Could this wild-haired, pathetic creature be her mother? She was usually so well groomed, with her hair shampooed and set.

'She will improve. Please don't worry.'

Norma clenched her hands together, but what else could the nurse say? She sat awhile and held her mother's hand. It was warm but lay lifeless in her own hard-worked palm.

Before Norma left she went to the nurse's desk.

'She's paralysed down one side, isn't she?'

'Yes. I'm sorry. Hemiplegic.'

'I'll come tomorrow.'

'Anytime. Goodbye,' and the girl was immediately caught up with the next anxious visitor. Norma trailed home to her Aunt's. Her whole body ached, her inside felt bruised and her eyes wanted to weep but somehow they couldn't.

She stayed ten days. Each evening she rang Noel. Each time she said, 'She's improved, but only a bit.' Then one evening she said, 'She knows me now. She said my name and her eyes focused.' Then her voice faltered, 'Noel?'

'Yes?' His voice crackled on the phone.

'I don't feel too good. I think I'd better come home.'

So she went back to Eastchurch. She knew now her mother wouldn't die but she also knew her mother would never be able to live alone again. What would Noel say if his mother-in-law came to live with them? He'd lose his 'study' and...she winced. Her inside was troubling her again: a deep-down grumbling ache. She knew really what it was, but pushed the thought as far away as possible. She raised her chin and stared defiantly out of the train window. She was going to be all right.

Noel met her at the station and rushed forward to take Helen from her arms. 'You shouldn't be carrying Helen,' he cried. 'And put that suitcase down!' Norma was so surprised to hear him shouting at her that she dropped the case like a hot potato. What on earth was wrong with him? He put his arm round her and guided her to a taxi. They went back in silence and she put her head on his shoulder and began to weep. He stroked her hand and tried not to keep looking at her dead-white face, pinched cheeks, the black circles under her eyes and her lustreless hair.

When they got back he put the girls to bed and then Norma, but in the middle of the night she woke him.

'I've got the cramps in my stomach.' He rang the doctor, who came almost at once. After he'd examined her, he called Noel out on to the landing. 'I'm afraid she's bleeding heavily.'

'Can you save the baby?'

The doctor's shoulders drooped and he put his hand on Noel's shoulder. 'I only wish I could.'

'But Norma?'

'She'll be perfectly all right. Why you could try again next month.'

Noel stared, perplexed. 'Try again?'

The doctor rolled his eyes upwards. 'To start another baby!'

'Oh. I see.'

But when Noel got back in the bedroom, she was sobbing into the pillow and moaning. At last, when the sleeping draught took effect, she fell asleep in his arms, but he lay awake the rest of the night gazing dry-eyed at the curtains. He'd lost his child. He clenched and unclenched his hands under the sheet. His child was gone. A son perhaps, lost for ever.

The week dragged by. Norma felt as if darkness had shut out all the light in her life. She felt empty, hollow, barren.

'Let's have another,' suggested Noel desperately one evening.

'I can't. I can't,' she said and ran sobbing into the kitchen. He forced himself to go after her, but he was angry. No one seemed to care about him. She got all the sympathy, all the flowers. It was his child as well as hers they were mourning for. Then he was ashamed. He'd never forget her agony that night as she laboured with the dead child.

'Come and sit down,' he said. She came and sat next to him. He switched on the television. It was a programme about the Yorkshire Dales and sheep. It went through the seasons and at the end, showed lambing time.

Suddenly she rushed out into the kitchen again, crying. He willed himself to go after her. 'Why? Why?' she sobbed. 'Why, those sheep can have as many lambs as they want. Why can't I have my baby, alive?'

'But you can at least thank God you've got two lovely daughters.'

'I know. I know. But I wanted this baby.' And she pressed her hands on to her thin body. Noel grabbed the kettle.

'Go and sit down. I'll make you a cup of tea.' He banged the cups on to the saucers and splashed the milk on the table. She heard him and was upset. 'It's not my fault.'

'No, I know…it's nobody's fault.' He passed her her tea and slopped it in the saucer. He was tired of always being the stalwart one, the supportive one. Who was there to support him? She sniffed and drank it in silence.

He blustered and banged about but eventually they both

calmed down and went to bed.

He couldn't settle, so when he was sure she was asleep he crept downstairs again. He tried to read but every time he looked at the page, instead of the story, he saw Norma in bed at Haughton-Le-Skern, ill with rheumatic fever and trying to give Susie her bottle. He tried to push the memory away. But it stayed. Norma saying, 'You'd love me more if I was well, wouldn't you?' And he only half-listening, saying of course he would, and then wondering why she was in floods of tears. He sighed. He never got it right.

He paced up and down the lounge. Other memories came crowding in, and he was too tired to resist them. He thought of Stanley and then Mac. He half choked when he remembered Mac and his stumps. Then there'd been Sammy dying on the operating table after the football match. Was all that why he was so understanding at funerals? He knew. He understood. And now there was this next loss. He clenched his hand, but as if a nail gashed it open again, he made himself stop and say the words out loud, 'Dead. Our baby's dead.'

But with each death there'd been new life, he argued with himself. People had found faith, or they had other babies. Why, he himself had been the new baby to help his mum through.... His thoughts trailed off and met a dead end. He thought about his life, his incessant work, as if he were trying ...to do what? Had he been trying to make it up to his mum, trying to compensate for the loss of Stanley? And had the habit now stuck? What was he trying to do? Erect a huge barricade of life and liveliness and song and meaning against death? Don't be daft, he thought. But he knew. It wasn't daft. He'd thought he could beat death. Now it seemed to be beating him.

Suddenly he sat down. Then a moment later slowly rose to his feet. Well death *wasn't* going to beat him. Yes, he'd still work and work. They'd have another baby. He'd let his mother-in-law come and that would take Norma's mind off things. Oh no! He'd not let death defeat him. He realized his hands hurt and he looked down at them in surprise. He'd clenched his fists so hard that his fingernails had chafed a red mark on his palms. He rubbed them together. He'd better go to bed. There was work to do in the morning. And with that thought he dragged himself upstairs.

Very slowly Norma came to terms with the loss of their baby. Noel insisted her mother come and live with them, even though the little chance he got to talk to Norma alone dwindled to the few minutes in bed at night before they turned out the bedside lamp.

Norma found she had to rehabilitate her mother, 'Come on now, Mum, can you wash the kitchen floor for us?'

'Yes, dear.' And old Mrs Long swilled the easycare floor and then tried to mop it up, often breaking off in the middle for minutes at a time to gaze unseeingly out of the window. Norma bristled with impatience but managed to wait till her mother had gone pottering in the garden before she dried up the pools of water. How often she had to bite her tongue these days. Poor old Mum. She watched her fumbling over Helen's shoelace and stopped herself from offering to do it. She wished she'd bitten her tongue more when she'd been nursing.

'I just used to churn out the same old glib phrase, the slick reply, Noel, to women who were weeping over their miscarriages, or who sat holding themselves so tensely still.' She shook her head. 'Now I *know*. I'll never be glib again.'

He patted her arm absentmindedly.

'Are you going to your surgery tonight?'

'Yes, dear.' He looked at her and smiled. His old ever-ready grin wasn't much in evidence these days, but the smile lit up his face and glowed in his eyes.

'Don't work too hard.'

'I'll try not to,' and he walked slowly out of the house, clambered on to his bike and freewheeled to work. He turned his head when he got to the corner and then waved to old Mrs Long.

On the way he wondered why he was so tired. It wasn't just the unending work, the girls and Norma's mum, it was...he sighed. Perhaps it was middle-age? And he wasn't sleeping well. The snag was the business of losing the baby had reminded him of things he thought he'd forgotten. He pushed the thoughts away irritably and scraped his front wheel on the kerb. Blow! He willed himself to go into the waiting-room. Before he opened the door he made himself smile and he forced his steps to have a spring in them. Then he opened the door. At least twenty men sat there, a few biting their nails.

'Evening, lads!'

A few muttered hellos.

'I won't keep you a minute.' And he strode briskly into his office, shut the door, then slumped down in the chair. He was early and so he tried to pray for the prisoners waiting to see him.

It was hopeless. The mountain of things to do kept pressing in on him: prepare two sermons, make endless arrangements, try and sort out the mess of broken marriages amongst the men. He groaned and pressed his fingers on his closed eyes. Having a 'surgery' had seemed a good idea: prisoners came in their dozens and he knew he often did help them and the numbers were building up at chapel, but it was exhausting. The well of human need was so immense, it seemed bottomless. He never felt he'd finished, there was always one more person to see. Always. He felt squeezed at both ends and utterly drained. 'Help me,' he mouthed and reached for his bell. The first man came in.

Two hours later he said goodbye to the last man, locked up his office and trudged down the path. He decided to push his bike home tonight, after doing a call at Ninety-Eight Block.

'Hello there, Chaplain,' Noel jumped and looked around. Brian MacLean was jogging past him round the football field, his leg muscles rippling below navy shorts.

'Evening, Brian. Out for your evening stint?'

'Yes.' Noel shook his head. Really Brian was fanatical about physical fitness.

Next morning Noel was in his office early and was one of the first to hear the news. He rang Norma.

'Brian MacLean's absconded. I was the last to see him. So it looks as if I won't be in for lunch.' He went down to the football pitch, with Mr Shute, the Chief Officer and Tiny Townsend, the Governor. 'Yes, he always jogged round here every evening if there wasn't a match on. And I saw him after my surgery last night.'

The Chief stared at the fifteen foot high fence, with barbed wire strung along the top. 'What I want to know is, how did he get over there?'

Noel looked round vaguely and then Tiny Townsend said, 'What's that?' They went to look and found the pole from the goal post lying near the fence. 'What's that doing near here?'

'Well it's needed mending for some time...that's it!'

'What!'

The Chief was furious. 'He used it to pole-vault the fence!'

'Wow,' said Noel. 'He took a risk didn't he?'

'Well he can't have planned it because all his things are still in his locker.'

The Chief snorted, 'We'll soon find him. He can't get far. Someone will pick him up on the bridge.'

But four days and nights passed and no one found Brian.

'What's he in for?'

'Petty thefts, I think.'

The police did not pick him up on the mainland and no one saw him cross the bridge. On the third day the police sent out search parties on to the marshes. They had to pick their way carefully with Ordnance Survey maps because of unexploded mines. On the fifth day they found him. Noel chuckled as he told Norma about it that evening. 'He was standing on a little patch of solid ground in the middle of a quaking swamp when they found him. Everytime he tried to step off it he sank into the brackish water.'

She shuddered. 'Poor chap.'

'He'd jumped the fence on the spur of the moment. He'd not looked at any maps, and he went the wrong way on the other side. Instead of going right to the road, he went left, and spent half a week wandering on the marshes. He was blue with cold. He only had shorts and a vest on!'

'He had a lucky escape, then!'

Noel threw his head back and roared with laughter.

'Well, you could call it that!'

She watched him laughing. Do him good to have a laugh. He never seemed to laugh these days.

Things settled down into a routine. They both worked hard, he with the men, and she with her family, mother and friends. And they began to feel things were looking up. Soon they'd been there two winters and a new spring was just round the corner.

## Chapter Ten

# Good Friday 1972

One day the phone rang. Noel came back in the room, sat down suddenly on the settee and buried his head in his hands. Norma flew to his side.

'What's happened? What's happened?'

'That was my mum on the phone. My dad's...'

'Is his heart worse?'

He nodded and couldn't speak for a moment.

'Is he...?'

He shook his head and then got up. 'The IRA or somebody planted a car bomb on the Protestant side of the Grosvenor Road earlier today.'

She went white and put her hand over her mouth.

'It blew up. No, no one was killed. They telephoned a warning, but,' and his voice was like ice, 'no one thought of telephoning 3, Roden Street where my old dad was ill in bed. The bomb-blast, and falling glass and women screaming, gave him such a shock, he's had another attack.'

'Oh no, no,' she said, and tried to comfort him, but she knew she couldn't reach him.

'You'd think the IRA would leave people alone on Good Friday wouldn't you!' and he strode up and down and then slammed a whole pile of magazines onto the floor and flung upstairs.

'I'll have to go and see him,' he called down the stairs to her. 'It'll have to be after the service on Sunday. I won't be able to miss the Easter Sunday service. Anyway Mum says she thinks he's fairly quiet at the moment.'

He preached of resurrection at the packed Easter service and a hush fell over the men as they listened to him telling a story:

'There's a lad sitting here this morning who told me something very interesting when I was interviewing him about his parole. He said how he'd broken into a house one night and when he'd climbed through the lounge window he got the shock of his life. There in the middle of the room was a coffin and in the coffin was a dead body! He realized he'd broken into a house where the family was in mourning. He was so upset about doing this he climbed back out again, then rang the front door bell and apologized to the widow for disturbing her grief. Then he went down to the Station and told the Police all about it and asked for a lot of other offences to be taken into account.

'It would be nice to think that his confessing like that let him off the hook, but unfortunately, he still got "time" and was sent here. When he got in here, he found he was troubled at night and couldn't sleep. He kept thinking about all the folk he'd robbed. Well one day he came to see me and we got talking and I told him straight that it was guilt that was troubling him, and that there was only one way to get rid of it.'

Noel paused for effect. They were rapt, hanging onto his every word. He went on, 'I told him, "Confess your sins, lad, and make Jesus Christ your Saviour. Then the slate will be wiped clean." Well he did just that and there's a much happier young man here today because of it.'

And so the service went on. Norma watched him, standing with his head erect, with his back to Wally Clarke's cross, while the Easter hymns swelled joyously round the chapel. She marvelled at his self-control. He knew his dad was so ill, yet he still gave all he'd got for the men, even making an impassioned appeal at the end. After the service he took down the cell numbers of the men who'd asked to see him and then tore home and grabbed his bags. 'Goodbye, darling,' and he was off. The Prison farm manager was waiting to give him a lift to Heathrow Airport in his car. When they arrived Noel thanked him and hurried to his plane. The Manager watched him go and then turned sadly away.

All the way on the flight over the Irish Sea Noel sat upright in his seat. How on earth had he managed to preach about joy, new life and resurrection that morning? It still felt like Good Friday to him. 'Please let him stay alive till I get there. Please!'

Then the plane touched down and he looked at his watch: half past nine.

He took a bus from the airport and got off at the stop on Grosvenor Road. His footsteps echoed down the wide street. There was no one about and all the street lights were off. He was about to cross the road when a black shape loomed up out of a doorway. His heart nearly stopped but he forced himself to stand still.

'Will you open your case, please, sir.'

He stood for a second, completely bewildered. Then it dawned on him. The black shape was a British soldier. He looked down at his battered case.

'Yes, of course.'

He half knelt down and opened it. The soldier never took his eyes off Noel's dog collar.

'Step back.'

Noel left the open case on the ground and stood back. The young soldier went behind the case so he could see both its contents and Noel at the same time. He kept his hand on his gun and with the other shone a torch in the case. Its circle of light played over Noel's clothes and then picked out his Bible. The torch light rested on the Bible for several seconds and then the soldier said, 'I'm sorry, sir. But it's orders. We've got to stop anyone with a suitcase.'

'That's all right. I've just come off the bus from the plane. My father's very ill.'

'I'm sorry, sir. Carry on.'

He fastened the case and walked steadily on, crossed the road, and came to Roden Street.

He reached the door, went up the two steps and knocked hard. He noticed the edges of the steps were white. So his mum still used a donkey stone, did she? Well perhaps things weren't so bad after all. He heard footsteps scurrying down the hall-way and then the door opened.

'Mum!'

She threw herself at him and buried her head into his arms. He half carried her in and then got the door shut.

'How is he?'

She lifted up her head and shook it hopelessly from side to side. He stared at her. She lifted up her hands to him in a

beseeching gesture and he held them and let her clench and
unclench them in his palm. He put his arm round her and they
went into the back room. She wiped her eyes on her apron.

'When?' he asked.

'About six o'clock this evening,' she whispered. He slumped
into the old chair by the fire. So he was five hours too late. He
wanted to ask, 'Why, why? I wanted to see him, to say
goodbye. Couldn't you have let him wait?' But instead he got
up and filled the kettle. 'Have a cup of tea, Mum.'

They stayed up late, sitting in silence together. Then he
said, 'Do you want to sit in the parlour at all?'

'Parlour? What for?'

'Well you used to go...in there.'

She stared at Noel. 'Why should I want to go in the parlour,
when you're in here?'

He said nothing, but a corner of his heart was warmed.

On the Tuesday the funeral came and went. He'd taken
hundreds of funerals, but this time he just sat with the family.
He hardly heard a word, his mum kept close to him and
Robert, and she held both their arms. On the way out she said,
'He died in peace. I read that psalm to him, you know,
twenty-three, and we said a prayer together and he died in my
arms.'

Later all the relatives came back for tea and sandwiches and
Noel kept them going with plenty of talk and news from
Eastchurch. Then they gradually went off home and Rosie,
their Roman Catholic neighbour, came round to 'sit with our
Edie'. She looked at Noel and waved her hand in his face. 'Get
off upstairs and have a sleep. You're all in.'

He climbed the stairs and stopped on the landing. Instead
of going into the little back bedroom, he turned and went into
the front room. He stood for a long time, just looking at the
narrow double bed. His dad had died in that bed. Now it was
stiff with clean sheets and the faded bedspread was unwrinkled.

After a while he went and knelt by the edge of the bed.
'Dad,' he said, but there was no reply. The room was quite
empty. His dad had gone. He put his head into his hands and
began to cry.

The tears ran onto his hands and onto the bedspread. He
wept until he was exhausted. Finally he pulled himself onto

the bed and lay and stared at the ceiling. 'Dad, if only I could talk to you....' After a while he jerked awake and realized he must have dropped off into an exhausted doze.

He crept downstairs and managed to get to the sink without his Mum and Rosie hearing him. He washed his face in cold water and then put the kettle on. He leaned against the sink. His chest and heart ached so much he felt as though someone were trying to push a stake through them.

He took the tray of tea into the parlour and gave a cup to the two women, and his mum darted a glance at him.

'I've got a fruit cake in the back,' she said and went to fetch it. She closed the door and then trotted upstairs to her bedroom. She straightened out the bedspread and noticed it was damp. She let her hand rest on the damp patch for a moment, then turned and scuttled downstairs, rummaged, and found the cake. She hesitated over the chocolate biscuits before taking them in as well.

She cut him a huge slice of cake and put two biscuits on the plate. 'Eat this love,' she said and then, shyly, hesitantly, patted him on the arm. 'Go on.' He stared at the plate, then looked up as her. 'Go on,' she said again. So he chewed through the food and drank another cup of tea. Then Rosie went. And Noel and his mum sat on by the fire.

## Chapter Eleven

# Rebekah

When he got back he plunged into a round of activities that left him no time to think. He even started working on his day off. 'I wish you wouldn't visit folk on *that* day,' said Norma. 'Well I won't have far to go! They're all waiting for me outside!' She glanced through the window and then at the clock. The prisoners always came on gardening working parties to her house or to Nana Shute's at coffee time.

'I've never had such a well brushed path,' she said and went to put the coffee on, saying as she went, 'Why does the Governor make them work so hard?'

'Well you can't keep eighteen men locked up in a dorm for twenty-three hours a day, can you?'

'Honestly, I feel invaded by them, even though I've put "nets" up.'

Noel whirled through his life. Every day on the campus he visited the metal recovery shops, the farm, the dining-room, the games-room and the TV room, and the other workshops, as well as doing his statutory duties, interviewing men and visiting the hospital and the Punishment block. He cycled twice a day up to Ninety-Eight Block at the top of the hill, where the Category 'C' prisoners lived. Sometimes he'd have a bit of fun with Brian MacLean, who had now settled down after his ordeal on the marshes.

'I'll give yer a Mars bar if you can cycle all the way up the hill without getting off!' And Noel would shoot off. He won the Mars bar more than once, too!

The men got to know that they only had to go to his 'surgery' if they wanted any help. The work load was great, especially as he held classes nearly every night. He even got a recording of church bells and rigged up a record player and amplifier outside the chapel and then played it each Sunday morning.

But the need was so great that he felt sucked in, drained, exhausted and empty. He felt like the empty rind of an orange that had been squeezed of all its juice. All his drive had flowed out of him with the tears he'd shed on his dad's bedspread. He spent hours trying to mend broken marriages, phoning up men's relatives, spurred on and driven by he knew not what. And all the time he couldn't look inside himself because he knew he was empty. Empty—and nothing helped. He couldn't pray, but he knew the language of a preacher, and so he carried on.

A few days after he'd come back from Belfast the emptiness oozed away for an hour as he sat in the chair and wept for a time over his dad. Norma gave him a cup of coffee. He dangled Helen on his knee and read Susie a story. He'd had a letter delivered by hand and it stared at him invitingly from the sideboard. It had no stamp and eventually he opened it.

Inside was an enormous hand-made card and someone had painted a rose on it. He opened it and read over sixty signatures. 'In sympathy,' he read out, 'in your sad loss.' He couldn't speak for a moment.

Then Norma said, 'Is it from the cons?' He nodded.

She said, 'Haven't they been kind and thoughtful. I wonder who drew it?'

He swallowed. 'There's a chap called Mick. He's good at art. Perhaps he did it.'

She smiled, 'Do you know what? A gypsy-looking con came round today, at coffee time. Well, he offered to plant me some flowers. He said he'd heard your dad had died. I thanked him very much and said yes. An hour later he knocked again. I came out and he'd put in some very nice forget-me-nots. I said, "Those are lovely," and he said...' she burst into laughter, 'He said, utterly deadpan, "I pinched them from the Governor's garden!"'

But only too soon the pleasant hour was over and he had to go out again on his bike and struggle up the hill to Ninety-Eight Block with the wind against him all the way. And as he cycled slowly along, the old emptiness hollowed him again.

One day in late summer Norma said, 'I think it's happened at last!'

'What dear?'

'I think I'm pregnant again.'

And it was so. They were all delighted. The new baby was due in April and as the time drew nearer old Mrs Long tried to do some knitting and Noel began to feel happier. He whistled as he painted the old cot. The wind seemed less bitter, and the marshes less bleak; he felt less tired now a new baby was on the way.

Norma was well and assisted at the Christmas nativity play. The Officers and wives who came to chapel helped to put it on and the performance was so popular that they gave it twice to the cons. A lot of the men wept over the tinsel angels. 'It's a sad time for men to be in prison,' said Nana Shute as she and Norma were trying to stop the angels from falling off the wobbly platform. 'Christmas is a bad time to be away from family and friends.'

Then one day in February Noel was called to the Governor's office. When he got inside several Officers were standing around, all gazing at something on Tiny Townsend's desk. Noel peered at it. It was a large brown paper parcel and clearly as anything, his name was written on it.

Tiny Townsend said, 'It's for you Noel, but we're worried.'

'Oh?'

'Yes. Every time we pick it up, it sort of gurgles, or ticks.' Suddenly Noel went white, and remembered that only on the News that morning there'd been a warning about a renewed IRA bombing campaign. A security man had been called in. Cautiously he undid the parcel. Noel felt the sweat trickling down the back of his neck. Surely no one would....First one wrapping fell to the floor and then another. At last all the paper was off. The men stood in absolute silence gazing at the contents. There in a cardboard carton were six bottles of best Scotch. Noel broke the tension by bursting out laughing. He read the card on the carton.

'It's from that businessman who was in for smuggling Pakistanis into the country!'

'I hope he came by it legally!'

Tiny grinned. 'It's a pity, but it'll have to all go back.'

'Well, it was very kind of him.'

'Mmmmm.'

Several pairs of eyes gazed wistfully at the bottles. Noel chortled to himself as he left the room. He was the only one that didn't drink!

Early on Mothering Sunday Norma woke up with labour pains. Noel rang the midwife and Nana Shute came to look after the girls and old Mrs Long.

He said, 'I'll come as soon as the service is over darling. Try and hang on to the baby till I get back home.'

She groaned. 'I'll try, but I don't think I can.'

As he dashed into the chapel he suddenly noticed Wally Clarke's cross for the first time. The sun burnished the crown of metal thorns with light. At the height of the service, the door banged at the back and the Chief yelled 'It's a girl!' A cheer went up from the men and several knowing grins.

'You been busy Mr Proctor?' He went bright red, rushed through the service and then flew off to see Norma.

'How are you?'

'Fine. Isn't she lovely. Let's call her Rebekah.' She smiled, 'You've got Rebekah at last!'

The baby held tightly on to his little finger with her fist.

'Where's she got all that brilliant red hair from?'

'Every time I have a baby, their hair gets lighter and redder!'

'It'll be gold next time!'

'What do you mean: next time! I'm not going through that again!'

'Was it bad, my darling?'

Norma lay back on the pillow and closed her eyes. 'Well, it was quick anyway.'

He kissed her. 'Well done.'

He ran downstairs and realized halfway that he was singing at the top of his voice.

It was to be the last time he sang like that for months.

## Chapter Twelve

# 'It's Nothing to Worry About'

With the trees and flowers breaking out all around him, and a new baby snuggled in Norma's arms, Noel felt his old self again. He trotted down to Masons, the corner shop, one Friday evening soon after Rebekah was born. He waited at the counter, jingling the coins in his pocket.

'Two packets of plain biscuits and some tea bags, please.'

'Choir practice again?'

'Indeed it is.'

The door banged and Noel looked round. A bloke had slouched in and was hanging round near the pet food shelf. Noel stared. Surely he knew him? Suddenly he remembered, nipped over the shop and tapped the man on the shoulder.

'If I were you, Phil, I'd get back up on the Campus as quickly as you can. You'll be done if anyone finds you in here.'

Phil gazed bleary-eyed at him. 'Yes, sir.'

He went back and paid for the biscuits and tea. He frowned and glanced over his shoulder at Phil. Why on earth was Phil wearing home clothes? 'Shall I come back with you Phil?'

'Yes, sir. I'll just buy some fags.'

He waited and then Phil came back and they walked slowly up the drive. Noel had to make himself walk really slowly to keep back to Phil's dragging pace. He wanted to half run and sing, but Phil went slower and slower, he shoulders bowed with an invisible weight.

He said, 'Are you all right?'

Phil sighed. 'I'll have lost my remission!'

'Pardon?'

'I had to go. You see, the wife wrote. My lad's been in trouble with the police. I had to go. She couldn't stand it any more.' Light began to dawn on Noel. So Phil had absconded.

'You mean you've, er, been home?'

'Yep.'

'When?'

'Last Sunday.'

'Last Sunday!' Noel stared in amazement. It was the first he'd heard of it.

'A few of us went. I think they must have got the others.'

'Oh yes. I heard about that. One of them thumbed a lift. Only when he got in the car he realized it was Wally Clarke behind the wheel!'

A ghost of a smile played round Phil's unshaven chin.

'You don't mean the Deputy Governor?'

'I do!'

'Oh.'

'What you in for, Phil?'

Phil stared across the marshes.

'A few bounced cheques. And I got a suspended sentence. Then I went and forgot to pay my National Insurance stamps. I was self-employed you see. So they sent me in here.'

'Forgot?'

Phil drooped even more. 'Well, you know what I mean. I got twelve months.'

Noel was amazed. He remembered carefully buying his National Insurance stamps every week at Byers Green and sticking them in the card.

'It's very easy to get on the wrong side of the law, isn't it.' Phil nodded. 'Too true, sir. The missus thought I'd got permission to come out. Anyway, I decided I'd better come back.'

'Come on, then. We'll go and see the Chief.'

Noel whistled as he went on his rounds next morning. He popped into the Punishment Block as he knew there was one man in there at the moment.

'Morning. Who've we got here?'

'James Paynton.'

'Oh.' He remembered James. The last time he'd seen him he'd been standing in the dining-room, bright-red in the face and shouting, all because another fellow had said they had one hundred head of cattle on the prison farm. James said two hundred! Then he blew his top at the other fellow who carried on doggedly eating his fish and chips, while James threatened him with a jug of water. Noel sighed as he read James' file. Even at twenty-two he was very immature. In and out of Borstal and Approved Schools. Now here. All because of his silly temper.

Noel unlocked his door and James sprang up like a scalded cat. 'Come on, lad, calm down,' said Noel and gave him a drink of orange.

'I can't stand it in here!'

'Why don't you sit down?'

'I won't stand it in here.'

He sat down and stared out of the window, one foot kicking at the iron legs of the bunk.

'Now look, James, you know why you're here.'

James began to roll a cigarette.

'You just lose your temper and wham! You're in here. The Governor's got no choice. How long you got this time?'

'Fourteen days.'

'How many have you done so far?'

'Three.'

'Oh,' said Noel. 'Well, don't be so stupid next time.'

'Nope.'

'Anything I can get you?'

'Nope.'

'Books from my library?'

'Nope.'

Noel sighed and got up to go.

'Chaplain?'

'Yes?'

'Ta.'

Noel grinned. 'You're welcome. See you tomorrow.'

He left and locked the door behind him. A pity about James, but there it was.

On the way back to the office he met a big, burly lad called Mick. 'Hello there. Hey weren't you the lad who did that card for me when my dad died?'

Mick coloured up and said, 'Yes, I did.'

'It was beautiful. I really appreciated it. Thanks a lot.'

As Noel set off again Mick called after him.

'Excuse me, but do you have, er, a discussion group on Monday evening?'

'Why, yes, I do. Would you like to come?'

'Yes please.' Noel was pleased. Mick didn't seem the usual type who came to the meetings. He was an ex-bouncer or something. Mick hovered on, so Noel said, 'Is anything wrong?'

Mick took a step nearer. 'I've got my wife and two young kids. It's her birthday today and I wish I could talk to her. I've sent her a card...and that, only she's been real good to me. Waiting for me and not taking any notice of the neighbours, spiteful lot.'

'Are you busy?'

'No, it's free time. I was just going for a walk.'

Noel said, 'Come with me. The Governor's given me an open phone. You're not allowed to speak to her direct, but I can phone her for you, with you sitting there. O.K.?'

A big smile lit up Mick's face. 'Oh, great. Thanks a lot.'

The first few weeks of Rebekah's life passed in a whirl of feeds and nappies, but the family didn't mind and anyway she slept soundly at nights. Norma said to him one day, 'You know we are such a happy family, especially with Mum with us. Isn't it lovely?'

'Yes my darlin'.'

'You Irish rogue!'

Late one evening she was doing the late night feed and he was trying to pray. But he couldn't. He felt drained inside. He'd nothing to say in chapel but remembered phrases. He'd given everything he'd got to the cons, poured it out on them day after day, and now it had all trickled away and left him in a drought. The still small voice that once spoke to him in quiet moments and refreshed his spirits, or came to him with a gentle force when he read the Bible, seemed to have deserted him now. He couldn't remember the last time he'd heard it...and in any case when he read his Bible he was so tired the words danced up and down on the page, or else the baby cried and he couldn't concentrate.

He wanted to pray for James, still in Punishment: he'd asked for a Bible. And there was Mick, too; he'd come each

Monday to the discussion group and seemed very interested. Noel walked restlessly to the window. Really Mick ought to go to Art Classes, and he'd see if he could arrange it. He sighed. Not only could he not pray, he could hardly say a 'thank you' either.

Norma gave a sudden cry and the baby, jerked awake, began to wail. 'Oh no! Noel come here!'

Obediently he turned from his reflections at the window and reached for a clean nappy.

'Feel that.'

He put the nappy on the bed and looked to where she was pointing. Then he prodded her breast. 'Is it sore?'

'No, silly. Can't you feel it?'

All of a sudden he felt it. A hard, round lump, like a pea under her delicate skin.

'Do you think it's…?'

'Oh no, it's only because you're breast-feeding.'

Norma stared, white-faced, at him.

'I've nursed people who've had lumps you know. They die.'

'Norma, stop it. It must be something to do with the breast-feeding. There's nothing to worry about. Have a good night's rest and it'll be gone in the morning.'

The next morning the first thing she did was feel for the lump. It was still there. Noel reassured her. 'It won't be anything at all. Yes, ask the doctor if you like.'

And so she did. The doctor said, 'There's nothing to worry about, Mrs Proctor. It's only a blocked milk-duct.'

But she couldn't stop worrying and went back to see him three times, and each time he said, 'I've no doubts about this lump. But would you like to see a Consultant?'

'Yes please.'

When she went to see the Consultant, he wasn't there and a House Surgeon examined her instead. 'There's nothing to worry about,' he said.

'But it keeps niggling at me,' said Norma. 'I was always trained that lumps should be excised and analysed.'

He shrugged. 'Very well then,' he said. 'I'll make you an appointment for surgery.'

When the day came for the operation to remove the lump, Norma had to sign a form that asked her whether she would be willing for a mastectomy if the lump was found to be malignant. She stared at the impersonal words on the impersonal form. What a question. She could wake up and find herself breastless, only half a woman. She winced. She remembered women she'd nursed, with their set faces and tremulous lips and the flattened side to their bodies, neatly stitched in half, with the flesh rising a little as if in protest, on each side of the stitches. She shuddered. 'Lord Jesus, help me to sign this form.'

She forced herself to reread the form, as if her life could be measured by the small letters that went to make up the words, as if life itself was so small and fragile that it fitted into the spaces inside the written words. Life! She recalled her tutor at Musgrave Park saying, 'Mastectomy is a life-saving operation.' And all the nurses listened, quietened as if a shadow had fallen across the room.

'A life-saving operation....' She thought of her three girls, then picked up the cheap ballpoint pen and wrote her name. It sprawled bold and black on the paper, a pathetic defiance against the scales of time. So now she was ready for the operation. Noel crept into the room and kissed her goodbye. 'Now don't worry. Marjorie's coming to look after your mum and the kids. And I'll fetch you this afternoon.'

'Goodbye.' She clung to his hand and then turned her face away. 'Goodbye.' He stood, a small man framed in the doorway and then went quickly.

He crossed the car park and clambered into the old Morris Traveller and then chugged off. He couldn't believe that Norma might have cancer. No, no. Such things never happened in their family. 'All things work together for good to those who love God,' he kept repeating to himself. But suddenly he amazed himself by hearing his mind say, 'Do they? Did all things work together for good when your mother-in-law had a stroke, when you lost the baby, when your dad died, and now when Norma has this...lump? Do they?'

When he got back to Eastchurch he parked the car near the house. Oh, no! What were those two doing on his step? Karl and Big Roy! Karl was peeping hopefully through the lounge window trying to see if Norma was in the lounge, behind the 'nets'. Noel sighed deeply and got out of the car.

'Can I help you two lads,' he called. Then he noticed
Norma's sister Marjorie peeping from behind the bedroom
curtains, rocking Becky in her arms.

'Well, I'm sorry lads, but there's no coffee today. Mrs
Proctor's in hosp....'

But Big Roy turned round and Noel swallowed his words,
hesitated and then carried on up the garden path. It was *his*
garden after all. Big Roy said nothing but put the sweeping
brush in such a position that Noel would have to climb over it.
Quickly Noel noticed some sweet papers on the grass, and
skirting the brush, went to pick them up.

'Good morning,' he said and then glanced up at Big Roy.
Very slowly Big Roy turned his back on him and then inched
his way down the path.

'Come on you lot,' shouted an Officer who seemed to appear
from nowhere and was obviously in charge of the gardening
working party. Noel breathed a sigh of relief. Karl trotted off
obediently down the path but Big Roy stood stock-still, as if
bound to the pavement. Nearly everybody was afraid of him,
but no one knew why. He had an aura that hung like a shadow
round him, like a black smell. His first and only words to Noel
had been, 'I've no time for God, no time for the church, and no
time for you. In that order.' And he'd flung past Noel's
outstretched hand. The other prisoners kept their distance or
else sucked up to him. Noel watched as Big Roy finally
slouched down the road, his spade over his shoulder. There'd
been rumours of violence at night in the dorm. Something
about sleepwalking. Noel always spoke to him, even though at
best he got a surly nod in reply. He often felt tempted to cross the
road if he saw him coming, but he'd will his feet to stay on the
same side. 'The snag is,' he'd told Norma, 'he's bigger than
me.'

Well he couldn't stay out on the drive all day. And he made
himself go into the house. Poor Norma. He wondered how she
was faring.

'It'll be all right,' he kept on saying all day to himself. Late
that afternoon Marjorie rang him at the office. 'The Ward
Sister's been on the phone. She says Norma's tired, so can she
stay in overnight.'

'Oh, I see.'

'It's quite normal, I think.'

'Righto.'

He sat at his desk and stared out of his window at the campus. So she was all right. But his heart didn't leap for joy and, fleetingly, he wondered why. It must be tiredness and he began to pack up and go home. Just as he was leaving there was a knock at the door! He ground to a halt in the middle of the room. Couldn't they leave him alone, even today? 'Go away, go away!' he wanted to shout. But his backbone stiffened. 'Come in,' he said.

An inmate stood in the doorway and then started to come in. Noel said, 'I'm not doing a surgery tonight. My wife's in hosp…'

But the man, unhearing, grabbed his arm. 'Oh please, sir, please help me,' and he began to tremble.

Noel stared back at him. Somewhere in a tiny back corner of his heart pity stirred. He gritted his teeth. 'Very well, then. Sit down,' and he removed the man's hand from his arm. The man came forward and slumped in the seat. Noel didn't remember seeing him before and certainly didn't know his name.

The man put his head in his hands, but Noel was detached. He'd seen it all before.

'It's my wife,' said the man. 'She's going to divorce me.' Noel sighed inwardly. He'd heard it all before.

'Go on,' he said.

'She, I mean I wrote to my wife and, er, I wrote to my secretary as well and the Censor's Office made a mistake and put the two letters in the wrong envelopes and now my wife's got the letter meant for my secretary…and so my wife's going to divorce me. She wrote me this' and he held out a letter to Noel. He took it but he didn't bother to read it. The writing sloped angrily in all directions and looked as if it had been in a puddle, or been wept over. He'd read them all before. He dredged a smile from the bottom of his consciousness and managed to lift his hand to give the man a friendly pat on the shoulder.

'Well, why was your wife furious?'

The man hung his head. 'It was lovey-dovey.'

'What was?'

'The letter to my secretary.'

'Oh...I see.'

'No, you don't see!' Noel blinked in surprise.

'My secretary's got enough on me to keep me in another four years. My wife doesn't know that. I've *got* to keep in with my secretary.' Noel slowly opened his desk, drew out a sheet of paper and an expensive ball point pen Norma had given him for Christmas. Was this man telling him the truth? How could he ever know? He was probably so mixed up he didn't know what the truth was. Noel began to write and then looked up.

'What's your wife's name?'

'Angela.'

'No. Surname?'

'Dyer.'

He wrote the letter, explaining to the wife, asking her to think again, telling her Dyer was heartbroken. He let Dyer read the letter and then sealed it up. 'I'll post it tonight,' said Noel. Automatically he picked up an invitation to the Chapel services and gave it to Dyer. Dyer stared at it and then, without a word, stuffed it in his pocket, and set out back to the dorm. Then, pausing on the threshold, he said to Noel, 'They said you'd help me.'

Back in the hospital Norma was coming round. She found herself in the ward, with bustle, noise and brilliant white all around. No one had drawn the curtains round her bed. Then, like a lump in the throat, it all came flooding back to her. She lay for about five minutes in the bed and then her right hand began to creep up her body. First across her stomach, then to her ribs. She stopped. Supposing...she pushed her index finger upward and her slender fingers felt round and round. And round.

There were so many dressings and bandages she couldn't tell. She half sat up and propped herself on her elbow. She felt for her good breast. Yes, nice and firm and she cupped it in her hand. Then for the other side. She made her hand caress the whole of her chest and, yes, the shape of a breast was there. She lay back on the pillows and a couple of tears made trails down her cheeks. So she was all right. But her heart didn't leap for joy. Must be tired. She lay down on her good side. Try and rest. Rest.

Next morning Noel came for her.

'They want me back on Monday to do the dressing,' she told him. 'Yes, all right.'

Norma stared at him. 'Aren't you pleased to see me?'

'Of course I'm pleased.'

'You seem so quiet.'

'I'm sorry. I've had to see to Becky.'

Norma bit her words back.

'Come on then,' he said. And they dragged themselves to the Morris Traveller.

## Chapter Thirteen

# Death Sentence

On the Monday Norma came back. A nurse took off her dressing and then left her to wait in the Consultant's sideroom. She waited. She lifted up the hospital gown and examined her breast. It was very bruised. They'd certainly handled it, to make such bruising. She lay back, waiting. They'd obviously had a jolly good look round.

Suddenly the door opened and the Consultant strode in. She struggled to half sit up. 'Good morning,' he said, without lifting his eyes from the paper in his hand. She glanced at it and saw it was a Pathologist's report. She knew from her Musgrave Park days that when a patient had been as worried as she'd been, they often showed them the report just to satisfy them once and for all that all was well. Tears of joy welled up in her eyes.

The Consultant pursed his lips. Then, 'Well, now, Mrs Proctor, I have the pathologist's report.' She gazed at him, bright-eyed.

'The lump which we removed from you was, unfortunately, malignant.'

Norma gazed at him helplessly from under the sheet. Her eyes were frozen with shock. 'But I've got three children....'

He seemed not to hear her. 'You've got breast cancer. It's as simple as that.'

'But I've got three children....'

'You can either leave it as it is and have radiotherapy. Or I can give you a mastectomy. That means take your breast off. And you might still have to have radiotherapy afterwards.'

'But I've got three....'

He snapped shut his file. 'You have twenty-four hours to

decide.' Norma felt as if she were stuck to the bed.

'But I've got....'

He was gone.

She lay a long time. Breast cancer! How could she have it? A nurse came in and tried to help her up.

Norma said, 'I must phone my husband.' She picked up the phone but couldn't remember the number. The nurse stayed with her and looked it up for her. At last she heard Noel's soft voice on the other end of the line.

'Noel, I...I....'

'What is it?'

She couldn't answer at first and then it all came out in a rush. 'I've got cancer. Cancer. The Consultant just told me. And I...I've got three children. Who's going to look after them?' She began to cry and her tears ran down the phone.

'Noel? Noel?'

He didn't reply and she looked up at the nurse. 'He's gone. Oh, he's there. Hello? Noel?'

His voice sounded hoarse on the phone and all she could hear him saying was, 'Norma, Norma,' and a noise like crying. Then he said, 'I'll come for you.'

'What about your interviews?'

But he'd rung off.

They drove home almost in silence. When they were nearing the prison, she said, 'Noel, I'm dying.'

He half turned to her and she saw that his eyes were red. He swung the wheel violently, lurched round the corner and then slowed up. 'No, Norma,' he said. 'No!' But she didn't believe him. And neither did he.

When they got home she went straight up to their bedroom. 'Tell Marjorie I'll see her upstairs,' she called over her shoulder to him, then she went into their room and slumped on the bed.

Marjorie came in and Norma faced her: 'The lump was malignant.' Marjorie's hand went over her mouth and she came and sat by Norma. 'Mother *mustn't* know,' said Norma and got up.

Marjorie stared after her and then jumped up and said, 'Why is it that Christian people have this, this cancer? Why doesn't God protect you?' and she flounced out of the room.

Why indeed? Norma pressed her forehead to the cool hand-mirror. As if being a Christian gave you some sort of insurance against the onslaughts of life. She wanted to say, 'I didn't become a Christian for what I could get out of it, but because I loved Jesus Christ.' But Marjorie had gone. Norma sat on in the room darkened by twilight. 'Why?' her spirit called out in anguish. Then she got off the bed and made herself go down-stairs. Mother mustn't know. She *mustn't*.

As she sat at the tea table she ate mechanically and only old Mrs Long, Helen and Susie tucked into the buns and cakes. Noel was rocking little Becky as if his life depended on it, his tea undrunk, his sandwich uneaten. Norma wanted to say, 'Give her to me. She's my baby. I want her. I won't be here much longer!' But instead she went in the kitchen and got the baby's feed out of the fridge.

Somehow they got the tea over and then Norma went to bed. Noel helped Marjorie with the children and his mother-in-law and then finally he crawled in by Norma. He lay awake a long time, stiff as a ramrod beside her and while she slept he tried to settle his thoughts. He pressed his hands to his eyes but they kept opening and scanning the darkness as if the answer were somehow written there. He felt as though someone had attached weights to his body and he ached all over with sadness. Again he remembered the verse 'All things work together for good, to them who love God.' He thought about the words, but they seemed to rise up and mock him, as if spoken by sleek, well-fed people raised in warm, detached houses, who were satisfied they knew the truth.

He buried his head in the pillow. If only he weren't so tired. If only God would speak to him, show him why all this was happening. But the darkness gave no reply. He felt so wrung out from pouring himself out for other people that he dreaded the next morning. Norma would be weepy, he knew that; the girls squabbling, old Mrs Long dribbling over her tea, the baby wailing and Marjorie to be taken to the station. And then he had to prepare a sermon for the cons, and think of some-thing for the Sunday School.

What would happen to him if he really went beyond his tether? Would he go mad? Or just turn into a cabbage? Some more words from the Bible came into his mind: 'In all these things you are more than conquerors.' More than conquerors? Over cancer? Over death? He clenched his fists under the blankets. How often had he trotted out that text: at funerals, at accidents, by hospital beds, in the Punishment block. He groaned inwardly. He hadn't known then how much it could hurt being human.

He inched his way out of bed and crept downstairs: half past four. He sighed. It wasn't the first time he'd had a sleepless night, nor the last no doubt. He put the kettle on and waited in the kitchen for it to boil. The whole room was redolent of Norma: her curtains, her china, her plants, her lists pinned to the wall, her clothes airing on the rack, her postcards from her friends, her homemade cakes in the tins. He couldn't weep, but his shoulders were bowed as if they carried a great weight. He forced himself to put his fear into words. His wife was dying. No, his wife could die. She might die, and one day he would die. He looked out of the window at the daffodil leaves straggling over the flower bed, and the faded tulips beside them. They'd end up like that. Faded. Then dead. They'd disappear, go into darkness so to speak.

All his parson's training rose up in argument against such an idea. The words 'Resurrection' and Eternal life' blurted into his mind, but jangled and tinkled and fell meaningless to the floor. His heart only knew one thing. He loved Norma and she was under a sentence of death.

When he awoke it was seven o'clock and he was cramped and cold in a kitchen chair. Norma was shaking him and he rubbed his eyes and yawned. Then with a sickening rush his memory quickened and he grabbed her hand. 'I wish I could have the cancer for you,' he said. She didn't answer but the ghost of a smile stirred in her eyes. She'd been going to bang about the kitchen and say, 'Why didn't you get Becky up? And where's her feed? Fancy leaving it all to me?' But instead she said gently, 'There's something funny about Mum. She's awake, but she doesn't know me. Her speech is slurred.'

Together they went upstairs and gazed at the shell of the strong woman they'd once known. Her spirit still flickered feebly, but her body was that of a thin bird.

'She's had another stroke?'

Norma nodded and then looked at him. 'You know what

this means? I can't have a mastectomy tomorrow. I can't leave her. *I can't*. I promised her I'd never send her to a hospital after the last time. She was petrified.' She pulled the covers over her mother and they went on to the landing. 'Well, at least it's made up my mind for me. I'll have the radiotherapy treatment instead and I'll nurse her at home.' She peeped into the room again. 'At least she doesn't know about me.'

Noel said, 'How can you talk so calmly about radiotherapy? You'll get sickness and depression.'

Norma shook her head. 'Because I'm going to fight.'

'Fight?'

'Yes. Fight for my girls. Fight for my life. I don't want to die.'

He stood helplessly as she went downstairs. She said, 'This stroke of Mother's is all the guidance I need. God's hand must be in it because it's taken the decision off my shoulders.'

He stared after her. How could she talk about God like that?

But by teatime she was exhausted and all the fight had drained out of her. She lay sobbing on the settee while he struggled with the girls and his mother-in-law and at last got them all settled for the night. Then he went and sat by Norma and put his arm round her. She pulled away from him.

'Can't you say something to help me?' she asked, eagerly demanding, as if he could feed her with life, as if she wanted to suck out the very hope from his marrow.

He pondered.

'Tell me it's God's will!'

He bit his lip.

'Well surely you know something from the Bible to tell me?'

She flung his arm away. 'Surely a preacher ought to be able to give me hope!' And she burst into bitter sobs.

He opened his mouth to tell her the texts he'd remembered from the Bible the night before when he couldn't sleep. He tried to say them but they stuck in his throat. He gazed helplessly back at her. 'Shall I make you some tea?'

'Tea!' she screamed. 'Is that all you can think about! Tea!' And she buried her head in the cushion.

He got up and walked over to the window and stared out over the marshes. It was dark and he sensed rather than saw the rough grass bending in the salt wind. The chill gusts seemed to enter his very soul. There was a movement beside him and he looked round. It was Norma. 'I'll have that tea now please,' she whispered.

'O.K.,' he said. 'In a minute.'

As he lingered on near the window all he'd ever hoped for and dreamed of seemed to flame up suddenly and then, in a blast of bitter wind, snuff out. Something in him had died.

## Chapter Fourteen

# The Cross Behind Bars

The week dragged by and Noel discovered he could go on, even in the job he was in, because he still believed God existed and he still had the will to survive. But one evening, as he was preparing to go and do some extra visiting in Ninety-Eight block, it suddenly dawned on him what God was trying to tell him.

'Oh, I think I understand now. You've no further use for me. My ministry's over.' Well, he'd face up to it at last, but there was a lump in his throat and he still didn't feel any more peaceful. Strange, and he frowned. He shut the front door behind him. All that stuff about power and evangelism seemed like dust and ashes to him now.

He began to speak to God as he set off down the path. 'How do you expect me to carry on? I'll have to give up my calling and just do a nine till five job. I'll have three girls to rear alone.' He was no longer angry, just spent with care. 'After all I've done for you. And you can't even let Norma see little Becky grow up.'

His garden was bursting with late spring flowers and blossom lay in drifts on the grass. He was shocked by the cheek of it all, by the course vibrancy of the birds, by the daring of the plants. It was too cruel that spring should burst out with greenery at the moment.

A few moments later he passed the chapel and on a sudden impulse got off his bike, propped it against the wall and went in. He collapsed on to a seat and tried to think. It was very quiet inside. He waited. He couldn't speak a nice prayer to God. He couldn't talk to him at all and he simply bowed his head. After a while he looked up and then, as if for the first time, he noticed Wally Clarke's cross, empty and stark on the wall above the altar. The sun was shining on it, lighting up the nails. He put his hand to his head; yes, he had an inkling now of what a crown of thorns could feel like. He saw the stakes driven through the wood, where the hands and feet should have been. He'd had a taste of something a bit like a stake lately.

All at once he half rose from his seat and then sank down on to his knees. The God he'd been blaming had actually died himself. The Jesus he'd preached about so often, knew all about it; he knew so much more about suffering than he did. Noel bowed his head. 'Forgive me,' he whispered. And then he looked up at the cross again and through a blur, it seemed as if he were on that cross for a moment. Then he was himself again, back in his seat.

He got his New Testament out and towards the end of Romans chapter 8 he read the texts he'd tried to say to Norma. 'All things work together for good to them that love God.' And, 'In all these things we are more than conquerors.' He sighed and half closed the book, but something suddenly riveted his attention. Between the two sentences the word death was mentioned twice, no, three times. He dropped the Bible on to the seat. What did it mean? What was the connection?

And then he saw it. He'd known it all along really...only now it was etched into his heart. The bridge to power, success, victory and to all that was good and eternal was through death; Christ's death. And seemingly he had to learn about that path as well. He remembered himself as a younger Noel, leaping on to platforms and going on about power and repentance, and he blushed. He'd wanted all the salvation there was, for himself and for others, but he'd forgotten the cost, the terrible cost. No wonder they'd called him arrogant at college! And why had Jesus gone to that terrible cost? He frowned. He knew the answer to that, it was so we could be saved from our sins...he found the page again and re-read it. 'Because he loved us.'

He closed the Bible and sat on quietly. A love that was prepared to go to the very limits and beyond. It made his own love seem a ragged, poor thing in contrast. He got up and walked slowly out of the chapel. As he went he turned once more to look at Wally's empty cross: the emptiness was its hope. As he left, he knew; he'd never be the same again.

On the way back he saw Big Roy coming down the road on the same side as him, but Noel neither hurried nor slowed up. As he got nearer to Big Roy, he said, 'Good evening to you.' Big Roy scowled and his tawny eyes glared at Noel. The black aura still hung round him like a smell, cutting him off from the other men. It struck Noel that Big Roy was never seen walking with anyone, but was always on his own. This time Noel didn't care what Big Roy could do to him. He'd been staring death in the face for so long that the problem of Big Roy seemed simple in comparison. Noel looked him straight in the eye and then strode on. Big Roy moved slightly to let him pass and then stared after him as he went past, his eyes narrow slits.

The week passed somehow. Despite his new-found understanding in the chapel Noel still felt empty although underneath the emptiness there was a sense of quiet, which hadn't been there before. Norma began her radiotherapy treatment at Rochester hospital. The trouble was that it was a fifty-mile round trip and on top of that they had a young baby and a dying mother to look after and in the end Norma broke down under the strain. She wept constantly and clung to him for help. He tried to give it to her, but in his own heart he kept crying out, 'Who'll help me? Who'll support me?' It seemed there was no one.

By the Thursday he was spent, but he had to keep going on. And on and on. And on. As he cycled to and fro on his bike he heard himself muttering, 'The cons have finished me, sucked me dry. And what have I got out of it? A couple of Mars bars!' Then another thought surprised him. It was his own fault. He'd conned himself that he was the great and mighty Noel Proctor, able to work and work and bring peace and hope and salvation to the men. 'A trio,' he'd thought boastfully, him and Norma and God. Well there was only God left now. He was finished and she was, well, poorly. It served him right for thinking too much of himself.

But even as he stood here outside his office, fiddling with his bunch of keys, he knew God wasn't punishing him, nor waiting for him with a big stick. 'He's letting me see life as it really is, for some folk at least,' and the thought staggered him.

He got through the morning, automatically cycling round one old RAF hut to the next. Would the incessant struggle never end? Was this what came of putting God first? It was as he was cycling back that the full force of what he'd refused to think about, really hit him. It wasn't that he'd be left alone with three kids and a different job to find. No, it wasn't that.

He clambered off his bike and walked. He noticed Mick working on a flower bed, deftly turning soil with a trowel.

'Hello there.'

'Hello, Mr Proctor.'

Noel watched him tying up the old daffodil leaves into loose knots ready to wither down. Soon no one would ever know there'd ever been any bulbs at all. But Mick was whistling.

'We'll have a marvellous show next year.'

'Oh?'

'Yes. You'd never know the bulbs were there during the summer. Underground in the dark, just biding their time till next spring.' He grinned and plucked up a few weeds.

As Noel watched him, something stirred in the back of his mind.

Then he said, 'How you doing these days?'

'Oh,' and Mick was very busy with the trowel, 'I've made my mind up.'

'Pardon?'

'I'm going to get stuck into this religious thing.'

'Oh?'

'Yes. Well I always did think Jesus was a good bloke when I was at school. It was just that no one ever told me.'

'Told you what?'

'That he was still around.'

Noel said nothing, but he shook Mick by the hand. If only Mick knew....

'Oh and my wife liked her birthday card.'

'Why did they put you in here, Mick?'

Mick flushed. 'I was a Bouncer at the King Kade Club in the East End. It, well, I got into a fight. Stupid really.' He shifted the earth about a bit more.

'Actually Mr Proctor, I've heard all about this Jesus stuff before.'

'Oh?'

'Yes, I used to go to the Mayflower Centre run by this chap called David Sheppard.'

Noel nodded. He'd heard of the Centre.

Mick went on, 'My wife wrote and told me he's been made a Bishop now.'

'Yes. Mick?'

Mick looked up.

'I think you ought to go to art classes. You're good.'

Mick smiled. 'I've just enrolled, sir.'

'Good lad.'

Then Noel set off and trudged home with his bike. Mick gazed after him, a puzzled frown on his forehead. Poor old Chaplain. He looked as if he carried the cares of the world on his shoulders. And by the time Noel got to his front door, he'd faced the issue he'd been shirking all week. How could he live without Norma? It was as simple as that. He knew he couldn't.

Next day he got Norma into the front seat of the car and Becky in her carry cot at the back. Then he set off for St Williams hospital, Rochester. When they arrived she got out and he carried the baby in his arms and they went to the waiting-room full of patients. They all had cancer. Noel and Norma sat together and waited for her name to be called out. The place was dark and dreary and needed a coat of paint.

Eventually her name was called and she went off. Noel got up and took Becky and waited in the car. Somehow it seemed easier than avoiding the half glances of the other patients.

Norma walked down the interminable corridors to the radiotherapy room. She was alone, alone as she'd never been before. She took her clothes off and lay on the high bed. Dr Jenkins, the radiologist, came in and marked out her body with a blue marking pen as he needed to be sure which parts were to get the treatment. Then a nurse covered the rest of her body up with bags of small lead pellets. Then they both went out and closed the door, operating the machine from beyond closed doors. Norma lay utterly still for the twenty minutes and then Dr Jenkins came back in. As he began to lift off the pellets she shivered.

He said, 'Are you cold, Mrs Proctor?'

'No, I'm terrified.'

He took her hand and spoke gently. 'I think your surgery went well. Try not to worry.'

She struggled to sit up. She had to know. She had to have it in black and white. 'How long have I got, Doctor?'

He looked at her and she was aware of the sorrow behind his brown eyes. 'I can't really say. I wish I could.' He piled up the pellets on a trolley and the nurse wheeled them out. 'We did have one patient who lived seven to eight years. But,' he looked away, 'I must tell you, Mrs Proctor, that that is exceptional when the cancer has spread as far as this.'

Norma pulled her clothes on mechanically and then he said, 'We'll see you tomorrow. Everything we can do, we *will* do.'

She nodded. He was kind and she knew he'd do his best. She went back to the waiting-room and then to the car. Somehow she had to fight it; she had to trust, there was nothing else to do.

Then Friday came and Noel was idly flicking through his diary when suddenly he groaned.

Norma looked up. 'What's the matter?'

'I'm preaching at Sittingbourne on Sunday evening.'

He ran his hand through his hair and she watched him as he started hunting for a book of sermons. He was quite grey now and a bit thin on top. She went and looked at her own face in the mirror and touched her hair; it was lank and lustreless. She remembered herself and Noel as they used to be. He fair-haired and full of zest, prancing up and down on various platforms with his cornet. She in lacy blouses, crowned with glowing, bouncy hair, giggling at him from the back row. She turned away from the mirror. What had they come to now? Was this...all there was? No, she couldn't believe that. She *had* to trust, somehow. Then she pulled herself together. Noel was saying, 'I just can't go. I can't. I can't.'

'But you've promised.'

'I can't,' and he buried his head in his hands.

'Well phone the pastor, then.'

'No, I'll have to go. I can't let him down.'

Later he crept out of the house and went to the chapel. He slumped in a side seat and then looked up at Wally's cross. The cross stared back and as he gazed at it, it seemed to be trying to tell him something. What was it?

Then he knew: without meaning to, he'd always tried to keep the pain of the cross at arm's length. Oh, he'd preached about the empty cross often enough—its victory, its power, its success—and had been right to do so. But he'd not wanted to know about the pain and the cost. He'd fenced the cross in, put it behind bars, not wanted to get too close. But now he knew and he bowed his head. After a moment his shoulders sagged and he said. 'All right. All right. I give in.'

Then he got up and went back home and found the telephone book. He looked up Pastor Jones' telephone number at Sittingbourne and picked up the phone.

At last a voice answered, 'Pastor Jones here.'

Noel said, 'I'm coming to speak to you on Sunday night, about the prison work.'

Pastor Jones was pleased he'd phoned and they talked about arrangements. Then there was a pause. Pastor Jones said, 'Are you all right?'

Noel tried to say, 'Oh, fine,' but instead began to cry. He was horrified at himself and tried to stop, but he couldn't.

The Pastor was quite calm, 'Don't worry, friend,' he kept saying, 'You'll tell me when you can.' Then, 'Shall I come out to you?'

Noel managed to say, 'No,' and then, in a tangle of words, he said, 'Do you believe in divine healing? My wife, er, she's got cancer, and I, that is we, can't go on, and I feel as if I've died inside.'

Pastor Jones said quietly, 'We do believe in the power of Christ to heal.'

'Then will you pray for Norma?'

'We will. And gladly.'

There was a pause. Noel swallowed his pride.

'And...er...me. I need it, too.'

'Yes brother,' said the kind voice of the Pastor. 'We'll do it right after the service.'

When the Sunday came Noel and Norma drove to Sittingbourne in silence. When they were nearly there he burst out with, 'He's *got* to give me a sign!'

'Who?'

'God, of course. He *must*. I've got to have a sign.'

Norma was quiet. 'Got to?'

'Yes. Got to!'

'I've got to know he wants me to carry on with my work. And I've got to know you are going to get better.'

He preached somehow and then they were led into the vestry where the Pastor and the Elders were sitting round in a circle. They welcomed the Proctors with kind and gentle smiles, yet Noel felt there was a hint of steel there, too. No one could pull the wool over these men's eyes.

Pastor Jones said, 'Forgive me for asking, but we always do the prayers for healing in the same way.' He glanced round the circle of quiet men dressed in grey and they nodded in turn, then he turned back to Noel and Norma. 'Is there any sin in your lives? Any wrongdoing, or thoughts that trouble you? Whatever you say will be in utter confidence.'

They looked at each other and then she said, 'Er, no, I can't think of anything.'

Noel ran his tongue over his lips, 'Well, I suppose I've lacked faith. I've not believed God could, no, would, help me.'

There was a pause and then the Elders gathered round and laid their hands on Noel's and Norma's heads. Pastor Jones, still in his quiet voice, prayed, 'Almighty God, in your mercy, we ask you to please heal your servants.' He prayed over each one individually, asking for healing, wholeness and a restoring of joy. Then the Elders gradually began to say, 'Thank you. Thank you.' Noel bowed his head sadly. He still felt the same.

When they were alone again, he said to her, 'Do you feel better?'

She hesitated. 'No, not really. But Noel?'

'Yes?'

'I do trust the Lord. I trust. I'm in his hands.'

He concentrated on his driving. He wished he felt so sure.

## Chapter Fifteen

# 'Not Unto Death'

On the following Tuesday Karl came to do Norma's garden, on the dot of eleven as usual. She gave him coffee and then went in, while he drank it slowly. Mick came over from across the road and had a word with him. Karl's face broke into a grin and he nodded. He trotted back to the house and rang the bell. Norma leaned against her sink in the kitchen and muttered, 'Go away,' but she still trailed to the door and held out her hand for the cup.

Karl said, 'Mrs Proctor, me and my mate Mick would like to give yer somethink.'

'Oh yes?'

'We'd like to carve you a name-plate for this house, you know, with the name on a piece of wood.'

She was surprised. 'That's very kind of you.'

'Well what name do yer want?'

'Er...er,' she couldn't think at first. 'Oh, I know, "Bethany".'

'Betharny? What's that?'

'It was the name of a house where Jesus used to go and stay.'

Karl blinked. Norma half whispered, 'I'd like to think he would come to this house and stay here, if he were walking the earth.'

Karl nodded. 'Write down how you spell "Betharny" for us.'

As she wrote she said, 'Are you going home soon?'

He hung his head. 'Suppose so.'

'Don't you want to go home?'

He grinned uncertainly. 'Well...yes. But my stepfather don't want me. No, no, I'll get back in here as soon as I can!'

She resisted the impulse to smile. Poor, pathetic little chap, and obviously not all there. She gave him the paper and watched him trundle off with it. She shook her head. What was it he'd said last time? 'My Mam wanted a fur coat and I didn't see why I shouldn't help myself to one!' Noel used a word to describe inmates like him: 'recidivist' or 'unable to cope with life outside'. Her smile was gone now. Prison was the only real stable 'home' he'd ever had.

As she shut the front door an inner voice seemed to speak to her. 'Go and read the story about Bethany.' She pushed the thought away; she knew the story—why bother to read it again? But the voice persisted so she looked at her watch: Noel was out, her mother was asleep and Becky dozing. She went upstairs, protesting all the way. She knew the story, she didn't want to read now, she'd a lot to do....

She went into the bedroom, found her Bible and plumped down on the bed. She flipped through the delicate pages until she came to the story in John's Gospel and idly she began to read. Suddenly one of the verses seemed to jump out of the page at her. It shouted at her, it strode round the furniture, it filled the room. She began to tremble inside and then leaped up and ran to the window to hold the page up to the light. It couldn't be true, could it? Could it? She read the verse again:

This sickness is not unto death....
But that the Son of God might be glorified by it [John 11:4].

'Not unto death,' she whispered and then sank down by the bed. Was Jesus really saying this to her? Was he saying her cancer wasn't unto death? Was he promising her life? As she knelt there the hope that she had grew and grew, until like a great tree coming from a tiny seed, she knew. He had! He had spoken to her when she least expected it. She knew she wouldn't die. And she knew there was going to be a reason for her living. She didn't know yet what it was, but she knew.

She raced downstairs and grabbed the phone. Noel's weary voice answered. She cried, 'I've had a sign! A sign! You know you wanted God to give you a sign? Well he has! Only he's given it to me!' She told him about the verse and he listened intently. He could hear her voice breaking with her joy. And in his own heart something stirred; like the first streak of dawn light after a long and bitter night.

Life still had to go on. Norma still had to complete her radiotherapy and Noel still had to work hard every day. As he was opening his mail on the Wednesday he noticed with surprise he'd got a letter from David Sheppard, the Bishop of Woolwich. It was quite simple: David wanted to come and see his old friend Mick, from the Mayflower Centre days. Noel ran outside with the letter, went to find Mick and let him read it.

Mick was stunned. 'A Bishop! Coming to see me?'

A small crowd of men gathered round and Noel explained. 'Would you like him to talk to you?'

Several heads nodded. One lad said, 'Wasn't there a cricketer of that name?'

Mick and Noel exchanged knowing glances. 'One and the same!' said Mick, and Noel left him, the centre of an admiring crowd of lads.

As Noel got on to his bike again he saw James running to join the group and he shook his head. James was constantly in and out of hot water. He'd spent more of his time in 'Punishment' than anyone else. And yet? Noel watched him. Who could tell? He *said* he wanted to be a Christian: it was just that his behaviour didn't seem to coincide with his desire to be good! Noel sighed. After all, did anyone's? He decided he'd better not write James off too quickly; perhaps there was more there than met the eye.

He got home and backed the Morris Traveller out. Norma was ready and they set off for Rochester. It was already day four of the treatment. As she lay in the hospital room and the radiologist gave her the cobalt treatment, she began to tremble again. No, she mustn't give in. So this time she tried to focus her mind on Jesus and his great love for her. For *her*. She talked to him about the girls and about Noel and her mum and about herself. She repeated to herself the words, 'Not unto death.'

Suddenly the door banged and in came Dr Jenkins.

'Are you finished already?' asked Norma, amazed. Surely she'd only been in here a few minutes?

'Yes,' said Dr Jenkins and gave her a curious glance.

On the way home she relaxed in the front seat and watched the great horse chestnut trees with their pink 'candles' all lit, and the fields bursting with buttercups. It was all so beautiful and she drank it in, as if it were the first time she'd ever seen it.

When they got home she slipped up to see her mother. Old Mrs Long lay in a semi-coma and Norma kissed her. She sensed that her mother was trying to leave her feeble shell of a body behind. 'Goodbye Mum dear,' she whispered. And during the night her mother died peacefully in her sleep.

As the days lengthened into weeks and months and Norma grew stronger, Dr Jenkins became cautiously optimistic about her. When she'd finished her radiotherapy treatment the nurse said to her, 'We were surprised you didn't have any depression or radiation sickness.'

Norma smiled, as if the nurse had just given her a present. She *knew* why. 'Thank you,' she said. Then, grasping the table to give her moral support, Norma said, 'I wish I could stand by the sick and dying like you and help them. You see I used to be a nurse.'

At that moment Dr Jenkins popped into the room and overheard her. He thought a minute and then sizing her up and down said, 'If you promise me you won't do any heavy lifting, then I think you could go back to nursing. And it would be the best therapy in the world for you.'

Norma went pink with pleasure and rushed off to see what Noel thought.

As they were driving home she told him all about it.

'I know it sounds funny, me wanting to go back to nursing now. I know you need me and the children need me, but since I had this cancer I feel so urgent about everything. As if nothing can wait. And I feel I've got to go and comfort the sick and dying.'

He glanced at her and saw her old spirit returning in the toss of her head and glow of her hair. He patted her hand. 'How often would you go?'

'Twice a week at night.'

'All right, my darling, do whatever you like. I don't mind.'

She grasped his hand and smiled. It was all the thanks he needed.

## Chapter Sixteen

# Nightmare

Their life fell into a new pattern: she was out two nights a week while he minded the girls, and although they both got tired, her spirits were good. He marvelled at her. Most of the time she had an absolute trust that she wouldn't die; and when occasionally she had bad days Noel was able to help her through them. As for Noel himself, he didn't quite understand what had happened to him, but slowly and surely, as if after a great storm, he felt at peace. Every now and then a spurt of joy hit his eye. It would take time, he knew, for him to get back to his old drive and impetus, but at least where he'd felt so empty before, now he just felt quiet.

One morning he was walking briskly to his office when he saw Big Roy hanging round near the doorway. He slackened his pace momentarily and then carried on. Big Roy slouched up to him till he towered over him. He wiped his nose with the back of his hand and then said, 'Chaplain, can I speak to you?'

'Fire away.'

'Will you, er, pray for me?'

Noel stopped dead in his tracks, his key half way to the lock. He swung round on Big Roy. 'The only other time you ever spoke to me you said, "I've no time for God, no time for the church, and no time for you—in that order!" So why the change of heart?'

Big Roy shuffled his feet and shook his greasy hair that had been blonde and was now grey. He shrugged his shoulders and then said, 'Can I talk to you?'

'Yes. But you're supposed to be on a working party at the moment. I'll speak to you at lunchtime.'

'O.K.'

Noel watched him as he went. He didn't actually smell at all, in fact he was perfectly clean, but Noel wrinkled his nose. There was just something about him that was, well, *like* a bad smell. Noel shivered. Big Roy gave him the creeps.

Noel went into his office and spent a few moments praying about Big Roy before his day began. 'Please give me the grace to love even a man like Big Roy.' Noel knew now that he couldn't help God. There was no trio. It was simply a case of being the Lord's servant.

When lunchtime came there was a knock at his door.

'Come in.'

Big Roy lurched in and sat down without being asked. Noel was surprised. He'd wondered whether Big Roy would come at all. 'How can I help you, Roy?'

Big Roy began to bite his nails and his dark presence seemed to disturb the room, but Noel felt perfectly quiet about him.

'Yer see, Chaplain, I get these nightmares.' An ugly red stain crept into his cheek and his head fell on to his chest. Noel nodded. He'd heard about these nightmares, of men refusing to sleep near him in the dorm.

Big Roy looked up. 'Well last night I terrified the chap next to me in the dorm. And I terrified myself as well.'

'How was that?'

Big Roy stared at Noel. He seemed to be labouring with his words. 'I tried to strangle him.'

Noel held his gaze and looked into his tawny bloodshot eyes. A wave of pity for the fellow swept over him. Big Roy leaned forward. 'You see, I'm dreaming I'm strangling him in the nightmare, only I really *am* doing it. It's as if I'm in chains bound to the bed and my body gets up and starts doing awful things. I can't control it.' A great shudder went like a spasm through Roy. He said, 'Chaplain, I'm terrified. What'll I do next? Murder or something? I quite like the lad in the next bed, only I *couldn't* stop my body trying to strangle him!'

Noel frowned, perplexed. He'd never come across this kind of problem before. 'What about the M.O.?'

'I've had it all. Medical treatment; drugs; psychiatrist; nothing cured me. I'm getting worse.'

'What you in for?'

'Drunk and Disorderly.'

Noel thought a moment and then Big Roy leaned across his desk and said, 'Please pray for me. I've tried everything else.'

Noel got up. 'All right. Come on.' On the way he found the Officer in charge of Big Roy and asked permission to take him to the chapel and the Officer agreed.

Just before they got there Roy said, 'I think I know what's the cause of it all.'

'Oh?'

'When I was a kid of about nine my Dad fell out with a gypsy family and sent them packing. One of those gypsies came back and caught me in the lane. He cursed me, over and over again.'

'You mean "swore"?'

'No, Chaplain. A curse.'

Noel looked at him sharply. Was he taking the mickey? No. For a second Noel seemed to see the young Roy gazing desperately out of Big Roy's eyes.

'Do you think I'm daft?' he asked.

Noel shook his head. 'Come and listen to this story.' He got a Gideon New Testament out of his pocket, opened it at Luke chapter 8, and began to read Roy a story:

> There was once a man who wore no clothes, cut himself with knives, tore off his chains and roamed round a graveyard. One day Jesus found this demented bloke [Luke 8:26–40].

Big Roy was rapt, but then he began to tremble. 'Go on,' he said. Noel swallowed. In an instant he saw the trap he was falling into: if he told Roy he was demon-possessed like the man in the story, then Roy would for ever more blame all his lapses on the devil and take no responsibility for his own actions. Noel winced as he imagined Roy telling a magistrate that the 'devil' had made him drunk. On the other hand, if he didn't pray for Roy to be delivered, then he might never get right...and Noel might never get the opportunity again.

Big Roy shifted in his chair, 'Go on,' he said.

'Well Jesus cast out, er, Legion from him.'

There was a pause and then Noel said, 'Jesus utterly changed him. He stayed in his right mind from then on.'

Big Roy's eyes bored into Noel. Noel said, 'Shall I pray for you now?' Big Roy nodded.

They walked up to the chancel rail and Noel prayed for him: 'Please, Lord, forgive Roy's sins...and please take, take out of Roy's life whatever is causing these nightmares.'

There was a sudden movement by Noel's side and he looked round. Big Roy had knelt down. Noel drew himself up to his full height and laid his hands on Big Roy's head. With a firmness of voice that surprised even himself, he said, 'May you be healed and changed, in the name of the Father, the Son and the Holy Spirit.'

After a moment Big Roy looked up at Noel and there were tears trickling down his cheeks. He said, 'For the first time in my life I feel clean.'

Noel put his arm round him and gave him the New Testament.

Later that evening Noel was telling Norma about it.

'Do you know what was the most remarkable thing of all? He used the word "clean" to describe the change in him. Now how did he *know* that was the correct theological word when he would never be seen dead near a church?'

'Well something obviously happened to him.'

'Yes, I think so.'

She said, 'Have you ever prayed like that for anyone else?'

'No, it just seemed the right thing to do at the time.'

'How did you know God would answer?'

He stared down at his hands. 'I just *knew*. After all, he's healed you.'

Her face lit up and she took his hand, 'Let's pray for him, shall we.'

The next Sunday just before the service began the door at the back of the church banged and Noel looked up. Big Roy strode in and behind him came a gang of about twenty men, none of whom had ever darkened the doors of the chapel before. But they were all quiet enough during the service. At the end Noel caught Roy's eye and went to shake his hand.

Roy smiled. 'It worked!' he cried happily. 'I've not had another nightmare since.'

After a bit he joined his cronies and they meandered off, apparently carefree in the sunshine. Noel scratched his head.

Funny, he didn't feel creepy about Roy now.

Noel could never quite put his finger on what began to happen to him after all the bitter months of suffering in his family. In one way he'd never be the same again. In another, he was just the same hard-working Noel. But things were happening on the campus. Staff and prisoners came to chapel and when all the Sunday School kids were there, it was bursting at the seams. And he knew why. He blushed to think he'd once thought God would give him power. Who was he to have power? In one way he was much less confident. He knew who he was now; a servant. Oh yes, he was an evangelist, he knew that. But over and above that he was a servant.

In another way, he was more confident. He knew if he prayed and asked Jesus to help the lads as and when they wanted it, Jesus would answer the prayers. After all, he'd helped him and Norma, so he could help others. Big Roy never looked back. Neither did Mick. Even James stuck doggedly to the Bible class, though he was full of argument! And a man called Dyer whom Noel scarcely remembered came and told him that after Noel had sent his wife a letter she'd decided not to divorce him after all!

'You saved my marriage,' said Dyer, pumping Noel by the hand.

And there were many others who'd been helped, too. If he preached the gospel men listened and queued up afterwards to find out more about it. And in himself he felt at peace; deeply scarred but re-made.

So their lives went on. Norma's check-ups were good and despite moments of doubt she clung wonderfully well to her belief that her life now had a particular purpose.

Sadness was not at an end in Noel's life. His dear old mum never really got over the loss of his dad, and slowly she bowed out of life. About two years after his dad had gone she died peacefully.

'It's good how the Catholics and Protestants alike helped her when she was a widow in Roden Street,' said Norma.

He nodded. 'Yes, they've always been good to her. Religion made no difference to them.' He sighed. 'That's the sort of news that you never read in the papers.' Her funeral made them realize afresh the urgency of life and its precarious nature.

'We must use every opportunity for the gospel,' said Norma.

'Yes,' said Noel. They knew that life would never be the same again.

One Sunday in the New Year of 1974 the Chaplain General, Canon Lloyd Rees, came to visit Noel at Eastchurch, to take the services and to have lunch with them afterwards. After lunch he and Noel talked and he said that he could see God was blessing them so much there. He asked if they would like to stay on a few more years. They were delighted and agreed.

A few weeks later there was a phone call from the Canon.

'Hello there,' said Noel.

There was a pause and then Canon Lloyd Rees said, 'Look, I'd like you to go to Dartmoor as Chaplain!'

Noel stared at the receiver, thunder-struck. In a flash he remembered having seen 'Great Expectations' on the television a few days before. He thought of little Pip being chased over the marshes by the terrifying Magwitch, marshes swirling with mists and lurking with dangerous criminals. In a flicker of fear he remembered that hardened men and heavy criminals went to Dartmoor—for years. They weren't the petty criminals of Eastchurch.

'You mean... leave Eastchurch?'

'Yes.'

'Er, sir, you did promise us we could stay on here a few years.'

'I know. I'm sorry. But you see I was praying this morning and I felt, well, I felt that God was saying he wanted you to go to Dartmoor.'

'Me!'

'Yes, you!'

Noel's voice rose, 'But God never said nothing to me about it!'

'Well, will you think about it?'

'Yes, all right sir.'

He sat on at his desk. Dartmoor! 'That's not my idea of where you want me, Lord. Is it?' There was no answer so he phoned Norma. 'It'll be a nightmare,' he said.

She was quiet and then she said, 'You'll be all right.'

# PART FOUR: 'THE MOOR'

'He shared the fate of criminals'
(Isaiah 53:12)

Easter 1974 – Easter 1979

## Chapter Seventeen

## 'Only Eight Come!'

Noel took one last look at Eastchurch chapel, turned his collar up and strode back to the waiting Morris Traveller. He clambered in and glanced at the three girls on the back seat.

'Ready for off then?'

'Yes, Dad,' and they all started giggling.

'Be good!'

He turned the ignition and the car sputtered into life. Norma looked at him. 'But are *you* ready?'

'Well what do you think I'm sitting here with my coat on for?'

'No, silly! I mean are you *ready* to leave,' and she looked around the campus, 'to leave all the memories here?'

He went into first gear and the car jerked off down the road.

She flushed. 'Will you never listen! I'm trying to talk about something important and all you can do is put kangaroo petrol in the car!' And she turned and glared out of the window. He patted her knee. 'Well yes and no. You know. This place holds...well good and bad memories.'

Norma pulled her coat round herself more tightly. 'I wonder why we were so upset about leaving, then?'

He shrugged and they drove on in silence, past front gardens full of wallflowers and tulips and then on through the Kent apple orchards, all frothy with blossom.

'We're always upset when we leave anywhere.'

She sighed as they came to the single bridge from the Isle of Sheppey. 'Last time we'll ever go over here.'

'Mmmm.'

'Noel?'

'Yes?'

'I've got that cutting from the *Sunday Express* in my bag.'

He stopped his mouth from curving up too much at the corners. 'Which one was that then?'

Susan groaned on the back seat.

'Honestly, Mum, you'd think he was in the *Sunday Express* every week!'

Norma giggled and opened her bag. She unfolded the page from the newspaper, gently pressed the creases out and then began to read:

> More than three hundred prisoners at Eastchurch Open Prison signed a petition to try and prevent their Prison Chaplain, the Reverend Noel Proctor, being transferred to Dartmoor. Mr Proctor said, 'I feel very flattered by the petition but I am ready to accept the challenge of Dartmoor!'

Susan squirmed. 'I hope none of my friends read it.'

Noel chuckled. 'Oh, can your friends read, then?' And the whole car load burst out laughing.

But as he drove further and further west, as the girls settled down with their books, and little Becky fell asleep, and Norma studied her lists of things to do at the new house, he found he couldn't stop thinking about Dartmoor. There was a shivery feeling at the base of his spine and he tried whistling to make himself forget it. Every now and again he stopped whistling and Norma looked at him out of the corner of her eye. She frowned. He was always joking about being 'sentenced to "The Moor"' but...she shook her head. It was going to be a challenge.

The nearer they got to Dartmoor the harder he found it to keep his thoughts in order. The image of huge Magwitch chasing little Pip across the marshes ran round and round his mind. He clenched the steering wheel and stuck his chin out. Well, Magwitch or no Magwitch, he was going to Dartmoor and he'd have to make sure he liked it. Or lumped it.

They swung into a layby and the girls jumped out and scampered on the grass verge. Norma passed them some sandwiches through the car door. 'Do you know, Noel, it's such a lovely day we could eat outside. Just listen to those birds singing.' She shut her eyes and felt the sun warm on her face. But he didn't answer. She sat up again and put her hand on his arm. She saw his sandwich lying uneaten on the seat.

'Noel, what's the matter?'

He chuckled. 'Do you think I could play the part of Magwitch?'

She tossed her head. 'All right then. Don't tell me. Don't share.' She began to get out of the car. 'Anyway, I don't know why you make such a fuss about Magwitch. He was sentenced to Prison Hulks on the Thames. Not on to Dartmoor!'

'Norma...don't go.'

'Well, what is it, then?'

He looked at her and his shoulders sagged. Then he stared at his feet and began to pluck at his woollen pullover.

'Aw, I dunno. I guess, I'm frightened.'

'Frightened?'

'Yes. Of going to Dartmoor. They say it's a tough place. With hard men.'

Her eyes widened. She thought for a minute and then said, 'Well, if my cancer hadn't been healed and if I hadn't had the twenty-one doses of radium, you couldn't have gone to Dartmoor at all. I'd be...I wouldn't be here and you'd have to have taken on an office job or something.'

He listened, his eyes fixed on his shoes.

She went on, 'So there must be a plan in our going to Dartmoor.'

'Yes, I know.' He sighed. 'It's just that I'm still scared.'

He stared out of the window. Most of the time at Eastchurch when he'd allowed himself to think about Dartmoor, he'd managed to push the shivery feeling to the back of his mind. Now it had taken root and was growing up his spine. 'Anyway, my darling, we're going and that's that!'

She sniffed. 'Do you know I rang up David Dodds, the former chaplain, and asked what the house was like. He laughed and said, "Oh, it's like *Wuthering Heights*"!'

Noel looked up, startled.

She giggled. 'So I said, "Well as long as Catherine and Heathcliff aren't wandering about inside, I don't mind!" And he laughed and said, "No, they aren't"!'

She wrapped up the remains of the sandwiches and pulled out a packet of biscuits. 'So you see, Noel, I'll have my problems, too.'

'Well I'm thankful I've got you,' he said.

'You really mean it, don't you?'

'I do.'

She paused and then said, 'I used to wonder at Haughton-Le-Skern, if you were really thankful about me.' He sat very still and she rushed on, 'I mean, I knew you loved me, but I wondered sometimes, when I was low and ill, if you felt I was always moping and, er, hindering your work. But now I *know*,' and she floundered to a halt.

He looked at her out of the corner of his eye.

'Eastchurch changed all that,' he said in a low voice. Then he took her hand and their eyes met for a minute.

After a while he said, 'I'll have that sandwich now.'

It was still bright daylight when they came to a signpost which said 'Princetown'. Noel turned up the lonely road and they spun across the moors in silence. Norma gazed about her.

'It's very high up.'

'Yes. Fourteen hundred feet above sea level. It's the highest prison in England.'

'Will we ever stop climbing?'

At last they came round the corner and into the village of Princetown.

'David Dodds said the house was just next to the church-yard,' said Norma. Then her voice trailed to a halt.

Noel stopped the car. 'Here we are then.'

They sat in the car and stared.

'Do I go through the gates or park outside?' asked Noel.

Susan giggled. 'Oh, go on, Dad, sweep up the drive to the front door!'

'OK!' and he backed the car and then shot through the gates and up the drive.

Norma was too surprised to speak. She got out of the car and gazed at the house. Really it was more like a mansion: double-fronted, built of stark granite and set in grounds that were surrounded by a high wall and oak gates. He gave a mock bow. 'Come along, Milady. I want my supper.'

But she wasn't ready to go in yet. She shivered and thrust her hands into her coat pockets.

'It's like winter here. What a wind!' She turned and stared at the gravestones and bare trees in the graveyard next door. 'Noel, there's not even a single leaf on those trees yet. And look, there's a powdering of snow on the grass under the shadow of the wall.'

'Really?'

'The leaves aren't out yet. We set off in spring this morning and now it's winter here.' She turned round quickly, gathered the girls around her and marched up the twelve stone steps to the front door. And they all flocked inside.

Norma went into the house with her heart in her mouth but by the time they'd been all round and explored it her heart had risen. The house was gracious and welcoming and she knew that whatever it looked like on the outside she was going to like it inside.

The girls ran up and down stairs.

'Mum, there's seven cellars.'

'Mum, there's five bedrooms.'

'Mum, can I sleep in the attic?'

'No. Your father wants it for a study.'

He frowned. 'I don't want to trail all the way up there every time I want to prepare a sermon.'

Norma tossed her head. 'Oh, you'll like it. It'll be nice and peaceful.'

'But I don't want to!'

'Well I do. You'll be out of my way.' And she set off for the kitchen with a duster in one hand and a picnic bag in the other.

He opened his mouth to argue and then shut it again. He trailed up the two flights of stairs and peeped into the attic. Mmmm. Well, it wasn't too bad and it certainly was quiet. As he stood there he remembered David Dodds saying, 'There's twelve Lifers in, you know. It's not easy to do a spiritual work here.' Noel bit his lip. He hoped it wasn't going to be too quiet up in the attic, alone with his thoughts.

He glanced out of the window and saw Norma talking to a uniformed Officer in the garden. He sprang out of the room and flew downstairs. The Officer greeted him and jerked his thumb in the direction of a couple of men in prison clothes, standing behind him. 'I'm in charge of a working party sent to help you move in,' he said.

After breakfast next morning he walked through the misty village to the prison. The wind had dropped and it was quiet. He'd seen the building before when he'd come down to visit the Governor and have a look round, but this morning it was different. He slowed down and let his gaze rest on the great, granite oblong, the rows of windows and the massive gates. It was too misty to see the bars at the windows clearly but he knew they were there. Wandsworth had been Victorian, too, but this place was different. He'd be on his own, with the care of the souls inside. The very weight and mass of stone seemed to speak of serious matters. There'd be no light-hearted banter of winning a Mars Bar here.

He raised his head and set his chin. No use hanging around outside. There was a job to be done and he had to get on with it. He strode up to the granite gateway, passed under the arch and went to the second lot of gates. There was the usual business of identification and security and then he went into the inner courtyard and was shown to the Governor's office. As he went he noticed that the yard was set out with flower-beds and some daffodils were out. He smiled. The atmosphere was grim and stark, but it wasn't evil. He was glad they cared about plants here.

The meeting with Colin Heald went well and then Noel went on to meet the Chief Officer. After a few pleasantries they got down to discussing Noel's job.

'Have you seen the chapel yet, Mr Proctor?'

'Only briefly.'

'Well, you share it with the Catholics.'

'That's all right.'

'Actually, it was all arranged before you came, so you shouldn't have too much bother.'

'Oh yes.'

'Your service is at eight o'clock in the morning.'

'Pardon?'

'Eight o'clock. It's Holy Communion.'

Noel wasn't sure he'd heard properly.

'Eight o'clock?'

'Yes.'

'You mean that's the only Church of England service on a Sunday?'

'Yes.'

'But....'

'The Catholic priest has to do a service somewhere else first and he can't be here before nine. So you have eight o'clock, and he has nine o'clock and the men go out on exercise at ten o'clock.' The Chief got up and jangled his keys. Noel stared at him. 'But the men have breakfast at eight!'

The Chief shrugged. 'Well, it's difficult to fit it all in, sir. I appreciate your, er, concern, but as you only get about eight men at the service, anyway, I shouldn't let it worry you.'

Noel went pink. 'Eight!'

'Well, twelve sometimes.'

'I'll jolly well make sure I get more than that.'

The Chief half grinned. 'Yes, Mr Proctor.'

'Well, if I don't there must be something wrong with my services. Or with me!'

The Chief didn't reply but jingled his keys again.

They set off for the chapel and the Chief said over his shoulder, 'I'm afraid the men aren't much interested in religion. Not really. They think it's more for women.'

'Women!' said Noel and shoved his hands deep into his pockets. The Chief handed him the keys. 'Your set. I've got a spare,' and he stood back to let Noel go into the chapel. Noel half glanced round and then up at the Chief.

'Well, thanks very much for showing me round.'

'I'll do all I can to help.' He paused on the threshold, 'Don't let them get you down, Mr Proctor. It's not worth it.'

Then Noel was on his own. He switched on the lights and looked round the modern room. There were golden curtains and chairs and marble behind the altar. He turned to go, a lead weight pulling at his heart: eight o'clock! Only eight who come! During breakfast! He looked at the back wall and saw a black metal cross hanging there. It was spotlighted from behind and there were spiked shadows on the wall. He went over and had a look. It was made almost completely of metal nails with black spikes sticking out. On the cross the figure of Christ writhed.

He stared at it and then bowed his head: no congregation, and not even a sensible time to have a service. 'Well give me the grace to accept it....' Then he raised his head. 'But I don't want to accept it, Lord. I want to fight it. I want there to be interest in you and packed services and men finding peace... even here, at notorious Dartmoor.' His head drooped on his chest for a moment but then his chin came up again. 'Well, Lord, I'll fight for you and your name in here. And I'd be grateful if you'd fight for me, so to speak. But even if you don't I'll still go on, because...' and he looked again at the spiked cross, 'just because.'

The chapel was very quiet, serene almost. He set off back for his office and after a minute he realized he was whistling. He didn't know how or why, but somewhere between the chapel and the office the leaden depression had sloughed off and instead he had a quietness in him.

## Chapter Eighteen

# A Hard Place

The first few weeks were tough, but not in the way they'd expected. The mists and cold winds got Norma down and Noel realized the cons thought he was irrelevant, one shuffling chap going as far as to spit at him every time he passed by. The Officers didn't take much notice of Noel, especially as he'd politely turned down the invitation to join their club in the village. However, they were reasonably co-operative and he didn't mind too much. No, it was the apathy of the cons that he knew he had to break through. At Eastchurch he'd held a 'surgery' and it had worked. But what could he do here?

By the end of the first six weeks he'd visited every prisoner in the jail, invited them to chapel and offered to help them in any way he could. The numbers crept up at the eight o'clock service. Thirty men were willing to miss their breakfast. He thought and he frowned until his brow was furrowed with deep creases. He'd seen the Chief every Monday morning, reported the increase in numbers and asked for the service to be changed to ten o'clock. The Chief was pleasant, but firm.

'I'm sorry, sir, but the men musn't miss exercise.'

'But it's rained on the last two Sunday mornings and they couldn't have exercise! They might as well have been listening to me!'

The Chief cleared his throat and gazed at a point just over Noel's left shoulder.

'I'm sorry.' And he picked up his ballpoint pen.

Noel left the office quickly. The shivery feeling at the base of his spine was speedily giving way to a fiery glow in his chest. Why, it was as if a pall of apathy lay over the whole place. The long-termers certainly weren't bothered and the short-termers just rolled cigarettes when he mentioned 'chapel'.

By the time the week had passed by, Noel felt as if he'd run a marathon, uphill. He was sick of opening cell doors, begging men to miss their breakfast, seeing thirty men sit in a room well able to hold one hundred and twenty. And then hearing that exercise had been cancelled yet again. So he went and asked the Governor if he could change the time of the service, but the only reply he got was, 'I'm quite happy to do what the Chief says.'

By the following Monday the fiery glow filled his whole body and he wrestled with it.

'It's no good, Norma. Something's got to give. Either them or me.' And he jumped up from the table and paced up and down.

'And it's not going to be me!'

'All right. All right. Don't shout.'

He tore out of the room, grabbed his coat and marched up to the prison. He went straight to the Chief's office, banged on the door and then, without waiting for an answer, flung the door open and strode in.

The Chief looked up in amazement and half got up.

'Can I help...'

'Yes, you can,' shouted Noel. 'I'm just about fed up.'

The Chief sat down again and opened his mouth, but Noel rushed on.

'I'm beginning to think you don't need a chaplain at Dartmoor prison. You've made it pretty clear my presence isn't acceptable....'

The Chief stood up again. 'Now come on, Mr Proctor, don't get upset.'

'Well, I am very upset,' shouted Noel and glared the Chief in the eye. 'I want a ten o'clock service! I'm not putting up with this "Miss your breakfast" business any more. If you don't want me to stay on here, why don't you just give the word and I'll pack my bags and go!'

The Chief licked his lips and fiddled with his diary.

'I can't discuss it now, Mr Proctor. Will you, er, come to my office again tomorrow morning at nine?'

'Very well!' said Noel and turned and marched out again.

But by the time he got to his garden gates he was creeping

along with his shoulders hunched. The mist was blowing in yet again and the few late bulbs were drooping. Why, oh why, hadn't he kept his big mouth shut? He could just imagine the conversation in the Club later on that evening: a 'Holy Joe' who not only didn't drink, but who lost his temper as well! The old slur of 'arrogant' pricked back into his mind. He groaned, ran his hand through his hair and dragged himself up the steps.

The cosiness of the house inside usually lifted his spirits, but not tonight. What would Norma say when she found out they might be leaving? He trailed into the kitchen and slumped at the table. But to his surprise she flew into a rage on his behalf.

'How dare they criticize you!' and she tossed her dark red curls.

He had to grin, in spite of himself. 'The Chief's not that bad. He's just, well, doing his job I suppose. He's been quite friendly.'

'Friendly!'

Noel lay awake all night and when he got up next morning every joint ached and his eyes were bloodshot. He dressed carefully, refused most of his breakfast and then set off in good time. He got there early and inspected the flowerbeds until five to nine, whereupon he checked his watch yet again and walked over to the Chief's office. The old shivery feeling was back in full force. He knocked gently.

'Come in.'

He opened the door slowly and then closed it behind him with care. He cleared his throat. 'Good morning, Chief.'

'Sit down, Mr Proctor.'

Noel pulled up a chair and sat on the edge. The Chief pursed his lips and Noel said quickly, 'Look, I'm sorry I blew my top yesterday. I know you've got a job to do as well as me.'

The Chief seemed to expand in his chair slightly.

'I'll be honest with you, Mr Proctor, I was upset. But I've been thinking, and, I don't want to hear any more of this nonsense about packing bags. Anyway, I'll grant you have a point, so,' he paused and caught Noel's eye. 'I've changed my mind. You can have your ten o'clock service after all.'

Noel leaned forward and his grey eyes gleamed.

'Well I . . . thank you very much indeed.'

'Don't get too excited. Remember you'll have to compete with "exercise"!'

'Well, if I can't compete with "exercise" there's something wrong with my ministry.'

The Chief smiled faintly. 'You'll get full co-operation.'

Noel stood up, shook the Chief by the hand and then went back to his office. It didn't make sense, the Chief changing his mind like that. It seemed a battle too easily won, but he was glad. Perhaps he could get somewhere at last.

As lunchtime approached Noel went and stood, as he had made it his custom to do, by the hot plate near the kitchen. The kitchen staff hadn't been too happy at first when they saw him standing there with a notebook in his hand. He'd noticed their raised eyebrows and the fact that they wouldn't look at him, so he'd tried to explain.

'I'm not checking up on you or anything like that. Just the opposite. I like to see if any of the men look downcast or depressed, so I can give 'em a visit in their cell after.'

The kitchen Officer had shrugged. But now they accepted him, and understood why he stood there.

He watched the staff in the kitchen lugging the food on trays, or else piling it on trolleys and pushing it to the hot plate. When they were ready Principal Officer Jones shouted the order 'Open up!' to the Officers on each landing. This Tuesday the Third landing was first on the rota, then 'Fourths', then 'Firsts' and 'Seconds'. The Officers unlocked the cell doors in a few seconds and the lads marched out in single file downstairs, came straight to the hot plate and grabbed their heated metal trays. After the quietness of the morning with each man alone in his cell, the noise of boots, clattering trays and general chit-chat was like a blast in the face. The place was suddenly bursting with bodies and noise. Officer Jones patrolled up and down and watched as the kitchen staff plonked the soup, main course, sweet and cup of tea into the indentations or 'dinges' in the trays.

A giggling group of lads approached the hot plate.

'Ugh! The grub's rough.'

'You could stand yer spoon up in that rice pudding.'

'Starch yer collar in it, more like!'

'We're not on the same old rubbish again!'

Officer Jones was there in a moment.

'Come on, lads. Keep moving. Keep your voices down. No messing.'

Noel waited patiently, scanning the faces. It wasn't the chatty ones he was worried about so much as...yes...there he was again: a lad in a jacket several sizes too big for him, who wouldn't raise his eyes. Noel waited till he was almost at the hot plate and then said quietly, 'Would you like me to visit you after lunch?'

The lad looked up, startled, and stared bleakly at Noel. There were black circles under his eyes and his face was white.

'If you like.'

'What's your cell number?'

'Nineteen. On "The Threes".'

'Right,' and he jotted down the information in his notebook.

No, it wasn't the chatty ones who might do something silly. Noel scanned the stairs again. He'd been warned by the Governor not to step out of line at the dinner queue.

'It's a flash point, Noel. You've only got to get someone losing his temper, raising that metal tray and hitting out and we've got a potential riot on our hands.'

'Yes, sir.'

As he stood there he felt for the first time that he was being accepted. One or two of the lads who missed their breakfast on a Sunday morning said hello, and a round-faced man came up and asked for a cell visit. So that was two cell visits after lunch. He closed the notebook and let the conversation drift round him.

'I waited all day on Saturday for my missus to turn up. She never come. I bet she's having it off with someone else.'

'No....'

'Yep.'

'When I get out in ten years I'm going to spend all the money I've got stashed away.'

'Hey, did you hear that programme about football transfers....'

'Well, all my missus does when she comes is moan about money and the long journey up here. I ask you. What about me, eh?'

'Oh, they never think of that. Only browned off about their housekeeping.'

Noel frowned and opened his notebook again. He scribbled down the word 'Wives' and stood deep in thought. He might preach about it next Sunday.

Norma had told him about the wives she'd seen trailing up the village street, young girls, some of them. There was one in particular with long, blonde hair. She had two kids who squabbled all the way as she dragged them along with one hand while with her other hand she humped a heavy bag. Norma had watched her through the kitchen window one Saturday morning, as she stopped every now and again, utterly spent, before doggedly setting off again up the road. 'Noel, that poor girl comes every month for visiting. She'll make herself ill. And those two boys! They're beautifully turned out, but ever so naughty.'

He sighed. The trouble with the inmates was that they conned themselves. They considered they were badly done to and they never thought of their wives struggling to keep things going at home. Sometimes it seemed as if society punished the wives while the men inside had everything provided for them: food, warmth, clothes, peace and quiet in the single cells, television, a games room, the gym, education classes and goodness knows what. He snapped his notebook shut and pushed it in his inner pocket.

Later, when Officer Jones had counted all the men in their cells, Noel was allowed to do his cell visits and he went off to see the lad who wouldn't look at anyone in the dinner queue. He opened his cell door.

'Can I come in?'

The lad was sitting on his bunk staring at the bars at the window. He didn't look round. Noel came in and shut the door.

'How are you Mr...er...Lomax?'

The lad shrugged and then said in a hard voice, 'You know what I've done and what my cell number is, so don't Mr Lomax me!'

'I do *not* know what you've done because I never read your report until *after* I've visited you for the first time,' Noel paused, 'and I know you have a number on your front door, but so do I.' There was another pause.

'Well, aren't you going to ask me to sit down?'

The lad half turned. 'Suit yourself.'

'I can see you're a bit low and I wondered if you'd like to come to chapel on Sunday. It's ten o'clock now.'

The lad sniggered. 'Chapel! I'd be a screws' bloke then. "Go to chapel and get a good parole report,"' he mimicked in a falsetto voice.

Noel sighed and got up to go, but just as he was leaving, the lad turned and said quickly, 'Have you any radios?'

'Yes, I'm putting an appeal out to local churches for old transistors.'

'My wife said she'd heard about it at her church. If I got one she'd buy me some batteries.'

'Oh, very nice, too,' said Noel. 'Does she visit you often?'

The lad slumped down on the bed again and said, 'Yes, every month.' Noel frowned. He sensed he was getting close to something, but he knew it wasn't the time to ask.

'I'll get you a radio as soon as I can.'

'Ta, mate.'

'Shall I call and see you again?'

'If you like.'

'Cheerio, then.'

As he left he heard the Officers coming back from their own lunch. In a minute he knew the quiet landings would be a seething mass of noise as men queued up to rinse their trays under the hot tap and then sling them back onto the pile, then form another queue for the few toilets. So he went as quickly as possible outside to visit the workshops.

He stepped into yet another mist and pulled on his coat. Mist in June! And he shook his head. Often the mist gave him the illusion of being very alone. He crossed the courtyard and went towards the Blacksmiths' shop. There was a civilian worker there called Goodyear and Noel badly wanted to meet him. He peered into the workshop and spotted a man in beige shirt sleeves.

'Hello there. Are you Mr Goodyear?'

'I am.'

'Well how do you do. I'm Noel Proctor, your new chaplain.'

They talked about the mist and then Noel said, 'I've seen

that wonderful cross you made for the chapel. You must have a great faith to be able to make a spiked cross like that.' Goodyear turned away and stared at his tools and then ran his hand over his hammer.

'No,' he said.

'No?'

'No. I don't have a faith.' He turned back to Noel and gazed him in the eye, his face red from the work, his eyes clear and gentle. 'I wish I did, like, but I've thought and thought and I just can't believe.'

Noel was nonplussed.

'But your cross is so full of feeling.'

Goodyear smiled. 'The Governor said it "symbolized the sufferings of the Moor" but,' he shrugged, 'I just felt for the poor bloke on it. A bit like some of them in here. It was so unfair for him, wasn't it? No, I have no faith.'

Noel said, 'Can I see you working?'

Goodyear smiled. 'Come on, then.' Noel watched as he grasped some steel with tongs and then carefully hammered out the bar into a curve.

'What you making?'

'A flower-pot holder.'

'Well I'd be happy to talk to you sometime.'

Goodyear straightened up. 'Well, that's a kind offer and I don't mean no disrespect, but it'll do no good. My mind's made up.' He said the words with a simple dignity and then, his shoulders bent a little as if with a secret sorrow, he went slowly back to the fire. Noel watched him go. He knew he had no words to give and slowly, sadly, he turned away.

'Goodbye then.'

'Goodbye.'

## Chapter Nineteen

# 'A Taste of Mustard in My Mouth'

Later on in the same week Noel was standing by the hot plate again when he saw John Lomax once more, this time with his head hanging even lower. Officer Jones caught Noel's eye and beckoned him over.

'That lad's stopped eating, you know.' And he jerked his thumb in the direction of John Lomax.

Noel's eyebrows shot up.

'You mean a hunger strike?'

'No, I don't think so. He's not making any demands or statements or anything. No. I reckon he's very depressed. He sends his tray back uneaten.'

'I went to see him this week and he was a bit aggressive.'

Officer Jones pushed his peaked cap back and his keys jangled on the end of his chain.

'Yes, that's often the pattern. First he was Jack-the-lad, centre of the crowd. Then he got depressed, then angry and as you say, aggressive, and now this thundering, black depression.'

He looked at Noel. 'I don't like it at all.'

'I'll see him this afternoon,' said Noel.

'Good.' Officer Jones glanced up and down the row of chattering men and then put his finger to his lips. Noel bent forward and he whispered in Noel's ear, 'Ask him for his razor blade will you?'

'His...razor blade?'

Officer Jones nodded.

'OK then, I'll do that.'

Noel went back to the hot plate and pondered. Ask for his razor blade! Surely it couldn't be as bad as that?

After lunch he went to see John Lomax again. He found him sitting, head in hands, on his bunk. His dinner lay congealed on the tray and his cup of tea had a brown skin on top. Noel decided to get straight to the point.

'Look, John, there's one or two of us who are worried about you. You're so depressed. What's wrong?'

John shook his head and fiddled with a bit of paper on his table.

'Come on, it'd do you good to talk.'

But John sat on, quite still, except for the rolling and unrolling of the paper in the fingers of one hand.

'You can trust me, you know.' Then, 'I've not managed to get you a radio yet, but there's one in the pipeline.'

Still there was no response.

Noel sighed. 'Well, I'm sorry to have to ask you, but please will you give me your razor blade.'

John looked at Noel for the first time and Noel ached for him. He was only a lad. On his locker stood a photo of a pale-faced girl with delicate features and long blonde hair.

Noel said, 'That your wife?'

'Yes,' muttered John.

Noel picked up another photo, this time of two boys, one fair like the girl and the other dark like John.

'These your lads?'

'Yes.'

Something Norma had said stirred in Noel's mind. Something about seeing a long-haired girl dragging up the village street every month with two naughty boys.

'You said your wife comes every month?'

John nodded.

'Well, then you'll see her tomorrow, and the boys.'

For a second John looked at him with an expression of such hopeless despair and anguish on his face that Noel instinctively reached out his hand to pat him on the shoulder. But then the look was gone, frozen behind the tightly controlled features and the dark circles under his eyes.

'I'll try and see you and your wife in the visiting room,' said Noel and held out his hand. John looked at the hand and then rummaged under his bunk. He pulled out a sponge-bag and took out his razor. He undid it and let the blade fall on to the table. Noel gingerly picked it up.

Noel said, 'I'll hand it to Officer Jones until you feel better. The Officer on duty in the morning'll give you a blade to shave with.'

John turned away and sat stiffly on the bunk. Feeling defeated, Noel left, and locked the door behind him. He stood to one side in the corridor for a moment and then looked back at John through the peep-hole. He was slumped on the bunk, his face hidden in the pillow, his whole body saying, louder than any words, 'Go away. Leave me alone.'

Noel went straight to the chapel and let himself in. He stayed there some time and, as he prayed, his thoughts constantly turned to Mr Goodyear and John Lomax. 'Oh Lord, please reach these men.' He looked up at the stained glass window behind the altar. The shape of the cross was picked out in red glass. The sun had come out, making it glow like a fire.

Next morning he sought out the Officer on John's landing and asked how he was doing.

'Well, he did eat some supper and he seems reasonable this morning. He's in the visiting room at the moment.'

Noel hurried off to the visiting room and stood in the doorway. The noise was terrific. Children were bawling and squabbling and one or two couples were arguing. He stared round the room and finally his eyes rested on John. He was sitting hunched in a corner, with his back turned to his wife. Noel sauntered in amongst the couples.

'Good morning to you. Hello there!' He rummaged in his pocket and found the bag of boiled sweets Norma had got specially for him and began to give them out to the children. He didn't stop and talk to any of them because he knew they needed time on their own, but at least they'd know who he was because he always wore his dog collar.

He arrived at John's table and casually said, 'Hello'. John didn't reply. The girl looked up at him, her eyes too bright and her mouth set. Noel dropped some sweets on the table and the two boys dived for them. He said quietly to the girl, 'I'll be around outside when you come out.' Then, equally casually, he ambled back to the door.

Outside it was chilly and misty again, although a pale disc

in the sky showed it was summer time. Noel strode up and down, and kept glancing at his watch. Suppose the girl didn't want to see him? But he kept on waiting.

A few minutes later he felt a tap on the shoulder. He looked round and there she was, so pale and thin that she looked like a waif herself.

'He's told me he wants to go back to his cell. For some peace. He's told me not to bother seeing him this afternoon.' She turned her head away and brushed her cheek with her hand. He led her and the boys back to his office and made a cup of tea.

'He says I must be sucking up to the screws if I come and talk to you. I don't understand him any more.'

When she'd calmed down, Noel said, 'He's making himself ill with this depression. He's not himself. But he's got your photo on his locker and one of the boys. I've seen him staring at your photo again and again.'

She sniffed and a little light came back into her eyes.

'Have you really?'

'Yes.'

'Honest?'

'Yes.'

She found a hanky and blew her nose. One of the boys started playing about with the phone.

'Stop messing, Kevin,' she said in a voice sharp with tension. Noel got some paper and two pencils and gave them to the boys.

'Look,' he said, 'you're a good wife. You obviously love John. Have you *any* idea what's wrong with him?'

She shook her head. 'No. But he keeps saying he'll be out by Christmas and we'll have the best time we've ever had and new toys for Kevin and little John.' She sniffed. 'That's what he used to say. He doesn't say anything now.'

'Well you can rely on me to do everything I can.'

When she'd gone he asked for John's file and read it slowly. As he read a frown creased his brow. 'Early Discharge' and 'Home-Leave' had been crossed out. In their place someone had written 'Cancel all remission'. So John wasn't going out before Christmas. He'd lost all his remission, probably through fooling about and being cheeky. He wouldn't be going out until the following Easter at the earliest. Noel stared at the report. Surely three or four months more inside wouldn't make a man want to use a razor blade. Would it?

By Monday morning John was eating again and talking reasonably to the others and Noel tried to dismiss the whole thing from his mind. But he couldn't. He kept thinking of the girl, Lynne, getting up so early, struggling on trains and buses, trailing all the way through the village with the boys, only to have to hang about from noon till two o'clock eating sandwiches and trying to shelter from the rain. And after all that, all John could do was sit with his back to her. So many of the wives were like her: faithful and enduring. Slowly the week passed and still John was all right.

As the monthly Saturday visiting day came round again, Noel got in to his office early. He was settling down to read a report when the phone rang. The voice at the other end said, 'Will you come to the hospital wing at once. It's urgent.'

He ran all the way and was shown straight into the little operating theatre. He didn't recognize the man on the operating table. He peered forward and watched the doctor put the last two stitches into a long, nasty gash on the man's neck. The doctor turned round and shook his head. 'He was within a fraction of an inch of his jugular vein. If he'd cut that, I couldn't have saved him.'

Noel stared at the ashen-faced patient. He felt like crying. It was an inmate he'd failed. He sighed. 'Was it an accident?'

The doctor passed his hand over his forehead.

'No. A razor blade.'

'Oh no! It's not John Lomax?'

'Yes. He did it just before breakfast when he should have been shaving.'

'Will he be all right?'

'He should be.'

Noel took the unconscious John's hand and as he did so he suddenly realized that John had done it that particular day because he couldn't face Lynne and the boys. But why? She was so obviously determined to stick by him.

Noel had a difficult morning trying to comfort Lynne. In the end he took her back to Norma and Susan played with the boys. He dashed back to the hospital and went and sat by

John's bed. John opened one eye and Noel couldn't stop himself blurting out, 'Look young man, you've got a lovely young wife who's terribly upset about what you've done. She thinks you don't love her.'

John spoke with difficulty. 'I do. I do.'

'Well, shall I go and tell her that?'

John nodded and leaned back on the pillows. He touched his neck. 'I've been a fool, haven't I?'

'Well, don't upset yourself about that now. You're going to get better and that's the main thing. You've got two young boys playing with our Susan at the moment. They want yer. They look up to yer.'

'But I've let them down.' And the same agonized look flitted over his face again.

Noel thought for a minute. 'You've not told them about losing remission have you?'

John shook his head and his eyes filled with tears. Noel had to lean forward to catch what he said.

'They think I'm coming home for Christmas. I've broke my promise.'

'But don't you see they'd rather have you at home three months late, than never again!'

'Can I have a Bible?'

'A Bible?'

'Yes. You know.'

Noel hid his surprise and took out a Gideon New Testament from his pocket. 'Here you are. Keep it.'

'Ta, mate.'

'Now, have a sleep. Would you like me to tell Lynne about Christmas for you?'

'Oh, would you?'

'Of course.'

John sighed and his shoulders relaxed into the pillow.

'The Governor says she can come and see you in here later.'

'Ta, mate.'

By the time Noel left, he was asleep.

On his way back Noel called at the Governor's office and told him that John Lomax would recover and why he'd done it in the first place.

'You know,' said Colin Heald, 'I think I'll resurrect that

idea of a hostel in the village so visiting wives can stay overnight and leave their children there. Something has to be done.
I've been talking about it to the Probation Officer, and he's
keen. Oh, by the way, where's Mrs Lomax now?'

Noel grinned. 'With Norma.'

'Good for Norma. You know, the Probation Service might
even man the place with a Warden.' Colin Heald thought
again. 'If I get a committee together, would you serve, Noel?
Deputy Chairman perhaps?'

'I certainly would. But where could you have a hostel?'

'There's a disused Methodist Chapel down in the village.
I'll look into it.'

Noel rushed home and grabbed some very late lunch from
Norma. In a quiet talk with Lynne he told her the full story.

'But why didn't he *tell* me?' she said at last.

'I don't know. But being locked up all the time can play
funny tricks with a man's mind.'

Then he flew back to the hospital and saw John again. He
was sitting up in bed and his face was quite pink and rested.

'Hello, Mr Proctor.'

'Hello. I've told Lynne all about it and she's on her way to
see you shortly. She doesn't mind about Christmas at all.'

'Thank God for that.' Then John was quiet for a while. Noel
noticed that the New Testament was open on his locker.
'What've you been reading?'

'Well, I started at Matthew chapter one....'

'Oh, that's not a good chapter to start with. All those
genealogies!'

'...and I read on till chapter thirteen. It was something
about parables. I was reading about a mustard seed.' John
paused and looked at Noel. 'Well, then I must have fallen
asleep, because when I woke up, I had the taste of mustard
seed in my mouth.'

'Mustard!'

'Yes. Mr Proctor?'

'Yes?'

'Do you think God's speaking to me?'

Noel smiled. 'Yes I do,' he said. 'He saved your life. He kept
you from letting that razor blade get into your vein. Now he
wants to save you.'

## Chapter Twenty

# 'D' Wing

As Noel went through the inner courtyard on his way home, he noticed one of the inmates bedding out some plants. When Noel went past he heard the man spitting behind his back. It had happened before and probably would again, but it depressed him. He mentioned it to the Officer on the gates.

'Well he does it to anyone and everyone who smacks of authority.'

'So I'm not the only one?' said Noel.

'Oh no.'

'What's he in for?'

'He's a lifer.'

'Murder?'

'Yes. He's been in for twelve years already.' The Officer shrugged. 'This place, it changes them all in the end. They become recluses. It's the isolation. It gets through to them in the end.'

And to me, thought Noel. 'What's his name?'

'Marcus Blake.'

Noel walked slowly home, his hands thrust deep into his pockets. Now he'd got to grips with most of the prison, and the staff had got used to him popping into the workshops and visiting room and standing at the dinner queue, he knew what his next step had to be. The trouble was he kept pushing it to the back of his mind.

When he got home he was very quiet at the lunch table. Norma watched him out of the corner of her eye. 'What's the matter?'

He shrugged and fiddled with his knife. 'It's no use, Norma. I'll have to get to terms with these lifers.'

'What do you mean?'

'I've not really got to know them properly. I don't quite know how to react to them. In fact, if I'm honest, I'm a bit scared of them. They're sort of set apart from the rest.'

'You know what it says in the Bible about Paul. And David. They had blood on their hands.'

'Mmmm.' He looked up. 'Well, I've made my mind up not to read the men's files until after I've had a chat with each one.'

'Why?'

'Well then I can see them as people. And not just living crimes.' He shook his head. 'One spits at me every time I go past.'

'Oh no!'

'Yes.'

There was a short silence and then Norma said, 'Noel, you must go and see them. There might even be one who's interested in God. You never know. Noel, I've got such an urgency in me now, ever since I nearly.... You might not have much time left. I might not have. They might not have. I should go this afternoon!' And she jumped up and began to pile plates on a tray.

He grinned. Just like her, never willing to wait a minute, especially since... her illness.

'I'll go and see them this very afternoon. There's a new lifer just arrived this morning. I'll start off with him.'

She smiled and he took her hand. He felt better already, now he'd made his mind up.

The prison was quiet when he got back. Most of the men were in the workshops trying to earn the one pound maximum they were allowed per week. He collected his keys from the Duty Officer and went to the cell door. Outside he hesitated and bowed his head, all the time aware that the Officer was watching. Then he turned the key in the lock and went inside.

'Good afternoon Mr, er, Halliday.'

A slightly built man turned from gazing out of the barred window.

'Good afternoon?'

'I'm your Chaplain. It's nice to meet you.'

'You can't mean that!' Halliday gestured round the cell and

then pulled out the single chair for Noel to sit on.

'Do sit down.'

Noel was surprised but took the seat. 'Thank you.'

Halliday sat on the bunk.

'I'm sorry I've nothing to offer you to drink.'

Noel felt a great desire to laugh but managed to smother it in time. After all his fears, this was like meeting a business executive. Then he frowned. Perhaps that was what the fellow was. Or had been.

Halliday smiled urbanely and said, 'What can I do to help you?'

'I'm the one who's supposed to say that to you!'

'I'm afraid I'm not a churchgoer.'

'Well when you've settled down, you might be allowed to attend the afternoon concerts. And I've a Chaplain's library. Oh and I'm to get a library of radios, too. Would you like your name down for one of those? And if you do ever need any help or want to come to chapel, I'll be delighted to see you.' Noel stopped, aware he was talking too much. Halliday stared at him, and passed his tongue over his lips. For a moment he looked very tired and very old. Then he said, 'I have quite a lot of books. Perhaps you could borrow some yourself.'

Noel looked at the pile of books under Halliday's bunk. It looked like his memories of English 'O' level! Noel was non-plussed and felt out of his depth with this sophisticated man.

Halliday said, 'I do thank you for calling.'

'May I see you again?'

'Oh do.'

Noel left the cell. Obviously it took all sorts, but who'd have thought a man like that would end up in a place like this. He nearly bumped into the Duty Officer on the way out. The Officer grinned. 'How did you get on with him?'

'O.K. He's very well spoken isn't he?'

'Hmmm! Know what he's in for?'

'No. What?'

'Murder.'

Noel whistled under his breath. It seemed so unreal. The Officer lowered his voice. 'He did his wife in and hid her in the wardrobe. Then he took loads of pills. He took so many that he woke up and was sick. So then he gave himself up.'

'Poor man.'

The Officer went red. 'Poor woman you mean.'

'Of course, you're right.'

'That's what I don't understand! You're always on the cons' side. They do rotten things to innocent people and yet you people in the church stick up for them.'

'No I'm not on the cons' side.'

'Well whose then?'

'God's side, I suppose. And I suppose I do often feel sympathy for the prisoners.' Noel sighed and stared at his shoes. 'I should think more of the victims.'

The Officer's eyes bored into Noel and then he said, 'The funny thing about Halliday is that his children have stuck by him. Came to see him today and brought him books.' The Officer shrugged. 'Perhaps they think he did them a favour!'

'Oh no!'

'Who can tell?'

Noel had to go through the TV room on his way out so he stopped to chat to a group lolling on the chairs. He noticed a fat chap with a pile of books under his arm and went to have a word with him.

'What you reading?'

The fat chap leered. 'Wouldn't you like to know.'

Noel stared down at the cover, with its promise of dark, supernatural secrets and then looked sharply at the fat chap.

'What's your name?'

'Charlie.'

'What you reading that rubbish for?'

Charlie was taken aback for a minute and then said, 'Oh I love these books. You learn so much from them,' and his hands caressed the cover. 'I've lots more in my cell,' he said gloatingly.

Noel was not impressed. 'Evil rubbish!'

Charlie sniggered. 'Call yourself a sky pilot! You'd never get your tin pot religion to do the things they can do!'

'Who can do?'

'Demons of course. And Satan.' Charlie giggled and went and slouched in an easy chair. One of the other prisoners caught Noel's eye, glanced at Charlie's back and then tapped his forehead with his fingers. 'Barmy,' he mouthed. Noel stormed out and went to his office.

Nothing made sense: a lifer with an armful of classical novels who tried to commit suicide and then gave himself up; Charlie, an agitator sent from Liverpool jail and now in 'D' Wing because of subversion, who read books about Satan worship and was allowed free association. As Noel often did when he was upset, he went to the chapel and knelt down to pray.

After a while the peace seeped into him and his tensions and anger filtered away. He turned round and looked at Goodyear's cross. It moved men so much and yet it had been made by a man with no faith. Poor Goodyear, who was slowly dying of Hodgkin's Disease. Perhaps he was feeling after faith in spite of himself. Noel began to pray in a whisper. 'I'm glad you're a God of justice. One day each of these men will get true justice. Maybe unlike what they got down here.' He paused. No one deserved justice. No one was truly good. Not even himself. As he knelt on in the quietness some words of St Paul came into his mind:

For I was determined not to know anything among you, except Jesus , and him crucified. [1 Corinthians 2:2]

He thought and thought. Yes, there was only one place where all men could meet and be equal. And that was at the foot of the cross. No matter who they were or what they'd done, there was equal forgiveness for all... if they asked for it.

On the following Sunday Noel was due to hold one of the new ten o'clock services. He planned it very carefully as he knew the Officers would be watching. He asked his red-band, the 'trusty' Dennis, to read the lesson and he decided to sing a solo. At a quarter past nine he went up to the prison. The sky was a leaden grey and he wrestled with himself. Should he pray for it to rain? Or should he simply wait and see? Either way someone would be disappointed. He scratched his forehead and then grinned. Idiot, he said to himself!

By a quarter to ten he had to keep his mouth firmly in a straight line, but inside he was chuckling. The rain teemed down his office windows and he knew exercise would have been cancelled once again. He set off for the chapel and collected Dennis on the way. He knew Dennis liked to fuss round with hymnbooks, but he didn't mind, as Dennis was so keen to please. The only trouble was that Dennis did rather like to tell everyone he'd become a Christian, usually when they were trying to do something else, and he did seem to interrupt any conversations going on in the chapel after services and blurt out his own ideas, but he meant well. Noel was sure of that.

This particular morning Noel half-heard him say, 'The Lord's called me to be a preacher you know.' But Noel's mind was on other things so he nodded absent-mindedly and then went to the door to see how many were coming to the service.

About thirty men came and to his surprise and pleasure he saw John Lomax, still bandaged on his neck, but now with a relaxed air about him and no more black circles under his eyes. And then, surely that couldn't be Halliday sitting alone at the back? But it was. Halliday sat through the service and didn't sing. Noel ached to see the terrible shadows under his eyes and his too-still body, taut as if holding in great tensions.

He shook Halliday's hand at the end. 'I'd like to come and see your books.'

'Do call. Do call.'

'I will.'

Then John Lomax came up and pumped Noel by the hand. Noel smiled. 'How are you. How's Lynne?'

'She's great. Oh Mr Proctor, they don't mind about Christmas. My Mum and Dad are having them. It's all worked out.' His face shone and Noel put his arm round him.

John said, 'I prayed about it all and it's just as if a great weight has been lifted off my back.'

Noel drew him to one side. 'Look, John, you're not the criminal type. What you in for? A fight when drunk.' He shook his head.

John said, 'I've not had a drop of drink for two years while I've been in here and I don't miss it now.'

'Well make your mind up *never* to come in here again. *Never*. You've got the potential to make good. Some of these lads in here would give their eye teeth to have a wife like Lynne.'

John blushed. 'I know. I've realized a lot lately.'

In the afternoon Noel decided to go and see Halliday again. On the way he had to cross the TV room and out of the corner of his eye he spotted Marcus Blake. He listened as he passed. Yes, he'd been spat at again. Noel resisted the impulse to turn round and shout at Marcus, and so immersed was he in keeping his cool that he bumped into another man.

'I'm very sorry....Oh, it's you!'

Fat Charlie was there again, and the pile of books he'd been carrying had spilled all over the floor. He sniggered at Noel.

'Shall I tell you my horoscope?'

'Certainly not!'

'It's all right for posh folks like you. We've never had a chance.'

Noel stopped in his tracks and spun round. 'No, Charlie, it's not all right for people like me. My dad was an alcoholic, or as near as makes no difference. I was brought up in the back streets of Belfast and I left school when I was fourteen. So why is it all right for me?'

Charlie frowned. 'You don't know what it's like to have nowt.'

'Well if you call earning fourteen pounds a month in the Church Army for five years having "owt" then I'll agree with you. But everything I've got I've worked for. And hard. I didn't go round helping myself to other people's property. So I don't want to hear any more about it. Understand!'

Charlie took a step backward and gawped. He dug the fellow next to him in the ribs and said in a loud whisper, 'He's not soft, is he?'

The other fellow looked embarrassed and turned away.

Noel said, fully aware that half the room was listening. 'I could have ended up like most of you. My mates got into trouble with the police when I was a teenager and I was heading the same way, only my old dad gave me the belt. So if I could get off the big wheel and stop conning myself so can you.'

He let his gaze travel round the room, then picked up one of

Charlie's books about the devil and dropped it on the floor in disgust. 'You've no idea, any of you, what real power is, real power and real forgiveness.' He looked at Charlie. 'Your books on witchcraft and astrology. Hmmm! Just cheap counterfeit and pretence. It's a pity you don't know about the real thing!' and with that he turned and strode out. As he left he heard the sound of spitting again, but he kept going down the corridor.

When he'd seen Halliday and spent half an hour trying to lift his spirits from a leaden depression, Noel knew he'd have to walk back through the TV room. He set off quickly. By the time he got there his chin was held high and he practically marched through the room. But Charlie was too quick for him.

'Hey, can I come along?'

'Pardon?'

Charlie giggled. 'Can I come and see inside the chapel?'

'You mean come to a service?'

Charlie's eyes shifted slightly. 'Er, no. Just to *see* it.'

'Do you mean it?'

'Yes.'

'All right then. I'll ask permission and take you tomorrow.' Noel walked away thoughtfully. He doubted very much if Charlie would come the next day.

But next morning when Noel had got permission from the Duty Officer he found Charlie ready and waiting in his cell. Under his arm was another lurid cover.

'I'll not have that thing in the chapel,' said Noel. Charlie carefully put the book on the middle of his table, where the skull on the cover grinned through bared teeth. Noel shook his head. The cell was lined with similar books.

'Come on,' said Noel, and Charlie trotted along after him, plucking his elbow and offering to tell him his horoscope. When they got to the vestry door, Noel suddenly stopped, and went round to the main chapel door. He unlocked it and stepped inside, Charlie close behind him.

He walked in and the peace of the room embraced him. The sun was shining, filling the room with shafts of light, and the stained glass window gleamed and threw coloured shadows on the wall. In the middle window the great, ruby-coloured cross glowed like a fire.

Suddenly a sharp scream pierced the room. Noel whirled round and grabbed Charlie who had dropped to his knees, his hands clawing at his eyes. 'Oh my eyes! Oh my eyes!'

Noel dropped down, aghast. Whatever was happening? Charlie fell to the floor, moaning, and Noel half dragged him to a chair.

'I can't see! I can't see! Oh my eyes!'

Noel prised Charlie's hands away and looked at his eyes. They stared back at him, blue and clear.

'There's nothing wrong with your eyes, man!' He pulled Charlie up and led him to the vestry where he sat him down.

'Here, I'll make yer a cup of tea.'

Noel got the kettle on and stood, perplexed, gazing at Charlie, who had put his head in his hands and was muttering, 'I'm blind! I'm blind!'

Whatever could have happened? If Charlie was blind, and it had happened in the chapel, then, and Noel groaned, that would probably mean the end of his ten o'clock service. After a while he said, 'How are you feeling now?'

Charlie wiped his nose with the back of his hand.

'It's blurred now.'

'But what happened?'

'I dunno. I just followed you in here and then,' Charlie's voice dropped to a whisper and he plucked at his sleeve and shifted in his seat. 'I looked up and...the light...it pierced my eyes.'

'What!'

'A red light. In the window. It pierced my eyes.'

Eventually Noel got him back to his cell, where he had to leave him huddled on his bunk, still rubbing his eyes. Noel went straight back to the chapel, entered by the main door again and stared up at the window. The light streamed in through the centre pane and lit up the empty cross to a brilliant red. He stared and frowned and the cross shone back.

He went back to his office and picked up the phone. After a moment he got through to Father O'Driscoll, Charlie's priest, and told him what had happened.

'It was some light, something in the chapel window, something about the cross, that made him, er, blind for fifteen minutes.'

Father O'Driscoll said, 'I'll stop in and see him this afternoon. He always refuses to come to Mass, so it'll be an opportunity to speak to him.'

When Noel had time to tell Norma about it later, he said, 'Strange that I took him in at that entrance at the back. I never use that door normally.'

'Can he see now?'

'Oh yes.'

Norma thought for a while and then she raised her head. 'Perhaps he met a power greater than all his witchcraft and stuff. Perhaps there was a collision between good and evil.'

Noel started with surprise. 'Well he's not exactly become a Christian, but he has started going to Mass. And Father O'Driscoll said he's got rid of some of those books.'

'He ought to burn the lot,' said Norma.

'Perhaps it's the beginning of something.'

'It certainly shook him. Jolted him up!'

'Mmmm. And me!'

## Chapter Twenty-One

# *Alone*

As the months went by they gradually settled down, despite the weather and the isolation of the place. Norma had a grumble about the weather every now and again: 'Nine months of winter here! And only three of summer! If you can call it summer!' But the edge was taken off her loneliness when she made friends with Liz who had been appointed as Warden of the hostel for the prisoners' wives in the village.

Life settled into a routine. Each morning Noel met Dennis, his 'trusty' red-band, and had prayers with him in the chapel, then went off to do the interviews with the new prisoners, the hospital visits, and the 'Punishment' visits. The Sunday ten o'clock service caught on and often he had ninety or more men there. It was one thing to be thankful for, he told Norma, that the weather was so bad on Dartmoor. It meant as often as not that rain caused cancellation of exercise on a Sunday morning and the men could go to chapel instead.

It was one evening after supper that he had his great idea. He slapped his knee with his hand. Why hadn't he thought of it before? He'd arrange a sing-song for the men on alternate Sunday evenings.

Next day he went to see the Chief about it.

The Chief stroked his sandy moustache and stared out of the window.

'If you had this "Sing-along", Mr Proctor, would it put the Salvation Army people out? After all they always do cell visits on Sunday evenings. And...' The Chief smiled to himself, 'they also have a little service every fortnight. About six go I think.'

Noel put his hands carefully behind his back. 'I think it's

more than that. But they don't mind. I've asked them. I'd alternate with them, you see.'

The Chief seemed deep in thought and Noel couldn't read his expression. With a slight shrug the Chief said, 'Very well. It can't do any harm.'

'Thank you very much.'

When Noel left the office he was bubbling with excitement. But underneath he wasn't sure. Was it all too easy?

By Sunday evening Noel had arranged for a local choir to sing and had told nearly every man in the jail about it. He got to the chapel early and waited. Suppose no one came? Then the doors opened at the back and a file of prisoners came in. He began to count and after a few moments a tingle of anticipation shook him. He suddenly remembered that first night at Durham jail and the four hundred men filing in there. He clasped his hands together and bowed his head. Then he opened his eyes again and stared round the chapel. Yes, there was Halliday; and fat Charlie, who was quite recovered now; and John Lomax; there were well over seventy there. Then the Chief came in and stood at the back. He kept glancing at his watch and then counting. He caught Noel's eye but made no sign of recognition.

The hour passed at a sparkling pace and Noel gave a five minute talk at the end. He punched his words home. These men weren't interested in Churchianity. No, he'd give it to them straight.

'There's no point in you lot thinking of running away. Look at Jonah. He ended up in the belly of a whale! Even Dartmoor isn't as bad as that! Ay, he thought he could run away from God, but he found out he couldn't. There's two people you can never run away from: yourself,' he paused, 'and God. God knows your life from the beginning to the end. And somewhere in the middle is the cross.'

In the silence he could have heard a pin drop. Then quietly he said, 'We'll be here in a fortnight, so make sure you put your names down on the list. Or you might not get a seat.'

By the third 'Sing-along' one hundred and fifty prisoners managed to squeeze themselves into the chapel. Noel was thrilled. And bewildered. Later he said to Norma, 'It's nearly a third of all the inmates. Where else in our society do nearly a third of the population come to church? After all most of these cons have free association on a Sunday evening, so I haven't got a "captive audience"! And these cons are supposed to be the dregs!'

She caught his eye and then looked away.

'What about the other two thirds?' she asked.

Noel flushed and his chin fell on his chest. There he was, falling into the old trap again, secretly congratulating himself, when it wasn't him at all who'd drawn them in.

Norma crossed over the room quickly and patted his arm. 'I know it's the Lord who's drawn them in, Noel, but he has used you to do it and don't you forget it.'

'No, but…'

'No "buts"!'

'He's used you as well, Norma.'

'Me?'

He stared at her. She got no bouquets and no paragraphs on the front page of the *Western Morning News*, yet she'd sacrificed herself as much as he had. She'd given herself to the work and hardly ever grumbled. She was left alone in the house so often, while he got all the praise and excitement of leading men to Christ. All she got was even more babysitting. He knew he could never do the work he wanted to do without her behind him. They held hands, but into the moment rich with meaning, came the sound of the phone.

When he answered it, he heard the Chief's voice. Noel swallowed. So this was it.

'Mr Proctor, there's one or two things I'll have to discuss with you. Can you come and see me tomorrow?'

Noel put the phone down and frowned. He scented trouble in the wind.

Next morning the Chief came straight to the point. 'I appreciate what you've done, Mr Proctor. And I'll be honest, I don't know how you've done it. Your Sing-along isn't exactly modern, but the men like it.' He cleared his throat. 'I'm sorry, but it can't go on.'

'Can't go on!'

'No. Not in its present form.'

'Why ever not?'

'I'll be honest. I'm worried. There might be a riot.'

Noel stared at him. 'But why on earth should there be a riot?'

'Well some new prisoners have been transferred here from Liverpool and they might be agitators. Don't forget the old chapel was the scene of ugly riots.'

'But that was in the 1930s!'

'Yes. I'll grant you those riots happened in the *old* chapel. They barricaded themselves in after a service and wouldn't come out. And well, we aren't used to big numbers in the new chapel.'

Noel bit back his angry words and sat in silence. The Chief had a point. Supposing there was a riot during one of his services? What could he do? He shuddered and looked up.

'I never allow clapping, or too much singing at once. I know there's always your "inadequate" there who might get excited and start something...'

'...and then be used by an agitator,' added the Chief.

'Yes.' Noel bit his lip. 'But I'll be terribly upset if I have to pack in the Sing-along. The cons have all behaved perfectly.'

The Chief sat back in his chair. 'Some years before you came one bloke knifed another in the cinema. As you know the cinema is housed in the old chapel building.' The Chief paused. 'That bloke died of his stab wounds.'

Noel stared hopelessly at him. 'I only want to bring a bit of cheerfulness to their lives. And tell them about Jesus.'

The Chief winced slightly. 'I've discussed it with my Officers. We, er, appreciate your concern. And I'll grant you have planned everything very carefully. So we've decided to allow it to continue,' Noel looked up quickly, 'but with only seventy maximum.'

'Seventy!' It was at least a partial reprieve.

'But how can I select them fairly?'

The Chief relaxed in his chair. 'How about one of your famous lists Mr Proctor? The first seventy to sign up and you're away.'

Noel fought the decision and tried every way he could to get extra men at the service. He even swelled the numbers one Sunday by bringing in men from the hospital. But he had to accept the ruling in the end.

'You're just not sufficiently security conscious, Mr Proctor!'

'Well that's your job, not mine! My job is to introduce men to Christ.'

Despite the big numbers coming to chapel and the Sing-alongs, Noel still hit the hardness and apathy of the 'Moor' every day and it made him feel very alone. It was during cell visits he felt the hardness the most. Occasionally men would say, 'Get the hell out of it!'

But the more usual response went: 'Why shouldn't I rob them rich folks? They don't deserve to be rich any more than I deserve to be poor. Why shouldn't I have colour TVs and fast cars, and furs for the wife, like them? No. If I can lay my hands on anything I'll take what I can.'

'There's no justice. I'm done for five years in here. I got four hundred and thirteen "taken into considerations" and I never kept anything what I stole. I gave it all away.'

'It's my *right* see! I've got a right to what I want. Thieving's the only trade I know.'

'Coming in here's simply one of the risks of my job. Chaps take risks working on oil rigs. Well I risk it by thieving.'

Noel sighed and ran his fingers through his hair. Some of the men obviously looked upon themselves as 'Robin Hoods', robbing the rich to help the poor. There were some men who'd never change, he knew that. Marcus Blake still spat every time he went past.

But some did want to change and try and build themselves into a new routine of life. Noel marvelled at the ones who stuck doggedly to their new faith in Christ in spite of the backchat from the other prisoners.

The usual taunts they got were: 'You became a Christian so Mr Proctor'll write you a good parole report!' And, '"Screws" bloke! Sucking up for Home Leave!'

One day a Welshman called Tom had been working on a brick laying course in the Works Department. He had just got interested in Christianity and tried to convert the man working next to him. The man got so fed up of Tom singing and preaching at him that he made his mind up to get his own back. He waited till tea time and then just as Tom walked past him with his tray, he picked up his plastic jug full of water and poured it all over Tom's head. 'Now I've baptized yer,' he taunted. Tom rounded on him and swore loudly, using a choice number of oaths. The other man sniggered. 'Ha ha ha. I've made yer break your religion!'

Tom walked off to his cell, put his tray of tea down, walked back and said to the man, 'I've asked Jesus to forgive me. Now will you?'

The man bent down to pick up his jug and muttered, 'Get lost.'

But Noel noticed he left Tom alone after that. And he was in chapel next Sunday.

One Sunday evening after the Sing-along a prisoner called Mick asked to speak to Noel. 'I was washing my hands, Mr Proctor, when I saw a black thread in my soap. I looked at it more carefully and do you know what it was? A razor blade. Now who put it there, that's what I'd like to know. Nothing like that ever happened to me before I "got religion" as they say.' Mick winked at Noel and wiped his nose with the back of his hand. He leaned forward and whispered, 'I used to nick bacon and stuff from the kitchens when I worked in there and put it in big pockets I had sewn inside my underpants. No one ever missed it and I'd quite a following of long-term lads I could flog it to for cigarettes in exchange.' He sighed and pushed his black hair back. 'Now I'm religious I won't pinch. So they're on to me. Badger me to death.'

'Bless you, Mick, for your courage,' said Noel. Mick grinned.

'My prison visitor's coming to see me tomorrow. He's getting me a job in a hostel in Plymouth. Helping down-and-outs. So I've got something to look forward to when I get out of here.' Noel watched him lope down the corridor. He knew it was the faithful prison visitor and his family, who'd come year in and year out to visit Mick, who'd finally got through to him and broken down his shell of apparent uncaring. And who could blame Mick? He'd been in orphanages all his life and never known a home.

At that moment Dennis came fussing up, displaying his red-band for all to see. 'Can I tidy up the hymnbooks now?'

'Yes, please.'

Noel stood and watched Dennis, while seemingly very busy tidying up the library of Christian paperbacks he'd started collecting. Dennis was so keen to come to every meeting, to pray, to push in, almost. He'd started saying lately, 'The Lord's called me to be a preacher.' Noel shook his head.

Almost as if Dennis had read Noel's mind, he trotted up and said, 'I'm going to Bible college.'

Noel started in surprise. 'Pardon?'

'Yes. The Lord told me.'

And before Noel could open his mouth Dennis was off again, humming to himself. Noel watched him.

'Dennis,' he called.

Dennis almost ran to his side. 'Dennis the Dachshund' the other men called him. He gazed bright-eyed at Noel.

'Yes, sir.'

'Sit down Dennis, Bible college can be…tough. You know the Bible says people who used to steal should learn to work with their hands and pay back what they took. Maybe you should be thinking in those terms and then, perhaps, in the future, you could go to college.'

There seemed to be a glass wall round Dennis that stopped him taking in what Noel meant.

'Yes, sir,' he said mechanically.

Later on that evening Noel overheard him saying to the visiting choirmaster, 'I'm going to Bible college. The Lord's told me.'

Noel sighed. He couldn't stop him. He would be a free man soon, but surely it wasn't wise?

He locked up the chapel and walked home through the mist. When he got in it was very quiet, almost too quiet, and Susan came creeping out of the lounge to meet him.

'Mum's gone to bed.'

'Oh? Susan?'

'Daddy, she's been crying.'

He dropped his coat and his briefcase on the floor and ran upstairs two at a time. He burst into the bedroom and saw Norma huddled in their bed. She turned her back on him and blew her nose.

'What's the matter?'

'You're never here when I need you. Always helping the cons.' Her voice went sharp. 'Always putting God first.'

He said nothing. After a bit he said, 'Tell me what's the

matter.'

She screwed her hanky up into a wet ball and then said. 'I was having a bath this evening when I,' suddenly she burst out crying again.

'What? What?'

'I felt my breast was all little lumps...down the scar.'

Noel clutched at her elbow. 'Are you sure?'

'Yes.'

'We'll ring the doctor first thing tomorrow morning.'

'Noel, I've lost my faith.'

'No you haven't, darling. It's the spiritual battle. I'll go and make a cup of tea.'

He went downstairs and put the kettle on and as he did so the full force of what she'd said came home to him. He leaned on the sink and stared out at the misty darkness. Only last week he'd buried the gentle atheist, Goodyear, who'd made the spiked cross in the chapel. Goodyear, who had died too soon of Hodgkin's Disease. He sighed and reached for the tea pot. Goodyear's cross reminded him of so much suffering, so many deaths he'd known and of their own suffering at Eastchurch. Surely Norma couldn't have...it...again. Surely God wouldn't lead them all through their troubles at Eastchurch and bring them out on the other side, only to dump them back into the problem again. Surely not? It wouldn't be like the Lord to do that. Would it?

They visited the doctor and then the hospital. Norma had detailed X-rays done. The results were hopeful. 'It's simply fibrous tissue, Mrs Proctor. But you'd better come again in six months to make sure.' So Norma had to learn to live her life at six-monthly gaps. It wasn't easy.

Then Noel was asked to 'look after' Princetown Church as the vicar had left. Norma threw herself into the work with him.

'It's like being in Parish work again,' she said. 'I must make the most of every opportunity. At once.' He looked at her out of the corner of his eye. In case she might not be here next year, that was what she meant, he knew that. But he didn't say anything. They did visiting together in the village and began a Sunday school.

At the back of Princetown Church hung three flags: American, French, and British. After a while Norma discovered why they were there.

'Noel, those flags are in memory of the men who built this church. They were French prisoners of war, after the Napoleonic wars. Oh, and some American prisoners from California, I suppose after the War of Independence. They had to march across the moors from Plymouth, chained together and they slept in the prison.' She shuddered. 'The poor things had no heating. Can you imagine that in a Dartmoor winter? And there were nine thousand of them!'

He shook his head. Sometimes the very weight of the presence of the 'Moor' and the moors themselves, the wind and the isolation so got through to him that he wished desperately he could get away, back to pleasant, flowery suburbs and a nine-till-five job and at home every night with Norma.

She giggled when he told her. 'You! You wouldn't last five minutes. I know you. You'll never change now. You might not be very tall but you've got a big heart and a restless spirit, always "putting God first" and fighting for poor people!'

He went pink and then grinned as she said, 'I don't know why I ever took you on, Noel Proctor! But I did, and I wouldn't change you!'

Princetown Church needed money so Norma organized an August Bank Holiday mini-market. The tourists flocked in, especially when they heard that Clive Gunnell, a local ITV personality, was going to open the proceedings. By the second year they had raised over a thousand pounds. The Governor was so impressed that he suggested the prisoners should start exhibiting their own handicrafts at a prison craft fair.

In order to get plenty of stuffed toys and handiwork to sell Norma organized sewing parties throughout the year and so began to get to know several local ladies. She became very friendly with one girl called Sheila, who helped her constantly with the sewing. One day they were sitting together in Norma's lounge with a work basket between them, when Norma said, 'Have you always lived here, Sheila?'

'Oh no. Only after I got married last year.'

'Last year! But your son is five, isn't he?' Norma blushed when she realized what she'd said and her needle flew in and out of the apron she was sewing.

But Sheila laughed easily and said, 'Don't be silly. I'm Don's second wife.'

'Oh, I see.'

'His first wife died, poor thing. She'd only just had the baby when she found a lump in her breast. Her doctor was convinced it was only a blocked milk duct.'

Norma's needle stopped darting in and out of the flowery cotton and her hand lay very still in her lap.

Sheila said, 'It was terribly sad. She turned out to have breast cancer.'

Norma bent her head over the apron and made her fingers push the needle.

After a moment Sheila said, 'Have I upset you?'

Norma paused. 'No, not really. Only, it...could have been me.'

'You!'

And Norma told her. When she'd finished Sheila burst out with, 'How can you believe in a God of love after all that? I know I couldn't. I don't anyway.'

'Well I do trust him.'

'But it's like a lottery. You live and Don's first wife died! It doesn't make sense.'

Norma looked up and said, 'I am scared at times, but I trust him. I trust there's a purpose in my life continuing.'

'But...but,' and Sheila flung her patchwork down. 'I don't understand you.'

Norma leaned forward. 'He died on the cross and he knows what suffering's all about. That must have seemed meaningless at the time. But now we know it was the cornerstone of history.' She sat back, pleased to have said so much.

Sheila frowned. 'Don't try and convert me.'

'Not if you don't want to.'

They both sewed very fast for a few minutes and Norma pricked her finger.

'Sheila?'

'Yes?'

'If you don't believe, why do you help me so much to raise money for the church?'

Sheila went red. 'I'm not doing it for the church. I'm doing it for you, Norma. You're my friend after all.'

Norma touched her on the shoulder. 'Thank you ever so much.'

They sewed on, sharing the same box of pins.

'Norma, is Noel going to be on TV?'

Norma's chest swelled. 'Yes. In a film called *Chaplain of Dartmoor*. It's directed by Clive Gunnell, you know, the chap who opened the mini-market last year.'

Sheila giggled. 'Not only is Noel like The Bionic Man on a Sunday, rushing round doing five services. Now he's a film star as well.'

Norma laughed. 'Yes.' And she gazed out of the window at the churchyard. Who'd have thought the skinny little lad from the back streets of Belfast would end up as the star of a television documentary? A smile hovered round her lips and the half-finished apron fell unnoticed onto the carpet.

## Chapter Twenty-Two

## Another Funeral

One Monday morning Noel collected Dennis and took him to his office. Dennis immediately started darting round the room tidying up the already neat desk and shelves. Noel forced back his irritation.

'Look, Dennis, sit down. I'll get to the point. I want to talk to you. I'm not happy about you applying straight to Bible College when you get discharged.'

Dennis stared at him. 'But I've got my red-band, sir.'

'I know. I know. And I trust you completely. You're the best red-band I've ever known.'

Dennis sat up a bit straighter.

'But the point is, can you trust yourself outside? It's a long time since you had to cope on your own. And you were an alcoholic before you came in here.'

'But I've put in to do my exams now.'

'Well you can still do them. The College'll hold your place open for a couple of years.'

Dennis' brow puckered. 'But the Lord's told me to be a preacher!'

'But has he told you to be a preacher at once?'

Dennis' mouth set in a firm line and he sat very still. Noel sighed. Obviously that tack was getting nowhere. He tried again. 'Did you know John Jenkinson? He used to be on "B" Wing.'

Dennis nodded.

'He was a Hell's Angel and got involved with drugs and witchcraft. He did four years for stabbing some youths and almost blinding two of them.'

Dennis interrupted. 'I've never done anything like that.'

'No, no, I know you haven't. But, as I was saying, his prison visitor helped him and he became a Christian.'

Dennis fiddled with a pile of books and stopped looking at Noel. 'Well he thinks the Lord's called him to be a preacher, too, only he's determined to work three years first, save up, and pay his way.' Noel paused. 'I had a letter from him the other day. He's settled down at a Precision Tool Makers. He's paying his way with his landlady and he's kept out of trouble.'

'Yes, sir.'

Noel searched Dennis' face for any sign of real agreement.

The phone rang and as Noel picked it up, Dennis trotted off in the direction of the Chaplain's library shelves, with a duster in his hand.

'Hello there,' said Noel.

It was the Censor Office with bad news. 'I've received a letter from Marcus Blake's sister. Their mother's died. Could you break the news to him?'

Noel's mind was a blank. 'Marcus Blake?'

'Yes. The lifer. He, er, spits.'

'Oh no! Not him.'

Noel saw him in his mind's eye. A shapeless, shuffling figure spitting in the exercise area. He groaned. Well, there was nothing for it. He'd have to go and break the news.

Within five minutes he'd taken Dennis back to his cell and then arrived at 'D' Wing. He asked the Duty Officer in charge to come and wait outside Marcus' cell while he went in. Noel opened the cell.

The smell inside hit him in the face. Marcus Blake hadn't bothered to put his bucket under his bunk, or even to have it emptied at all.

'Get that thing under the bunk,' said Noel.

Marcus moved his toe towards the bucket and pushed it an inch across the floor.

Noel cleared his throat. 'Mr er, Blake, I've got some bad news for you.' He drew the letter out of his pocket. 'I'm afraid we heard this morning that your mother has, er, died. I'm very sorry.'

Marcus lifted his head suddenly. 'My mam?'

'Yes. I'm sorry.'

'But, I never knew. Was she ill?'

'No. It says here it was sudden.'

Marcus sprang up. 'But why didn't they send for me? I've never seen her for a year!'

Noel said in a low voice, 'I just missed seeing my father before he died, too. I know how you feel.'

For a second their eyes met and they exchanged a glance on equal terms. And then Marcus' brilliant blue eyes filled with tears.

'My mam,' he said.

Suddenly Noel felt pity for him. He was still young and slender, dwarfed by the shapeless clothes, the greasy hair and the smell.

Noel went and put his arm round him. 'Come on now.'

Marcus shook his head. 'It's all my fault.'

'How could it be when you weren't even there?'

'That's the whole point, I *wasn't* there. I were in *here*.' He paused. 'I were in here, where I shouldn't have been, if only I'd listened to her.' He put his head in his hands. 'My own stupid fault.'

Nothing Noel said could convince him. Years of depression, guilt and sluttishness threatened to swamp him. Noel was worried.

'Look, shall I arrange for you to go to the funeral with an Officer?'

Marcus looked up. 'Could you?'

'I'll try.'

When Noel got outside again the Duty Officer said, 'How did he take it?'

'Very upset. Cried his eyes out.'

'Did he spit?'

'No,' said Noel surprised. He'd forgotten about the spitting. 'He needs his bucket emptying, though. By the way, what's he in for?'

'Murder. A pub brawl. He's done twelve years already.'

Noel walked slowly away. Marcus had done a terrible crime. Somewhere in England was a widow, perhaps with children. Noel bowed his shoulders. He knew Marcus had been very bad. And Marcus knew that. And society had taken a terrible vengeance upon him. Noel shook his head. The Officer was following him so he stopped and turned round.

The Officer grimaced. 'I don't know how you can put your arm round him. He stinks.'

Noel groaned. 'I don't know either. All I know is that if my Christ could say "Father forgive them" when he was up on his cross, how can I *not* put my arm round him?'

The Officer was silent for a moment and then said, 'Talking of, er, religion, there's something funny going on in the Punishment Wing. Something about ghostly fingers! Would you like to go and see?'

'Ghostly fingers!'

'They're all scared to death down there!'

Noel frowned. 'After being locked in with a lifer who hasn't emptied his bucket, I don't think ghostly fingers'll worry me much!'

Noel strode to his office, made a phone call to arrange for Marcus to go to his mother's funeral and then went to the Punishment Wing. He went straight to the Officer on duty, an elderly man called Murray, and asked what was going on.

'It's Eric. He's been put down here on Rule 43B. You know, segregated.'

'What's he been up to?'

'Oh, acting the fool, messing about in the Mail Bag section. He's been getting in with those blokes from Liverpool, those agitators.' Mr Murray shook his head. 'Some of 'em never learn. Anyway he says that he woke up last night and someone . . . or something was clutching at his throat, trying to strangle him. He really was in a state.'

Noel stroked his chin. 'Perhaps I'd better go and see him.'

Murray seemed about to say something and then changed his mind. 'I'll see you afterwards,' was all he said.

Noel unlocked Eric's cell and walked in. Eric sprang up off the bunk and grabbed him by the arm. 'Please, please, sir, help me!'

Noel steadied him and took in the red, blotchy face. Eric certainly wasn't messing about now.

'Of course I'll help you. Tell me all about it.'

'Them fingers pressing at my throat. I thought I were dead.' Eric shuddered. Noel sat next to him on the bunk. He talked to him and then prayed: 'May any bad influences in this cell be taken away by the power of Christ.' They paused and then

Noel said, 'If you've any more problems Mr Murray will move you.'

Eric wiped his nose with a dirty hanky. 'Ta, mate.'

When Noel got out into the corridor again and the door had clanged behind him, he went and found Murray. Murray sized him up and down and then beckoned him down the corridor away from Eric's cell. 'Do you know what I think?'

'No,' said Noel.

'Well,' and Murray stared into the middle distance. 'I've been here a long time. It's years ago now, but it did take place in that cell.'

'What did?'

'Suicide. A lad committed suicide in there.'

'Oh I see.' But Noel didn't see. How could something that had happened years ago affect Eric last night? And in any case as the days went by Eric perked up. Soon he was back to his irritating self, the ghostly fingers seemingly forgotten.

When the day of Marcus' mother's funeral came, Noel went up to see him in the morning. He entered the cell with the keys jangling and then stopped. Something was different but he wasn't sure what. Marcus stood up. He still looked as if he were wearing jumble sale clothing, but he'd made an effort to be very clean and had shaved. Noel wrinkled his nose. There was something different.... 'Well, Marcus, are you ready?'

Marcus nodded, his eyes very bright. 'I'll see my sister at the graveside. She hates me.'

Noel sighed. 'Let's pray anyway before you go.'

Then he stood back as the door rattled, keys turned and a burly Officer came in and handcuffed Marcus to his brawny arm. Noel followed them down the corridor and it echoed with the sound of their footsteps. Then two more Officers strolled up and the four of them climbed into a taxi and sped away.

Noel suddenly felt tears pricking at the back of his eyes. He remembered going to his own mother's funeral. He'd been angry that she had given up wanting to live after his dad had died. And under his anger there'd been a deep ache, somewhere in the marrow of his bones. He forced himself to turn away, to push down his own grief. There was work to be done.

It was as he was walking briskly back to his office that he

realized what was different about Marcus' cell. There'd been
no smell! No dirty bucket half shoved under the bunk. There'd
been the scent of cheap after-shave instead. Noel was thoughtful as he went into his office. People were saying Marcus had
stopped spitting, too.

An Officer brought Dennis in and he immediately started
retidying the library books. Noel groaned inwardly. 'Look
Dennis, pick out two or three good titles: *The Cross and the
Switchblade*, something like that, and put them on one side, and
then, er, go and dust the chapel, please.'

'I dusted it yesterday.'

Noel grimaced.

'Shall I dust it again?'

'Yes, please.'

But Dennis hovered nearby, flicking a duster, so in the end
Noel said, 'Did you want to tell me something?'

Dennis' chest swelled. 'Oh, sir, the Bible College in London
will take me on. I just need references. They say I can go
straight from here.'

Noel's heart sank. So Dennis wasn't going to work in a
factory first in spite of everything that had been said.

Noel shook Dennis by the hand. 'You've done very well,' he
said.

When Dennis had gone Noel gathered up the books under
one arm and went back to 'D' Wing, intending to leave them in
Marcus' cell for him to read when he got back from the
funeral, but the Officer on duty met him and said, 'Can you go
and see Halliday? He's very depressed. Says he'd be better off
dead.'

'Why?'

'He's very intelligent and has nothing to do except remember
his crime.'

'Do you reckon it was a "crime of passion"?'

The Officer thought. 'Yes. I do. He's not the criminal type,
who'd rob a bank with a gun in his pocket. But if you murder
your wife you can expect to end up in here.'

Noel was quiet for a minute and then went to Halliday's
cell. He unlocked the door, stepped inside the cell and sprung
the lock behind him.

Halliday rose to greet him. 'Do sit down.'

'Thanks.'

Noel made some small talk but was really sizing up Halliday. He was very tense and his hair was streaked with grey.

'How are you, Mr Halliday?'

'Very well indeed.'

Noel bit his lip. So poor Halliday didn't want to talk about his problems. So Noel tried again. 'Can you help me?'

'How on earth can I help you?' asked Halliday.

'You could help me to run a "Mastermind" competition next Friday evening?'

Halliday was staring at him but Noel rushed on. 'You could think of some good questions to ask. Nothing too hard. Some of the lads aren't too, er, quick. I'm desperately busy and I promised them I'd run it. If you were interested I might be able to get permission for you to be the Question Master.'

Halliday was looking at him intently. He knows why I'm asking him, thought Noel. He must have seen me through the spyhole in his cell door as I was talking to the Officer.

But Halliday had jumped up and was pulling a small encyclopaedia off his shelf. 'Yes, I'll do it.'

Noel grinned. 'Good lad!' and slapped him on the back. Halliday was surprised and moved away slightly. Oh no, thought Noel. I forgot he wasn't a working bloke like me. However Halliday carried on leafing through his books.

Noel said, 'Do the other prisoners accept you? Do they ever gang up on you or call you names?'

Halliday thought a minute. 'No, I don't think so.'

'Will you be the Chairman, then?'

'Yes I will, if you can get the permission.'

'Ta, mate. Er, I mean thank you very much.'

As Noel got up to go Halliday said, 'Did you bring those books for me?' Halliday pointed to the three books Noel was still carrying under his arm.

'Oh, these. Would you like to borrow them?'

'Yes, please.'

Noel handed them over and wondered what the literary Halliday would make of the stories of down-town, drop-out teenagers in New York who became Christians and came off drugs.

Late that afternoon Noel got a phone call from 'D' Wing.

The Officer said, 'Marcus Blake wants to see you. He's back from the funeral.'

'OK.'

Noel pushed away the files of Home Leave reports he was doing and went straight to Marcus' cell. He was prepared for Marcus to give him a rough ride, to shout and swear. Men often used him in that way when they were upset and angry. He squared his shoulders. Better that than men blowing up with an Officer, who'd have to put them on report.

He got inside Marcus' cell and locked the door behind him. 'How are you?'

'How can *I* become a Christian?'

Noel sat down suddenly on the bunk. 'Pardon?'

Marcus stared at him and ran his fingers through his hair impatiently. 'Me. I wants to be a Christian.'

Noel stared back, nonplussed. 'Look sit down and tell me about the funeral.'

Marcus took out a faded, black book from his pocket. 'She gave it to me. It says *I* can become a Christian.'

Noel gently took the old-fashioned New Testament. It was open at John's gospel and underlined in red were the famous words:

> For God so loved the world, that he gave his only begotten son, that whosoever believes in him, should not perish but have ever-lasting life [John 3:16].

Someone had crossed out 'whosoever' and written 'Marcus' over the top in blue ballpoint. Noel looked up at Marcus.

'She said, "It means you, Marc."'

Noel sat back on the bunk. He had the feeling he was a bystander at some preordained event, a greater and more far-seeing plan than he could ever have envisaged.

'Tell me,' he said.

'Well I went to the funeral, handcuffed, and sat at the side in the church. I saw the coffin and everything. My sister and her family were there but she only looked at me once. I felt nothing when I saw the coffin. Nothing.'

'I know.'

'Then we went to the cemetery. The Officers took me to the graveside, and she threw some earth in. Then we all stood quiet, but as we turned to go my sister rushed up to me and pushed this little, black book at me. She looked straight at me, with tears in her eyes, and said, "Read what I've underlined, Marc. It means you. This was Mum's Bible and she gave it to me and now I'm giving it to you." And then she rushed off again.' Marcus was silent. Then he said, 'I read it on the way back in the car. I couldn't turn the pages over because I was handcuffed and I had to ask the Officers to turn the pages over for me. One said, "It's a bit late for you to get religion, isn't it?" But the other said, "Leave him alone. If he wants to read it, let him read it."'

Noel stared. 'Go on.'

'Well, when I read what she'd underlined I suddenly realized it meant *me*. It wasn't just for toffs and them on the right side of the law. It meant the likes of me as well.'

'Yes,' said Noel.

'Go on then.'

'What?'

'Say what you have to. The prayers and that. I'm ready.'

Noel knelt down by him and they prayed.

As Noel left the cell and locked the door behind him, he wondered whether Marcus would stick to his new-found faith. Could Christ really change a murderer, who'd become a recluse, and had no other prospect than the grim, granite walls of Dartmoor for years to come?

## Chapter Twenty-Three

# 'I Learned to "Fight" at the Moor'

The months sped by. Soon they'd been at Dartmoor three years. Every six months Norma had her check-ups at the hospital. Each time she was still clear of the cancer. And one day Noel realized with surprise that for all his initial fear before he came his main work had been done amongst the men in 'D' Wing, his main response had come from the long-termers, the lifers and the men in Punishment. There was something else he realized too: he had learned to fight both circumstances and people at Dartmoor, fight until he won through.

The girls liked the life at Princetown. They enjoyed school and had lots of friends. But the poor weather and the isolation did affect the whole family in the end.

'There's only one bus a week to Tavistock,' said Norma. 'Hard luck if I miss it. You know Noel, Dartmoor really is a hard place.'

'Do you know what one of the ex-cons said to me recently?' Noel asked. 'He said, "I know of nowhere that can so finally break a man's heart as Dartmoor."'

'Imagine being locked in that grim place. Nothing but wind and mist outside and locks and bars inside.'

Norma tossed her head. 'But there is good news as well. You told me that John Lomax was giving his testimony at Newquay recently and a woman there said his face shone so much she wanted the same Christianity he had!'

'Yes. And his wife, Lynne, has become a Christian as well.'

She smiled. 'What about that chap at Eastchurch? James who was always getting sent to Punishment for losing his temper. Well he's got married, stayed out of trouble and gone to Oakhill Theological College. He's made good.'

'I know.'

'And Mick who won that big art competition and sent you the picture. He says he's still a Christian.'

But Noel wasn't listening, so Norma tried again. 'They say that 20% of first-time offenders go straight afterwards.'

Noel looked up at last and he had shadows under his eyes. 'People are always asking me if Christ can miraculously change a man once he's been in prison. They seem to expect him to wave a magic wand.'

'Life's not like that, is it?' Norma responded.

'No. For a man who's been in prison, to pull himself back into society, to get and keep a job when no one wants him and he's no family behind him and the church is distant,' he shook his head. 'It's a fantastic achievement. Someone from the Education Department said only yesterday how few prisoners can read well. Most of them can't read as well as an average nine year old child!'

Norma stared at him, silenced.

He sat up very straight. 'Folks outside have no idea of the pressures the cons face when they come out. Often the only place they can go to is a hostel. And all their old cronies will be there. Those are the only people who'll accept them. So back they get into trouble. It takes years, Norma, for an ex-con, who's usually from a broken home or an orphanage, to get practised at living a decent life. The snag is he often falls by the wayside.'

He flung a letter on to the table. 'Here's a case in point. A thief called Nick gets converted...he sticks to his faith. I believe he means it, so when he's due to be discharged I write to three different churches in his home town.' He snorted with disgust. 'The Church of England chap doesn't reply. The Baptist chap writes to the Governor and asks for a list of his crimes! And the Pentecostal pastor writes and says, "What train's he coming on? We'll meet him, give him digs, and find him a job."'

Norma was silent. He got up and scraped his chair against the wall. 'It certainly makes you think! I don't know why I bother with the Church of England. A lot of middle-class toffee noses!'

Norma laughed. 'You can't altogether blame them. They're right to be wary.'

Noel sat down again heavily. 'Well, they've no right to be wary. Jesus isn't wary!'

'But remember that poor old retired vicar in London? He wrote and told you he trusted an ex-con who came to his door telling him how he'd been "converted". But when the old vicar went out the con helped himself to the wife's jewellery! You see that vicar was too trusting!'

Noel groaned. 'Do you know, that particular con, a good-looking chap, actually pinched and used the story of the conversion of his cell-mate! And as a matter of fact the cell-mate really did become a Christian and has gone straight!' He sighed. 'The cons do live on their wits, I know. I suppose you're right, Norma. I do get too impatient. But I see these men day in and day out, stuck in their cells. Usually there's only a bucket to use for a toilet. They all wear the same clothes. Often they've no hope left.' He hit the table with his fist. 'No wonder they say prison breaks a man's heart.'

'But you've done good work Noel.'

But he rushed on. 'It would be easy if it were all cut and dried, and neatly tied up in parcels. Then I could say, "Fifty's been converted and they'll never get into trouble again." But real life's not like that. Just a seething mass of men up there. I can only do my best.'

Norma was concerned. 'You're tired.'

'People always ask me about the failure rate. But society itself has a big failure rate. Even Jesus expected a failure rate. Look at the parable of the sower! We all call on God when we're in trouble, but when things perk up a bit, we forget him.'

'You *are* tired.'

'I don't know, people are cynical about cons becoming Christians. Yet why shouldn't a con find Christ? Inside, they get rock bottom and if they can get a straw to cling to, and find faith, they can get hope back, and confidence and assurance. Maybe it's the first time *anybody's* ever loved them. The trouble is when they come out, there's no Officer to knock on the door and ask 'em to meetings. There's a certain importance in prison in having your name on a list—even if it is the choir list.'

Norma grinned and then went serious. 'You can't do it all,

Noel. In the end they have to make up their own minds.'

He yawned and stretched. 'You're right, dear, I am tired.' Then he brightened up. 'Do you know, when I asked that evangelist Dick Saunders to come he gave an appeal at the end for men who wanted to follow Christ and twenty-eight men raised their hands.'

But she was fiddling with her fork. 'You know what you said about that Pentecostal church being the only church to befriend that ex-con?'

'Yes?'

'It's interesting, isn't it? Pentecostalism, I mean.'

Noel groaned and then laughed, 'If you start speaking in tongues, there'll never be any peace at all!'

'The cheek!'

'Well actually the pastor of Plympton Pentecostal Church is coming up to speak at the prison one Sunday morning. So perhaps you'll find out then!'

Later on in the week Noel had more to worry about than speaking in tongues. He kept hearing the odd snippet of conversation, and the odd snatch of prayer. There was always the same word in the middle of it: 'trouble'. So he went to see Officer Murray in the 'D' Wing.

'What's going on, Mr Murray?'

For an answer Murray took Noel to a cell door and unlocked it. Noel stepped in and Murray stayed close behind him, jangling his keys on the end of his chain. The prisoner inside stared sullenly at them. 'Get lost!' he growled.

Noel said nothing but stood his ground. The man was cleanshaven and had a bruise on one cheek. Suddenly he sprang forward and lifted up his shirt. 'See that!' he said. Noel peered at his chest. There were some bruises, yellowing at the edges. 'See them bruises!' and he pointed at Murray. 'Ask him how I got them!' Then he turned his back on them.

When the two men got outside in the corridor and Murray had clanged the door to and locked it fast, Noel said, 'What's it all about?'

Murray pushed his peaked cap further back on his head. 'He'd been misbehaving in the TV repair workshop. Shouting and carrying on. The Governor said he'd got to be put into

Punishment to cool his heels. Well he fought and fought when they tried to get him down here. And of course he got bruised. Now he's kicking up a right old fuss.' Murray wagged his finger at Noel. 'No one seems bothered that one of the younger Officers got bruised as well.'

Noel sighed and then pursed his lips. 'Well the prisoner doesn't look too bad to me. Is the Officer OK?'

'Yes.'

'Why was the prisoner put on Punishment again?'

'Mainly for agitating and complaining. He was transferred from Hull, you see. He's become a sort of ringleader to the others now.'

'Hull. Haven't they had riots and prisoners on the roof lately?'

'That's it. The Governor here doesn't want any of that kind of trouble spreading to the Moor. We've got a good reputation.'

As the days passed Noel kept his ear finely tuned. Rumours were flying round that some long-termers were going to create a disturbance because their leader had been wrongfully put into Punishment and had got bruised. Noel realized that someone might get hurt and finally he went to see the Governor about it. Colin Heald said, 'He claims he's been beaten up.'

'Well he's got bruises, but I think that's natural when he fought all the way down. No, there's nothing to the extent the rumours say.'

'Hmmm.'

'Can I have permission to go and see him?'

'Certainly.'

Noel went up to 'D' Wing and his heart was beating rather fast. Murray raised his eyebrows when he saw him there again but said nothing. He let Noel into the cell and waited outside.

Noel said, 'Mr Bailey, there's rumours going round this prison that trouble's brewing. Your name keeps being mentioned.' He paused. 'There was no trouble before you came.'

Bailey didn't answer.

'Well?' Noel demanded.

Bailey shrugged, 'So what!'

'You've nearly done your sentence. Why chance losing remission now? If there's a riot you'll get the blame even if it's not your fault. Why chance it?'

Bailey glanced at him. 'Who said anything about a riot?'

Noel leaned forward. 'Can I have your permission to see the other ringleaders and ask them to cool it?'

There was silence.

Noel said, 'If all this dies down there'll be no repercussions. You'll still get the same remission if you've earned it.'

Bailey looked at his shoe. 'OK,' he muttered and named two cell numbers.

'Right,' said Noel and left the cell.

He decided to see the other two ringleaders at once while he was in the mood, but Murray stopped him. He locked up Bailey's cell and then said, 'There's trouble with ghostly fingers again.'

'Oh no! Not that again!'

'You can laugh. But that lad Eric's been sedated by the MO. He's so upset, I've decided to move him. He says,' and Murray frowned and took a step nearer Noel, 'he says he didn't learn his lesson last time, he didn't bother to go to Mass or confession with Father O'Driscoll and now the ghost's trying to kill him.'

Suddenly Noel shivered. Badness in men's hearts was one thing, it tarred all men, including himself. But this supernatural, evil brooding, was...it was uncanny. He walked quickly after Murray to Eric's cell.

The cell seemed ordinary enough as Noel stepped inside. The door clanged behind him and he sprang round. 'Don't lock me in!' he yelled.

Murray heaved open the door. 'Sorry,' he said. 'Force of habit. I won't be far away.'

Noel stood alone in the cell: so grey, so quiet, so small. Surely he didn't need to bother...then he realized he was afraid, but he did not know why. He had to force himself to pray. As he did so and the familiar words of the Lord's prayer rolled round his mind, he suddenly remembered Big Roy at Eastchurch who'd had the gypsy's curse put on him. He gathered himself together and began to pray out loud. He heard his own voice, strong and sure saying: 'In the name of Jesus Christ, begone you...you evil thing....'

The cell was very quiet. He knew he wasn't afraid now. He carried on:

'And may the peace of Christ rest in this cell.
And may the blood of Christ protect it and all who
     sleep here from all evil.
And may the Spirit of Christ rest here.'

He stood with bowed head. His fear was gone, and in its place was an upsurge of joy and a sense of the restored rightness of things. He opened his eyes and looked round.

Whatever 'it' was, had gone. He strode across the room and let himself out. 'You won't have any more trouble in there,' he called out to Murray jauntily as he trotted past. Murray watched him go then pushed his cap even further back on his head. He grinned and shook his head. It certainly took all sorts...!

Noel was late home and it wasn't till they went to bed that he was able to tell Norma all about his day. 'I managed to see Bailey and the other two ringleaders and warn them. I'm hoping they'll see sense.'

'What did they say?'

'Absolutely nothing. But at least they didn't tell me to get lost. So you never know.'

He paused. 'Then I saw Eric. He was in a terrible state. White-faced and with staring eyes. I prayed over him in the end. You know, Norma, evil is a funny thing. Ghosts and witchcraft and all that. It's as slippery as an eel. You can't put your finger on it. But, my word, you can see the results. People walking round terrified out of their wits, suicidal and despairing.'

'What's happened to Charlie? The one that was "blinded"?'

'Oh, he settled down into one of Father O'Driscoll's groups. I don't know about him being converted but his life is slowly changing direction. He's always at Mass on a Sunday now.'

Norma was very quiet. Then she said, 'Noel, it's a good thing Jesus died on the cross, isn't it? And rose again and defeated all death and darkness and,' she shivered, 'all the evil things.'

He looked at her. 'Yes?'

'Otherwise I'd have given up when I had the cancer.' She raised her chin. 'Now I *know* why the gospel is called "good news".'

## Chapter Twenty-Four

# 'The Only Sin God Cannot Forgive'

On the day Dennis was discharged Noel and Norma invited him to breakfast. Norma found him a pile of old sheets and blankets to take with him and then Pastor Jack from Plympton came to take him to the station. Someone from the College was going to meet him at the other end. They waved the car goodbye and then went back into the house, Noel to prepare a sermon, and Norma to clear up the breakfast things. As he pored over his concordance Noel couldn't concentrate. His heart felt heavy every time he thought of Dennis.

Life went on as normal at the prison. One day came the news that Marcus Blake's mother had left him a little money in her will. When Noel next saw Marcus he said, 'Mr Proctor, will you buy me some model kits of aeroplanes and things, with some of my mam's money?'

'Yes. But why?'

'I thought I'd make 'em up.'

'OK then.'

Soon Marcus' cell was alive with models, the first ones shakily assembled, but the later ones quite good. Noel was pleased with him. He'd stopped spitting and behaved properly with his bucket now. He was still a recluse but was a lot happier now he was using his hands.

One day Marcus said, 'Can you give some of these models to hospitals for sick children?'

'Yes, I can arrange it.'

Then he made his best model. It was a boat with batteries at the back to propel it through the water.

Noel said, 'You'll be wanting to keep that one.'

Marcus thought. 'No. I've made my mind up. I want it to go

to a mentally handicapped child.'

Without thinking Noel said, 'Officer Murray has a slightly mentally handicapped son. The lad'd be thrilled to receive it.'

There was a very long pause. Marcus gazed at the boat and held it tightly in his hands. Noel wished he'd kept his mouth shut. He knew Marcus hated all authority, especially the Officers, and that the last family he'd want to give his precious boat to would be an Officer's family. Then Marcus sighed and his fingers uncurled from the boat.

'OK.'

Noel put his hand on his arm. 'Are you sure? I know you've put a lot into that boat. I won't think any less of you if you want to change your mind.'

Marcus frowned. 'No, go on. I want him to have it.'

'Thanks ever so much.'

That same evening Noel took the boat round to where Murray lived in the village and the lad whooped with delight when he saw it. Murray said nothing but as Noel was leaving he said, 'Tell — Blake — I'm grateful.'

'OK.'

Then Murray pointed to the house walls, where some pretty wallpaper was hanging off the wall in one corner. 'See that! These prison houses are all the same. All damp! We're fed up of them. I'm thinking of buying my own place in Tavistock and motoring up each day.'

'Are you really?'

'Yes. And the weather's so awful here.'

Next morning Noel popped in to see Marcus and tell him how thrilled the lad was with the boat. But when he got in the cell he gazed at Marcus in astonishment. For the very first time Marcus Blake looked human again: he stood erect, his eyes were bright and his hair neat.

'You'll never guess what, Mr Proctor! Officer Murray came to see me after breakfast. He asked me all about the model kits and how I made 'em and what glue I used.' Marcus' smile seemed to fill the cell. 'He sat down where you're sitting, Mr Proctor, and he said, "Thank you Mr Blake, for making my son happy." He called me "Mr Blake". He says he's telling the other Officers in "D" Wing about the boat.'

'That's great.'

And for the very first time Marcus looked him straight in the eye and smiled.

On his way back to his office Noel made a detour to see Murray. 'Marcus Blake is tickled pink by what you said.'

'Humph!' said Murray going red.

'You've made his day.'

'Poor devil,' said Murray, but Noel couldn't help noticing that Murray was whistling as he went off down the corridor. Noel watched him go. Dartmoor wasn't really a whistling place and a little light gleamed in Noel's eyes as he thought of Marcus Blake and Murray.

The letter Noel had dreaded receiving came a few days later. It was from the London College: did Mr Proctor have any idea where Dennis was? He'd been missing several days and, sad to say, items were also missing from other students and from his digs. If Dennis could return, explain and give back the items, the situation could be reviewed. Otherwise his place at the college was closed. Noel shut his eyes and groaned. Why, oh why hadn't Dennis listened to him? Why hadn't the college insisted he worked first? He rang the college principal, who was understanding. 'The trouble was, Mr Proctor, he never seemed to fit in.'

Over the next few weeks the failure of Dennis weighed heavily on him. Even the Chief told him to forget it. 'You can't win 'em all, Proctor. Let it drop. No one's perfect.'

But Noel couldn't sleep at nights. He blamed himself. The whole episode highlighted the major social problem of his work. What were the men to do when they came out of prison? Of course many he'd known had gone straight and a few had done very well indeed.

Norma kept reminding him of the man who'd worked his way up from sweeping out a bus station to managing a cafe. John Jenkinson was in his second term at his Bible College and sticking the course. And James from Eastchurch was now a curate in the North of England. But nothing she said would help. Noel put his head in his hands. Dennis had only been at the college six weeks before he disappeared. He was obviously in a mess.

In the afternoon post a dirty envelope arrived for Noel. It

was postmarked Southampton and written in a sprawling hand. He opened it and stared at the splotchy writing, the pathetic signature with the twirl under the first letter. 'Yours sincerely, from Dennis,' he read. The letter ached with repentance, with sorrow that he'd stolen china from his landlady to get a bit of cash. 'I just couldn't stand it at college. They watched me all the time. Do this. Do that. It was worse than prison. I just didn't fit in. So I ran away and now I'm living in a hostel with some of my old mates....'

He showed it to Norma and she said, 'I don't think he's deliberately turned his back on God. But he was weak and had no family.' She shook her head. 'It's too easy to blame the college. They did try to give him a chance. But there again, what about the landlady?'

He didn't reply but went and stood by the window. He remembered his own time at college. The slur of 'arrogant' that clung to him; the students who all talked 'posh'. He remembered getting a note from John Jenkinson saying, 'The other students here are giving me a rough ride. I can't read and write as well as them....' He ran his hand through his hair. What was the answer? He replied to Dennis begging him to go back. He got no reply so he wrote again. But still there was no reply.

In September he set about preparing yet another group of men for Confirmation. The Bishop now came about twice a year to the Moor to take Confirmation services because, as Noel explained to Norma, 'We're getting one or two men every week who are serious about becoming Christians.'

'How on earth has the interest arisen?'

'Well there's the services and the Sing-alongs. They're always asking me to pray for them if they can't sleep, or have a pain or whatnot. And, well, the prayers are answered. So that creates interest. There's one negro chap who kept bleeding from his penis and he got very upset and asked me to pray. Well, ever since he's been OK.'

'Spare me the gory details!'

Noel groaned, 'He went and told the M.O. they didn't need a doctor any more. I'd do instead!'

'Oh no!'

Then Noel went serious. 'This time I've got a problem.

Halliday wants to be confirmed.'

'Halliday!'

'Mmmm. I can't refuse and I don't want to refuse. But,' and he sighed, 'he was a murderer. And he's shown no sign of remorse.'

When he went to see Halliday, he wasn't quite sure how to approach him. He wasn't like the other long-termers; Noel could see if their behaviour had changed along with a change of heart. He was not like Marcus Blake where the change was plain. No, Halliday behaved perfectly. He never swore, or spat or caused trouble. Yet he had never discussed his crime, never actually said he was sorry. So Noel got straight to the point. 'Mr Halliday, are you really sure you want to be confirmed?

'It's a big step. It means turning your back on your old life and stepping out into the new.'

'Yes.'

'It means totally committing your life to Christ.'

'Yes.'

Noel swallowed and took a deep breath. 'It's no use conning yourself or conning God. Confirmation is the end of the road. Or to put it another way, a new start.' There was a pause. Then, 'You know as well as I do that your offence was vile.'

There. He'd said it at last. The words were out in the open.

Halliday was very quiet. Noel waited. Then Halliday cleared his throat, 'Does, er, God forgive, er...' and his voice dropped very low, 'Does he forgive murder?'

'Yes.'

'Does, er, God give you peace of mind?'

'Yes.'

Noel waited again, but that was as much as Halliday would say. And it was as much as he ever did say in the Confirmation classes.

Noel decided to let him go ahead. After all, he wasn't Halliday's final judge.

On the night in November when the Bishop came, Halliday was ready and waiting with all the others. As Noel went past he touched him on the arm. 'Excuse me, can I speak to the Bishop privately?'

'I'll try and arrange it.'

The Officer gave permission and Noel led Halliday into the

vestry and shut the door. Noel said to the Bishop, 'Excuse me, sir, this candidate would like to ask you something.'

The Bishop smiled at Halliday. 'Yes. What is it?'

Noel moved to the other side of the room, but Halliday spoke in a clear voice and Noel could hear him.

'I wanted to ask you, my Lord, is there a sin God cannot forgive?' Halliday's voice sounded even more upper-crust than usual and the Bishop glanced at him quickly. Noel held his breath. He never told the Bishop what any of the men were in for.

There was a pause and then the Bishop said, 'The only sin God cannot forgive is the unconfessed sin.'

Halliday's shoulders seemed to relax. 'Thank you, my Lord. That was all I wanted to know.'

Noel let out a sigh of relief. And then they all went into the chapel.

## Chapter Twenty-Five

# 'Good Lord Deliver Us!'

The winter of 1977–1978 was so cold that the ice froze on the tree branches and the ground in the churchyard was littered with broken twigs. For seven long days the snow was so heavy that there was no electricity and no phones in the village. Noel and Norma had a coal fire in the lounge. They hugged it whenever they could and Norma struggled to heat pans of soup over the hot coals. Some of the elderly villagers were cut off by ten feet of snow at their front doors. The Governor sent working parties of inmates to dig them out and as the prison had its own generator they were able to take hot water bottles to the oldest inhabitants. The Governor also allowed bread baked in the prison bakery to be sold at the village shop, and he had extra milk sent down.

'In fact,' said Noel, 'the prison's really kept the village going. Perhaps it'll help to make the villagers more accepting of the prison Officers and the prisoners.'

It was the worst winter Princetown had known for years. Norma shivered. 'I hope this'll be our last winter here.' But Noel was fiddling with his diary and seemed not to hear her. She tried again. 'It's so upsetting for me now my friends Paul and Denise have moved on. I feel lonely.'

He nodded. It was one of the problems of running Princetown Parish Church. He would just get good numbers of Staff families there, when they would be promoted and move on. No one, it seemed, wanted to stay too long at the Moor.

'There's the Mission to look forward to next April,' he said.

She sighed heavily. Sometimes trying to get through to him was like knocking her head against a brick wall. If he was planning a Mission she knew she'd just have to put up with the weather and the loneliness until it was over. Her mouth went into a firm line and she stirred some soup quickly. No way was she going to put up with another winter like this one. He carried on fiddling with his diary. He knew she was upset and he'd have to talk it through with her later. Yes, later would do.

The ecumenical Mission was planned for Holy Week, 1978, and there was a lot of co-operation between the different denominations. The Catholics were sending a Redemptorist Father, called John, to take their side of the Mission and Noel marvelled at him. He was so simple and so direct with the men, so full of fun and humour, so pleased to work with Noel. Ivor Earl, the Methodist minister, was also enthusiastic about it, and there was support from the Governor and the Chief as well. Noel had been praying for God's blessing on the Mission for eighteen months and as the time drew nearer he got excited. At every opportunity he told men about it and invited them to come. Yet he wondered: with almost half the inmates on free association in the evenings, able to chat, watch television, listen to the radio or read, would they bother to come?

On the first night the chapel was full. Noel counted. There were at least one hundred and twenty there to hear the Chaplain General preach. By the Good Friday, which was the Church of England night, two hundred men were squashed inside.

At the end Noel said, 'If anyone would like to follow Jesus Christ will they please rise to their feet.'

At once there was a scraping and shoving of chairs. Father John tensed and leaned forward, while Noel clasped his hands behind his back and blinked very fast. For a second their eyes met and Noel knew, evangelical that he was, and fiery Roman Catholic that Father John was, that they were united at that moment by a deep bond.

Noel asked those who'd stood up to wait behind to be counselled, while the rest left. It took an hour for the chapel to be cleared while the Chaplains counselled the men.

'Between a third and a quarter of them stood up,' said Noel at last.

'Bless God,' shouted Father John and Officer Murray looked back, startled. Noel grinned and began to make a list of the men. As his eye ran down the list he suddenly looked up. It couldn't be! But it was. That foul-oathed giant of a chap had waited behind with the others. Father John raised an eyebrow and Noel explained.

'One day last week I was called to Reception to interview a new prisoner. When I got there it looked as if a tornado had hit the place—chairs broken, a vase smashed, papers everywhere and a table upturned. I set off to find the prisoner when one of the Officers tried to stop me. 'Don't go in there, Mr Proctor. He's a wild animal. I'm warning you, don't go in. You'll get hurt!'

'Well,' continued Noel, 'I half turned to leave when something made me turn back. I decided I would have a go at talking to the prisoner. So I asked the Officer why the man had wrecked the Reception and he replied that the prisoner's mother had just died. I went to the cell door and put my key in the lock and turned it, a bit slowly, and then stuck my head round the door.

'The prisoner was sitting hunched up with his head in his hands. When he heard me he sprang up, and honestly, he seemed to fill the cell, he was so tall, so broad, like a giant. I said, "I hope you don't mind me calling on you, but I heard that your mother had died and I wanted to tell you how sorry I was."

Father John interrupted. 'Weren't you scared, man?'

'Yes. Terrified. He was twice as big as me, but he suddenly slumps down and starts howling like a baby. So in I goes and stays about half an hour. I found out through all his tears and oaths, that his mother had died at four o'clock the previous afternoon. He'd been very close to her and she'd stuck by him and given him hope. Then, out of the blue, it was very unfortunate, he was told he was being transferred to Dartmoor, hundreds of miles away from his family. So he went beserk when he got here.'

'How long's he been in?' asked Father John.

'Eighteen years.'

'Eighteen years! What's his crime?'

'Must be murder. I've not looked up his file yet, but I have found out he's called Graham. And now,' Noel's voice went very Irish in his excitement, 'he's stood up to give his life to

Christ. He'll be the first one I'll visit tomorrow morning.'

When Noel got home Norma rushed across the hall to meet him. 'How did it go?'

'Fantastic!'

When he'd finally finished speaking, she said, 'Do you think we'll be able to leave soon? I mean now you've done so well, someone else could take over.'

He grinned. 'You know what the Chaplain General said when he came to dinner on Monday? What about being a travelling prison evangelist? Or going to Parkhurst on the Isle of Wight?'

'Near my sister,' interrupted Norma. She clapped her hands. Summer would be a lovely time to leave, especially as Noel had done so well.

'We'll just have to wait for the official letter.'

'I've made my mind up, I'll not stay here another winter!'

'You've been a wonderful support to me Norma. I couldn't have done any of it without you.'

'What kind of a life would I have had without you?'


When Noel went to visit Graham next morning he found him very quiet.

Noel said, 'I was thrilled to see you stand up last night at the service.'

'Yes.'

'Did you...really want to become a Christian?'

'Yes. But,' Graham's face was set in dark lines, 'no one'll believe us. Especially after I blew up in Reception.'

'I do.'

'Yes, but them Officers don't believe in us.'

Noel knew very well what he meant. Officers were understandably cynical about prisoners who were 'converted'.

'Graham it's up to you. You've said you want to be a Christian. If you stick to Christ he'll stick to you. So let the Officers see the change in you, over the months. And the years. That'll speak louder than any words.'

Graham sighed and twisted his hands. Then his Geordie accent filled the cell. 'The years! I've been inside for eighteen years. And I've got a lot more to go. When I come out I won't know anybody, the places I knew they're all changed. My mam said so. It'll be a different planet. I'll have no job. My lads won't want me. Us whole life's been wasted.'

Noel put his hand on Graham's arm. 'Some of that's true and I'm glad you're a realist. But you've forgotten one thing.'

The heavy, set face stared back and Noel said, 'Don't forget you've got a friend now who'll stick closer than a brother. Your life can change.'

'It could only change for the better. Go on then, us'll give us life to God.' He sagged. 'No one else wants it.'

But as Noel left he had a sense of peace about Graham. Perhaps because he was so honest and so realistic, perhaps because he'd scraped the bottom of the barrel and even had to put his hand up and stretch to feel that bottom. But whatever the reason, Noel believed in Graham.

Slowly the summer came. Noel visited all the men who'd put their names down on the list. The numbers at all his weekly meetings doubled and then trebled. There were reports of 'Religion Taking Off At The Moor' in the local papers. He was thrilled and amazed. Men were asking for counselling all the time. They asked for a prayer group instead of football on Saturday mornings and he got permission. For the very first time since he'd entered the prison service he began to find fellowship amongst the men. He chuckled to himself, much as a proud father would do over his toddler, when he heard their prayers:

'Lord I feel so free, I feel as if I'm doing society out of retribution.'

'Hang on a minute, Lord, I've forgotten what I was going to say. I'll be back in a minute.'

'Get Paul to shut up a bit will you, Lord, so's I can have a pray as well.'

Yet hadn't these men, so completely unaware of religious clichés and pretence, hadn't they something to teach the church outside, something to say about having a relationship with God, as if he were a real person? As the summer days lengthened, invitations poured in for him to speak at clubs, churches and schools all over the South West. And he went. He went to challenge the Christians and to tell them about the prisoners. There was a big response. People and organizations offered to help, to give money, books and radios. It was the beginning of a move that culminated in the organizing of the Prison Christian Fellowship. Noel flung himself into it all, rushing here, there and everywhere, absorbed and very happy. And as high summer came and went Norma gradually grew more and more silent, her mouth set into a firmer line and her eyes constantly searching the moorland horizon.

One day in late August she cornered him in the attic study. 'Look, Noel, that letter's not come yet and I'm *not* staying on here another winter.'

'What letter?'

'What letter! The official one, saying we're leaving.'

He frowned. 'I can't leave now. There's so much happening.' He gazed out of the window and avoided looking at her. 'Actually, er, the Chaplain General did, er, mention on the phone only yesterday....'

'What?'

'That it hadn't worked out as he'd hoped, but he'd move me when he could, er, er.' He floundered to a halt.

She sat very still. 'Why didn't you tell me yesterday?'

He stared miserably at his desk. 'I knew you'd be upset and I felt awful because I'm so happy.'

She looked at him for a long time and at last he looked at her.

'Noel, I'm glad you're happy. It's just that,' suddenly her face crumpled and she wiped her eyes with the corner of her apron, 'I feel so lonely here all day on my own. The girls are all out at school and I was so looking forward to moving...and... I want you to put God first and I love God, too, and I want to put him first, only my life's not easy. I can't drive and...and I hate the wind coming down the chimney.'

He got up and put his arm round her. 'What can I do, darling? You know I love you. I'll just keep pestering to move.'

She blew her nose. 'But you really feel called to stay, don't you?'

He began to pace up and down. At last he said, his words halting as if they were being forced out of him, 'No. I don't honestly feel called to stay indefinitely. I'd like to, but that's a different matter. No. I'm willing to move.'

She was thrilled. It would be all right now. And for the next few months she hummed her way round the house.

Then the winter set in again and this time the snow started even earlier than the year before. Noel was always out, or on the phone or in his study. In spite of what he'd said before, he was more immersed than ever in the follow-up work at the prison. It got that every conversation they had either began or ended with her saying, 'But when are we leaving?' and him saying, 'Don't nag, I'm doing my best.'

Best not to talk to him at all, she thought one day as flurries of snow hit the window. She cried a little on her own in the twilight, while the girls squabbled over their tea in the kitchen. 'I can't stand it, Lord,' she prayed. 'I feel like Elijah in the wilderness. And who is going to help me? At least Elijah had an angel. But I've got no one.' There seemed to be no answer so she got up, drew the curtains and put the lamp on and—as always in that strong, granite house—she felt slightly cheered by its warmth and strength. By the time Noel came home she felt better. He was full of it as usual.

'Do you know, Norma, almost a quarter of the men in prison have made some kind of profession of faith. I was only talking to Father O'Driscoll today and he says that Charlie and Eric, those two lads who got involved with the supernatural, haven't slipped back into their old ways. There's been no more ghostly fingers in that cell, either!'

'Oh. Lovely. You'll be after the other three-quarters of the men now, I suppose!'

He looked at her sharply and went quiet. He waited, tense in his chair, for her to start nagging, but for once she didn't say, 'When are we leaving?' and finally he relaxed and dropped off to sleep in his chair.

The December days were dark for Norma. The friends she'd made moved on. She still had to have the detailed X-ray every six months and then one day the girls came home from school saying their friends had got head lice and asking her to check their hair. Hours later, her eyes red with searching, she pronounced them clear. She switched on the television to hear of the ambulance men's strike, and all the while the wind was howling round the house. Noel was late home and by the time he got back she was close to tears. 'I can't stand it. I can't take any more.'

He slung his briefcase down and didn't answer. He went through to make a cup of tea and she followed him.

'Why don't you ever listen, Noel Proctor?'

'Oh stop it, woman! Nag, nag, nag, all day at the prison with Officers fussing me about security. Now all I get at home is nag, nag, nag.' And he stumped upstairs to his study.

She flew back into the kitchen, slammed the door, got out the broom and began to bang round the floor with it. For five years she'd stuck the Moor. How much longer could she go on? After a while she heard the door open. She looked up and saw Noel standing in the doorway.

'Er Norma?'

'Well?'

'Would you like me to run you to Plymouth tomorrow to do a spot of Christmas shopping?'

She examined the handle of the broom carefully. 'I might.'

'OK then. I'll take you out to lunch.'

'Oh.'

The next day as they sat in the cafeteria of the British Home Stores in Plymouth, with mountains of parcels at their feet, Norma suddenly opened her handbag and took out a pen and a screwed-up old envelope. She began writing furiously and Noel watched, fascinated, until at last she said, 'Right. Read that.'

> 'From this awful snow and ice,
> And now an influx of head lice
>     Good Lord deliver us.'

He looked up and grinned.

> 'From pickets who are out in force,
> From friction, violence and worse,
>     Good Lord deliver us.'

As he read on his grin faded.

> 'From Princetown with its endless snow,
> There *must* be a better place to go.
> It's time we moved, so let us know
>     You have delivered us.'

He put the paper carefully on the table and looked at her, a slightly puzzled expression on his face. 'You really mean it?'

'I do.'

'Oh.' He frowned and blew his nose. 'Right.'

'What do you mean, "right"?'

'We'll move.'

'But...what if the Lord wants us to stay?' She fumbled suddenly for her hanky, 'and I'm just grumbling all the time ...I keep praying to do the right thing.'

His hand covered hers, 'I've got peace about moving, dear. It's just that, well, I enjoyed the Mission. I've seen the Lord work like I've never done before. But if he can work here he can work anywhere.'

'You're very popular here, Noel.'

He went pink, 'But I've not been popular with you have I?'

'Aren't you called to put God first?'

'I've thought about that. Sometimes putting him first means putting the work first. You've been good about that, Norma.' It was her turn to go pink.

'And sometimes it means putting family first,' he said and rose to his feet to go.

She grabbed his arm. 'Noel, what made you say all this today?'

'I've known it for a while, but kept pushing it to the back of my mind. Hey come on! If we don't get a move on we'll get cut off by snow on the moors!'

Next morning he went to the prison with a heavy heart. Everything he'd worked for and dreamed of would have to be given up. And then he rounded on himself. He'd promised to love and cherish Norma at the wedding service and he knew he did love her. And he loved his work. Especially now, with jostling services and a bustle of men at the meetings and the crackle of excitement during the prayers. There were reports of 'revival' in the local papers. As he crossed the courtyard he prayed earnestly, 'Lord, I only want to please you. If it's right to leave, give me peace about it.'

As he got to the security check on the inner gate he noticed several Officers bunched up together. When he called out, 'Good Morning,' they turned their backs on him, only one mumbling, 'What's good about it?' He stared at them. Their collars were up and their heads bowed.

He went to the Governor's office.

Colin Heald said, 'Noel, they've gone to the gates!'

'What! Who?'

'The Officers. They've stopped work!'

'Why?'

'Oh, they're fed up of their damp houses and the wallpaper hanging off. The Department haven't done anything about altering them yet.' The two men came out of the office in time to see the Officers coming away from the gates again.

'Look, they're going back to the Landings now.'

'Yes, Noel. But I don't like it.'

'Couldn't you have a word with them? And telephone the Department? It can't be much fun living in damp houses this weather.'

Rumours flew round the prison all day and Noel began to get worried. He tried talking to the Chief, who said, 'Keep out of it, Mr Proctor, it's best that way.'

Next morning as he went into the main building Noel heard a dull banging. It thudded on and on, like a gigantic heart beating.

'What on earth's that?' he asked one of the Welfare Officers.

'The prisoners. They're banging their food trays on to the walls of their cells.'

'Why?'

'They've heard on the local radio station that the Prison Officers' Association has called an overtime ban or strike or something. They think they aren't going to unlock them for dinner.'

'Oh no!'

Noel ran to the Governor's office. Several men were in there with him. Colin Heald looked worried. 'Look, there could be a riot. And we've had such a good record until now. Will you help, Noel?'

'To feed men who are hungry? I certainly will.'

'You realize you might get accused of strike breaking?'

One of the civilian farmhands said, 'Yes, but even animals should be fed.'

'Come on,' said Noel, 'the kitchen staff have decided not to strike, so we mustn't let them down.'

They set off down each landing, calling out through the cell doors, 'Don't get worked up. You'll be getting your dinner and we'll try and get you out on exercise as well.'

Some of the prisoners called out in reply, 'Thanks very much.'

Others yelled, 'Get the hell out of it!'

By quarter past eleven the kitchen staff had got the food on the trolleys and the Assistant Governors, Noel, a Welfare Officer and some farmhands were waiting to hand it out. Suddenly there was the sound of footsteps echoing down the corridor, a door banged, and then up strode one of the Union Officials. He scarcely stopped in his tracks, but made straight for Noel. 'Chaplain, if you open the cell door of any one of these prisoners to feed them you need expect no more co-operation from the Officers of this prison!'

Without thinking Noel stepped forward and said, 'I don't think that'll worry me all that much as I haven't had a lot of co-operation in the past!'

There was a sudden dead silence. Noel groaned inwardly. Why had he said that? The official seemed to back away from Noel, then swung round on his heel; the door banged behind him and they heard his footsteps fading away down the corridor.

Much later that evening Noel was telling Norma about it, 'I don't know what happened exactly but five minutes afterwards all the Officers came trooping back in, gave the lads their dinner and let them slop out their buckets. And that was an end of it.'

She looked at him hard. 'It won't be,' she said.

'Well, the Governor's been on to the Department and they've promised to alter the houses.'

She shook her head. 'It won't be.'

'It' came on Sunday. Obviously some of the Officers were upset by the dinner queue affair because they cancelled all the church services in the prison. Noel heard the news in silence and stood with his head bowed. Somehow he managed to swallow his anger and apart from pushing his clenched fists into his pockets, he didn't answer back. Then as ten o'clock drew near he set off with his bunch of keys and his Bible and made for the landings. He began to visit every man who had ever come to chapel and he made as much noise about it as he could until everyone on the landing knew how upset he was there were no services. One of the Officers said, 'We thought you'd refuse to come in.'

'Me?' said Noel. 'Never! I'd be here on a Sunday, even if it killed me!'

Officer Murray joined them. 'I never heard of prisoners being refused their *only* right before!' he said and stumped off down the corridor muttering to himself. Noel's heart warmed to him as he watched him go. So many of the Officers were like Murray: decent and caring. Noel didn't blame them for getting fed up, but he had his own job to do. So he set off for the next landing.

By the Monday morning the strike had fizzled out and Noel became aware of the fact that his meetings were now 'on' again. Yet as he went on his daily rounds he realized he'd started to get tired of continually fighting the Moor. For the very first time it struck him how Norma must feel, how difficult it was when you never made any headway.

There was still no news of them moving so he sat down and wrote to the Bishop of Liverpool and asked about a Parish post in that diocese. Even as he dropped the letter in the post he knew he had a great sense of peace.

Christmas was approaching so he made arrangements for a big carol concert with lots of visitors expected and a choir. A few hours before it was due to begin, it was suddenly cancelled because of an Officers' overtime ban. Noel was furious and so were some of the Officers who had offered to work voluntarily to man the service. But the Prison Department refused, saying that by law the Officers must be paid. It was hopeless and in the end the service was cancelled. The next morning, on Christmas Eve, this cancellation was to make the headline in the *Western Morning News*.

Noel was still angry as he walked home that night. He'd had the embarrassment of turning away many visitors whom he'd been unable to inform about the cancellation; he'd had to run a make-shift cup of tea service from the vestry—and then say goodbye to people who'd travelled miles to be at the service. He'd given the Moor five years of his life and the rewards had been great. And so had the fight, and the toll on Norma.

Enough was enough. He was suddenly immensely glad he'd written off for a new job and his anger melted away. The weight and the problems of the Moor seemed to slip off his shoulders and he half ran up his drive. It was weeks since he'd had a night in with Norma. Well, he'd have a night in with her tonight and as he flew in the house, it enveloped him with its Christmas sparkle. Toast and TV, that was what was called for. And, grinning, he went into the lounge.

Christmas came and went and then one day in January the Chaplain General rang up. 'Noel, I've heard from the Bishop of Liverpool that you, er, want to leave the prison service. Is there anything I can do to persuade you to stay?'

Noel swallowed. 'Yes. Move us from Dartmoor.'

There was a pause. 'If I can get it arranged within three months, will you stay on?'

'Yes, if my wife's happy. You see, sir, she means too much to me for her to go on being upset, and she's been ill, so....'

The Chaplain General cleared his throat, 'Leave it with me.'

'I would like to stay in the Prison Service if it's possible. I do have a sense of call. But at the moment my family comes first in the priorities.'

There was another pause. 'I'll do my best, Noel,' and he rang off.

## Chapter Twenty-Six

# The Gentle Giant

A couple of weeks later Noel heard from the Chaplain General again. Would Noel like the job of Senior Chaplain at Strangeways Prison, Manchester? The job entailed being head of a team of Chaplains and was vacant after Easter 1979. He stared at the letter, deep in thought. Strangeways, he knew, had one of the biggest prison populations in the country. He'd been told that there were about one thousand, seven hundred and fifty inmates, including five hundred boys under eighteen. He picked up his phone and spoke to Norma. Then he phoned the Chaplain General: 'Yes,' he said, 'we'd like the job.'

When the prisoners at the Moor found out many were upset and some tried to persuade him to stay. The local paper carried an article, 'Prisoners want Chaplain to stay behind bars!' But Noel knew the time had come for him and his family to leave. He thought about it one evening as he left the granite walls of the prison behind and walked home. He remembered his first morning there and grinned. He'd come to the place with fear in his heart and he'd had to learn to stand up to himself and his fears and trust God to help him. And he'd come through on the other side. He knew that. He'd learned both to fight with himself and with situations until he was sure the work of Christ was going forward.

He reached his own granite garden walls and went through the gate. He thought about the hard men he'd feared before he came. None of them had attacked him. Of the twelve lifers, three had become Christians. And of the five hundred or so other prisoners, about a fifth had asked to follow Christ. And many others were showing a lot of interest. All the organizations he'd got going were doing nicely and the Christians in the surrounding areas were showing a lot of interest and offering practical help. At the flight of steps he stopped and bowed his head. He looked up and saw Norma through one of the windows and she gave him a wave. It had all been God's grace. If it hadn't been for God's grace, Norma wouldn't be here, he couldn't have done the job he'd done. It was all God's grace. He bowed his head again. 'Thank you, Lord,' he said simply and then disappeared into the house.

When Graham found out Noel was leaving, he asked permission to talk to the men in the chapel one Sunday morning. Noel was silent for a minute and the huge prisoner waited quietly.

'Graham, I'd like to say yes, and certainly over the last fifteen months you've stuck wonderfully to your promise to be a Christian, but,' Noel looked him straight in the eye, 'I don't usually allow it.'

'Why not?'

'In case the other lads start taking the mickey out of you afterwards. They could make your life a misery.'

Graham smiled. The light in his eyes spread out over his whole face and Noel couldn't help smiling back.

'Well Mr Proctor, I'm not scared of a few little fellas. I don't think they'll bother us.'

Noel could well believe it. He'd heard the hush fall on the other prisoners as 'Graham the Killer' walked past. He'd seen them edge back to give Graham room.

'Well, er, since you are such a big chap—with a big heart—why not? I'll give you the chance.'

Graham stood up and his enormous shoulders seemed to fill the room. 'Thanks Mr Proctor,' he said and then turned and eased himself through the door. They'd called him 'Graham the Killer' at first but recently the change in his life had become so obvious that people couldn't help noticing it. Now they called him, 'The Gentle Giant'.

The Sunday morning service came and it was thronged with prisoners. Word had got round that Graham was going to speak. At first Noel had wondered if the Chief would give permission, but he'd whistled between his teeth and said, 'Yes, provided the Officer on duty that morning agrees.' Noel looked at the Officers on duty in the chapel. They stood, arms folded, faces impassive, with the silver chain that ran from their belts to their pockets, thick with hidden keys. Only their eyes were never still as they darted glances too and fro amongst the prisoners.

Everyone sang and then, as the music died away, Noel came forward to introduce Graham. Over a hundred pairs of eyes fastened on Graham as he clambered to his feet and went and stood at the front.

He cleared his throat, 'Well, lads, Mr Proctor's given us permission to give yer a quick estimate of my life. In 1954 I got married and the wife had two or three kids. But in 1960 things started to go wrong. I went and got a gun and robbed a few places and I got money. I got a few thousand pound. But then one time the police came and I shot a few of them. They got George medals for capturing us. But in 1960 my life came to an end.'

His thick Geordie voice filled the room. Many of the men were leaning forward. He drew breath and went on, 'Well, I was very hostile. I wouldn't accept the system. I was usually on my own in the "Block", and,' his voice trembled but he carried on, 'I've been in Wakefield, Hull, Parkhurst, now here. I've been inside for nineteen year. But my family stuck by us. My mam visited us every week. She never turned away from us. She gave us hope.

'Then I went on a visit to Durham to see her and on the Monday they told us I was coming to Dartmoor.' He raised his voice. 'No ways was I coming. I didn't want to. My mam was old and I knew I might not see much more of her, so I said no. Then,' his voice dropped, 'at four o'clock that afternoon she went and died.'

Noel looked at the men who were rapt with attention. He noticed Marcus Blake nodding sympathetically. Graham went on, 'Well it were a big shock to us. I loved my mother. Then I came down here. They kept saying, "You can't do this!" "You can't do that!" So I blew up in the Reception.' A ripple went round the prisoners, a silent snigger, as they remembered the shadow of the old Graham.

Graham paused and then he said, 'Well, this bloke, Mr Proctor, came and told us about the Mission. I'd never been to church before in all the prisons I'd been in. But I thought, is there anything in this? So I read my Bible and every night I came to the Mission.' A hush fell on the men and they stopped fidgeting.

'Well I decided to give us life to God. I couldn't do any worse. No one else wanted it. And he's give me peace of mind. I've new hope for the future. I know I've got a future now. I didn't before. My eldest son says to me, "Dad, there's a change in you," and I know there is a change in us. My burdens and sins have gone. I know I'm a sinner at the cross. But I'm more happy in my mind. He'll see me through if I carry on with the teaching of Jesus. I love him. And I can love my enemies. I have a few of them. I only hope my enemies can forgive me...the people I shot...and the people that died.... I can only hope my Lord can forgive me what I've done....'

Into the hush Graham shed a few tears, wrung as it were from his very heart. Noel glanced quickly round the room, but the men sat still. No one whispered. No one fidgeted. The Officers stared at Graham, as he quickly turned his head away and wiped his face with his sleeve.

He sighed and then struggled on, 'I know I can take us troubles to him. Don't get me wrong, I don't like these buildings and I don't like Dartmoor, but I like to come to chapel and to the prayer meetings....' As abruptly as he had begun, he finished and swung back into his seat.

But before he had time to sit down, the men began to clap. They clapped and clapped and then, in a final burst of solidarity, they all stood to their feet, pulling Graham up with them. The clapping went on and on and on. And Noel joined in. Finally it died away and stillness descended. At the end of the service Noel shook hands with every man as he left. Soon he had about a dozen names of prisoners written down in his notebook. 'Can you tell me how to get like Graham, please?' 'Can I become a Christian?'

Then, almost last out, came Graham. Four Officers were near him, one to escort him back to his cell. Suddenly one of the Officers stuck his hand out at Graham. Graham stared at the hand and then looked down at the Officer. For a moment their eyes met and then Graham lifted up his hand and grasped the Officer's. As Noel watched the other three Officers each came up to Graham and shook him by the hand.

Then they all turned away quickly and left, taking Graham with them. Noel gazed after them. In all his years in the Prison Service he'd never seen Officers shake hands with any prisoner before least of all when that prisoner was a lifer.

Later, when he told Norma about Graham's talk, he said, 'It's funny how many men are affected by their mothers, especially when the mothers die. There's Graham, and Marcus Blake. And at Eastchurch there was many a chap who had a girlfriend ten or twenty years older than himself; as if they were searching for something.'

'For love?' she asked, 'And security?' Then she said, 'What about you? You did everything you could to get your mum to take notice of you when you were young!'

'Me?'

'Yes, you! Always trying to make up to her for the loss of Stanley.'

'I never did.'

'Oh, you couldn't see it as I could. But you were always trying to shine: to get her to be pleased with you; to love you. That's why you were always on the go,' Norma sighed. 'Unfortunately the habit's stuck!'

He stared back at her nonplussed.

She went on, 'It was only when we were at Eastchurch and I nearly…it was only after that you seemed to realize I was, er, the love of your life. Oh, I don't know, you changed.'

Suddenly she blushed, 'You no longer strove to shine, you just…lived. Oh, I don't know what I mean!'

He didn't reply at first but looked intently at her. Then he said, 'I realized I was simply a servant at Eastchurch. We weren't a trio on a par with God, if that's what you mean.' There was a pause. 'And I realized I couldn't live without you.'

They sat together by the fire, quietly, and after some time he said, 'Would you like a cup of tea?'

The Sunday before they were due to leave Dartmoor they were invited to the evening service at the Pentecostal Church in Plympton. Norma sat, her back very straight and her eyes firmly closed as the service went on with one excited prayer tumbling on the heels of another. She shifted slightly in her

seat. They were lovely people and very genuine. Pastor Jack
had helped Noel a lot, but she did feel so much more at home
in the stately Church of England.

Then a deep quiet fell, a quiet so intense, she felt she could
almost touch it. Into the quiet came the Pastor's voice. 'If
Brother and Sister Proctor will come forward we'll pray for
them in their new work in Manchester.' Norma stiffened. 'You
go, Noel,' she whispered, 'I'll stay here.' Noel looked at her but
she shook her head. Then he got up and walked the few paces
to the front. The Pastor smiled gently, 'And if Mrs Proctor will
come forward as well.'

Norma blushed and then, with head held high, she went
after Noel and knelt beside him.

For several seconds they stayed there in silence and then the
Pastor's wife began to pray quietly. At first Norma was
puzzled. Why was she praying in Welsh? Or some other
language? Suddenly it dawned on Norma. The Pastor's wife
was praying in 'tongues'. Norma glanced up quickly at the
serene face of the other woman, whose quietness and relaxation
of spirit seemed to reach out and touch Norma. There was no
hysteria, no excitement, nothing funny at all. Simply the
gentle, pleasant voice and a slow peace spreading out into the
room.

After the prayer was over the Pastor beckoned his wife and
they both came and lay their hands on Noel's head and
Norma's head. The Pastor sighed, his hands quivered and he
said, 'The Lord says to you both, I go before you to Manchester, I have a work for you to do there....'

In the car, going home, Norma said, 'That speaking in
tongues was...beautiful really, wasn't it?'

'Yes, lovely. A lovely promise for our future. It was great!'

'I didn't think it would be so powerful and so quiet.'

He laughed, 'Well don't forget that Saint Paul recommends
it highly!'

She didn't answer. Her whole being felt warm with God's
promise. There was far more to this Christian faith than she'd
realized.

# PART FIVE: STRANGEWAYS

'A Human Warehouse'

April 1979 to the present

## Chapter Twenty-Seven

# The Chaplains' Meeting

Noel and his family quickly settled into their new life in Manchester. They liked their spacious house in the Salford suburbs, the girls accepted their new schools and Norma found a part-time nursing job.

Noel rose to the challenge of Strangeways. His task was huge and daunting but he threw himself into the work. He discovered that ever since the visit of David Watson to the prison in 1978, interest in Christianity had been simmering amongst the prisoners. The numbers in chapel on Sundays were always increasing, even though about two hundred men were re-allocated to other prisons every week. 'You know what that means,' he told Norma one evening. 'New men are coming to chapel each week.'

Only the Sunday before the chapel had been cram full, with over five hundred men, and boys from the Borstal Wing, at the Church of England service alone. There was so little room that a further one hundred and thirty men had to be turned away. On top of that the Catholic services were well attended and the Methodists had good numbers, too. Norman Brown, the Governor, backed him and his team of Chaplains, and was pleased with their efforts, 'We've somehow got to give these men moral rehabilitation,' he told Noel. And yet Noel was not as happy as he should have been.

One morning he got up early and made himself some tea and toast. If what was happening at Strangeways had happened at any of the other places where he'd worked, he'd have been thrilled. Not only were the numbers huge on Sundays but all his evening groups and classes were full; with waiting lists, often as not. And the local churches were interested and helpful. Only, somehow, here...he stirred and stirred his tea, until finally he made himself admit it. Somehow, here, something wasn't quite right.

He drank his tea and it tasted bitter. He pushed a few strands of hair off his forehead and set off for work. When Norma came down she found his toast uneaten on his plate.

Later in the morning he clattered down the stone stairs from his office and into the main courtyard. He had to visit the 'Block' before lunch.

When he got there it was very quiet and his footsteps echoed down the corridor. An Officer stepped forward to greet him and then waved him forward. Noel opened up the first cell door, 'Hello, there, Roger. Can I see you?'

A burly man with a crew cut shifted slightly on his seat, so that Noel could see even more of his broad back under the blue pin-striped shirt. 'Would you like me to give you some more books?'

There was no response. Noel picked up the three books from exactly the same position on the table as he'd put them yesterday. He put three more he'd chosen from the chaplain's library in their place.

'Are you going to talk to me?'

The silence burnt Noel's ears. He sighed and turned to go, saying, 'Well, reading a few books would be a darned sight more interesting than staring at the kitchen wall through your cell window. Or don't you ever bother to read?'

Noel swung out and locked the door behind him. That must have been the tenth time he'd visited Roger. And the tenth time Roger had ignored him and his books. Noel's shoulders went very straight. Even if he were ignored a hundred times he knew he'd still keep going.

The Officer on duty came up and said, 'How's Roger the "tobacco baron" today? Silent as ever?'

Noel nodded. 'Is he still on Rule Forty-three B?'

'Yes. He can have his radio et cetera but the Governor is waiting for him to make his promise.'

'Promise?'

'Yes. No more violence and aggression.' The Officer spread his hands out. 'Only our Roger hasn't made any promises yet;

one way or the other.'

Noel said, 'Does he still frighten the other men?'

'Quite a few. He lends 'em cigs and then demands twice as much tobacco in return. He used to have a little book and jot their names down. I've known prisoners snivel with fear because they can't pay their tobacco debts. So, for the time being, he's down here.'

'It's very quiet.'

The Officer laughed. 'How I like it. There was a rumpus yesterday because one of 'em enticed a pigeon into his cell and was feeding it with his breakfast bread. Droppings everywhere!'

'They aren't allowed pets are they?'

'No,' said the Officer and set off to patrol his corridor.

Noel watched him go. What must life be like for the men on the Block? They were locked in, alone, for twenty-three out of every twenty-four hours. Alone, with no visitors, no pets, no chit-chat with other prisoners. Some got so up-tight that they paced up and down the twelve foot cell for hours. Others tried to make friends with the pigeons on their cell window sills. Sometimes they dangled things on bits of string through their windows and tried to attract attention from the prisoners on the floor below. But that wasn't allowed. Sometimes they made friends with a spider, if they were lucky enough to find one in the corner of the cell. Noel grasped his Bible tightly in his hand. No, he'd come a thousand times if necessary. He was the only person all day who had the opportunity to stop and talk to men in the Block.

On his way back from the Block Noel saw Garth Rogers, the Methodist Chaplain, coming towards him down the front entrance hall. When he saw Noel he grinned, 'Hello there, Noel, what's up? You look as if you've got the cares of the world on your shoulders!'

Noel said nothing. He looked at Garth and shrugged, 'Oh, you know. Here from seven o'clock in the morning till eight o'clock at night. It's got me down over the last day or two.'

'What time do you normally get here?'

'About ten past eight.'

Garth moved closer. He seemed to size Noel up and down and then he said, 'You're not happy are you?'

Noel stared at the tiled floor and slowly shook his head. 'I know I ought to be,' he said at last, 'only somehow....'

'You aren't used to being part of a team, are you?'

Noel's head jerked up and he stared at Garth in surprise. 'How did you know that!'

Garth grinned. 'Perhaps we aren't used to having a human tornado around!'

Noel looked at Garth bleakly. But all at once Garth's tawny eyes crinkled at the edges and he chuckled gently. After a moment Noel's shoulders relaxed slightly and he managed a grin.

'Look,' said Garth, 'why don't you arrange a Chaplains' meeting? We'll all get together and sort things out.'

Noel thought a moment. Then he said, 'That's a good idea.'

'Make it soon, OK?'

'Yes. I'll get onto it right away.'

The day of the Chaplains' meeting came and after the first greetings and a few jokes there was an awkward silence. Finally Noel cleared his throat, 'I've called this meeting so as we can, er, share our feelings regarding the, er, team. And then we can see where we're going.'

The silence grew heavy. Noel glanced at Ian Ferguson, the Church Army Captain, and he began shuffling through some papers. The silence continued. Noel waited. Obviously no one wanted to be the first to air their complaints. He looked at Garth who was calmly staring at his finger nails. He stared at Bill Tabarn, Garth's assistant, and he got up and began to set cups out on a tray.

Noel sighed and took a deep breath, 'Well, I suppose I'm at the bottom of it. I'm not used to working on a team, or delegating, and I'm sorry if I've offended any of you.'

Ian looked at him quickly. Noel went on, 'But you're a good team. You care. And you work hard. I want to stay here and I'll try and give you as much leeway as possible. But....' Several pairs of eyes were fixed on him by now. 'But in the end, I carry the can with the Governor. So I'll have to make the decisions in the final analysis. It's not easy sometimes.'

He looked round the circle of faces, 'We've seen things happening in the chapel we never thought we'd see. God's beginning to work. So let's get ourselves sorted out and then we can give him a hand.'

Someone laughed. What on earth had he said that for?

'Well, you know what I mean,' he added quickly, but still the silence hung over them. Then he said sharply, 'Isn't that what we all want?'

The silence was becoming awkward. At last Garth cleared his throat. He let his gaze travel round the circle of men. Then he said slowly, 'But *is* it what we want? *Do* we want to see the prisoners finding peace and an understanding of Christian things? Or are we afraid in case our "own-little-ways-of-doing-things" might get upset? Because, make no mistake,' and Garth's eyes swept the room, 'Noel is here to stay. And you, Noel,' and he turned to Noel and the twinkle in his eyes took the sting out of his words, 'you, Noel, are the catalyst. You demand reaction. And you get it!'

A sigh seemed to run round the group, as if each man were relaxing and thinking, thank goodness someone's said it at last! Garth laughed and repeated his phrase, 'We aren't used to having a human tornado round here! I don't know how you do it all, Noel Proctor, but you do. Something drives you on.' Noel opened his mouth to speak but Garth raised his hand, 'Let me finish. Isn't it the truth that we've all been...jealous of Noel? Perhaps we still are.'

The silence suddenly became sharp with tension. The Chaplains shifted on their seats and carefully avoided looking at each other. 'Yes,' said Garth, 'jealous. And I'll tell you why. He's so singleminded. He only cares about one thing: to spread the Good News. Men have found *our* Lord to be *their* Lord. And we've been jealous.'

Into the hush Noel said, with his eyes fixed on his knees, 'I've been at fault, too. I've not understood about team work....'

There was a long pause and then Garth said quietly, 'Let's each of us do what God has given us the gift to do. We're all different. That way we'll make a better team.'

Several heads began to nod and Noel found he could relax in his chair again.

Garth said, 'OK? Anyone still unhappy?' There was no reply. Garth waited. Still there was silence. After a moment he smiled and waved in the direction of the tea tray. 'How about a cuppa?'

When they'd all gone Garth hung back. Noel said, 'Thanks, Garth. There's only you who could have said what you said.' Then, 'Will you be offended if I ask you something?'

'No, go on.'

'Apparently last Sunday one hundred and thirty men were turned away from my ten o'clock service. The Governor's worried in case they write to the Department and complain. Practising their religion is one of their few rights and he's concerned if they don't get it. He brought it up at the "Heads of Department" meeting.'

'One hundred and thirty were turned *away*?'

'Yes.'

'That's amazing!'

Noel's face lit up, 'Yes, er, Garth, would you consider having everyone in "E" Wing that wants to come to your Methodist service? There'll be at least a hundred men. We could call it a United Service. It could be exactly as you always do it, Methodist Hymn Book and so on. We could swap as preachers once a month. Only, what do you think? Would you be offended?'

Garth's face was one huge grin, 'Don't be daft, Noel! We'd be thrilled to bits. I only had twenty last week. It'll be a great opportunity. Yes. Yes. Yes!' And he rubbed his hands together.

Noel smiled back, 'Can I tell the Governor, then?'

'You can indeed!'

## Chapter Twenty-Eight

# The Beasts

On the morning Norma was due to go to Christie's Hospital for her six monthly check, Noel went to the prison with a heavy heart. He knew he ought to trust. The lads in the prison prayer meeting had prayed for her the evening before, some quite simply, others with deep feeling that spilled out in the rough Lancashire accents. They believed that all they had to do was ask God to do something and he'd do it. 'Please, Lord, heal Mrs Proctor.' 'Ta, Lord, I know you will.' He wished he were quite so sure.

He got to Reception early and began to interview the new prisoners. The first man in was very young. He hummed as he walked to the desk, sat down carefully and looked at Noel.

'Hello, young man. What's your name?'

'Peter.'

Noel was looking through Peter's sizable file. He glanced up with a puzzled frown on his face. 'You were discharged from here three months ago?' Peter nodded. His brown hair curved delicately round his face and his eyes were dreamy.

Noel said gently, 'Why are you back inside?'

'Can't pay my fines.'

'Oh.' Noel read on in the file. 'It says here you were down on $C_1$ for nearly four months. Why was that?'

'I was segregated,' said Peter and his tapering fingers suddenly clenched.

Noel chose his words with care. 'Did you have any, er, trouble with the other men?'

Peter's fingers began to tremble and he put them behind his back.

'They used to hiss...things at the dinner queue.'

'Oh?'

'Yes.' His voice went very quiet and Noel had to lean forward to catch his words. 'I was segregated with men who had...had done things with children and that. And they called, "Beasts, Beasts," when we went past.'

'Who did?'

'The other prisoners. And sometimes when I went to wash the dinner trays with our "Tray Party" they, they...' and his head fell forward.

'Go on,' said Noel.

'They twisted my arms and Roger the Baron gave me a black eye a couple of times because I couldn't pay my tobacco debts. They used to say things, like, "He's practising the trade again," and mince along behind me and call out, "Here comes Daddy's girl," and, "He'll play the bitch," and things.' Peter's tremulous voice trailed away.

Noel said nothing. From the mixed up words and jumble of facts he knew Peter's was a common enough story. He thumbed through Peter's file slowly. Homosexuals were the 'untouchables' of the Prison system. They often had to be segregated for their own protection. He knew that Norman Brown, the Governor, had publicly voiced his fear for men who were 'straight' when they were locked up twenty-three hours a day with two others who turned out to be gay. And if the gays were bigger and stronger, they could corrupt and rape a youth locked in with them. Who would know in time? Who would care? What could the officers do? There'd been trouble on the landing only yesterday and a pair split up because the third man couldn't stand their behaviour any more. Noel snapped the file shut.

He looked at Peter and his chest tightened. He said, 'How did you get into all this, Peter?'

Peter said, almost too quickly, 'I want to love someone. I wanted to be a woman, to be accepted and loved and protected. I wanted the operation.' His head went high and his voice strident. 'I am what I am.'

Noel knew Peter had probably said it all before, that he had his reasons off pat, and gave them almost slickly. Noel knew he had no illusions about Peter. And yet? He stared at Peter's slender face. What might Peter have been, with a good home behind him, and love and discipline?

Suddenly Peter looked up and for a moment, behind his careful pose and real fear of the other prisoners, for a moment, Noel saw the true Peter.

Peter held his glance and leaned over the table. 'I just want to love someone and have someone love me. That's all.'

'That's what we all want,' said Noel. 'And need. But you're not going about it the right way. What you're doing won't make you truly happy. There's only one way I know of and....'

Peter interrupted and his voice had gone harder, 'I am what I am. Anyway, you're paid to say what you say.'

Noel said sharply, 'I might get paid. But no one tells *me* what to say. Besides, what's wrong with getting paid? I've got to live haven't I?'

'Suppose so.'

Noel sat quietly for a moment. Should he say anything or not? He frowned and then decided. 'Peter, I don't believe God intended you to be as you are now. But he loves you and me, sinful though we are. He died for you, Peter.'

Peter's eyes shot open very wide. 'For me?'

'Yes. For you. And if you put your trust in him, you'd always have someone at your side who loves you.'

Peter was gazing at him with astonishment. 'I've never heard of all that before. Never. 'But...' and he flushed.

Noel said, 'There's no "buts". With Christ you can have a new start.'

'But what about me being...?'

'Well, God might not take away your drive for, er, other men, but in the long run I believe he'll give you the strength to overcome it.'

'But you don't know what it's like.'

Noel stared at the desk. It was true. He didn't. Yet he wanted to say, 'No, but I do know what it's like to wait seven years for the woman I love. And now she's on the bus going to Christie's Hospital.' Instead he said, 'Can I come and see you tomorrow and give you some books?'

Peter's attention had wandered. 'Yes,' he said dreamily and gazed out of the window. Noel sighed. He'd better get on with the rest of the reports.

An hour and a half later he'd finished and was about to start on his hospital round when the phone rang. It was Norma.

'Noel,' she said, 'the doctor thinks I'm doing fine.'

A hot flood of relief swept over him.

She rushed on, 'I had the usual checks and the test result will be coming out in a few days, but he thinks I'm doing fine. He says there's only a year or two before I'll be completely discharged. Oh, Noel, I feel so happy!'

He smiled into the telephone, 'That's wonderful news. I can't wait to see you tonight.'

'Yes! The doctor says he's no reason to doubt my recovery at all. Oh, Noel, it's wonderful!'

He almost ran to the Block later on that morning. He was whistling and the Officer on duty raised his eyebrows behind Noel's back. Noel stopped short outside Roger the Baron's cell. He tried to set his face into a sober mask and couldn't. He burst into the cell, put his hand out for the three books he knew were always left unread on the table, and then stopped dead. The books weren't there.

And Roger had turned round to look at him for the first time. He thrust his jaw out at Noel and said, 'Where were you yesterday?'

'Round and about. Why?'

'You didn't come and see me.'

Noel was remembering fast. 'It was my day off and I went to see my girls performing their school play.'

'Humph!'

'It's the truth.'

'Humph!'

'Did you miss my beautiful Irish voice?'

Roger half turned his back on Noel, then leaned forward and picked up the three books from his bunk. 'I'll have three more of these.'

'OK. I'll go and get you some and pop back with them as soon as I can.'

Roger grunted and turned away. Noel locked up behind him and stood still for a moment. Perhaps something was stirring at last in Roger's mind. At least Roger could read well, unlike so many of the others. Noel sighed and walked slowly away.

It was the hardest of hard places down here on the Block.

Not all the men were sex offenders, but a lot were. He was glad Ian was organizing some films for these men on Friday afternoons. But how could he get across to them what he believed? He hated what many of them had done. Everything in him was against sex offences. He believed what the Bible said against homosexuality and sex abuses. But he cared about them as people. Yes, that was what grieved him. They were people whom Christ loved. And they were in this mess.

As he was about to leave, the Officer came down the landing and jerked his thumb in the direction of the end cell. 'There's a new lad in there. He's very depressed. Could you give him a minute?'

'Of course.'

Noel unlocked the end cell and went in. A tall young man rose to his feet and nervously adjusted his glasses.

Noel said, 'Hello, there. Can I sit down?'

The young man swallowed and nodded.

'What's your name?'

'Richard.'

'Oh. Why are you, er, down here?' said Noel.

'Well, it's the nature of the offence you see. So I've been put here, until I can see a psychiatrist. He'll talk to me about the nature of my problem.'

Noel shifted on his seat and glanced round the cream painted brick walls.

'Do you want to, er, talk to me about the nature of your problem?'

There was a long silence and Noel was on the point of making some small talk before leaving, when Richard said, 'I did phone the ambulance. The Risley psychiatrist said that would be an important factor in my defence.'

'You phoned the ambulance?'

'Yes. He was badly bruised on his back. So I phoned the ambulance.'

Noel leaned forward, 'Who?'

'Oh, her little boy.'

'Whose little boy?'

'My girlfriend. She had a toddler and then I moved in with her and she had my baby. I was unemployed so she worked nights and I looked after the children.'

Richard pushed his specs back on to his nose but they kept falling forward. 'I couldn't stand it in that room with those two yelling kids and them nappies draped all over the place.' He blinked. 'I lost control.'

Noel's mind felt numb and he couldn't think of anything to say. Richard finally took his specs off and examined them. 'The offence is Grievous Bodily Harm. GBH they call it down here.'

Noel said, 'God can forgive you. If you ask him.'

When he got into the corridor again his hands were clenched. The Officer sauntered up. 'How was he?'

'How was *he?*' exploded Noel. 'He's in a nice, quiet cell with all his meals put on. He's bashed up his step-son and all he can talk about is how long a sentence he'll get!'

'It gets you, doesn't it?' said the Officer.

'Yes. I'll tell you what gets me. He shows no sign of sorrow or remorse. Only thinking of number one! He goes on about "The Offence" as if he's got no responsibility for it. It's incredible.'

'Yes. The child nearly died, too.'

Noel marched back to his office and sat down to do reports, but something kept niggling him. Child abuse was the one offence he felt he couldn't stand. Or understand. He could find it in his heart to understand and forgive the gays and even the dirty old men. But men who did violence to children...a great shudder ran through him. He noticed his hands were clenched. He stared at his two fists: they looked like fists ready to fight. As he stared at them, he realized, with an unwelcome jolt, that he was a hypocrite. He'd fight the baby-batterers if he could. And yet wasn't he falling into the same trap of violence they'd fallen into? For a long time he sat motionless. At last he heaved himself off his chair and slowly climbed up the steps to the chapel.

He knelt at the side of the altar rail and looked at the great cross with the carved figure of the risen Christ on it. He put his head in his hands. Some words he'd rather not have remembered came into his mind. 'Father, forgive them. They know not what they do.' For some minutes he wrestled with himself and, at last, the words were wrested from him: 'Lord, I'm sorry. I feel nothing but judgement and anger over that

Richard who harmed his toddler. Help me to have your love even for him and the likes of him. Help me to hate the sin, but love the sinner. I'm incapable of doing it on my own.' Then he sat down and rested. It was only when he was on his way out he realized he'd forgotten to have any lunch.

The following Sunday, after Chapel, one of the men from C1 landing asked to see Noel. So after dinner had been served, Noel set off.

As he made his way down the narrow, iron staircase, on to the walkway and started down the landing he heard a noise that sounded like an animal howling. Officer Marsh came up to him and said, 'Can you do something? That man in there is thoroughly upsetting his two cell mates. I've had no trouble on this landing before and I don't want any now.'

'What's the problem?'

'It's all in his mind. It was a sex offence against a girl.'

'Right,' said Noel.

He unlocked the door, but even as he opened it a man half fell out and threw himself on the floor sobbing and moaning. Noel and Officer Marsh got him on to a chair.

'Help me. Oh, help me. Help me,' cried the prisoner and his hands clutched at Noel's coat. Noel put his arm round the man and gradually he subsided. Every now and then a sob shuddered through him. Officer Marsh leaned forward. 'He's not drugged. And he couldn't be drunk. And he's not really a bad lot. He took all the blame for his offence and didn't let the girl's name be mentioned in court. He's been working up to this attack of hysteria for days. He keeps howling like that in his cell and his cell mates can't take much more. He's normally a meek and mild chap.' Officer Marsh shrugged, 'He seems to be going off his head, crying all the time.'

Noel looked up at the clock. In five minutes the tea bell would go and the landing would be about as private as Euston station. And as quiet. 'Can you talk now? Tell me your name.'

The prisoner shook his head. 'You don't want to know the name of the likes of me.'

'Come on now.'

'David King.'

David looked like a hunted dog. 'It's this black weight that presses on me at night. I can't hardly breathe. I keep remembering.' He threw his head back and howled. Mucus poured out of his nose and he kept wiping it away with the back of his hand. He put his head into his wet hands and shook it from side to side. Saliva spattered onto his sleeve and on to Noel's jacket. 'Oh God help me. I'm going mad. I can't stand it.' He clutched at Noel, beside himself. 'I didn't mean no harm. My wife had died you see. Seven years ago. And I was so lonely and this neighbour's girl kept coming to see me and I just wanted to be friendly. And it all went too far and I...' and he cried again. 'I feel so awful. I've done wrong. And there's no pills, nothing in the world, nothing to take that wrong away.'

Noel stood up and cupped David's chin in his hand. 'Listen to me,' he said gently. 'You *are* sorry. And I know how you can get rid of that black weight, that guilt.'

David stared at him.

Noel said, 'Jesus will take it away.'

There was a long silence while the words went home.

'How?'

'We'll pray.'

David clung to Noel's arm. 'Will you do it? Here and now?'

Noel looked up and down the corridor. Officer Marsh was watching.

'Er, all right then.'

David threw himself onto his knees by the side of the chair. Noel hesitated. Marsh would think he was daft. He sighed. Well, he'd better kneel if David was kneeling. He laid his hands on David's head and said as firmly as he could: 'If you confess your sins, Jesus is faithful and just to forgive you your sins, and to make you clean from *every* kind of wrong. Be clean for now and always.'

David was weeping quietly and Noel became uncomfortably aware of heavy footsteps approaching. They stopped. He was dying to look up and to get up. But he did neither. He waited till David was ready and then helped him to his feet. At last he looked round and saw Marsh staring at him with a puzzled frown.

He looked round at David and his heart nearly missed a beat. David had gone quiet but his tear-stained face was shining.

'It's gone,' said David. 'That black weight. It's gone!' He

turned and rushed into his cell and Noel followed him. He heard him say to his cell mates, 'That black weight's gone off my chest. It's gone. I'm free. Jesus has made me free!' He gazed at his two cell mates and his head was high. 'I'm free,' he said.

Officer Marsh said, 'But he's still two years to go.'

Noel smiled. 'He doesn't mean that,' he said.

When Noel got home that evening he was whistling. Norma heard his key in the lock and ran to meet him.

'Hello there,' he said, but suddenly his smile faded. 'What on earth have you got on?'

Norma went bright red and twizzled round, 'Do you like them?'

Noel slowly took off his coat. What was she wearing shorts for at this time of night?

'Well it's er, fine for the tennis court!'

'Tennis court! What do you mean?'

'Er, well, you know.'

'No, I do not know. But I'll never wear them again!' And she flounced upstairs.

Susan and Helen came out of the lounge. 'Oh Dad! Those were Mum's new culottes. They're smashing. Do you think she'll let me borrow them?' asked Susan. 'Rust-coloured corduroy. Mmmm.'

A few moments later Norma marched downstairs with a face that gave nothing away. She was wearing a respectable pleated skirt. Noel stood, feeling foolish, with his briefcase still in one hand. 'I'm sorry, darling. They were very nice. Only I'd have to get used to seeing you like that. You looked so, er, young.'

Norma pushed past and strode into the kitchen. 'Tea's ready,' she said tartly.

Later that night he tried again. 'Look, I didn't mean to upset you over those...shorts.'

She sniffed. 'I was so thrilled when the doctor gave me a good report, that I went to Kelshaw's and bought them, as a little present for me. But when I was trying them on, I had to undress of course, and my underskirt strap fell off one shoulder. And I saw the assistant's face in the mirror. She looked away quickly. But she'd had a look of horror when she saw my breast and the...marks left by the Radiotherapy and,' Norma began to cry and buried her head in the cushion, 'suddenly I felt so ugly. So half a woman. And then, when I came home the girls were so excited about the culottes that I felt happy again.'

There was silence. 'Then you walked in and didn't like them.' Her voice petered out and she moved closer to him. He put his arm round her. He couldn't say anything. He stared at the fireplace. How could he have been so thoughtless? What could he say?

He swallowed: 'I'm sorry darling. You're the only woman I've ever looked at. You're still beautiful to me. That's why I forgot about your...because it's so unnoticeable. It's...you're the only woman for me.'

She blew her nose and said, with a ghost of a laugh, 'Only one who'd have you, you mean.'

He lay awake a long time that night, grieved by his lack of thoughtfulness. He'd buy her something really pretty. Yes, he'd do that, on his next day off.

## Chapter Twenty-Nine

# The Forgotten People

After the Chaplains' meeting things began to settle down on the team. Noel got used to working along with the others and they accepted him. In the months afterwards some good ideas began to surface amongst them.

'Shall we meet every morning for prayer?' asked Noel and several heads nodded in agreement.

'Why not involve others too?'

So other people working in the prison, like Probation Officers Stan Gibbs and Harry Hobbs, joined in the morning prayers. They all found it set the tone for the day. They also decided to send out a monthly prayer letter with news and daily prayer requests.

As the months went by Noel and the team worked hard. One Sunday alone Noel, Garth and Ian counted in nearly eight hundred men at their three services.

'Over half the inmates,' said Garth and shook his head with delight. 'And every day prisoners are asking for counselling!'

Noel accepted speaking engagements all over the area. And people outside became very interested and supportive. They gave books for the Chaplains' library and began to ask for the Prison Prayer Letter. Eventually over fifteen hundred were being sent out each month. Noel also invited many outside speakers and choirs to come to the prison and help at the services.

A branch of the Prison Christian Fellowship started up in Manchester under the auspices of the Manchester City Mission and they met monthly for prayer and to support ex-offenders. Some ladies there offered to help at the creche in the prison, so the prisoners' wives could leave their babies in proper care, while they visited their husbands.'

'I'm sure,' said Noel to Norma one day, 'that the reason God is blessing us so much at Strangeways is because all these people are praying.'

Lionel Cook, the Manchester City Mission missioner, re-started his Bible Class, with good results.

Then Peter Shepley, a prison visitor of long standing, found out that a few of the young men in one of the dormitories he visited, were wanting to learn how to pray together. 'All because one of them had the courage to say his prayers at night in front of the others. He was on his own at first. But now,' and Peter grinned, 'three of his pals want to join in!' And this sparked off the beginning of Noel's Wednesday evening prayer meeting with the prisoners.

On one of Noel's routine visits to the Block, he came to Roger's cell and unlocked it. Roger was sitting hunched over his table with a book open in front of him. Noel said, 'Oh, I see you do like reading after all!'

Roger grunted, 'There's a lot of hypocrites in the Church of England!'

Noel grinned, 'Not such big sinners as you lot are!'

'They've got all that money stashed away in banks. And they've got chalices and that! Hypocrites!'

'Oh,' said Noel, 'and I suppose you've never stashed any away!'

'Humph!' Roger pushed two books at Noel. 'Get me some more of them.'

'A few thank-you's wouldn't come amiss!'

'Humph!'

'OK, I'll bring you some.'

The next prisoner Noel visited wasn't interested in paper-back books. His eyes kept darting round the cell, combing the brick walls, as if somehow he could find a chink in the armour of the prison there.

'My mate's got it,' he said finally, and his eyes rested momentarily on Noel's face. His hands were fiddling the whole time with a bit of paper. Noel noticed his nails were bitten down to the quick and rimmed with dirt.

Noel said, 'Your mate's got what?'

'The money. Fifty grand! Oh God!'

'Pardon?'

The man put his head in his hands, 'Fifty grand and I'm stuck in here. And that woman. I didn't mean her to get killed. It were an accident.' And his eyes started roaming again.

Noel sighed. Occasionally he met cons like this, whose stories sounded like extracts from cheap newspaper serials. And yet, sometimes their stories were true. 'Are you on remand?'

'Yes.'

'Why are you down here?'

'They said they'd get me. I asked for protection.'

'Who?' asked Noel, but the man didn't reply.

'You're three times a prisoner,' said Noel as he got up to go. 'A prisoner in this cell; a prisoner to fear of what the others'll do to you; and a prisoner in your mind to money.'

The man did not answer but shifted to and fro in his seat. Noel took a card out of his pocket. 'Why not come to chapel on Sunday? You'll be escorted so you'll be quite safe. You'll hear something worth thinking about.'

The man turned away and looked out of the window.

Noel stood by the cell door. 'You'd not be alone. There's between four and five,' he paused for effect, 'hundred other men come.' The man looked round, startled for a moment, and then slumped back to the tiny window, biting his nails.

When Noel got back to his office there was a message on his pad in Ian's writing. 'Norma rang. Ring back at once.'

When he got through, she said, 'I've just heard from Nora Hall.'

'Oh yes?' Nora was a Magistrate and also on the Board of Prison Visitors at Strangeways.

Norma said, 'Something awful has happened, she's just rung me. She's really upset because the doctor says she's got to go back to Christie's. She's got,' there was a crackle on the phone, 'she's got cancer on her face.'

'Oh no.'

'She asks for prayer. She wants you to ask the prisoners to pray for her at the prison prayer meeting this evening. Noel, she's...she's had it before and she thought it was better. Only now she might have to have another operation. And she feels she can't go through it all again.'

He sighed, 'That's terrible. Of course we'll pray. It's little enough to do.'

He got to the prayer meeting and an Officer brought in the prisoners. There were about twenty of them, mainly under thirty years of age but a few older men as well. When they'd finished the few pleasantries and the reading, Noel told them about Nora Hall.

'She asks us to pray,' he said.

There was a sudden silence. At last someone said, 'Well what are we waiting for?'

They sat in a circle, Noel amongst them, and they prayed.

'Lord, help that woman.'

'Let her get better soon.'

'Don't let her have that operation.'

'It's not right, Lord, that she should be suffering now.'

'Come on Lord. I know you won't let us down.'

'Heal 'er Lord. We believe.'

Somehow they couldn't stop praying for Nora. One prisoner wept. Another spoke in tongues and a young lad interpreted. Noel listened. It was a message of peace and comfort.

Noel was deeply moved by their prayers. For the very first time he felt there was a bond between him and the cons that went deep. They were his brothers in Christ. They were no more important and no less important than he was in God's sight. And although he must smack of authority, and The Authorities to them, they had accepted him. It would be wonderful for God to hear and answer the prayers of these criminals, 'The Forgotten People', as they sometimes called themselves. They'd be the last people anyone else would choose—but supposing God had chosen them to fulfil his purpose?

When he got home it was late, but Norma ran down the path to meet him. 'Nora's been on the phone. She says did you pray for her at about half past six this evening?'

He struggled to get out of his car. 'Yes, it was about then. Why?'

'She says she was in the kitchen washing up. She noticed the time because the radio was on. She said she was so depressed. Her husband was ill, too, and she felt in despair. She couldn't go on. She felt as if she were drowning in blackness. And she was feeling terrified of going to Christie's on Tuesday in case they say the cancer's eating into her brain.' Norma suddenly stopped for breath.

Noel couldn't speak. He knew what it must be like for Nora and her husband.

Then Norma said, 'Nora told me that she was feeling so awful when all at once she felt as if someone were there; as if they took the burden of despair and blackness from her back. She felt it lift. And in its place came a peace, so strong, she knew she could trust again. And go on. It was so unexpected she was amazed. Isn't that wonderful!'

'Praise the Lord!' said Noel and quickly turned his head away, hoping she wouldn't notice. But she took out her hanky from her pocket and gave it to him. 'We know what it's like,' she said. 'I told Nora that.'

He blew his nose and then said, 'Just think of it, Norma, God has chosen to use the prayers of criminals, the down-and-outs, the drop-outs, the "no-goods". He's chosen them.' He shook his head. 'It's amazing.'

Norma gazed out across the garden. 'That's typical of God,' she said.

When Noel got to the prayer meeting the following week he told the men about Nora's phone call, 'And I'll bet you'd like to hear the rest of her story!' he said.

Their eyes riveted on him as he carried on speaking. 'Well, she phoned Norma and told her she'd gone to Christie's on Tuesday of this week. The doctor examined Nora carefully. She was calm—and had been ever since we prayed for her last week. Then he called for his notes and read them through slowly. Then he examined her again. After a pause he said there might have to be a biopsy to make sure, but,' Noel said, 'he was puzzled. He'd been so sure before that her cancer was spreading. Now he could find no trace.'

The prisoners burst into an excited murmur and a relaxed joy spread amongst them.

'Ta for answering our prayers, Lord.'

'Thanks very much.'

'Isn't it great!'

## Chapter Thirty

# 'If You Haven't Tried It . . .'

Next morning Noel went as usual to Roger's cell in the Block. Roger looked up when he heard the key in the lock.

'Morning,' said Noel.

Roger said, 'Hey, Mr Proctor have you read this book about this girl called Joni?'

Noel stared at Roger as if he were seeing him for the first time. Roger had rolled his shirt sleeves up and the muscles rippled in his arm. He swung round on his chair, faced Noel and looked him straight in the eye. He jabbed his finger at the book on the table. 'This girl Joni what had the accident and got paralysed from the neck down. She's got real courage.'

Noel sat on the bunk and tried to think of some response. 'Er, yes.'

'Do you know, when I read she'd learned to paint pictures with a brush in her mouth, I thought to myself, Roger, she's got more courage than you've ever had.'

Noel said without thinking, 'I don't know how that book got in the pile really. It's a woman's book.'

Roger's face puckered into a frown. 'She's some woman. You know, you sit here in these four walls and strange things pass through your mind. You start thinking, why am I down here? What's the point of all this?' and he waved his hand round the cell. 'What's it all for, eh? And I started thinking: I've always had to be "Number One". Number One in my own life and Number One in everyone else's. It's been like that for a long time.'

Noel sat quietly. He knew Roger had the reputation for being a bad lot. He'd been in and out of Borstals and prison for years. Men were afraid of him. It was well known that he had to be Number One. He spent more time in the Block than on the landings. He was a hard man. Noel looked at him, 'Go on,' he said.

'Well, I read that book and I got to thinking, what's the point of all this Number One business? That girl Joni has more courage than I've ever had. She's got something I haven't got.' Roger was leaning back in his chair and his head was held with ease and confidence, the stance of a man who only had to hold his hand out to get what he wanted. Fast. He was a man other men kept on the right side of.

He looked at Noel.

Noel said nothing. Roger suddenly crashed forward on his chair. He flung his hand out towards Noel. 'I want what that girl has.'

Noel said. 'I'm delighted to hear that, Roger. And I'd like to come and talk to you about it again. Tomorrow perhaps.' He spoke slowly, as if calculating the weight of his words.

Roger flushed and his hand fell back to his side. 'I want it now.'

'It's not always a good idea to rush into a big decision, Roger. "Getting what Joni got" is a big thing. It needs thinking about very carefully. It would involve you in decisions that would change the outcome of your life.'

Roger was scowling and fractionally turned his back on Noel.

Noel said, 'I'm delighted you've had the intelligence and maturity to say what you've said to me. I only wish there were others on this landing able to speak as you've spoken. Will you let me come tomorrow and speak more about it?'

Roger sat on in his chair, his face heavy and his hand on the book. He seemed deep in thought. Noel waited, tense on the edge of his chair.

Then Roger's face cleared. He turned back to Noel, 'OK. You're on. I'll see yer tomorrow.'

Noel left the cell and scratched his head. Was it possible that Roger of all people was in earnest? Surely a man like him would find it almost impossible to change. And yet he'd clearly been moved by Joni's story. Noel was thoughtful as he got to his office. He'd have to tread very cautiously with Roger.

The next morning when Noel got to the Block Roger was

ready and waiting for him. The three books were in a neat pile on the table.

'How are you today?'

'I've been thinking, Mr Proctor. It's funny you get time to think down here. It's so quiet. But I still want what Joni's got.'

Noel bowed his head, 'Well let's run through it all again shall we. Why are you down here?'

Roger shrugged. 'A fighting charge. I was found "not guilty" as I knew I would be but the Governor said I'd got to be quiet for a bit. I'm on Rule 43/B. I can have my cigs and radio and that.'

'Hmm.'

'I've been thinking. I've always had to be Number One. Everything I've ever wanted I've had to fight for. Fighting to be Number One has been like a religion to me. I've made enemies. People wanted to fight me for the reputation I'd made. People were always challenging me for my name. It's got bigger and bigger over the years.'

Noel looked at Roger. 'If you *really* want to change your life you'd have to let go of being Number One. You'd be involved in a fight, but it's a different kind of fight.'

Roger frowned and carried on as if he hadn't heard, 'A lot of people have got hurt through it. And I've lost my feelings. Pain is a four-letter word to me. I don't care if I inflict it and I blank pain if someone else is gunning for me. I blank it.'

Noel sighed. 'I know you're sincere now. You really want a change of heart. But do you know what it would mean? No more Tobacco Baron. No more getting tobacco debts off other lads. The other inmates will snigger at you and think you're daft. I'm telling you the truth. Being a Christian isn't easy.'

Roger went red and turned his head away.

Noel pushed his point home, 'No more robbery and violence. Can you face it, Roger? You're thirty-five now and you've spent over twenty years going in one direction—the wrong one. Can you want to change so much that you'll turn your back on all that and start to live again? It'd be like getting born all over again. You'd have it all to learn.' He paused. 'Can you really stand doing all that?'

Roger fiddled with the three books and kept his face turned away.

Noel stood up. 'Think about it very carefully and I'll see yer tomorrow.' He paused on the threshold, 'You've read the good bit in *Joni* and I've told yer the bad bit. Now put both bits together and see how you feel.'

He walked away down the corridor and his footsteps echoed. Had he been too hard on Roger? But Roger had to understand the challenge very clearly. Otherwise he'd be worse off in the end than he was now.

When he saw Roger the next day, Roger was still convinced he wanted what Joni had got, so Noel prayed for him and laid his hands on him. But as he left he still wasn't quite sure if Roger meant business.

The following morning he got to Roger's cell as soon as he could and unlocked the door.

Roger was up at the cell window and turned round quickly. Noel shut the door and was about to say, 'How are you?' but stopped short. Roger was smiling uncertainly but his face was...it was the same but different. Something must have happened. He gazed at Noel and his eyes were almost shy. He hesitated and then sat down on the only chair. Noel sat on the bunk. Roger put his hands in his lap and Noel stared at them. They were resting loosely on his knee and there was something different about them....

'What's happened?' asked Noel.

'How do you know?'

Noel laughed. 'I've not been reading men's faces for nearly thirty years for nothing. I can see something's happened to you.' He didn't add, 'and your eyes look as if someone's washed them clean from that hard stony stare.'

Roger cleared his throat. 'Well something happened, only, like, I don't quite know how to say it.'

'Try.'

'When you'd gone yesterday I began reading that book *Joni* again and I thought, she's got more nerve than I ever had. So why don't I ask to get that "something" she's got. I want it. So I asked and asked.

'Then in the evening I sat on my bunk and I said to myself, why don't you try this? See what it can do for you. I knew how to pray as I've seen people pray before, so I put my hands together and I said, "I will make a deal with you, Lord, if there's such a person. If you can take the violence and aggression away from me, I will follow you. I will be one of your servants."

'Half an hour went by and I started,' Roger stopped and stared straight at Noel, 'I started calming down. I felt very calm and I've been so uptight all the time from being a kid. I felt very quiet and I lay on my bunk. A strange feeling came over me, what I've never experienced before, of being relaxed, of being so relaxed, it was unbelievable. Something seemed to speak to me in a whisper: "The change is yours. You can take it or leave it."' Roger stopped again. Then he said, 'I thought, well, why not? I'll take it. I'll follow you.

'Then it was just like,' he spread his hands out, 'just like waves of the sea washing over me. It went on and on. And I was getting calmer and quieter and more relaxed. All my aggression and hatred, it seemed to flow away with these waves that were flowing over me. Until I lay there like you said, like a little baby waiting to start again.'

Noel didn't speak. He gazed and gazed at Roger's hands. He knew now what the difference was. Before they were tense fists, or fingers drumming on the table, or thumbing through a book. They were never still. Today they lay, quiet and open on Roger's knee, all the tension gone. He put his hand on Roger's shoulder.

'You've met with Jesus, Roger. You've met with him.'

Roger stared back and shook his head slowly. 'I don't really understand what you mean, Mr Proctor. Only I know now I've got what Joni got. All my life I've felt like I was standing in a cold street gazing in at toys and things in a shop window and if I wanted anything I'd have to smash my fist through and grab. But now I feel as if I'm on the inside of the window looking out. And if I dare mention it, that as I'm on the inside, I'll not need to grab again. Everything's by me.'

Noel was silent. Then he said, 'That's wonderful. Can I tell the other chaplains? And I'll be back tomorrow to do a bit of Bible study with you.'

Noel half hoped the Governor would let Roger out of the Block soon, but he didn't. Roger stayed another two months in solitary confinement. At the end of that time the Senior Officer on duty on DI landing came up to Noel one morning and said,

'I don't know what you've done to Roger but he's made his promise to the Governor now. No more violence and aggression. He says he's made his promise to someone else as well. Do you know who it is? It can't be his wife as they're divorced. His mum maybe?'

Noel grinned. 'No. I know who it is.'

'Who?'

'Why don't you ask him?'

Officer Dalby pushed his cap back on his head. 'I've worked here for nearly twenty years and I've known Roger almost that long. He's been in and out of prison all his life. You might say a "hopeless case". I never thought I'd see the day when he would calmly come to communion every Sunday and sit there by me quietly, taking it all in. I might almost say, something's happened to him. Or is happening. I've not heard him use a mouthful of oaths lately, either.'

Noel's grin split his face in half. 'I'm delighted you've noticed,' he said.

'Yes, but...' and Officer Dalby's mouth closed, he shook his head and walked away.

Noel frowned. He guessed there was someone on C3 who didn't get on well with Roger and Officer Dalby was worried about repercussions.

Next day when he and Stan Gibbs, Bill Tabarn, and Ian and a few others got together to pray before work Noel asked them to pray for Roger. 'It'd be so easy for him to forget now he's been moved back off D1. It would be so easy for him to get annoyed and sock someone on the nose.'

So they prayed and prayed.

Ian said, 'It's funny to think a tough guy like Roger has become our brother in Christ. An actual brother.'

Noel had to laugh. 'We're quite a family.'

Bill said, 'Think who we've got as a Dad.'

The weeks went by. There were no repercussions on C3. Officer Dalby kept raising his eyebrows when he saw Noel. And Noel began to feel as if he were walking round with a permanent grin on his face. One day he was popping into the cells to get to know a few more faces, when he heard an Officer call down the landing, 'How's your halo Roger?'

Noel swung round and saw Roger walking down the landing with his bucket to take to the toilet. It was a young Officer and he kept up a banter behind Roger all about vicars and Holy Joes.

Noel winced and waited for the inevitable mouthful to come from Roger. But Roger, not noticing Noel, kept on walking.

Noel decided to follow them and as he came to the corner he heard the Officer say, 'What's got into you? You never answer back now.'

Roger planted the bucket on the landing and swung round on the Officer. 'I've become a Christian.' He shrugged, 'So my hatred for you has gone.'

The Officer laughed. 'Don't be so stupid! How do you know it's gone?'

Roger said, 'I've tried being a Christian. And it works. Have you?'

The Officer suddenly went red. 'Er, no.'

'Well, if you haven't tried it, don't knock it.' And Roger grasped his bucket and strode off.

Noel tapped the Officer on the shoulder, 'Makes you think, eh?'

'Hummph,' said the Officer and followed on after Roger.

Roger's changed behaviour on the landing wasn't the only change. 'He's begun to talk to the men with him and they all listen,' said Noel to Norma one day. 'Perhaps it's because he is who he is, or rather was, but they listen anyway. And four have decided to become Christians.'

Norma's face lit up, 'Wonderful.'

He grinned. 'This move of the Spirit seems to be taking a hold at Strangeways. Those four I just mentioned have all been filled with the Spirit. Three when they were on their own in their separate cells. They can speak in tongues and it's given them such assurance that God loves them. And two of them,' Noel chuckled, 'two of them decided to fast and pray till midnight recently. They stuck it out and collected all their food into their locker.'

'Why didn't they refuse it?'

'Not allowed to. In case it's a hunger strike. Anyway, at midnight they dived into the locker and had chip butties, lettuce butties, and goodness knows what!' His deep laugh filled the room, 'But they meant well, Norma. Now two more lads up there have decided to become Christians as well and these two think it's because they fasted and prayed, which no doubt it is!'

'That's wonderful, Noel. Just think. They're society's forgotten people. Society's bad people. And yet the Spirit of God loves even them, and changes them and uses them to help others. It's amazing!'

## Chapter Thirty-One

# Ex-Offenders

As the months went by Noel and the other Chaplains saw the momentum of interest amongst the prisoners gathering ground. Noel invited in speakers like Colin Urquhart, Tony Powell and Don Double. At the end of their sermons some of them invited the prisoners to respond to Christ. And Noel himself did the same. Scores of prisoners responded. When an American evangelist, David Gomez, came in, over eighty men and boys stood at the end of the service wanting to know more about Jesus Christ.

The follow-up work to all this was exacting but exciting. Day after day men on the landings were asking to become Christians. Noel and the other Chaplains were kept busy.

Invitations to speak poured in from all over the North-West and Noel accepted as many as he could. He took his excitement with him and challenged his hearers. His stories of prisoners and prison life became a talking point in the region. Church people began to pray. And Noel believed that God was blessing the prison work because of this prayer.

He tried to vary his talks. At one he spoke about the ex-cons who conned their friends: 'There was a fella in a cell who was only in for fines—he said! He said that when he got out he would pay for his cell-mate's wife to go on a holiday. The cell-mate agreed readily as his wife was a cripple. Well, the fella went round to the wife, explained about the holiday and asked for a £30 deposit. She paid. And that was the last she saw of him and her money.' A groan ran round his audience.

Noel warmed to his theme: 'There are so many difficult situations in prison. So many pressures. One prisoner went on a hunger strike, when it got fashionable to do so after the events in Northern Ireland. I tried to talk him out of it. In the end I told him he was damaging his liver by not eating so he started again!'

Noel shook his head. 'Some of these poor lads have no idea. His basic reason for stopping eating was that no one was taking the trouble to listen to his worries and he couldn't cope any more.'

At another meeting Noel tried to explain to his audience the plight of a segregated prisoner: 'I had a man only yesterday who asked to see me after the Communion Service. When I got to his cell he was sitting with his head in his hands. Finally I got him to talk and he had a sad story to tell: he'd been living with his girlfriend and she had had his baby. They decided to get married and go out to Germany as he was with the forces. But he only got a single man's pay. He tried and tried to get it changed but the computer wouldn't cough up, so they got deeper and deeper into debt. At last it all got on top of him and one night he couldn't stand his kid yelling any more.' Noel paused. He remembered his own previous difficulty in having any compassion for child abusers. He looked round the audience and said quietly, 'He hit the kid so hard he ruptured him. The child nearly died. The father got the doctor and confessed. But he still had to do time on a charge of Grevious Bodily Harm.'

The hall of people was silent. Noel went on, 'Meanwhile the man's wife had another baby. When it was eleven weeks old it died of a cot death.' A shudder ran round the listening people. 'Now when I'd listened to all this I started to tell this man that if he was truly sorry God would forgive him. But he interrupted me. "You've been talking about forgiveness, Mr Proctor, and I know God would, only," and he buried his head in his hands, "the trouble is I can't forgive myself." I had to tell that man that if our heart condemns us, God is greater than our hearts.'

Noel paused a moment and then moved over to his tape recorder. He'd decided to play them the tape of Graham, 'The Gentle Giant' from Dartmoor. He watched the faces of his audience as they listened to Graham's Geordie accent crackling into the room.

When it was over he switched off the tape and said, 'I had a letter from Graham recently. He's at Preston Prison now. He's been inside for twenty-two years and he's being rehabilitated for his release in another few years. His letter was full of the Lord.' He paused. 'And I met a man recently in the Strangeways reception who had travelled up on a coach with Graham, when he was being escorted to Durham to see his relatives. That man on the coach was so impressed by Graham that he asked to see me as soon as he got to Strangeways. He wanted to know how he could get like Graham.

'When Norma and I went to see Graham at Preston, we found he had stuck to his conversion. He was quietly carrying on, going to chapel, reading his Bible and so on. He's come a long way from the day he wrecked the Reception at Dartmoor!'

After the meeting Noel drove home. Before he got out of his car he checked in his diary. There were three more meetings this week: Bury, Middleton and Bramhall. Next week was Cheadle. Then Altrincham and Didsbury. He grinned and shut the diary. He'd blast them all and give them something to think about. He'd challenge them with the needs of the ex-offenders.

A piece of paper fell out of the diary and he bent to pick it up. It was a message from Garth and he re-read it slowly: 'Noel, Roger the Baron wanted me to tell you he knows what he's going to do when he comes out. He says he wants to help other ex-cons. I think he's serious. Garth.' Noel stood a minute in the drive and then walked up to his iron door. Perhaps Roger was going to be part of the answer of what happened to the ex-prisoners.

Next morning Noel was down at the prison early. After his duties were done he decided to do some cell visits. He got the usual mixed response. Most men smiled vaguely. One man swore at him. A thin man with a Birmingham accent said, 'Hey, Preacher, you're a con man like me!'

The other two men in the cell looked uncomfortable and turned away. But Noel grinned. 'How do you make that out?'

The thin man smirked. 'Well you sell invisible stuff!'

'What do you mean?'

'I sold two lorry loads of nylon sheets that didn't exist! And you sell your line and that doesn't exist!'

Noel's laugh filled the cell. He wagged his finger at the man,

'Aha, but my stuff does exist because my stuff changes lives!'

'Huh! My sheets didn't keep anyone warm!'

Noel was still chuckling when he left the cell. He shook his head. He couldn't win them all!

He went to the next cell. Inside a youngish man with dark hair was sitting hunched up by the cell window. Noel recognized him as a regular at the CEMS meeting.

'Hello, Lance. What's troubling you?'

Lance began to bite his nails. 'I'm going out next week. I've been inside two year and I'm scared to death of going out. I know it sounds daft but I'm really uptight about it.' He stopped biting his nails and stared miserably at Noel. 'I'm not ready to leave.'

Noel was nonplussed. 'What about your wife?'

'Oh, she's coming to meet me.'

'Come on, man. You're a lot luckier than some. There's no one to meet them. When they're discharged they shuffle off down Southall Street to the Bishop of Middleton's shelter under the railway arches or somewhere else like that. No one bothers to meet them. No one cares. All they've got to look forward to is a bottle of meths.'

Lance stared at the floor and his shoulders sagged.

Noel said, 'They turn back to their old cronies because they're the only friends they've got. The Police lock them up when there's a crime in the area and before they know where they are they're back inside.'

Lance's head fell further forward on his chest. 'I know all that, Mr Proctor, and I'm sorry for them gaffers but I still feel scared of going out.'

Noel came up and put his hand on Lance's arm. 'Look, I think you'll be all right when you've adjusted. Where'll you live?'

'My wife's mother's.'

'Oh.'

'Mr Proctor, I don't want to come back in here ever again.' Lance shuddered. 'It's like doom when you hear that cell door clang behind you. Anyway, what I want to say is that my wife's stood by me and I don't want to let her down. If only I had a job....'

Noel put in sadly, 'There's not many of those.'

'But if I prayed for a job, would I get one? Like they said at the prayer meeting. Ask....'

Noel's face was set into deep lines and he paused. Then he said, 'I'd like to say yes. Only sometimes God tests people and doesn't seem to answer at once. What I can promise you is that he'll never let you down, only he might help you in a way you don't expect.' He stopped, waiting for Lance to grumble and say the God-business was a con trick.

There was no reply so Noel looked the other man in the face.

Lance said, 'That's fair enough. I didn't become a Christian for what I could get out of it. But because I thought he were a good bloke.'

Noel said, 'Look, when I first left Ireland to go to college in London I was scared like you are now. And when I got there it wasn't easy. They thought I was, er, bumptious.' He grinned. 'I realize now they had a point! But as I look back, I see it was all part of the plan for my life. So don't worry. We'll keep in touch with you. The thing is, do join a church.'

Lance said nothing.

Noel said, 'Keep out of bad company. And keep away from the pub, man. It doesn't do you any good.'

Lance nodded slowly. 'I'll try.'

'There's an organization called "Contact For Christ". Shall I put your name down? They'll visit you the same day you're released.'

'OK.'

Later that day in the office Noel asked Garth, Ian and David to a meeting. They'd hardly sat down before he began. 'Look, the problem of the ex-offenders has come to a head. Lance Williams is worried sick about leaving. Can we review the situation? What can be done?'

Garth said, 'There's our six Methodist flats at the Central Hall. That's going well. The ex-offenders there are doing fine.'

'And "The Beeches" at Didsbury,' said Ian. 'A sort of Half-Way House.'

Noel waved his hand impatiently. 'I didn't mean that. He's already fixed up with accommodation.'

There was silence round the table. Noel was deep in thought.

'Look,' he said at last, 'I'm going to take Roger the Baron at his word. He says he wants to help other ex-cons. He's been out some time now and has joined a church. I'm going to suggest he links up with Lance. Perhaps based on the Prison Christian Fellowship monthly meeting. It would be a point of focus.'

'Mmmm,' said Garth. 'You mean a Self-Help group? A sort of Inside-Outside group.'

'Yes.'

'But it'd be a drop in the ocean.'

'You've got to start somewhere.'

'True.'

Ian was fiddling with his tie. 'Doesn't the problem lie with the churches as much as anything? If only they'd welcome in an ex-con.'

'But they're suspicious.'

'Don't lets be too hard on them,' said Noel. 'A Christian business man I know offered jobs to two ex-cons. One is making the grade. The other left after a few months and found a better job because he had a reference. You see, humanity can't be tabulated and bundled into slots. It's all so complex.'

But Ian was insistent. 'No, but the churches look down on the ex-cons. They'd never think they could learn anything from an ex-prisoner either!'

Garth frowned. 'Do the churches, or church people want to have anything to do with them? Would we? Would I? Wouldn't we be a bit afraid?'

'Jesus had plenty to do with them,' said Noel.

Ian got up and walked to the window. When he turned round his face was troubled. He shook his head. 'I've remembered something,' he said. 'When I was at my last prison the Chaplain had an early Communion Service on a Wednesday morning. One day there were only four of us there. He and I. And two red-bands. He had this idea that instead of him giving out the bread and wine, we'd all kneel round the altar and pass it one to another. Great, I thought. I saw myself giving these marvellous symbols of bread and wine to the poor cons and it gave me a warm feeling.' Ian snorted. 'I was *very* superior. But the Chaplain passed the bread first to one of the cons and I realized with a shock that it meant the con would have to pass it to *me*! Do you know at that moment I was flabbergasted! All my preconceived ideas suddenly bounced in my face. I was ashamed. And I realized I had the attitude, albeit unconscious, that no one could help me. I'd not realized that before God all men are equal.' Ian pushed his floppy hair back from his forehead. 'I was humbled that day.'

'We're all one before the cross,' said Noel.

'Right,' said Garth. 'And we've all got one to carry as well.'

Some time later Noel got a letter from Middleton. He opened it and saw it was from Lance.

'I left the first church I joined,' he read, 'but now I've joined another and I like it. They said they'd pray for me to get a job and they did. At first there was nothing. Then an interview at the Motorway Service Station. I were so excited and so were my wife. Only I didn't get the job. I were disappointed and kept thinking about what you said about trusting God.

'Then a few weeks later the Service Station rang me and asked me to go again. Well I did. When I got there they offered me a cleaner's job. Cleaning the garage forecourt. On nights.'

Noel put the letter down and looked at Norma over the breakfast table. Without speaking he passed her the first page of the letter.

He settled down to read on: 'It were hard on my wife and I was a bit sick. I saw I'd come down in the world and all I were worth was being a night-time cleaner. But I'd prayed for a job and here I was being offered one. So I took it.'

They read on in silence.

'He's got guts,' said Norma.

'It's a shame,' said Noel. 'His wife's at work during the day and he's on nights. And they've only just got married.'

She smiled. 'At least he's not too proud to work. What was his offence?'

'Drunk and Disorderly.' Noel was quiet a moment. Then he said, 'I think I'll invite him to give his testimony at a meeting in Manchester, if he can get the night off. And I'll arrange for him to meet Roger again.'

'Is that Self-Help group working out?'

'Yes. It's not large and it's not organized but they mean well.'

At the meeting Lance spoke and Noel was pleased.

'Will you come again in two months' time?' asked Noel.

Lance went pink with pleasure. 'Oh yes. Can I bring my wife?'

Noel laughed. 'Sure thing!'

There was a pause and then Lance said hesitantly, 'Mr Proctor?'

'Yes?'

'The Police have visited me a couple of times, when there's been a fight at the pub.'

'Well?'

'It's a bit hard like.'

'You can't blame them. They don't know you've become a Christian and are keeping out of trouble. It's up to you to prove it to them.'

'Mmmm.'

About a week before the second meeting Noel got another letter postmarked Middleton.

Lance wrote, 'I wouldn't want you to ask me under false pretences to speak at your meeting. There's something on my mind I feel I ought to tell you first.

'The other week I met some of my old cronies and they persuaded me into the pub. I promised myself I'd only drink orange but when it came to it, I drank the usual stuff and they had to help me home. Fortunately there was no trouble.'

Noel groaned and read on: 'But during that night I had a terrible nightmare. I saw myself back in Strangeways. I heard the locks, and the bolts being drawn and the keys jangling. I woke up and I was sweating and shaking. I threw myself on my knees and begged God to forgive me. It struck me that God had sent the dream to warn me. Drink had sent me to Strangeways the first time and now I was being warned. Drink could send me there again.

'I've not had a drop since. If you still want me to speak, I will. Only I felt I ought to tell yer what had happened. I'm still working and am happy at home. Also the Police haven't been round recently....'

When Norma read it she said, 'That's fantastic!'

'Fantastic! It's terrible!'

'No, it's not. It's fantastic that he's realized without anyone telling him, that he's got to be honest with you. He's "walking in the light". How many Christians do that?'

Noel thought. 'I do believe you're right,' he said.

They sat together and then he took her hand. 'You go for your final check-up at Christie's soon, don't you?'

'Next week.'

He squeezed her hand. 'You've done wonderfully well,' he said.

The week that unfolded was quite unforgettable. On the Sunday the Gideons came into Strangeways, bringing with them over one thousand New Testaments. Noel was stern with the prisoners at the Chapel services. 'No one must take a New Testament unless he *really* wants one. I'll not have God's word abused.'

Afterwards when he asked the Gideons how many had been taken there was a quick exchange of smiles. Then they answered, 'Over the thousand!'

On the Wednesday Noel preached at a church in Middleton. At the end of the service two young lads asked to see him. After some nervous pushing they both said they wanted to become Christians.

'How's that?' asked Noel.

'It's because of our brother. He's changed so much.'

'He's never been drunk on a Saturday night for ages—you know after closing time.'

'He even says sorry occasionally.'

'Doesn't grumble even though he's got a crummy job.'

'Yes. On a garage forecourt.'

'Working nights.'

Noel carefully set his face. 'Is he called Lance?'

The brothers exchanged glances. 'How do you know him?'

Noel gave a great laugh. 'Oh he's a friend of mine. And now I see you two want to join the extended family!'

Then came the day that he and Norma had waited for. Over the long years they had waited for the day when she would make her final journey. To Christie's on the bus.

'Let me take you in the car,' he said.

'No. I'll go as I've always gone. I'd rather.'

She gave him a quick peck on the cheek and was away. He watched as she went off down the garden path. Then he turned and forced himself to get ready for work. He knew he ought to trust, only supposing...and he shook his head.

The morning got under way pretty much as usual and in the middle of a clutch of phone calls he heard a voice he knew better than his own.

'Noel?'

'Yes. What...?'

All he could hear was her laugh, like a burst of sunshine down the phone.

'I'm discharged. I'm clear. I'll never have to go again!'

'Norma!'

'And I've so much to tell you!'

He looked at his watch. 'I'll come home for lunch and meet you there.'

'OK.'

He sat for a moment and then put his head in his hands. There was nothing to say. The glad spurt in his chest said it all. And he knew his Lord understood.

When he got home she was waiting for him. 'Oh, Noel, won't the girls be thrilled!'

'I'm thrilled.' And they threw their arms round each other. After a minute he said, 'I've been meaning to get you something after I made that gaffe about the, er, culottes.'

She laughed.

He went on, 'And I want you to buy yourself anything you like at Kelshaws.'

Her eyes brightened. 'There was a very nice fine woollen skirt and waistcoat I saw recently. In pale green. No, it's far too expensive.'

'You're having it!'

She looked at him. 'On one condition.'

'What's that?'

'You buy a new jacket for yourself. I've seen a brown velvet cord one.'

He swallowed and shut his eyes. Well, if it pleased her....

'All right,' he said.

After a while she said, 'You'll never guess what. The doctor who examined me was Chinese. Or Korean or something. He was very solemn and precise. After he'd discharged me he said, "You must have had a lot of fight, Mrs Proctor." I said, "I don't know about a lot of fight but I had a lot of faith." And his face lit up, as if a light had been turned on behind his eyes. He said, "You have faith?" I said, "Yes." And he said, "So do I, Mrs Proctor. So do I." And he wrung me by the hand as if his life depended upon it.'

As Noel drove back to work after lunch he began to sing loudly. What a day! What a week! He'd never been so happy. And he roared away down the Bury New Road, ready to face anything. The sun was shining and his light baritone voice sounded golden in his ears. Surely nothing could stop a revival breaking out now. Everything was wonderful! And still singing loudly he shot into the prison car park.

## Chapter Thirty-Two

## 'What Is Your Life?'

One Saturday morning a few weeks later Noel was woken up early by the sound of the phone. He struggled out of bed and down the stairs to his study. He grabbed the phone and heard a voice say, 'Is that Mr Proctor? There's been a fire. Will you come at once!'

'You mean at the prison?'

'Yes. A cell fire. Two dead. One critically ill in Withington Burns Unit. The Governor wants you down here.'

Noel's throat was dry. 'Right. I'll come at once.'

He rushed back upstairs, flung on his clothes and flew down again. Norma followed him, still yawning, and put the kettle on. He swallowed some tea, refused a slice of bread and marmalade and was gone. She was left in the hall, white-faced at the news.

When he got to the prison he went straight to his office. David Goldspink, his Assistant, was already there.

'What's happened?'

'A cell fire. Late last night. In the Remand Wing.'

'Oh no!'

'Yes. The Governor thinks it was a protest against conditions and that somehow it got badly out of hand.'

'You say two died?'

'I'm afraid so. The other's in hospital. Apparently the staff couldn't get into the cell in time. The prisoners had barricaded the door. Then used their cigarettes and matches...and you know what those mattresses are like. I don't suppose they realized.'

Noel was numb. He knew that once the alarm had been raised, the staff would try and open the cell door. They'd find it barricaded, so would have to rush down to the basement to get the hydraulic Jack; drag it upstairs; lift the door. The fastest possible time would be about twenty minutes. And he knew that those mattresses gave off poisonous fumes when burning and could suffocate a man in fifteen seconds.

He said, 'I'll get up there now and see what I can do.'

When he got to the Remand Wing he asked the Officer on duty if he could do cell visits and talk to the prisoners. The Officer stared at him. His face was white and there were black circles under his eyes. He nodded and suddenly said, 'The two dead prisoners have been taken to the City Morgue. The third's fighting for his life in Intensive Care.'

Noel nodded. The Officer's shoulders sagged. He looked at Noel and all at once said, 'Why? That's what I want to know. Why?' And he stumped off down the landing. Noel stood there, quite still. The same question kept troubling him.

He set off to do the visiting, passing the burnt-out cell. The blackened shell gaped on to the landing and an acrid smell hung in the air. He stared at it and then looked away, his face set in tired lines. But there was something else about it that worried him. He glanced back at it and frowned. Whatever was it? He visited the cells on either side and then saw the other men. He found the prisoners subdued and talking in whispers. He listened mainly, letting them talk it out. As he did so he kept hearing one word over and over again: why? Why had they done it? Why couldn't they be rescued? Why were they protesting? Why were conditions so bad? Why? Why? Why?

It was only as he was leaving the landing that he realized what had worried him about the burnt-out cell. No, surely not! An agony, as strong as a hand clutching at his heart, made him stop dead. Surely not. He ran back and checked the numbers on the cells either side. His head fell on to his chest. So he was right. Very slowly he turned away. He forced his feet to walk, to go down the corridor, to return to the office.

David looked up when he came in and half got to his feet. 'What's the matter?'

Noel raised his head and spoke with difficulty. 'That cell; there was a man in there. I visited him only yesterday. I've been visiting him all week. He was in D1, the Punishment

Block, till yesterday. He wanted to join the CEMS.'

Noel suddenly sat down. He felt very old and very defeated. He put his head in his hands. Why O why? It made a mockery of everything they were trying to achieve. What was the point of it all?

David gazed at him awkwardly. 'Er, would you like a cup of tea?'

Slowly Noel pulled himself up and looked at the younger man.

'Yes, please,' he said. Then, 'How am I going to face that lad's family at Withington this afternoon? He's only twenty-two and the hospital doesn't think there's much chance.' He groaned. 'And then I'll have to go to the City Morgue as well and meet those relatives.'

David said, 'Look, I know it sounds corny, but you can do it, Noel. And think of them. It's much worse for them. You'll be all right. You've had a shock, but you'll be able to manage. You'll see.' And he passed him his tea.

Somehow Noel got through the day. The media got hold of the story and while he was at Withington Hospital, the Governor was interviewed for *Nationwide*. When at last Noel came home in the evening Norma was waiting for him.

'Why?' he said to her as he got into the hall. 'Why? What's it all about?'

'What's what all about?'

'Life. And death.' And he trailed off into his study.

She called after him, 'Why don't you come to bed?'

'I've got a sermon to do for tomorrow morning. What I prepared before won't be any use now. What am I to say to the prisoners?'

When he got to the Chapel the next morning he found the Governor, Norman Brown, there. 'They want me to speak, Noel. So many Officers and prisoners have asked that I've decided to do it. Can I go on before you?'

'Of course.'

'You know the third lad died at quarter past three this morning?'

Noel bowed his head. 'I was expecting it.'

Norman Brown shook his head. 'Why on earth did they do it?'

The Chapel was crowded with men and there was a hush of expectancy in the air when they saw the Governor. After the first hymn Norman Brown took his stand in front of the hundreds of men and plunged into his talk:

'Some of you have asked me to come here this morning and speak about the cell fire. What I want to say to the majority of you, is pack it up! What do you expect to gain from this cell fire business? It's futile and it's stupid. It's no easy task the staff have had to perform, believe me. It's a pretty dirty, lousy job for staff to go into a burning cell. But they did it. Strictly speaking it's not legal for them to do it. The Fire Service should do it. But they and some of the inmates risked their lives, got burnt and made every effort to revive those people.'

He looked round the prisoners who were sitting very still and he said quietly: 'Unfortunately we lost them. And I know what I'm talking about. I've been through it. I can speak from experience about the horror of being burnt. And I don't want to be in the sad position again of having to go to someone's wife, father or sister with news they haven't got a son or a husband or a brother. That's not easy either.'

Noel sat and listened. It was known in the prison that the Governor had been burned in a tank accident in the War. He certainly held the men's attention. There was hardly a movement in the Chapel.

The Governor said: 'I know the appalling conditions you're in. I'm on record in the Press and the media as standing up for better conditions for you. Not for me. I can't help the conditions you're in at the moment. I also have bosses above me and I've tried to get certain conditions for you men but those conditions were denied me. To achieve them the Officers had to take industrial action for over a week. It was on your behalf. They got nothing out of it for themselves. They won their case and better conditions were promised for the Trials and Remands Wing.'

Noel bowed his head. Conditions were bad on that Wing. There were three men to a cell. Only an hour's exercise every day. Only eight toilets for three hundred and fifty men. And buckets at night.

In the visiting room a man had to speak through a pane of glass to his visitor and there were only fourteen booths. It was intolerable and degrading. As Garth often said, even though the men might have done wrong it was still like carrying a cross for them to have to bear these conditions. They still suffered.

Noel looked across at the Governor again, who said; 'In three to four weeks, by the beginning of June, I promise you that you'll be moving to better conditions. And the visiting room is being rebuilt. You will be able to have open visits. I give you my word.'

He paused and looked round the silent Chapel. Then he went on: 'I'm aware that it's only half a dozen or so who are giving instructions to demonstrate. But you are the majority. So be responsible. I don't want any more dead prisoners. The Board of Visitors are working on the mattress situation with the Home Secretary personally. So please be responsible.'

He stopped talking as abruptly as he had begun and swung back to his seat. A burst of applause followed him and he sat and stared straight ahead.

Then the service went on with hymns and prayers. When the time for the talk came Noel got to his feet and walked to the lectern. He looked at the sea of faces, took a deep breath and began to read from James 4 verse 14:

> What is your life? 'It is like a mist that appears
> for a little time and then vanishes.'

He shut the Bible and raised his hand.

'What is your life?' he asked again. 'Yesterday was a very unhappy day for me. Yesterday I got the terrible news about the cell fire and the deaths. Ever since I've been plagued by the futility of it all.

'Yesterday afternoon I went to Withington Hospital where that third lad was in Intensive Care. His liver, his lungs and his brain had ceased to function. I went to the waiting room and sat with his mother, his aunt and his sister.'

His throat ached but he was determined to carry on: 'His mother couldn't face going in to see him but she went in with me. When she saw her son on the bed with his face enlarged to twice the size by the burning, she collapsed. And I helped her up. We took her back to the waiting room and the nurse gave her brandy.

'We finished up in that waiting room praying out loud that God would help us. I'll never forget it. I've never heard such despair as in that mother's prayers. And I felt an utter failure. Every day in that week past I'd visited that lad. I'd given him books from the Chaplains' Library. I spoke to him about Christ. Yet here he was in Intensive Care.

'We wept together as we sat in that waiting room and, strangely, I felt the closeness of God in a way I'd never felt before. But what could I say to them? There was nothing I could say. I could only sit there and share their agony.'

He paused.

'At quarter past three this morning that lad died.'

A shudder ran round the prisoners in the Chapel and sorrow hung in the air. Noel went on: 'And this verse I read out to you pounds in my mind. "What is your life?" On Friday night, through stupidity, three lives have been snuffed out. Is there an answer?'

He waited and then said, 'I believe the only answer is the one I tried to give that mother yesterday: that Christ is the surpreme answer to death. Everyone of us in this Chapel is going to face death, if Christ doesn't return before that. But when we go through that valley, Jesus said, because of his death we can have life. Jesus went through it. He died a ghastly death. He knows what it's like.

'Three young men took their own lives. And we keep asking, why? Why? The most precious possession we've got is not money, not even freedom, although that's very precious to you fellas. Our most precious possession is our life. Once that's snuffed out, what is there more? We can't bring it back. Those three lads were only in their early twenties and they've gone into eternity. For what? That question digs into me all the time.'

His eyes swept round the hall and he clenched his hands on the lectern: 'The Governor is trying to improve things and so are the staff, so for God's sake, don't do things like this. It was a tragedy to comfort that mother yesterday and to hear her cry, and to feel so helpless, "What is your life? It's only a mist that appears for a little while and then vanishes." What can I offer that mother?'

He looked round. No one moved. No one spoke.

'God is speaking through this tragedy. But some of you have built up a wall and say God should never have let it happen.' Noel paused.

'God didn't let it happen. Human nature did. When that cell door was jacked off finally last Friday night, there were tears of frustration running down the face of one of the Officers because he couldn't get in quickly enough to drag them out....'

Suddenly there was a stir amongst the prisoners. A loud booing interrupted him. It echoed round the Chapel. Its sneer filled the room. Noel locked his hands together and shouted, 'Ah yes, you can make noises, but you ask some of the lads up there. They saw that Officer. And he did get in, in the end. But it was too late.'

As quickly as it had begun, the booing stopped and Noel carried on: 'You're so cynical, some of you. You have a silly, stupid grin on your faces because you haven't faced up to what your life's all about. And the sooner you do, lads, the sooner you'll find fulfilment. We all get confused. We've got no security and no sanctuary. But,' and he paused, 'there is sanctuary at the cross. This is the great message of the Christian church. That Jesus took your place and my place on the cross. His one desire is that you trust him.'

His voice was quiet. 'I'll tell you a story. There was once a great King at a big court. He had servants and everything. And he had a jester whom he called his "Fool". One day the King gave the "Fool" a gift of a golden rod. "You are my best and most faithful servant," he said. "Keep this rod and only give it away if you ever meet a greater 'Fool' than yourself."

'The years passed and they both grew old. Then the time came that the old King was dying. He sent for his "Fool" who was by now bent with age.

'"Fool", he said, "I'm going on a long journey." The "Fool" cleared his throat, "Master, have you made any preparations?"

'There was a long silence. Then the king said, "No." The "Fool" bowed his head. "Excuse me, sir." And he went from the room. When he returned he was carrying the golden rod. He put it on the bed cover and gestured with his hand towards the king. "Take it, sir," he said. And there was silence in the room.'

The silence too was intense in the chapel. Noel said, 'Each one of us has to go on that journey. God grant us the ability and power to be prepared.' He gestured behind him to the great wooden cross with the figure of the risen Christ carved upon it, the arms outstretched in welcome.

'God comes to us and says, "Repent. Turn from your old ways and old life. Begin again." I remember when I was seventeen years old. I had a job in the Royal Victoria Hospital, Belfast and I saw suffering and death. It moved me. I met a man who had had thirty-four operations. He told me he'd got peace because he had Jesus in his life. And then that man died. I couldn't forget him so in the end I knelt down in my little back bedroom in Roden Street and I asked to follow Jesus myself.'

He paused and waited. Hundreds of eyes were fixed on him. 'It was then I remembered a verse that made me warm inside. Jesus said, "He who comes to me, I will never cast out."'

## Epilogue

# Salford 1982

### 'That the Son of God might be glorified.'

A few nights later Norma suddenly woke up. She sat bolt upright in bed and peered through the darkness at the pale glimmer coming through the curtains. Why had she woken up so early? Noel was breathing evenly beside her and she kept very still so as not to waken him. She turned over carefully and tried to go to sleep again. But it was no use.

As she sat up in bed, completely awake, she remembered her joy when the Chinese doctor at Christie's had given her the 'all-clear'. Her cancer was dead. And buried. She leaned against the pillows and thought back to their agony at East-church. All those deaths in the family: first their baby lost, then Noel's father died, then her mother, then the cancer. And there had been other, older memories to trouble Noel. His brother Stanley dying before he was born, Mac's death at The Royal Victoria, Sammy's death on the football field in Belfast. It had all been too much for them. It had broken them. Eastchurch had been their Gethsemane.

She remembered the day when the prisoner, Karl, had knocked on her front door on the Eastchurch campus and asked if he could carve a name-plate for her house.

'Bethany,' she had whispered back.

And later on, when she finally turned to the Bethany story in John chapter 11 and read about Lazarus being raised from the dead, a verse had leaped out of the page at her: 'Not unto death...this sickness is not unto death.' Words that strode round the room and sent her running to the window to read them again. 'Not unto death.' It was the beginning of a hope that had seeded and grown and flourished. 'Not unto death.'

She smiled in the darkness and snuggled into the pillow.

Unbidden the rest of that verse came into her mind: '...this sickness is not unto death, but that the Son of God might be glorified.' She frowned. It had never struck her before but the more she thought about it, the more appropriate the whole verse seemed.

She'd looked death in the face at Eastchurch. And something in Noel had died there, something deep and spiritual. But somehow they had come through and started to live again. God had promised it wasn't unto death and they hadn't died. They'd lived on and worked and....Suddenly it dawned on her. The second half of the verse was a promise, too. They hadn't died and the reason was because—no—she wasn't bold enough to believe *that*! A quiet insistence prodded her on. But she and Noel were too insignificant. Too ordinary. And yet Lazarus had been ordinary, too. Except that no one is ordinary.

At last she nodded. Yes. It was so. The reason they hadn't died was because God had planned...she drew her breath sharply. God had planned to glorify his Son through their lives. Through their sufferings. Was it too much to believe?

What was it Noel had said that day of the cell fires? 'What is life all about? And death?'

She leaned back on the pillows and a quiet peace welled up in her. So Life was not a meaningless hurtle through hollow days with the darkness of death its boundary; death was not a bracelet around life. No. The cross put a stop to that. When Jesus was raised from the dead he made a path of light, leading from his life, through death, into eternity. And those with the faith could walk on it. Slowly she raised her cupped hands into the air and her spirit cried out in the night: 'Glory to God!'

# Light Through Prison Bars

JENNY COOKE

KINGSWAY PUBLICATIONS
EASTBOURNE

This book is dedicated to all those who give
their time and energy to bring light into prison.

# Acknowledgements

Noel and I would like to thank the following people:
  Tony Collins, literary agent
  Francis Cooke, some interviews
  Michael Deaves, formerly of Prison Office Press
    Office
  Edward England, literary agent
  Robin Halward, Governor of Strangeways
  John Hargreaves, Assistant Chaplain-General
  Beryl Pipes, for secretarial work
  Susan, Helen and Rebekah Proctor.

## Contents

# Author's Preface

*Light Through Prison Bars* is the second book about Noel Proctor, prison chaplain, and his wife Norma. It is a sequel to the first, *The Cross Behind Bars*, which was published in 1983, and goes on reprinting.

This second book takes Noel and Norma's story on from 1983 to the opening of the new Strangeways prison in 1994. The period of Noel's professional life (1970–1982) is briefly referred to in Chapter 5 and fully covered in *The Cross Behind Bars*. Yet *Light Through Prison Bars* also looks back to Noel's early years in Belfast and to his life as a teenager at home with his parents. Some readers may find this surprising in a sequel, although much of the material is new and only a very few incidents are taken from the first book. I have done this for two reasons: I wanted this second book to stand alone for a new generation of readers, and to show how Noel became the man he is today. And I wanted this story to live again for people who have read and enjoyed the first book, and to remind them of Noel's early life.

*Jenny Cooke*
*October 1995*

# Foreword

I have worked closely with Noel Proctor during two periods of my twenty-one-and-a-half years in Her Majesty's Prison Service, from mid-1984 to mid-1988, when I was Deputy Governor at HMP Manchester, more commonly known as Strangeways, and from September 1992, when I returned to the prison as Governor, until the time of writing this in March 1995.

Noel's impact on the prison community has been and continues to be immense. That community over the years is many thousands strong, embracing as it does prisoners and their families, staff and their families, and all the many visitors who come as professionals or in a voluntary capacity. Yet Noel's influence reaches further still, through newsletters, through videos, through this book and the earlier one (*The Cross Behind Bars*) to the thousands of people who believe that all of us, whether we are connected with prisons or not, have some responsibility towards those in prison—a responsibility which condemns the crime but not the criminal, and in the interests of our society seeks to encourage every prisoner to find a way of life which avoids crime.

Why has Noel made such an impact?

- Because he combines an acceptance of situations and people with a passionate desire for change for the better.
- Because he seeks for and nurtures the good in everyone, with his (as his wife Norma described it in her journal) 'naive faith in human nature'.
- Because of his commitment and sense of duty.
- Because he cares.
- But above all because of his faith. He has had a far from easy life, but his faith has enabled him to cope with everything and has made him ever stronger.

This moving account of Noel and his work cannot fail to inspire all who read it.

I am glad to have this opportunity to thank Noel publicly for all his support and care for me over the years.

Robin Halward
*Governor HM Prison Manchester*
*March 1995*

# *Prologue*

## Buckingham Palace—9 March 1993

The air struck chill as Noel shut the front door behind him. 'You got everything?' he said in a half-whisper to his two daughters, who were waiting near the car. They looked over to him. 'Come on, Dad. It's freezing.'

'Better not miss the train, Dad.'

Noel grinned. 'Let's be off then. London here we come.'

The three of them climbed into the car and he drove away through the quiet streets to Piccadilly Station.

The bustle of parking, ticket buying, finding seats and sitting down carefully so as not to crease their best clothes was soon over. Noel leaned back and contemplated his two daughters. He was glad Helen and Becky were with him, even though he was sorry Susan had not been able to come as well, because she had an exam to take that day. Who would have thought in the old days that the paper boy from the back streets of Belfast would have fathered such a gang of beautiful girls? Helen caught his eye and he smiled back. Each of them had Norma's red hair, though Susan's was dark, Helen's auburn and Becky's a bright, reddish gold.

'Drink sir?' The British Rail steward hovered at his elbow with a trolley.

Noel started. 'Er, yes. Tea please, if you have it.'

The train gathered speed and raced beyond Stockport and Macclesfield, past gardens of daffodils and through fields greyish-green in the early light. He leaned back and drank the tea. The girls were chattering together and he felt quiet, but quietly excited also. It was going to be a day to treasure; a day in which to let his mind slip back into the past. Norma would have been so thrilled to have been coming with them. And what would his father have said to a son who was at this moment travelling to London to be honoured with the MBE by the Queen at Buckingham Palace? Noel half-smiled as he remembered back to those early teenage years in Roden Street, West Belfast.

Early one evening his father had heaved himself out of the fireside chair in the back room. Noel had sidled in, hoping not to be noticed.

'That you, Noel! Where've yer been?'

'Er, out. Selling papers. Messing about.'

'Oh you have, have you!' And his father rolled up his shirt sleeves until the tattoo on his forearm stood out blue and bulging in the firelight. 'Messing about with that Davey. I told yer. Police were at his house last night!'

'I didn't pinch the bike, Dad, and anyways, Davey's all right and . . . '

'No!' His father unbuckled his belt, holding his trousers up with one hand while the belt flopped in the other. He lowered his head and lurched towards Noel, grabbed him and shook him. 'Don't bring no trouble on this house!' he shouted. 'Remember the hole from which you were dug, lad. Remember it.'

'Yes, Dad.'

There was a short pause. His father sucked his breath in. 'Oh, get on with you!' He pushed Noel away and put the belt back on. Suddenly he swung round and Noel jumped. 'Remember it!'

Now as the train travelled on Noel gazed through the window without seeing the view. Yes, his father would have been pleased and proud of him today. All at once Noel chuckled. Becky touched his arm. 'What are you laughing at, Dad?'

'Oh, I was just thinking how's when my old mum and dad came to London once when I'd passed my exams at the Church Army College. And they were coming to the Commissioning Service and I introduced them to Donald Lynch, the Principal, just too late realising how Dad had left his teeth in a glass by the bed upstairs. He hadn't a bar in his grate! It gave Donald Lynch quite a start, I can tell you!'

They all laughed and Noel relaxed in his seat.

Yes, he had come a long way since those days. His father had spoken more wisely than he knew when he had challenged Noel never to forget his roots: his life's work, his purpose and his meaning had all grown up with him from those hard and communal years in Belfast. His call to serve the Lord as a prison chaplain drew strength and understanding from those early experiences. Norma, his wife, had come from a similar background. She had understood so much, so very much . . .

'Dad?' Helen's voice was urgent.

'Mmm?'

'We'll be there soon. What'll you say if she speaks to you?'

'Who?'

The two girls groaned. 'The Queen, of course!'

'Oh, not to worry. I'll think of something.'

So the three of them got off the train at Euston and took a taxi to Buckingham Palace, chatting excitedly all the way. When its mellowed and columned magnificence came into view they gradually fell silent. As they climbed up the palace steps, mingling with the well-dressed crowd, Noel said to himself, 'Dad, you never thought your son would ever get to this place. Fancy the paper boy from the back streets of Belfast coming here.' He smiled to himself, tongue in cheek. 'I should have brought my cornet and played them all a tune!'

# Part One

## A Life's Work

*'And we know that in all things God works for the good of those who love him, who have been called according to his purpose . . . to be conformed to the likeness of his Son' (Romans 8:28–29).*

# 1

## *The Cornet*

On the 12th July 1947 Noel was up early and joined the Boys' Brigade Brass Band, ready to march in the Orangemen's Parade. All the bands from West Belfast massed until the signal was given and the parade started. They marched for four hours, past narrow streets decorated red, white and blue, with bunting and Union Jacks waving; under the huge wooden archways erected over Sandy Row, with the words 'Remember 1690' and 'King William of Orange' emblazoned on it; past the smouldering remains of bonfires that had burned effigies of the Pope the night before.

Behind the bands came the row of marching Orangemen, each one clutching his black-backed Bible. 'King Billy's Day' meant a day off work, chips and bags of sweets, hazy remembrances of the siege of Derry and the Battle of the Boyne, when the Catholic James 2 of England was finally defeated by the Protestant soldiers, under William, Prince of Orange.

Noel was the solo cornet player in the 46th Old Boys' Band and was kept fairly busy with his music. His friend, Jimmy Robinson, played next to him. Their band leader dropped his baton and gave them a few minutes off playing. Jimmy looked at Noel: 'What's it like living in Roden Street?'

'What d'yer mean?'

'Well, with all them Catholics moving in round yer.'

Noel rested his cornet on his shoulder and rubbed his mouth. 'Well, we live on the Protestant side of the Grosvenor Road, and anyways, most of 'em live in the Falls Road and I'm used to cycling up that way.'

'Why?'

'Well I sell newspapers at the hospital.'

'Which one?'

'Royal Victoria.'

'What they like?' asked Jimmy.

'Who?'

'Catholics.'

'They're all right. We never think of 'em as any different from us. My mum and dad's friendly with all the neighbours and them with us. We never think about what religion they are. Why?'

Jimmy frowned. 'There's no Catholics round us.'

The band leader gave a sign with his baton and Noel raised his cornet to his lips. 'They're all right,' he said.

'Well what you marching for then?' asked Jimmy.

''Cos I'm in the band, you idiot. What you marching for?'

Jimmy grinned. ''Cos I like playing in the brass band.'

So off they went, to a rousing tune and laughter in the crowd; two teenagers, soon lost in the surging marchers and onlookers.

'Noel?'

'What?'

'Do you want to join the Orange Order?'

'Dunno. Do you?'

'Dunno.'

But as the weeks went past Noel began to worry about being in the brass band. He had become interested in Christianity now and surely Christians were supposed to be involved with things like bands and influence their friends to join the church, weren't they? Noel sighed. He could not imagine any of his friends wanting to join the local parish church. 'Always arguing about infant baptism and confirmation,' said his mother.

And then there was the question of joining the Orange Order. They were a nice enough crowd, but he was not sure.

So one Saturday afternoon, after he'd finished playing in the band before the football match began, he went for a cycle to the river. He dropped his ancient bike into the long grass and threw off his jacket. It was hot and the river banks were a mass of dusty dandelions and red campion. He lay down in the grass and listened to a lark singing. All at once he raised himself on one elbow: 'But I don't want to leave the band,' he said to himself. 'I like being in it. I *want* to stay in it.' He lay back again. Playing the cornet was one of the few things he was good at. 'And I like marching in parades and playing at the football matches.'

He could just imagine Jimmy's face if he told him he was leaving. What on earth would the others say? 'Stuck-up!' 'You can't leave. You're the solo cornet player!' 'Flippin' heck!' 'Religious nut!'

Noel stared out across the water. So why was he making all this fuss anyway? It was as if all the time someone were giving him a gentle tug at the elbow and saying in his ear, 'Don't stay in the band. There's nothing wrong with it, but I want you to leave it.'

'Why?' asked Noel. He had been asking 'why' for weeks, and there was still no answer to it. He hauled himself to his feet and flung a stone into the water. It sank at once.

The sun was lower in the sky now and he turned to go. He put his jacket on, picked up the bike from the long grass and then grasped the cornet case. He clambered onto the bike, steering with one hand and carrying his cornet under his other arm. He would have to hand the cornet in if he left. He grasped it all the tighter.

He cycled slowly and by the time he got to Roden Street it was quite late. He cycled past the houses at the top, past their neat front gardens and red brick walls. Then he came to his end of the street. They didn't have gardens. Slowly he got off his bike, cradling the cornet case in his arms, and opened the front door. He had made his mind up. He knew what he was going to do.

The following Friday evening there was a band practice. Noel hardly spoke to the family over tea. He was still smarting from the reaction of the lads at work when he told them he was not going to the bookie's at dinner times any more. 'You'll have to place yer own bets. I'm through with all that now.' There had been various mutterings of 'kill-joy' and 'religious maniac'. They didn't send him to Coventry, but they were a bit cool. He knew they would get over it in time, but he sighed. Life was becoming rather hard going.

He waited until the band practice was over and then stood up in the lull while everyone was getting their breath back.

'There's something I'd like to say.'

But no one took any notice, so he cleared his throat and tried again. 'I like being in the band, but, er . . . I'm handing in my resignation.'

'What? When?'

'As from now.'

'What the heck for?'

'Well I'm, er, a Christian now and I feel there's other things I ought to be doing.'

The silence hung heavy in the air. Noel looked round. If only someone would say something.

'But you're the solo cornet player!'

Noel bit his lip. 'Yes. I'm sorry.'

'Sorry!'

'Aw come on, Noel. Don't leave.'

'Don't go, Noel.'

They all tried, even Jimmy, to persuade him to stay. But he stuck to his guns. Several of the lads cold-shouldered him on his way past them.

Jack, the band leader, said nothing as Noel handed over the cornet in its case. Jack took it out and examined it closely. It gleamed in the electric light. 'I've taken care of it, sir,' said Noel.

'I can see that,' said Jack. He put the cornet back in its case, and snapped it shut. Then he turned away, and never gave Noel a second glance. Noel hovered for a moment and then turned to go. Out of the corner of his eye he saw Jack shaking his head, and then he was out through the door and into the street.

He walked along, pushing his bike. It felt funny without the cornet case to carry. There was nothing much to do and no one to walk with, so he might as well go home.

He meandered along, one hand thrust deep into his pocket, his shoulders hunched. The bike wobbled over the cobbles in the gutter as he plodded on, one grey stone after another. Idly he kicked at a sweet paper, and it fell down the grid. So what was he going to do at the weekends now? He shrugged and sighed deeply. He heard some footsteps running behind him, but did not bother to look round. Kids chasing, probably.

'Noel! Noel!' He stopped and looked round quickly. Who on earth . . . ? Then he saw Jimmy puffing along down the street, waving to him.

Noel's face lit up. 'Hello, Jimmy.'

'Hello. Can I walk with you?'

'Yes. Course.'

They walked on a bit. Jimmy seemed stuck for words and would not look at Noel. At last Jimmy stopped. 'You'd tremendous courage back there, Noel.'

Noel shrugged. 'Aw, no I hadn't. Anyway, I don't feel very brave now.'

Jimmy drew breath and then his words all came out in a rush. 'Well, I want what you've got!'

'Pardon?'

'I want it.'

Noel stopped dead and his bike scraped on the pavement. 'What?'

'Being a Christian.'

Noel put his hand on Jimmy's shoulder. 'You do?'

'Yes. I made my mind up as I was running after you.'

'Oh Jimmy! That's wonderful!'

They stood together on the pavement, grinning at each other and then shook hands. Noel slapped Jimmy on the back. 'Good for you, mate.'

Jimmy grinned. 'I've left the band too. Tell you what, I'll come and call for you tomorrow afternoon.'

'Shall we go on a bike ride together?'

'Yes. Smashing.'

They went off home in the twilight. Noel held his head high and his eyes shone. He was really glad he had said what he had said after the band practice now.

# 2

## The Hallelujah Postman

The following afternoon Jimmy was round at the Proctors' as soon as dinner was over, his brown eyes bright with excitement.

'Hey, Noel! You'll never guess what!'

'What?'

'My mum says she knows a chap called Billy Johnson.'

'You mean the postman?'

'Yes. He told her about a male voice choir at Sandy Row Methodists. Oh, and he runs meetings and things. So why don't we ask to join the choir?'

Noel chortled and slapped Jimmy on the back. 'Why not indeed!'

'It's not quite as good as the band . . . '

'But it's the next best thing!'

So the two lads cycled off to Sandy Row. As they turned into the Row, they saw a wiry little man getting off his bike outside the Methodist building. Jimmy touched Noel on the arm. 'That's him.' They crossed the road and leaned their bikes against the wall, and then slowly walked over to him. Noel pushed Jimmy in front of him. Jimmy cleared his throat. 'Excuse me, sir, but we'd, er, like to join the, er, choir.'

'Please,' added Noel.

Billy Johnson turned round. His eyes twinkled behind his National Health glasses and he took

Jimmy's hand and shook it for ages. 'Bless you, lads,'
he said. Then he took Noel's hand and pumped it up
and down. 'Well, can you sing, lads?'

'Noel can play the cornet,' blurted out Jimmy and
Noel dug him in the ribs.

'Jimmy played in a band as well, sir.'

Billy ran a hand through his crisp greying hair and
then beckoned them to follow him into the hall at the
side of the church.

Suddenly he swung round: 'But do you know the
Lord?'

Noel and Jimmy halted in their tracks, almost falling
over one another and Jimmy went pink. Noel stepped
forward. 'Yes, sir. We do.'

Billy looked at Jimmy. 'And when did you get to
know the Lord?'

'Last night, sir.'

A smile lit up Billy's face. 'Bless you both.'

They got into the hall and Billy took off his jacket.
'Give us a hand with these tables, will you? We're
having a meeting tonight.' After a while they had all
the tables down one side of the hall and the chairs put
in rows in front of the stage. Billy was whistling 'The
Old Rugged Cross' and the two lads joined in the
chorus, Noel singing tenor and Jimmy, bass.

While they were singing Noel noticed Billy had
stopped whistling and was standing with his head on
one side, listening to them. 'What is it, sir?'

But Billy would only smile and shake his head.
'You're good at singing, you two, aren't you?' was all
he'd say.

Billy brewed some tea and opened a paper bag of
sandwiches and shared them with the lads. They sat
round the rough wooden table together, munching the
potted meat sandwiches and then sucking some treacle
toffees that Jimmy found in his pocket.

Noel listened wide-eyed as Billy told him about what went on at the Methodist church. Night after night was crammed with meetings: the Bible class, the men's meeting, the Saturday night open-airs, the follow-up visiting, the male voice choir practice, the visits made to other churches. And Billy, it seemed, had a hand in them all.

He seemed to grow a bit taller as he told Noel and Jimmy about it all. 'Best thing of all, lads, is the half-night of prayer.'

'The what?'

'We have 'em every now and again after the open-air on a Saturday night. They're wonderful. But,' he wagged a finger at the lads, 'no girls allowed at the half-night of prayer. I'm not having no girls hanging around here after midnight.'

Jimmy smothered a giggle. As if he and Noel were bothered about girls! They sat on at the table, looking up at Billy.

Finally Billy stood up and put his jacket on over his hand-knitted pullover.

'I must be getting along. Shall I see you two again?'

'Oh, yes,' said Noel and Jimmy together.

'And you like singing?'

'Yes.'

'Cheerio then.'

'See you tonight.'

'What a smashing bloke,' said Noel on the way home. 'I wish I was like him.'

'Yes,' said Jimmy. 'My mum says he's always singing "Hallelujah" when he delivers her letters. And if he goes on the bus at weekends, do you know what he does?'

'No.'

'He starts talking about being a Christian to the people he's sitting next to. My mum's seen him.'

Noel was silent and hunched over the handlebars. 'I could never do that.'

'No, neither could I.'

They got to Roden Street. 'See you tonight then.'

'Bye.'

At 8.00pm prompt they were back in the Methodist Hall. Billy and a few lads were singing on the stage and several men were dotted about on the rows of chairs.

'Come on up here!' called Billy, and they stumbled up onto the stage, Noel trying to hide behind Jimmy. It seemed to Noel as if the whole population of Sandy Row was gazing at him. He opened his mouth to sing and no sound came out. He swallowed and tried again. Then an arm came round his shoulders. It was Billy's. 'You're doing fine,' Billy whispered. 'Wonderful voice.' Noel glowed, opened his mouth and sang as he'd never sung before.

When they had finished the hymn, sparse clapping came from the hall. "Burdens Are Lifted at Calvary",' called out Billy, and they began to sing again.

As the evening wore on the hall filled up. And after closing time it got really full. One by one, Billy let the singers on the stage have a 'go' at talking about their faith. 'Just for a minute, mind,' he said.

Noel didn't have a notion of how to speak in public. He stuttered and stumbled over the words. 'Well, I once won a Sunday school prize. It was a big black Bible. Inside I read these words: "He who comes to me, I will in no wise cast out." This made an impression on me. Then when I was selling newspapers on the wards at the Royal Victoria I met a man called Mac. He'd had to have thirty-four operations. But he was always cheerful. When I asked him why he'd helped another patient, he said it was because he wanted to. But when I asked him again, he said . . . ' Noel swallowed. 'He said it was because he'd got Jesus in his life. Jesus had given him peace.' Noel stopped. 'Then afterwards, he . . . he died. And then I had a friend—a footballer called Sammy—and he died too. It all made such an impression on me. These deaths. And our Stanley's death, my brother, when I was only a few days old. I couldn't make it out.'

Quite a few men were listening by this time. Noel faltered and then hurried on. 'The Sunday school teacher said you met your Maker when you died. And I realised I'd never talked to God before, so in the end, one night, I knelt down on the bit of mat between the two beds in our back bedroom and asked God if I could be a Christian. Er, that's it.'

Noel stepped back from the mike and hid behind Jimmy. He wiped his forehead with the back of his hand. Phew! Thank goodness that was over.

Billy got the audience singing and clapping, even a tear or two flowed, and then, as if by miracle, everyone was utterly quiet while he prayed.

As he came to the end of his prayer, someone shouted out at the back of the hall, 'Holy Joe!'

'Shut up!' called out several of the men.

Billy stopped praying at once, motioned the singers to sing again and then ran down to the back of the hall.

Noel watched him. How on earth did Billy keep all this lot in order? He could tell a lot of them had rolled in from the pub, and even one or two of his dad's cronies were there. Yet they all sat quietly enough.

Billy was leading a drunk chap back with him. 'You Holy Joe,' sang the drunk.

'Poor old man,' whispered Jimmy. Tattered, torn and smelling, the drunk was led up to the platform.

'We're glad to see Ted here tonight, aren't we?' shouted Billy.

'Yes!' roared the crowd.

'He likes to tease me and call me Holy Joe, but you don't mean it, do you?'

The drunken Ted attempted to shake Billy by the hand. 'No, no,' he said, and swayed very close to the mike. Billy had his arm round Ted, and keeping him upright, turned to the crowd. 'The Lord Jesus is pleased to see Ted here tonight, isn't he?'

'Yes!' roared the crowd.

'And he can utterly change Ted, can't he?'

'Yes!' roared the crowd again, and then they all stood to their feet and sang the closing hymn.

Later, when everyone was going home, Noel noticed Billy take Ted into a back room, and he followed. In the back room Billy was giving Ted strong tea and was washing his face. 'Come on now,' he said and took off his own jacket and put it round the drunk's shoulders. Billy darted round the drunk, preaching to him, cleaning him up, praying for him and giving him tea all at the same time. He glanced up and saw Noel.

'But he can't understand a thing you're saying about putting his trust in the Lord,' said Noel.

Billy sagged for a minute and then brightened up. 'Use every opportunity,' he said and then, 'Do you want to come with me and get him settled for the night?'

Noel nodded.

So Billy put one arm round Ted, and Noel supported him on the other side. Ted let them lead him out, grumbling and grousing all the time.

'Come on, Ted lad,' said Billy. 'There's nothing doing here. Your old cronies can't take you back to their homes. Their missuses wouldn't have it.' So Ted gave in and came with them.

Jimmy Robinson pushed through the crowd at the

door and grabbed Noel's arm. 'Hang on a minute, Noel. I want you to meet Jim Long.'

Noel glanced up, grinned at Jimmy, said 'hello' and shook Jim Long's hand with his left hand. 'See you tomorrow, lads. Sorry I can't stop now. Billy needs me.' Then they plunged outside. It was dark and cool and quiet after the heat and bustle inside.

They walked slowly down the pavement and Ted swayed between them, shuffling along in his dusty hobnail boots. The toe cap was flapping on one and some newspaper was peeping through. Then he stopped and lurched forward. Billy steadied him and propped him against a lamp-post. Ted leaned forward and retched into the gutter, and Billy kept his hand on Ted's shoulder. Noel stood his ground, but turned his head away.

After a bit Ted straightened up; his face was grey and the bristle trembled on his chin. He tried to speak, but the words would not come. Billy put his arm round Ted. 'Don't worry, lad.' And off they went at a snail's pace, until they came to the doss house in Matilda Street.

Noel had heard of the doss house before, but had never been inside. No matter how drunk or how late back any of the menfolk were in Roden Street, their wives always took them in and quietly shut the front door on their misery. Only down-and-outs went to the doss house.

Billy pushed open the door and a bleary-eyed janitor half got up from a wooden chair that looked as if it had seen better days in the schoolroom. Billy took out some silver from his pocket and the coins clinked on the bare table. 'Couple of nights, please, and food as well.' The janitor nodded and waved them past and then turned back to his newspaper. He had obviously seen Billy before.

They went down the passage to a big room at the
back. It was cold and smelled. Tramps lay all around,
some covered with newspaper, some on dirty sack
mattresses. Noel noticed a spare place and they lay
Ted down on a mattress there. He started snoring
almost at once. Billy undid the laces on his boots and
arranged his jacket over him. Noel stared at the jacket.
Billy had been wearing it earlier in the evening and now
it covered Ted's stained trousers and greenish jumper
that was more gaping holes and strands of wool than
jumper.

Billy tugged him gently by the arm. 'Come on, lad.'
They went out briskly and passed a foul little kitchen.
'Bread and soup,' said Billy and jerked his thumb in the
direction of the grease-spattered kitchen.

Then they were in the street again and the fresh air
was sweet. Billy sighed. 'The doss house is grim, but it's
better than nothing.' They walked on in silence for a
bit. 'That's why I make such a stand against alcohol,'
said Billy suddenly. Noel thought about his dad and
nodded. 'If I once touch a drop all them men who come
every week, they'd laugh at me.' Billy sighed again. 'I
know some of 'em laughs at me anyway, but it's a
different kind of laugh, and anyways, I don't mind. If
I can point 'em towards Jesus, I don't mind. And they
know where to come when they're in trouble.'

Noel looked at Billy's white shirt sleeves and hand-
knitted pullover. 'Are you cold?'

Billy laughed. 'I've got a good missus. If I don't get
my jacket back,' he shrugged, 'I'll have to do a bit of
overtime and buy another.'

They came back to Sandy Row for their bikes and
Billy stopped and shook Noel by the hand for a long
time. 'Well lad, goodnight. Do you want to come to
Sandy Row tomorrow morning?'

Noel hesitated. 'I usually go to the parish church, but I could miss it.'

Billy shook his head. 'No lad, that's not the way. There's always the open-air on Saturday night. Shall I see you next week?'

'Yes, rather.'

'Cheerio then.'

'Cheerio, and thanks.'

Noel stood and watched Billy until he had cycled round the corner of the street. Then he climbed onto his bike and cycled home slowly. He was tired but glad, even though his arm ached from supporting Ted. He whistled to himself. Billy was just grand.

# 3

## The Call

One Friday evening Jimmy Robinson called for Noel as usual and they cycled off two abreast for Sandy Row. All of a sudden Noel slowed up. 'What's that noise?'

Jimmy listened. 'It's music, I think. Or is it someone speaking?'

They rounded the corner, then saw a crowd of men and boys clustered round a small rostrum. A girl was speaking into the mike, and behind her were two other girls and a few lads. Noel did not know any of the young people on the rostrum.

'What on earth . . . ?'

'Redeemed Testimony Band,' muttered Jimmy.

'What?'

'Baptist.' They leaned their bikes against the nearest garden wall and inched into the crowd. The girl who was speaking was taller than the other two. Noel gazed at her, oblivious of all the pushing, shoving and whistles. He watched as first her scarlet coat swung round, and then swung back again. She gripped the mike with both hands and was rather pale. Hanging from under her red coat was a froth of white lace. 'Bet she don't know her underskirt's showing,' giggled a lad next to Noel.

'Shut up!' he replied so fiercely that the lad moved off. Then she started to speak again, her voice quavering slightly. Noel gazed at her dark hair, burnished with red lights. 'Who's that?' he asked Jimmy.

'Jim Long's sister.'

'Who?'

'You know, you've met him at Sandy Row.'

'Oh yes.'

Jimmy was serious. 'Would you like to meet her?'

Noel shrugged. 'If you like.' He took care not to be seen staring at the girl again. Yet he made sure he was near Jim Long when the clapping died down and the group began to pack up their things.

'This is Norma,' said Jim Long. 'And Eileen and Christine, her friends.'

'How do you do?' said Noel, looking at Norma.

Norma tossed her head. 'Pleased to meet you.' Then she and the other two girls burst into a fit of giggles and Noel went pink.

'Come on, you lot,' said Jimmy. 'Let's go and see if Billy's about.'

Norma hung back and touched her brother on the arm. 'Who's that awful chap?'

Jim Long looked surprised. 'Noel Proctor. He's all right.' Jim stroked his chin. 'I thought I'd invite him to the Christian Endeavour Society. Do you mind?'

'Mind? I'll never go again.'

But she and Eileen and Christine were there the very next Monday. Noel was the star of the evening. He sang a solo and then led the chorus-singing. He did all the actions to all the words and sang all the choruses twice. The people there loved it. All except Norma and Eileen and Christine, who sat on the back row.

'Isn't he awful!' said Norma in a low voice and sat on her hands. 'I'll *not* do any of those actions!'

Eileen grinned. 'He's coming over.'

Norma started flicking through her Bible, pretending not to notice him. Noel cleared his throat. 'Hello.'

Norma tossed her glowing hair. 'Hello, Noel.'

'There's just something I wanted to tell you. It's about last Friday evening.'

Norma tensed and looked up. 'Did I speak all right?'

Noel grinned. 'Great. You were very brave.'

Norma shrugged.

'Yes you were.' Then Noel was serious. 'But did you know your underskirt was showing?'

'Well, really!' said Norma on the way home. 'Isn't he the limit? Who does he think he is?'

Her brother chortled in the darkness. 'Well you'd better get used to him, 'cos he's coming to Christian Endeavour every week now. He's been asked to be on the Look-Out committee. If anyone can ginger up Christian Endeavour, he can.'

Norma groaned. 'Oh no!' And she and Christine and Eileen burst into fits of laughter.


So life continued for Noel, with his job as a cloth-cutter at Philips and Jones during the day, and most evenings spent at meetings or singing in the male voice choir. Yet underneath this busyness a longing grew within him, until it was like a voice calling him each day, very quiet but quite insistent. The call was not clear cut, but it had to do with his wanting to be like Billy; wanting to make something out of his life; wanting to get along-side the lads and men he knew so well in among the back streets, factories, churches and red-brick terraces of West Belfast. He wanted to tell them about Jesus; that there was something more to life than working so hard all week that they had to get drunk every Saturday night in order to forget it all.

He read deeply, particularly influenced by two books he had bought from the second-hand bookstall. One was about John Fletcher of Madeley, who had worn away his floorboards with his constant praying. The other was called *Helps to Holiness* by Commissioner Brengle of the Salvation Army.

In the end he became confused. Was God calling him to be like Billy and reach the men round him? Or to be like John Fletcher and be holy? Or to seek the power of the Holy Spirit like Brengle said? Or was God calling him to be a missionary?

He saw himself standing by a campfire in the jungle, with his Sunday school prize Bible in one hand. He was proclaiming with the other, making a huge embracing gesture, and somehow he seemed taller than all the Africans who were clustered shyly in the bushes. He preached his heart out: 'Repent . . . come to the Lord Jesus . . . be baptised . . . ' And they came, brown eyes trusting, and crowded round him, understanding the brash attempts he made at their language.

Noel closed his eyes. He could just imagine telling Billy. Yes, it was a lovely dream and perhaps one day. . .

The back door crashed downstairs. So it must be after 10.30pm and his dad had come home pretty well-oiled as usual. Noel could hear him muttering downstairs and then his slow, heavy tread upstairs. He paused on the tiny landing, hiccuped and then lurched into the front bedroom. Noel frowned in the darkness. Really, his dad was getting too bad these days. *Thank goodness I don't drink*, he thought.

He kept hearing the mumble of voices in his parents' bedroom and then their door opened. His mother was talking and then his dad said, 'First you moaning at me, and now there's that hypocrite son of mine who's always condemning me.' His dad flung his shoes onto the landing and they fell with a thump against the wall. Then the door slammed.

Noel lay very still for a long time. He tried to get to sleep, but couldn't. The dream about being a missionary in the jungle shrank and shrank until it seemed to fall into pieces round him. *How can I be a missionary if I can't even win my own dad?* he thought. The darkness was very still. It seemed to Noel as if he caught a whisper in the dark bedroom. 'How can you win your dad if you don't love him? If you don't forgive him? If you don't respect him?'

Noel sat up and then got out of bed. He pulled open the drawer of his chest and got out a hankie and blew his nose. After a while he rubbed his eyes. The trouble was, as fast as he rubbed them, they were wet again. He got back into bed again and thought for a bit. He knew what he would have to do. He shut his eyes and whispered, 'I'm sorry, Lord. I've made a right mess of things. I've been rotten about my dad.' He rubbed his eyes again. 'I don't know how to . . . please help me to talk to him . . . I really do want to respect him.' He lay quiet again and this time a sense of peace stole over him and he fell asleep.

It was quite late when he got home from work the next day, but his dad was back early from the pub. Noel wandered across the back room. 'Where's Mum?'

'In the parlour. At it again.'

'Stanley's photo?'

'Yes.'

Noel fell silent for a moment. His mother had never forgotten Stanley, the son who had died of diphtheria a few days after Noel was born. Even now she often stood in the parlour and gazed at his photograph for what seemed like hours. Then he said, 'Dad?'

'What?'

Noel swallowed and fixed his eyes on the hob. The words tumbled out. 'Dad, I want to go into full-time Christian work. I've thought a lot about it. I'd have to leave Philips and Jones and perhaps go to college or something.'

His dad sat dead still, gazing at the fire. Noel moved a step nearer. The words he wanted to say kept sticking in his throat, but he took a deep breath and forced them out. 'But, Dad, I want your blessing on it.'

There! It was said now. Silence hung between them in the back room, and then his dad's chair creaked as he struggled to get up. His eyes glinted in the firelight and he too seemed to have difficulty in getting his words out. Finally he said, 'Lad, I never thought you'd come and even talk to the likes of me about a thing like that.' He wiped his eyes with the back of his hand.

Noel went pink. His dad turned his head away and used the back of his hand again. 'I told her. I told your mum, "You'll be proud of that lad one day. You'll see."' He turned to face Noel again. 'You broke your legs often enough when you was small, but you're strong enough now. Bigger 'an me.'

Noel grinned. 'You wouldn't mind then?'

'Mind? No I would not!'

Noel grabbed his father by the hand and shook it hard, and then turned and ran upstairs two at a time. He felt warm all over, and in his heart he was singing as loud as he could.

Eventually Noel went to night school, passed his exams and was offered a place at the Church Army College in London, which he accepted. It was hard saying goodbye to so many friends and family; hard to leave them and the work they had shared behind.

Somehow, until that firm offer of a place came, he had not been quite sure he would get to London. So he had not said much about it to Billy and the others. They knew, of course, but as he would only be away a few weeks at a time, the break perhaps would not be very noticeable. He had seen Billy looking at him a

time or two though. And Noel knew the break was
coming.

It was the Saturday of the Orangemen's Parade and
Noel wandered to Sandy Row and saw Billy watching
the procession and went up to join him. He did not see
Noel at first. Noel swallowed and then touched Billy on
the arm. Billy swung round and his face lit up. He
shook Noel by the hand. 'Hello there, lad. How are
you?' He turned and gestured to the marchers. 'Look at
'em all, Noel. All carrying a Bible.'

'Yes, Billy, I . . . '

'Aren't you glad you left the band now, Noel?'

'Yes, but I . . . '

'I was so proud of you when you decided not to
march with the parade.'

'I'm not against them, Billy.'

'No, I know you aren't. And neither am I, lad.
They're our countrymen.' Billy stood proudly to attention as the strains of 'God Save Our Gracious Queen'
floated past. 'An' I'm proud to be British. But what I
says, lad, is, "Does what you do bring people to Jesus?
Does marching with the Orangemen honour Jesus
Christ?" An' if it don't, there's no point in belonging
to it, is there?' Billy stood back. His eyes were bright.
Men in the crowd kept waving to him. Noel had a lump
in his throat. All those men. And Billy had won so
many for Christ.

'Billy?'

He turned, 'Yes?'

'I'm leaving.'

Billy stared at the ground. 'When?'

'In September.'

They were silent.

'I'm going to college in London. It's definite.' But
Billy did not clap him on the back like his father had
done or scurry round telling people, like his mother

had done. Billy just looked up at Noel. 'I suppose I had heard about it. Well, you're a man now.' His shoulders sagged and he sighed. Then he looked up and said, 'You wouldn't think of not going . . . and sharing the leadership with me?'

But before Noel could answer, Billy shook his head. 'No, no. It wouldn't do. You go, lad.' He paused. 'I just wish that . . . ' He didn't finish, but turned and strode over to the church hall.

Noel followed him. 'I'll only be gone two years. And there's holidays. I'll be back then and be able to help you.'

But Billy did not look at him. He just put his hand on Noel's shoulder. 'Goodbye, lad.'

Noel stopped. 'But look here, I've not gone yet.'

Billy chuckled. 'Of course you haven't. Come on in and meet some new recruits.' Inside the hall was a knot of young lads. They were all about seventeen. They clustered round Billy, gazing up at him, their eyes bright, while he explained about the visiting scheme.

Noel hung back. Everything he knew, he had learned from Billy: how to visit the sick, to pray with them, to give up all his spare time, to lead a meeting, to preach, to testify. That was why he had put off telling Billy. He realised it now. He could not bear the hurt look veiled behind Billy's jokes.

So what was wrong with staying here, helping Billy, earning good money at Philips and Jones? He could go to Christian Endeavour with Jimmy, Jim Long, Norma, Eileen and Christine. It was just that he felt excited about going to London. And on top of that, there was the same insistent, gentle tug to go. He had felt it before—the night he had left the band, and even before that, on the night long ago when he had prayed to become a Christian. He knew. He *had* to go to London.

He looked round the little hall and smiled. It held
good memories. But he had to go on. He looked at the
lads clustered round Billy who was standing in the
middle of them, all gazing up at him. He turned
slowly, half-raised his hand in farewell, and went out
and pushed his way through the crowds towards home.

On the way home he met Norma. 'Hello there.'

'Hello, Noel.'

They stood looking at each other for a moment and
then sat down together on a garden wall. Norma put
her head on one side.

'What's this I hear about you going to college, Noel?'

'Yes, I am. In September. Church Army, in London.'

Norma smiled at him. 'That's wonderful.' She
wriggled her foot and then looked directly at him.
'I'm really pleased for you. I wish I could go to college.'

'Well, why don't you?'

'It's no good. I'm like you were. I left school at
fourteen, I've no "O" levels and I've got a good job
at the Post Office. My mum's a widow.'

Noel nodded. He understood all right. 'It'll come,
Norma. You've got to trust. The Lord'll bring it about.'

Norma giggled. 'You never miss an opportunity, do
you?'

'I beg your pardon?'

'To bring the Lord in!'

Noel went red. 'I am *not* always bringing him in!'

Norma patted his arm. 'Sorry, I didn't mean it really.
You've lots more nerve than me.'

Noel glanced at her. 'Will you take over my job as
leader on the Look-Out committee?'

Norma's eyes opened wide. 'Me? But I'm no good at
singing!'

Noel chuckled. 'You'd have to lead the choruses, *and*
use your hands for the actions. No more hiding on the
back row giggling at me.'

Norma flushed and Noel went on, 'I know I look funny.'

'You do *not*.'

Noel glanced at her. 'Oh thanks. By the way, can I write to you? About Christian Endeavour I mean.'

Norma said, 'Yes, all right. But I can't guarantee any replies. Well, I will reply, but not straight away.'

They got up to go. 'Shall I see you home?' asked Noel.

Norma shook her head. 'No, I'm on my way to Christine's.'

'Cheerio then.'

'Cheerio.'

Noel watched her go through the crowd, her red hair glinting in the sunlight. She was all right, was Norma.

# 4

## *And the Bike Came too*

The years at college were a challenge. Noel found he
enjoyed practising speaking at Hyde Park corner, but
life with the other students was not quite so straight-
forward. Somehow he did not feel as if he fitted in; as if
he did not belong to a world where you called the
others 'students' and not 'the lads'. However, he was
determined, settled down eventually and in June 1957
passed his exams with credits. He was commissioned as
a captain in the Church Army and promised to serve for
five years in the Durham Diocese.

It was while he was on the train coming home for a
fortnight's holiday after the end of his course that he
realised how much he was looking forward to seeing
Norma again. *I'm twenty-seven and I've never had a
proper girlfriend*, he thought. All the other girls he
knew were all right, but were nothing compared to
her. Every week she had written to him and he had
replied. She had been so faithful in that letter writing.
So, so lovely. His face grew pink as he thought about
her. *I'm going to say something to her*, he decided. *The
first night I see her, I'm going to speak.*

When Noel arrived home his mother and father
made a great fuss of him, and so did Robert, his
younger brother. Every evening he had invitations to
speak and at nearly every meeting he saw Norma. But

she was always at the other end of the room, or if they did start talking, her brother, and Jimmy Robinson, and Eileen and Christine were always clustered round them.

In the end it was the last night of the holidays and he still had not spoken to her. He arrived early at Jimmy Fowler's and soon all the Christian Endeavour gang were there. They talked and laughed and sang and ate. Noel kept glancing at Norma. She was wearing a big collar on her dress and an artificial velvet rose was pinned at her neck. She did not seem to notice him, but sparkled and laughed a lot. All too soon it was time to go home again and still he had not spoken.

Suddenly he thrust himself through the group and touched her on the sleeve. She turned round. Noel fixed his eyes on the rose. 'Can I see you home?'

'Thanks very much. Oh, but I always walk home with Eileen and Christine.'

'Oh, that's all right. I'll see them home too.'

The four of them set off walking home, Noel nearest the kerb, pushing his bike. First they saw Eileen home and Norma waited for him to say goodbye as well. But he said nothing, just doggedly pushed his bike along, his other hand thrust deep into his pocket. What on earth was he doing? At last they got to Christine's home in Sandy Row.

'Goodnight, Chris.'

'Goodnight.'

That just left the two of them and they walked all the way back to Norma's house. At last they got there.

'Well, goodnight,' said Norma.

'Wait a minute.' He leaned against his bike and his face was in shadow.

'What is it?'

'Well, there's just something I want to ask you, but first of all I'd better tell you . . . '

'What?'

Noel swallowed and took a deep breath. 'I love you.'

Norma stared at him. Her heart gave an enormous leap. It could not be true that Noel, the kingpin of Christian Endeavour, loved her.

She took a step nearer to him. 'Well I . . . '

But he interrupted her, his words tumbling out and jumbled up in his eagerness. 'You see, I'd like to marry you, only I've promised Church Army I'll work for them for five years, so I don't suppose you'd want to wait that long and I'm only home every six months, but if you did want to wait, I'll wait for you because you're the only girl I've had any dealings with, the only girl I've ever liked and now I know I love you, so will you marry me?'

The words hung in the air between them, opening up a whole new life to Norma, so bright, so unexpected, it sparkled like diamonds.

'Oh yes,' she breathed.

'Yes?'

'Yes. Yes. I feel the same about you. I think I love you.'

Noel took her hand. 'Do you really mean it?'

'Oh yes. I realised how much I missed you when you went to college. I couldn't understand at first, but when I realised, I said "goodbye" to my other boyfriend.'

They stared at each other. Noel held onto her hand tightly.

'I waited till tonight to ask you, in case you said, "Get lost!"'

'Oh no,' wailed Norma, remembering. 'You go back to Durham tomorrow.'

'I'll come round and see your mother first thing in the morning. Then we'll get engaged.'

'Engaged,' whispered Norma and clasped her hands

together. Then she said, 'By the way, who do you think you are? Jacob or someone?'

Noel flushed and then said, 'Well, you're not Leah anyway!'

'Who am I?'

'The most beautiful girl in the world.'

At last they said goodnight. Just as he was leaving she started to laugh and pointed to his bone-shaker of a bike. 'Did you have to propose leaning on your bike?'

'Well I needed the support!'

'And the bike came too!'

And so they parted. Noel cycled home, his heart bursting with song.

In her bedroom Norma lay awake a long time. She did not want to go to sleep in case she woke up and found it was all a dream.

But next morning she was just finishing her breakfast, when there was a knock at the front door. Her mother went to answer it and then she heard Noel's voice in the hallway. She swallowed her cup of tea and tried to sit still. She pushed her hands into her pockets and then took them out again. She jumped up, patted her hair, whirled round and then straightened her collar.

Suddenly the door opened and her mother led Noel into the room. 'Well,' said her mother. 'What's all this I've been hearing about you and Noel then?'

Norma blushed and opened her mouth, but Noel cut in quickly. 'I've explained everything to Mrs Long, I mean your mum, Norma, and she's very pleased.'

Mrs Long put her arm round Norma. 'I'm very pleased. Noel will be just right for you.'

Then her mother popped out of the room and he came and sat by Norma. 'I've got you a present,' he said and gave her a brown paper parcel. Norma opened it and the paper dropped unnoticed to the floor. Inside lay a brand new book: *Revelation* by J. B. Phillips. 'Oh, thank you!' she cried and looked at him shyly.

'Open it.'

Inside he'd written, 'With love from Noel.'

Later he had to dash for the boat to Liverpool. 'Write?'

'Of course.'

'See you at Christmas.' She watched him go cycling at speed down her road. At the corner he turned and waved. She waved back and then went indoors. If she wrote to him straight away, he would get it on Monday.

Their lives settled into a pattern: they saw each other every six months. While they were together they were in love, but when they had to be apart, they had to accept it, each believing the other to be called to put God and the job they were doing first.

Norma left the Post Office and was accepted by Musgrave Park Hospital for her nurse's training. 'I remember thinking all the way through the park on my first morning that I would never pass my exams,' she wrote to Noel. 'But I did. And now I've just got some wonderful news. I've won the prize for the exam in surgery! Fancy me, Dumdum, coming first! God is good, isn't he?'

Norma's letters were full of stories of the people she had nursed, of being late off duty so she could just see to that extra last patient. He was proud of her. She was really making something of her life. It was good that he had not pressed her to get married sooner and forget the idea of nursing. She was so obviously right for it.

As the five years of Church Army life drew to a close, Noel began to wonder what to do next. He loved life with the Church Army as he was his own boss. But he was not quite satisfied.

As he thought over his adult life, it seemed like one

long meeting, one long appeal, one long line of folk wanting to know more about Jesus, all interspersed with himself singing a solo, or playing the cornet, standing on soap boxes or beaches or narrow streets. He sighed and got up to make a pot of tea; he liked the life, yes, and he knew in his heart of hearts what his life was about. He was an evangelist. He rolled the word round his tongue. An evangelist.

He stared at the cup of tea and drank slowly. He had wanted to succeed, and he had. He had wanted God's power for service, and God had graciously given it to him. He had wanted to be like Billy, to make something of himself, to get off the big wheel that sucked you down, like had happened to so many of his mates when he had been a youngster in the tough end of Belfast. Where were they now? Some were in prison, he knew. A lot probably got drunk on Saturday nights, like their old dads had done before them. God had helped him, even though he did not deserve it.

He finished off the tea and then prayed, 'What do you want me to do?' The nagging thought that had kept coming back to him over the last few months, nudged at his sleeve again. He pushed it away hastily, knowing even as he did so that he was going to have to face it. 'Get ordained! In the Church of England! Oh no!' He would have to go to college again . . . and poor Norma had waited long enough. He had no money saved, and anyway he liked being his own man.

But by the end of the week Noel had decided: yes, he would go to theological college and get ordained. Norma was wonderful. 'I've still got a bit to go to complete my SRN. So perhaps it's best,' she said on the phone. 'And anyway, you'll be nearer to Belfast. Only a hop across the water from Birkenhead.'

'Could you get me a summer holiday job at the hospital? Then I can start saving up to get married.'

Norma was silent for a moment. 'Yes, as long as it's not Musgrave Park!'

'Why not?'

'Well, I'd not like to fall out with you over a patient!'

Noel was silent and then began to laugh. 'Well, what about the Royal Victoria?'

'I'll do my best.'

And so it was arranged. Noel would work every summer vacation at the Royal Victoria as a porter.

The two years at Birkenhead (1962–64) went by in fits and starts. Noel studied hard under Michael Hennel, burned the midnight oil, and ended up with a distinction in Old Testament studies, the only one in his year. Norma passed her SRN and was a staff nurse at Musgrave Park. They were able to see each other more often, but that made the waiting all the harder, and the settling down in between seeing each other all the more difficult.

One day Noel saw Norma off at the docks in Liverpool and she was very upset. 'I can't stand leaving you again. I'm getting too old. I'm sick of this waiting.' And she hung her head. Then she sailed away, a tiny hunched figure on the deck of the boat, gazing at the strip of water separating them.

He watched her go, heard the ship's horn and saw the seagulls flocking round the ship's stern. *Easy for them*, he thought, and jabbed at a stone with his foot. *They can fly*. He turned and strode away, his collar turned up against the wind, hands thrust deep into his pockets. He had decided what to do.

A few days later he rang her up. 'Hello, darling. Guess what! We can fix a date!'

'What? When?'

'Easter Tuesday any good?'

'But that's so near . . . yes, marvellous! But how did you manage it?'

'I wrote to the bishop and told him we *were* getting married then.' Noel swallowed and his voice fell. 'But er, Norma . . . '

'Yes?'

'I'll have to come back and do my finals here, in June.'

He waited, miserably aware of the tiny pause on the phone. Then she said, 'I don't care. It'll only be eight weeks and I can finish off at the hospital properly. We'll be married then anyway. Oh, it'll be lovely!'

Noel let out a gasp. He had wondered if she would be upset, but she was chatting on about a dress and whatnot.

'I've got plans for the honeymoon too!'

'Oh you have, have you!'

'Yes, a fortnight at Harriet and Derek's guest house in Dun-Laoghaire.'

'Oh, what a lovely idea! All the spring flowers'll be out.'

'Better take an umbrella as well!'

'Oh shut up!'

So they were married on 31st March 1964, and had a wonderful day. It seemed no time at all before Noel was back from college, working as a temporary porter at the Royal Victoria. He and Norma enjoyed those few months of summer before he was ordained at Michaelmas in Durham Cathedral. Their first home was at Haughton-le-Skerne where Noel was curate. Later he became Vicar of Byers Green, near Bishop Auckland. Their first two daughters, Susan and Helen, were born to them in these years, and the family thrived.

One day Noel was invited to speak at a mission meeting in Durham jail. The meeting went well and

Noel enjoyed it. Although he did not know it at the time, this turned out to be the start of twenty-five years as a prison chaplain in British prisons. This was to be a new chapter in their lives, which was to bring challenge, joy and unexpected heart-searching to them both.

# 5

# Prisons of the Mind
## 1970–1988

Whenever Noel looked back over his life in the early years of prison chaplaincy work, his first few months at Wandsworth stood out as a happy prelude to the harder times they were to have at Eastchurch Open Prison. It was at Eastchurch that a succession of tragedies rocked the family until each day became more difficult for Noel to drag himself through.

As a result of the shock suffered after an IRA bomb blast only streets away from Noel's parents' house, his father died of a heart attack in Belfast. Noel flew over to see him, but was a few hours too late. By the time his mother opened the door and took him upstairs, his father was already dead. Then Norma's mother had a stroke and needed to come and live with them at East-church. Norma struggled to look after her, but the strain was too much. Norma had a miscarriage and this loss of a child affected both Noel and Norma deeply.

However, they weathered these losses. Life settled down, Norma eventually had another baby girl, Becky, and everyone was happier for a while. Then one day, old Mrs Long died peacefully in her sleep. After the funeral, when they should have been trying to pick up the pieces and look forward to the future,

Norma was feeding the baby, white-faced. 'At least
Mum never knew,' she said. Noel looked across at
her and then down again. 'No,' he said. 'No.' Old
Mrs Long never did know that Norma had found a
lump in her breast one day while breast feeding. This
was diagnosed as cancer and Norma was now under-
going radiotherapy.

It was a severe blow to them, a time when their faith
was tested to the limits. Yet Norma clung to the belief
that the God whom she loved and served would grant
her the life and strength to raise their three daughters
to adulthood. Noel found this experience hard to come
to terms with. 'Something in me died then,' he was to
say later. 'There were so many deaths to cope with. And
then the cancer.' It was a bitter search for him to
rediscover faith and to rediscover the power of Jesus
Christ. Yet in their different ways they both did rediscover this and their faith grew stronger than before.

Noel went to Dartmoor as Chaplain in 1974 and
spent five gruelling but satisfying years there. In retrospect the mist and snow seemed to last most of the year.
The prisoners he worked with were hardened men.
However, he had the satisfaction of seeing the numbers
at chaplaincy services rising from eight to about a
hundred men. Despite the isolation of 'the Moor' and
the incessant wind, Norma did well physically and was
pronounced clear of the cancer at each of her six-
monthly check-ups.

In 1979 Noel moved to Strangeways Prison in Manchester, where he was made Senior Chaplain and where
he remains in the post until retirement. It was here that
he was challenged to work in a team with Ian Ferguson
from the Church Army and Alf Hughes, the Catholic
priest, who were full time at the prison; and Garth
Rogers, the part-time Methodist chaplain. There were

several assistant chaplains as well, who spent part of their working week with the chaplaincy team.

As the work developed, the chaplains were seeing over half the prison population coming to the several different services on a Sunday. Over eight hundred men were attending church or chapel. As Strangeways had a rolling population of prisoners, many were allocated to other prisons and sent on from there, so those attending services were not the same eight hundred each week. In spite of the tension, pressures and long hours, Noel loved the work as chaplain, preacher, evangelist and 'bridge-builder', forming relationships with prisoners and staff.

In 1983 Norma was pronounced clear of cancer and discharged from Christie's Hospital. The whole family was delighted and relieved. Things were good at work too: Noel felt revival was on the point of breaking out in the prison. Both Noel and Norma were full of hope and enthusiasm for the future. *The Cross Behind Bars* was published and opened the doors for a wider speaking ministry in which they were both involved. Norma returned to nursing full time as a Sister, and began to accept speaking engagements in the area, often talking about Christian healing at these evenings. At the prison chaplaincy a network of prayer partners, churches, prison visitors, clergy and other interested people slowly built up, to support the chaplaincy team.

At the centre of it all was Noel, pouring his heart out into the tough work he loved so much. Day after day he saw much to encourage and challenge him. By the nature of things, of course, some days were harder and less encouraging than others.

One morning Noel walked briskly from the Adult Wing towards the Punishment Block, or the Segregation Unit as they now called it. The bunch of keys was heavy at his waist and jangled slightly as he walked. He never knew who would be waiting for him in the cells, nor what to expect from these daily visits. He unlocked the first cell door and called out, 'Are you all right?'

There was no reply. So Noel stepped further inside and glanced round. A man was sitting, round-shouldered and head hanging, near the window. Clear morning light came through the bars and cheered Noel. It was apparently making no difference to the prisoner.

'Mr Clark, isn't it?' asked Noel.

The head moved an assent.

'Are you all right? Can I get you anything?'

There was no response. Noel looked round the cell. It was oppressively tidy. There were no books, no personal touches.

'I don't think we've talked before,' said Noel, carrying on in spite of the obvious body language from Mr Clark, which spoke as loudly as any words, telling him to go away. 'I'm always ready and willing to listen if that helps. There are books I can get you from the chaplains' library. If you need me to make a phone call, or get the Probation Service to speak to your family, I can do that for you.'

There was a slight quiver across the man's shoulders, but he remained silent.

'I expect you've already had visits from the Governor, the Chief Officer, the MO and the Hospital Officer today.'

There was no reply. Noel waited. 'I'll see you tomorrow,' he said finally. Then he turned to go. He walked back out onto the landing and locked the cell door behind him. The officer on duty was walking towards him. 'Hello, Noel.'

'Hello there.'

The officer nodded towards the locked cell. 'Get anywhere with him?'

Noel shook his head. 'Nowhere at all. He wouldn't even turn round.'

The officer shook his head.

'What's he been sent down for?'

'Oh, stealing from another prisoner's cell. And not for the first time.'

'He obviously isn't very happy in here.'

The officer frowned. 'If Clark breaks prison rules he can take what's coming to him,' he said tartly.

Noel grinned and moved on to the next cell. He went through the same routine, only this time the prisoner was more relaxed, and more polite. However, the response was the same: not really interested in a visit from someone representing organised religion.

He made nine cell visits in total that morning, to nine men who were all very different. Each one had broken prison rules, either by fighting, giving streams of verbal abuse, stealing or refusing to co-operate, and then being confrontational, often ending up by hitting a prisoner or an officer. Their punishment was twenty-three hours a day alone in a cell in the Segregation Unit, with one hour a day only for exercise in the yard. The problem with lending books too was that many a time a man would shake his head at the offer, and Noel knew it was because he could not read. It was so hard to reach these men, and yet the chaplain was in a unique position. He had all the keys and could wander from cell to cell. Men got to know him and at times they would talk. Noel had learned to listen and found that by letting them talk, they could often find the answer to their own problems. Sometimes he would pray with them. Sometimes they wept. Often he felt he was a buffer, a safety-valve between their angers, strains, and frustrations with the prison system. If a wife was ill in hospital or a girlfriend pregnant, Noel could organise a phone call and then come back with any news.

These visits were never easy, but they were part of a chaplain's statutory daily duties. On very rare occasions a man went on protest and made his cell almost uninhabitable by plastering the walls with his own excreta. The smell was unbearable. Fortunately no one had done that for some time now.

Sometimes, however, a man did respond. Noel opened the last cell door. 'Hello there, Derek.'

Derek turned round and smiled at Noel. 'Hello, Mr Proctor. Nice to see you.'

'And how's it with you today? I thought you'd gone back to the wing yesterday afternoon?'

The smile faded a little. Derek shrugged his shoulders and half-turned away. Noel came into the cell. He sat on the only chair and said gently, 'Are you in more trouble, Derek?'

Derek hung his head. He was a slightly-built man with short sandy hair and appeared much younger than his mid-twenties.

'Have you been shouting your mouth off again?'

The young man nodded.

Noel sighed. 'Do you want to talk about it?'

Derek spun round and said, 'I didn't mean no harm. It's just that the words come tumbling out of my mouth. I get so mad, I can't help it. And besides, that lad was having a go at me in the dinner queue.'

'Look,' said Noel, 'it's not the first time you've let your temper get the better of you, is it? Why can't you let the other lads alone? They only try and wind you up. And they succeed. Look at you now. Back in here again. Banged up on your own for twenty-three hours a day and all because you didn't take my anti-swearing tablets.'

Derek half-grinned and took one of the mints Noel was offering him. The atmosphere relaxed.

'Yes,' he said simply. 'You're right.'

Noel tried to size him up. He liked Derek, but he also knew that there was only so much he could do for him in this situation. He guessed Derek had thumped someone in the dinner queue. His fists and his having always to have the last word were Derek's own two worst enemies. He was constantly in and out of the Punishment Block on account of his temper. *He's a prisoner of his temper really*, thought Noel. And it was a temper that was even harder to control than usual, as he was getting over his alcoholism.

'How long have you got this time?' he asked.

'Ten days,' said Derek.

'Oh.' He paused, then—'Would you like some books from the chaplains' library?'

Derek considered this. 'OK.'

Noel made a note in his diary. 'I'll come back and see you later.'

'Ta. Thanks, Mr Proctor.'

Noel let himself out, locking the cell behind him. He wondered what it must be like in there for twenty-three hours. No radios were allowed. Only you yourself and your thoughts. And books if you could read. One hour walking round and round the exercise yard, and even that depended on the weather. The only views were high, rearing red-brick walls, with their rows of tiny barred windows. There was the industrial landscape against the skyline, but virtually not a tree to be seen. Some small areas of grass and plants grew around the prison and that improved matters slightly. Pigeons and starlings flew about and some men tried to feed them and make pets of them on the windowsills. This was not allowed, but officers often turned a blind eye to it.

Noel walked on to the Hospital Wing and made his rounds there. He frequently sat at a sick prisoner's bedside and this seemed to calm them. He knew he could call on one of the many prison visitors if a man was in need of human contact, and visits could be arranged. There were many men with psychological problems in prison. So much of his work was in listening. Often men were unsure of themselves in prison. It was a new environment and their emotions built up—sometimes to illness point, and they ended up in the prison hospital; sometimes into aggression, when they would wreck their cells and end up in the Punishment Block.

He looked at his watch and hurried on. The Governor had called a meeting about the new Home Office initiative called Fresh Start. As Noel listened, he realised that Fresh Start was going to sweep right through the Prison Service. Prison was to be a more caring place. It was to be a community prison, changing for the better. Many classes and groups which had closed down due to industrial action, were to restart. The government was to put in more money. Overtime for prison officers was to stop, in favour of a thirty-nine-hour week and a reasonable wage. Staff quarters too would now charge rent, or staff could buy their own houses. Noel's brow puckered. As soon as he mentioned that to Norma she would say she wanted them to buy their own house. And perhaps she was right. It would be something of their very own and she would love it, he knew that.

Afterwards he spoke to the Governor. 'Won't these changes mean smaller staffing at weekends?' said Noel.

The Governor agreed with him. 'I hope it'll work,' he said. 'I am very hopeful. And I'm keen to implement it all and get going on education and workshops.'

'And my classes—men's society, confirmation classes, choir, prayer . . . '

'Yes, yes,' said the Governor and laughed. 'You can carry on with your classes. Do you ever stop, Noel?'

'Er, well.' He considered it. 'My wife says I take the

pressure home at times, but she doesn't mind. She listens to me and then I make her a cup of tea! Then I listen to her and then we both put each other right!'

Later that afternoon Noel considered his day. There had been prayers at 7.45am in the chaplaincy, followed by reception. Here the chaplains interviewed every man or boy who had been sent down the night before. They worked in a team with the senior officer on duty, the probation officer, the Education Service and the industrial manager. Often these prisoners were anxious and Noel's job was to reassure them and then, if they wished, let their family know where they were.

Then he had done the Punishment Block, hospital visits, and more visits. He had taken books to Derek, who had been rather depressed that afternoon. There were classes this evening. It had been a full day, but Noel was at peace with himself. As he spent a few quiet moments with a cup of tea, he thought about prison. So many people were in prisons, not just of bricks and mortar, but prisons of the mind; prisons of their own personality, of fear of the future and insecurity, fear of life itself and the fear of not being able to cope. It was his job to show them the way forward, to point them to Christ who had died to set prisoners free. Of course such men had committed serious crimes and had to pay the price and take the punishment. That was only right. But no one could really be released from the prisons of the mind, apart from by the grace offered by God. And that applied to people on the outside as much as on the inside. Such grace was offered to all people, as Noel knew, but not everyone wanted it. The Holy Spirit never forced himself on people.

Yet in these days he was seeing a movement of the Spirit in the prison. He took a long drink of tea and relaxed in his chair. His work was hard, there was no doubt about that. But how he loved it.

# 6

## The Street Preacher

In the days that followed, Noel visited Derek in the
Punishment Block each day. He lent him books and
listened as Derek talked. *Yes*, thought Noel, *he is a
lad who'll always need to have the last word. Best if I
listen and let him get it all off his chest.* He could see
that Derek was sizing him up, waiting to ask a question, but unsure of how to put it. In spite of a torrent of
words somehow Derek never quite got to the point.

Then one morning Derek said, with rather a flush in
his cheeks, 'Can you get me a Bible?'

Noel looked at him 'Yes, all right. I'll bring it down
when I can.'

'Ta.'

Noel took it to him later on in the afternoon.
Inwardly he was shaking his head. He did not expect
a character like Derek to change, even if he wanted to.
In the life outside he was too used to alcohol and to
shouting with mouth and fists for any change to come
easily. Nevertheless, Noel gave him the Bible. 'Here you
are, lad. Don't forget to read it.'

'I won't.'

Next morning, as soon as Noel opened Derek's cell
door, he said, 'Mr Proctor, I've been thinking.'

Noel waited.

'I've been thinking. And the thing is, well I mean . . .'

For once he seemed stuck for words. Then out they came in a rush. 'What's my life all about? And how can I straighten it all out?'

'Well, lad . . . ' But Noel did not get chance to finish.

'Because I'd like to commit my life to Jesus.'

Noel sat down on the bunk. 'Look, Derek,' he said, 'let me give it to you straight. I respect you for what you are saying and I don't doubt you mean well—at the moment.' Derek made as if to speak, but Noel moved his hand authoritatively and Derek sank back onto his chair again. 'You see if you really mean it and really mean business with God, talk isn't enough. There's got to be action as well.'

Derek hung his head. Then he sprang up again. 'But I want to, I want . . . '

Noel sighed and said gently, 'If you become a follower of Jesus Christ, you'd have to give up your drinking. It wouldn't be easy. Could you do that? And you'd have to learn how to calm down and not let your tongue run away with you.'

Derek said nothing. He looked at his knees for some moments. Then he raised his head and his body went still. 'I want to, Mr Proctor. I want to.'

Noel smiled. 'All right then, lad. Once you are back on the Wings you can join in one of the groups. Maybe the choir. If you're so good at talking you might be good at singing!'

Derek jumped up and ran to the barred window. 'Ta, Mr Proctor.'

Noel let himself out, and locked the cell behind him. He walked steadily away, but inside he felt a little sad. He did not doubt the sincerity of the lad at all. But what would happen to Derek once he left prison and went back to his existence of wandering the streets? He had no roots, no family to speak of. He had nothing going for him. Anyway, Noel decided he would have to do as much as he could for Derek while he was inside.

At home that evening he found Norma on the telephone. She waved at him and he went on into the kitchen for a cup of tea. Charlie, the Yorkshire terrier, gave a yap and raced for the door, sensing a walk. Norma flew into the kitchen. 'Hello, darling. Just hang on. Back in a minute.' She grabbed the wall calendar and rushed out. Noel sat down and waited, knowing before she came back what it would be. He heard the phone go down and immediately it started ringing again. At last she came in, her face alight and her hands full of calendar and paper, envelopes and a pen.

'Oh Noel, that's the third invitation tonight.'

He looked up at her. 'To speak?'

'Yes.' She clasped her hands. 'I so want to do it, Noel. It's ladies' groups, Women's Aglow, Christian Viewpoint, all in the area. People have read *The Cross Behind Bars* and so many either have cancer or know someone who's got it. And they want me to give a talk about it and tell them how the Lord helped me. Well, both of us really. And to offer prayers for healing.'

'What are you waiting for then? Come on, let's take Charlie for a walk and you can tell me all about it.'

So arm in arm they set off. Norma said, 'Isn't it amazing how all that we lived through at Eastchurch and me nearly dying, has had this kind of a resurrection? It's wonderful. So wonderful.'

He squeezed her arm. 'And now I'm going to invite you to come with me for a change and give your testimony at a meeting.'

'Oh?'

'Yes. The Independent Methodists are having their

Annual Meeting at a room in Manchester University. And . . . ' he paused.

She stopped, waiting for him to go on. When he didn't, she picked up a stick and hurled it for Charlie. 'Well, do go on.'

He grinned. 'And they want it to be on the ministry of healing!'

She chuckled. 'I'm with you, Noel. I'll do it.'

Derek was discharged from the Segregation Unit and moved back onto the Wings again. His behaviour settled down and he kept clear of trouble. Noel spent many sessions with him in the weeks that followed. Derek studied the Emmaus Bible Correspondence Course and was eventually granted a certificate when he passed. The day finally came for his discharge. Noel shook his hand. 'God bless you, Derek. Keep rejoicing. And keep that Bible I gave you!'

'Oh yes, Mr Proctor, I will. Ta. I'll be all right now. I know I will. And ta for everything.'

After Derek had gone, Noel wondered about his future. Would such a lad manage to stay out of trouble? In spite of Derek's jaunty air, Noel knew he had never mentioned a family, or a home, or a job. Noel sighed, prayed for a moment, and then set off on his rounds again.

When Noel spoke at rallies and meetings he tried to explain about the movement of the Spirit in the prison that was happening during these years. Men were committing their lives to Christ through the testimony of cell mates. As he prayed in chapel with Ian Ferguson for groups of men, and they laid hands upon them, men would slip to the floor, touched by the power of the Holy Spirit. On one occasion Noel felt the wind of the Spirit so powerfully that he was caused to stagger under the weight of it. Some men were speaking in tongues during meetings. A Muslim officer came and asked him about two young men who were praising God and speaking in tongues in the prison showers. 'And,' he said, 'they weren't speaking any language used where I come from!' Some prisoners who had committed serious offences were granted the peace and joy to live quietly in the Segregation Unit, and then on the Wings, still witnessing as the years passed. Hundreds, as had always happened, came to the many Sunday services.

A man called Peter tried to commit suicide, but the sheets he had knotted together tore at the last minute and he fell unharmed to the ground. He was overwhelmed with darkness and remorse because he had murdered his girlfriend in a rage. Months passed and he had no freedom from his conscience. He lived in a state of dark terror, fearful he was going to die. In spite of a lot of prayer he remained in this condition, even sleeping under his bed because he was in protest at the psychiatric help being offered to him. Nothing helped. Then one day he asked to see Noel, saying, 'Last night I was under my bed again. It was pitch dark in the cell. I couldn't sleep. All at once I noticed this light. There was light all round me, a gentle light. It shone around me and reached me where I was lying under the bed.'

Noel was quite speechless.

In great calmness and quietness of spirit and demeanour Peter went on: 'I thought it must be Jesus.'

Noel bent his head and worshipped God.

Since his release Peter has lived a decent life and become a church caretaker.

So the stories of blessing, forgiveness, repentance and peace multiplied in what some in that tough, rough and hard place of Strangeways called 'the human warehouse'.

When Noel and Norma ministered together at meetings outside of the prison, there were also conversions and healings. An elderly man with a hearing aid announced that he no longer needed it because he could now hear. They saw the goitre on the neck of one woman shrink rapidly and disappear. A girl who had suffered greatly with eczema, cycled round to the prison and waited outside to tell Noel, shyly, that she had been completely cured.

James was in prison for burglary. One day he saw a man whom he did not know walking at the end of the Wing corridor. As soon as James saw this man he said to himself, 'I know I must find forgiveness.' Afterwards he could find no reason why he had thought in such a way. Later on he discovered the man was called Noel Proctor and that Noel could point him to the one and only source of true forgiveness. James found that the forgiveness of Christ was so real that in the ten subsequent years he has not been in trouble with the police again. He married his girlfriend and has given their four children a stable home. It is hard to go straight when there is no glamour and no instant access to a chaplaincy team. Yet James and his wife have managed it.

Another lad called Mark decided to become a Christian, even though he had been a robber all his life. After some time in prison he was ready to accept the words in the Bible which say, 'Let him that stole steal no more.' He admitted a series of thefts to the police, and because he would not give the names of his two accomplices, the judge decided that he alone would have to serve the sentences of all three men. The headlines in *The Manchester Evening News* said 'Born-again convict admits to robbery'. But Mark said, 'Now at least I can live with myself.'

A man called Bob Sutton had a vision for a New Life

Centre in Stockport, used to house and help ex-offenders. He had to work through many problems and difficulties, but eventually his vision has become a reality. Joe Whelan is a field officer for the Langley House Trust. There are the Adullam Homes and a house in Plymouth Grove. All these initiatives were part of the movement of the Spirit in the North West.

Over 5,000 prayer letters were being sent out each month. There were prison visitors and many interested people all over the North West giving, and helping ex-offenders.

In the midst of all this activity, both inside and outside the prison, Noel began to receive some post-cards. He studied the picture on one of them and turned it over to see which city this was. 'Oxford' he read. He sucked his lower lip for a moment and then propped the card up next to the others: Cardiff, Swansea, Bournemouth, Eastbourne. It was amazing how Derek had got about. Once he had come up to Manchester and met Noel for lunch. Noel had watched him afterwards as he had tramped into St Anne's Square, with a sandwich board at his front and back. He had stopped dead in the middle and preached the gospel, the sandwich boards telling the same story too. Noel had been surprised. Many would see Derek as a figure of fun, a caricature of the Bible preacher. And yet Derek, who had no roots, was wandering from town to town, using the one big talent he had. He always had liked talking and shouting his mouth off. Now, thought Noel, the man was using his mouth for God, preaching his heart out for British shopping crowds.

Derek's wandering life of a street evangelist had lasted now for several years. At times he phoned Noel for advice and support; especially when he had ups and downs. He often lived a fortnight at a time in

Salvation Army hostels and these addresses would then entitle him to DSS money.

One day the phone rang in Noel's office. He picked it up. 'Hello there.'

'Oh hello. My name is Nigel Sharp. I'm from Radio Wiltshire.'

'Oh yes!'

'Do you know a Derek Smith, an ex-prisoner?'

Noel was cautious. 'Er yes.'

'Would you be willing to say a few words about him on a live radio phone-in tomorrow evening?' The interviewer then went on to explain the story and left Noel chuckling.

'Right,' said Noel eventually. 'I'll be happy to join you by phone on the programme.'

The evening came and Noel was ready and waiting by the phone when it rang. Also linked to the programme was a bishop. The interviewer began with the bishop. 'Can you tell us what happened to you recently in Oxford?'

'Yes,' said the beautifully articulated voice. 'It was my day off and I was going into the town centre by bus. I wasn't wearing a dog collar. Once in the centre I caught sight of a young man wearing a sandwich board, and I could hear him shouting out about Jesus. I pushed my way through the small crowd of onlookers and decided to challenge him. "Surely," I said, "You don't believe all this stuff about the Christian message. It's 2,000 years old." Well, the man drew himself up to his full height, which wasn't very tall, and said, "I was in Strangeways Prison and I was an alcoholic. Jesus Christ came into my life and saved me and changed my life." He paused for breath and I tried to speak, but he rushed on. "And now I preach the gospel and Her Majesty gives me DSS money to buy tracts to give to people like you!" With that, he rammed the tract into my hand!'

Later on the bishop had gone home and rung up the radio station. 'In all my years as a minister of the gospel, I don't think I've ever been as challenged as I was by that naïve and ignorant young man who told me Jesus loved me. I came home and I said, "Oh God, give me some of the zeal and enthusiasm that young man has got."'

The interviewer then asked Noel to chat to Derek, which he did. 'Derek's a street preacher,' said Noel to the radio listeners, 'who became a Christian in the Punishment Block at Strangeways Prison.'

Now Derek has lots of contacts in many towns. Local church people often give him a bed for the night. The last time he spoke to Noel, some eight years after his conversion experience, he said he would like to think of settling down, and gave Noel the same address as before in South Wales.

Noel and Norma were happy and busy—he in his prison work, she as a Sister at Heathlands Nursing Home and a speaker at many meetings. The Lord was blessing them so much. It seemed as if nothing could come and spoil their happiness in his work, each other and the girls. 'Why,' said Norma, 'next year is our Silver Wedding Anniversary.' Her face lit up and her laughter encircled the room. It seemed that 1989 was going to be their highlight year.

# 7

# *The Highlight Year*
## 1989

The 31st March 1989 was a special day in the Proctor household. 'Fancy us being married for twenty-five years,' said Noel as he got up that morning.

'Well, you aren't grumbling, are you?' said Norma tartly as she sat up in bed.

He grinned. 'What do you think!'

'Twenty-five years ago today,' she said, remembering, and her voice softened. 'Oh Noel, haven't we got a lot to be thankful for?'

'Yes, we have. And if I don't nip downstairs and get you that cup of tea, neither of us will ever get going!'

She smiled, and as he ran downstairs her laughter followed him.

The day passed by in a crackle of excitement. By early evening the whole family was assembled at the Christian World Centre in Deansgate, Manchester, where they greeted the 100 guests to their Silver Wedding Anniversary celebration. Noel's brother Tom and his wife had come over from Canada for the occasion, and this was cause for a joyful reunion. Everyone joined in a communion service first, led by Tom Johns, a colleague, and then they sat down to a meal together. Noel and Norma both spoke, followed by Susan singing, Helen playing her clarinet and Rebekah saying a few words about her parents. In the end it seemed as if nearly everyone got up and said something.

Much later that evening, just before Noel and Norma settled down for the night, he looked at the plaque which his mother-in-law had given them as an engagement present, and which was hanging over their bed.

Norma followed his gaze and read the verse out loud: '"All things work together for good to them that love God." That's why it's been so special for us today, isn't it, Noel?'

'Yes. It's been very very special.'

They looked at each other, remembering the past.

Norma said, 'When I was told I had cancer in 1973 and that the prognosis was poor, it seemed as if we would never see this day together.'

He took her hand. 'It has been a very precious anniversary. We've had all these years together. Years we never thought we'd have.'

'And we've been able to see our three girls grow up and encourage them in the careers they want to take up. Noel, isn't it amazing how much God has given us in these extra years? So much we would never have realised about in life, if I hadn't had cancer. My ministry has sprung out of it. Noel, I really do thank the Lord, with all my heart.'

'And so do I,' he said. 'Every day together has been a bonus.'

In July of the same year the chaplaincy work of many years came to a culmination. A mission was planned centring around some videos relayed from the Billy Graham Mission in London. Thirty missioners came from all denominations of the Christian faith, along with some prison visitors and other helpers. They were given permission to scatter around the prison from 8 o'clock in the morning to 8 o'clock at night, visiting and speaking to men in the exercise yard, in the workshops, and wandering at will around the wings.

Many prisoners who normally never came to chapel were affected by the atmosphere in the prison and came to some of the meetings. By the end of the week over 1,300 men had seen the videos and heard the challenge to commit their lives to Christ. Men in the prison hospital and also in the Segregation Unit were able to see them. One evening over half the Rule 43 prisoners (those vulnerable because of their offences) who had watched Billy Graham, stayed behind for counselling.

Catholic priests, Methodist ministers, Anglicans, Baptists, Pentecostals, Salvationists and others all worked together to bring the gospel to the prisoners. One evening, in a quiet moment, Noel realised what a wonderful experience it all was. Many of the prison officers were saying quite openly that the whole atmosphere of the prison had changed. There was a peace there that had come in and calmed many men.

Those men who signed a card were followed up by their own local minister from outside. Inside, Noel and his team were running twenty-nine services and classes each week. It was a time of tremendous blessing and encouragement.

In November a video called *From Crime to Christ* was made of four men who had committed their lives to Christ in prison and who are now in full-time Christian work. The Governor decided that it should be played every morning on reception, as new inmates were waiting to be interviewed, so that they could gain an insight into the alternative to a life of crime.

But one Sunday afternoon in November 1989 a film was being shown in the chapel to the remand prisoners. As the film ended the prisoners remained seated. Within a few moments it became obvious that they had planned and were now putting into practice a sit-down protest. Over 200 men were refusing to leave the chapel, and the officers on duty knew that this was potentially serious and confrontational. Eventually one of the Governors went in and negotiated with them. He promised to listen to their complaints about conditions if they found a spokesman and then left the chapel quietly. In the end the men went back to their cells.

When Noel heard about it he shook his head. An officer said to him, 'There's trouble brewing. I don't like it.'

'Yes,' said Noel. 'I agree. It's worrying.' But then in the general rush of meetings the fact of the sit-down protest slipped to the back of his mind.

Soon the year which had brought Noel and Norma so much happiness, both in the family and in the prison work, was drawing to a close. Christmas preparations were well underway. Noel's birthday on the 23rd December passed, and he had got his trumpet down ready to play carols early on Christmas morning before breakfast in the prison. He joked with Norma about it the day before. 'They keep asking me when I'm going to play. And I know what'll happen when I do. Some of them will shout from behind the cell doors, "More! More!" and some of them will be saying something quite different!'

For once she did not laugh. 'Do I look all right, Noel?' she asked.

He stared at her non-plussed. He nearly said, 'You always look all right. You always look the same to me,' but managed not to, just in time. He studied her and saw she was wearing a flowered dress and a short coat. Her hair glowed with red lights and her cheeks were pink. She really did look the picture of health and smartness. 'You look simply great,' he said.

She smiled faintly. 'Thank you.'

'Come on then.'

They set off in the car and made their way to Elmwood Church near Hope Hospital in Salford, where they were to be guest speakers at the Christmas Eve service. Once inside the new building Norma's face seemed to light up as she took in the Christmas decorations, lights and the tree. Noel glanced at her on the platform. She had been a bit quiet in the car, but then sometimes women were like that for no reason. She caught his eye and smiled encouragingly. He grinned back. So that was all right then. She was quite happy.

He poured himself into a gospel message and finally drew to a close. 'I'd like to introduce you to the one who keeps me on the straight and narrow,' he said, amid laughter from the audience. 'Let me introduce you to my wife. When I joined the Prison Service, you know what they said? They said, "You've joined the Prison Service to get away from the women in your life." I've got three daughters and a wife. The only other fellow in the house is a dog, and he's a bit of an old woman too! Anyway, it's lovely to share the platform tonight with the one who gives me the encouragement. Norma!' There was a burst of applause as he sat down. Norma stood up and stared out momentarily at the people.

As he listened to her, Noel was surprised. Her voice was soft and she enunciated the words slowly. 'Christmas for me means "Christ with us". A Christ who recognises our frailties because he was man as well as God. I was born in the city of Belfast, which you will know from my accent, and I was born again when I was thirteen, through seeing the changed life of a school friend.' Her voice became breathless and tremulous,

and she paused. 'Although we look back to our beginnings we also need to think, "What does Christ mean
to me today?" Sometimes people think Christians have
a natural immunity to life's problems.' She took a quick
intake of breath, and then her voice and gaze became
intent. 'But Jesus never promised us that, did he? But he
did promise his presence with us in life's problems.' She
paused again.

Noel began to wonder if she had a headache and
whether he should take over. She seemed to be labouring under some strong emotion, and yet she looked so
lovely and confident. She began speaking again and he
sat back in his seat.

'Life was good to us. We lived in Eastchurch. Things
started going wrong there, but joy and sorrow are very
much part and parcel of our lives. In the joy of our third
child came great sorrow when I discovered that I had a
breast lump that was diagnosed as cancer. As a nursing
Sister I thought cancer only happened to the people I
nursed.' There was a long pause. 'Cancer didn't happen
to me. But here I was faced with the fact of cancer and
an unknown future. When we married and left home
my mother gave us a text from our family home which
she knew was my favourite: Romans 8:28, "All things
work together for good to them that love God."

'There were times when I wanted to break the glass
round the plaque and underline in red "ALL
THINGS"—even cancer? Could that possibly work
for my good? I was absolutely shocked to learn that I
could die and could leave my three children of eight,
five and four months old—but I wasn't quite prepared
for how Noel would react to my diagnosis. He went
totally to pieces and became very embittered and
rebellious, and he questioned God's dealings with us
as a family. Oh yes, he's an ordained minister, but he's

got great big feet of clay. And he was rebellious against God.

'You know, God moves very mysteriously in our lives. As if having cancer was not enough, two days after I came out of hospital while I waited to have twenty-five treatments of radiotherapy, my mother had a second stroke and died. What was God trying to tell me? He was knocking from me all the props I had ever known: the prop of my good health, the prop of my mother's love, the prop of my husband's spirituality. They had all gone. And I was to learn again total and absolute dependence upon him.

'On the Sunday Noel was asked to preach at a Baptist church in Sittingbourne and he rang the pastor and asked to be excused. He said he had nothing to give. Something in him had died and he couldn't be a hypocrite. The pastor encouraged us to come and Noel said to him, "Well, do you believe in the laying on of hands for healing?" And he said he did. And Noel said, "Will you minister to Norma for physical healing and will you minister to me for spiritual healing?" And after the service we were both ministered to by the deacon and pastor of that church.

'On the way home Noel said that he needed a sign from God that I was going to live. He needed a sign that I was healed. I thought this was rather a bold thing to say. But Noel was like a drowning man and he needed something to take hold of.'

Noel listened as she spoke, her voice quicker and lighter now. The old sparkle was back and he knew everything was all right now. He heard her retell the story of how she had read the verse in John's Gospel, 'This sickness is not unto death', and had believed it applied to her own situation. 'I held on to this verse,' she cried, her voice strong and powerful, 'even when I still had to have twenty-five treatments of radiotherapy, and I still had to go every three months, six months, twelve months, for check-ups. But gradually God let me see the whole of the promise that he'd given me. "This sickness is not unto death but that the Son of God might be glorified."'

Her voice broke suddenly and Noel saw her hands were gripping the table. 'I realised that God had healed me for his glory. That is why I am on this platform tonight: because I want to glorify Jesus Christ.' Her voice halted again. Then she carried on: 'I want not to be seen, but I want the healing power of God to be manifest in this church tonight, and realise that although "cancer" is a word we are terrified of, the name of Jesus is greater than the name of cancer.' She paused again. 'And I cling on to the promise of God. Many people say to me quite candidly, "Why do you think you are still alive, when God has taken people like David Watson, and many others?" I am still alive because my ministry is not complete, and when it is, then he will take me as well.' Her voice quivered. 'I've had sixteen years I never thought I would have. I can honestly say that the quality of life I've had in these years far surpasses the quality of life I had before.' Her voice became shaky. Then as she spoke again the words were slow, quiet and deliberate. 'When you've had an encounter with the living God, your life is never the same because you get things into perspective.'

She sat down, her face glowing. The congregation began to sing the well-loved words of a carol. She turned and smiled at Noel. He grinned back. *She's a wonderful speaker*, he thought. She had such an understanding of spiritual life. What a lovely talk she had given. It was the crowning moment of the highlight year. He sat back on his chair and relaxed.

## Part Two

## *The Siege of Strangeways*

*Our God of the past.* Eleven years have done great and mighty things at the prison. We rejoice in that. Satan has tried to destroy eleven years of faithful ministry, but Jesus has promised, 'I will build my church and the gates of hell shall not prevail against it.'

*Our God of the present.* God has noted our tears, our questioning, and our brokenness. And his love is healing us by reminding us of his promise, 'Don't struggle, but be still and know that I am God.'

So wrote Norma in the front of the new Bible she gave to Noel in May 1990 to replace the one ruined by fire and water in the burned-out Strangeways chapel.

# 8

## Passion Sunday
## 1st April 1990

Noel shook his head as he waited to collect the men who wanted to come to one of the Lenten Series meetings. Usually it was a simple job for the prison officer in the centre box to read the list and send for the prisoners. He could see clearly down all the wings. But at the beginning of March twenty tons of scaffolding had been erected in the centre so that redecorating could take place. Noel looked at the scaffolding. He had seen the inmates looking at it too, especially when the men erecting it had been clambering up and down it like monkeys. He had heard one or two daring each other to climb it. The scaffolding blocked visibility for the officer on duty in the centre box. The planks made the third landing dark too, and lights had been put underneath to enable the officer to see more clearly. Somehow tempers became frayed when the lads were gathering to be taken to different classes and the chapel. It caused tension, which later dissipated as the classes got underway.

Things did not feel quite right in the prison either. Ever since January there had been a build-up of lifers—men who had been given a life sentence and transferred from other prisons to Strangeways; men who had been given no date for release and therefore no reason *not* to be rebellious. Their bad tempers were the cause of some confrontation. A lot of staff began talking about their concern. Pressure was mounting, not least because over-crowding was becoming an issue again. Prisoners were 'banged-up' for long hours. They only had buckets in the cells. Often the stench was appalling. The tiny cell windows had wire over them. Conditions inside the cells were not good. Slopping out was not pleasant.

On Mothering Sunday Norma came in and spoke at the main chapel service. As she left she nudged Noel. He looked at her. 'Noel,' she glanced round and shrugged helplessly. 'Noel, there's something wrong in the church.'

'What do you mean?'

She closed her eyes momentarily and then said, 'The atmosphere, it's . . . not like before. Well, it's just not there any more. And the lads didn't respond the way they've normally done in the past.'

Noel nodded. 'There's a lot of pressure at the moment,' he said. 'Maybe you've picked that up.'

In spite of Norma's words God blessed that service and a number of men asked for counselling at the end. During the following week some committed their lives to Christ. Yet, even so, as the week progressed Norma still felt that something was wrong.

On Saturday 31st March men were brought into the chapel as usual to see a film. After it was over they remained seated. Almost immediately one officer realised that this was a planned refusal to leave. Some even charged the gates at the back of the chapel. And there was trouble as the staff endeavoured to get them back onto the wings.

Noel arrived at the prison at 7.10am on the Sunday morning of 1st April. As he came into the prison to give out his list for the 8.30am communion service, he was met by one of the Governors who said, 'Noel, there are rumours that we could have trouble this morning.'

Noel said, 'Well, what do you suggest?' They both knew that Strangeways lived with rumours. There were always rumours that there was going to be trouble.

The Governor replied, 'Well, we'll put some extra staff into the chapel for the services.'

'Right,' said Noel. 'Thanks for letting me know.'

All was well at the 8.30am communion service. In fact Noel felt surprised by how well the men behaved and how quiet they were. He knew they were all believers, and it had been a lovely service. As the men left one came up to Noel and without looking at him said in a low voice, 'I'm not coming to the 10.15—there's rumours of trouble.' And then he slipped away. Noel frowned.

At 9.00am he and the Roman Catholic priest, Father Smith, exchanged chapels and each took a service. Noel was in the Roman Catholic chapel for the service for the remand prisoners, and Father Smith was in the main chapel leading a service for the Roman Catholic prisoners. Both services went well and were trouble free.

Then Noel came from the chapel in the Remand Wing back to the main prison to take the 10.15am service for the convicted prisoners. Before it began he went to the back as the men were being brought in and spoke to the senior officer in charge. 'I'm concerned because there are rumours of trouble today. One of the Governors met me this morning and told me, and one of the lads mentioned it too after communion.'

'We think everything should be all right,' replied the senior officer. 'We've got the extra staff in.'

'OK,' said Noel, and went down to the front again.

As Noel waited for the 300 or so men to be brought in from the back, and the young offenders from the side, he noticed that when the Category A prisoners (those who had committed very serious crimes) were brought in, along with those from the Segregation Unit, a lot of men turned round to stare at them. There was tension in the air, but Noel shrugged it off and announced the first hymn. It was hard to put his finger on what was wrong, but Noel recognised that there was an atmosphere, a pressure, in the service. When the hymn before the sermon was announced ten prisoners refused to stand. Noel walked rapidly over to them. 'Come on, lads,' he said. 'Show some respect in God's house. When we come into his house we stand to sing.' At this most pulled themselves to their feet. A couple remained seated. Noel turned round and marched back. He glanced at Ian Ferguson, the Church Army captain who was leading the service with him. The singing continued. Then the visiting speaker gave a brief sermon. This was received well, with some clapping.

Finally, Noel moved to give out the last hymn and opened his mouth to say, 'When I Survey the Wondrous Cross.' All at once a young man shot down the centre aisle, straight to the choir's microphone, and grabbed it. 'We've heard this morning how God is able to deal with the hardness of men's hearts,' he shouted at the top of his voice. 'I want to talk to you about the brutality of prison officers.' A string of obscenities poured from his mouth. His face and neck were covered with small beads of perspiration. He began to scream into the microphone. Noel ran forward and wrestled the microphone back from him. He pulled it with such force that he banged it into his own eye, which later swelled up, bruised and painful. The young man immediately quietened. Noel grabbed the opportunity to speak to the inmates through the microphone.

They had all risen to their feet. A wave of restless energy crackled round them.

'All right, lads,' he cried. 'I know many of you do not want to be involved in a fracas. Sit down and we'll get you out as soon as possible. I know you don't want trouble and we'll get you back to the cells as quickly as we can.'

About three-quarters of the prisoners then sat down. One officer began to try and usher the young offenders out down a side passage.

As Noel kept talking, a Category A prisoner raced down from the back of the chapel, closely followed by another inmate who was brandishing two sticks. They tore off after the young offenders' officer and knocked him down the stairs in the passage. 'Right, lads!' a prisoner shouted. 'Let's get them now!'

The young man who had initially grabbed Noel's microphone had gone very still and quiet as he saw what was going on, but now he was suddenly galvanised into life again. He tore away from Noel's side and rushed towards an officer who had come in from the vestry to stand with Noel as he tried to calm down the men over the microphone. The young man hit the officer on the head and shoulder in one great swipe. The officer fell unconscious to the ground.

Suddenly all the prisoners were on their feet. Shouting filled the chapel. Fists waved. Feet banged the floor. *That's it*, thought Noel. *The balloon's gone up.* The orderly rows of seated prisoners disappeared as men milled, shoved and yelled. Some inmates rushed over to where the officer was lying on the floor. They began to kick him. 'No!' cried Noel. 'They're not going to put the boot in!' He rushed straight for the booted, kicking group. With a force he didn't know he possessed, he pushed and knocked some of them out of the way.

All around the chapel men were pulling out homemade hoods that had been concealed under their clothing, and thrusting their heads into them. Some drew out sticks or chair legs. One picked up a clergy chair and brandished it as a weapon. Another began to rip out a front pew. Windows smashed. Many prisoners were panic-stricken, desperate to get out and not be involved. But doors were locked. They could not escape.

'Help me, lads!' shouted Noel to the group of ten or so who were sitting, shocked, in the choir. Some of these choir lads raced towards Noel, and between them all, they pulled the officer out from under the boots and away out of the chapel. Then, in a flash, the first young man appeared at Noel's side, ran down alongside the officer, snatched at his keychain and pulled it from him. He turned and ran up the left side of the chapel, shouting, 'I've got the keys!'

*This is trouble*, thought Noel. He gave chase after the man with the keys, running up the stairs in the chapel. But halfway up a young lad confronted him, waving a fire extinguisher above his head. Without stopping to think, Noel shouted, 'Drop it! Immediately!' Much to Noel's surprise he dropped it at once. By then it was too late to grab the keys back. The young man clutching them was already at the back of the chapel, mingling with the gang of prisoners. The noise was deafening. There was violent movement everywhere.

Ian Ferguson found himself leading about sixty prisoners out to safety. 'Please let us out,' they pleaded. 'Let us out.' He was able to get them away to a place of safety, where each was accounted for.

Noel turned and found a crowd of young inmates from the choir following him. They surrounded him, their faces furrowed.

'Don't go up there, Noel. We don't want you to get hurt.'

'Noel, we don't want you to go to the back.'

'We don't want anything to happen to you.'

'Come on, let's get out of here. Let's get out to the vestry.'

'We want to get out as well.'

So they surrounded him and led him back down again.

It was only later that Noel realised he must have been in shock by then, as he could not recollect what was happening for a few minutes. Somehow the vestry door was open. Later one of the lads from the choir told Noel that the young man who had grabbed the keys had come back down again and unlocked the vestry door to let them out. But as things were happening Noel had no conscious memory of it.

Once inside the vestry the ten or so prisoners built a barricade against the door, using a table and chairs from in there. They were all agitated and upset and it took Noel about twenty minutes to calm them down. He put his hand in his pocket and it closed over his own bunch of keys. *Strange*, he thought. *I'd forgotten I had them in all the uproar. Funny that the vestry door had been open.* As he looked round the choir lads it struck him with some force that he was one among ten prisoners, and that he had the keys. 'Let me take a list of your names,' he said. 'And then I'll vouch for you that you wanted nothing to do with all this. I *know* I know you all, but I think I'd better write a list.'

'I were panic-stricken back there,' said one of the men. 'I were looking round and wondering, "Where can I go? We're all locked in."'

'Yes,' said another, 'I was scared to death. We don't want to get in with that Category A mob.'

After a few minutes Noel decided to go for help. 'You stay here,' he said. 'I'll go down to the office and see if I can get help.'

There was a banging and a thumping overhead and several of the men ducked and then looked up rather fearfully.

'It must be them. They've got to the roof!'

'Like that lad last Monday who had to be talked down.'

Noel started. It was true that a lad had gone up that day. He had forgotten that.

'Look,' said Noel, 'I'll have to lock you in, but I'll be back as soon as I can. You are at least safe here.'

A crash was heard, followed by another, and another.

'Slates!'

'Started on that game, have they? Chucking slates.'

The noises outside grew louder and the thumping more intense. 'I'll *have* to go,' said Noel. 'We need help.'

He tried his key in the gate leading to his office and it turned. Once there he phoned the security officer, who assured Noel he would get the men out as soon as possible. Noel grabbed some packets of biscuits from his cupboard and ran back to the vestry. 'Here you are, lads,' he said. 'It's long past your dinner-time.' They looked relieved and helped themselves.

It was three-quarters of an hour before Security were able to get through to reach them and lead them away to the Visiting Room, where everyone trying to get out had gathered. The room was full of prisoners and staff.

Suddenly Noel saw Ian Ferguson coming towards him. 'Noel, where've you been? We couldn't work out where you were.' Ian hugged Noel and the tears trickled down his face. 'We've been so worried. No one knew where you were, because you were unaccounted for. I was so worried.'

Noel took his arm. 'Are *you* all right?'

'Mmm. I got a group of about sixty out. The organist helped me.' Ian shook his head. 'What an experience.'

'They're chucking slates now,' said Noel. 'They are on the roof.'

Ian said, 'It's fire that worries me.'

They looked round the crowded room. 'None of them have eaten. It's going to be some job to look after this lot.'

'Yes,' said Ian. 'Quite a few prisoners have been withdrawn from the main prison building now. And most staff have been withdrawn to the gate.'

'Are they safe?' Noel asked, thinking of the slates.

Ian shrugged.

Someone tapped Noel on the shoulder. 'The Governor wants to see you straight away,' he said. 'He's in Security.' Noel looked at his watch. It was 1.00pm. He spent some time trying to explain to the Governor and the security team what had happened in the chapel that morning. It was gruelling to have to go over it—the first of many, many times he was to relive that event of Passion Sunday morning, April Fools' Day 1990.

Eventually the Governor asked him to go to the Remand Visits Area to help the Principal Officer cope with about eighty inmates from the hospital and the kitchen. 'Some of those lads have mental problems, Noel. Some are very ill. Can you go and give some help and comfort to them?'

Noel nodded. 'Of course I will.' He glanced out of the window and the Governor followed his gaze. Both men stood in silence and watched. Officers in riot helmets were holding up perspex shields to make a corridor from the Visiting Room to the main gate. Other shields were held on top to offer protection as prisoners and staff from the Visiting Room began to run the gauntlet to get away.

Up on the roof pranced a mob of prisoners. Many

wore bags over their heads with slits cut for eyes and mouths. Fists waved. Voices screamed. Tiles were hurled. Other missiles rained down from the roof. The shields were battered as men tried to get out of the way. Some staff and inmates had been injured on the wings. Friends and colleagues helped the injured to safety. A further shower of slates, stones and bricks clattered down. *What a lot of courage among the staff out there*, thought Noel as he saw a brick bounce off a prison officer's back as he hung onto his shield, covering two inmates, one of whom was limping. He was to reflect afterwards that he had seen heroism and wonderful professionalism among the staff that day. He also saw bravery among the prisoners.

By the end of the day the majority of the men had surrendered and been bussed away to other prisons. Of the men in the chapel, Noel was sure that about three-quarters had been taken by surprise; they had been so quick to sit down when he asked them to.

The opportunity of escape into Manchester must have been uppermost in some inmates' minds that day. What a security nightmare that would have been, with escapees all over the city. Yet amazingly not one prisoner escaped. All were accounted for. It amazed Noel afterwards that prisoners stood outside the prison waiting for buses to take them to other prisons or police cells, apparently quite content to abide by the law. Prisoners still inside were ringing up the switchboard from all parts of the main prison asking to be taken out, anxious not to be involved.

Noel looked at the Governor. 'I'll get over to Remand Visits and help the Principal Officer.' And off he went.

# 9

## 'All My Work Is Ruined'

At home Norma was lying in bed early in the morning, awake, and knowing Noel had already set off for his usual Sunday morning services at the prison. She stretched and then gave herself over to reflection. Today was 1st April, Becky's seventeenth birthday. Norma looked back over all those years with thankfulness. 'Thank you, Lord,' she breathed, 'for these seventeen years.' She remembered when Becky was a few months old, when she had been diagnosed as having cancer. She had wondered if she would ever live to see Becky grow up. *And I have*, she thought. *She is seventeen, beautiful and intelligent, and like Susan and Helen, very precious.* She paused. 'Thank you, God, for the blessing of life.'

Everything in the room seemed to quieten. Norma herself lay still. She felt her hands by her side. She knew her body through and through. It had served her well all these years. She lay on for a few moments, wondering. *No*, she thought, *not today. This day is to be a happy day, a birthday celebration for Becky's special day.*

Later Susan, who was off duty, was taking charge of lunch preparation. Norma knew Noel would be home soon for the birthday celebration. Helen was working at college towards her finals, but would no doubt be on

the phone sooner or later. Becky was upstairs. Norma
could hear the murmur of the radio on in the kitchen
beneath the clatter of dishes. She sniffed. The roast
smelled good too.

'Mum!'

Norma started.

'Mum! Quick!'

She ran into the kitchen where Susan was standing
staring at the radio. 'It's a newsflash, Mum.'

' . . . a riot at Strangeways Prison, which began in
the chapel . . . ' said the announcer.

They stared at each other. 'Oh no!' said Norma.
'What about Noel? What on earth has happened?'

They rushed into the front room and switched the
TV on. After a few moments the news was broadcast
and the familiar façade of Strangeways came into view.

'Hostages may have been taken. Hundreds of inmates
are on the rampage. Wild and senseless destruction is
taking place. Numbers may be dead. It started in the
chapel . . . '

Norma and Susan clasped each other's hands. The
dinner was forgotten. Norma stumbled to the phone. A
few days later she was to write in the journal she began
during this momentous year in their lives:

I rang the prison—no calls were getting through. I
rang my Christian friends and asked if they would
start praying for the situation. They assured me that
they would.

Where was Noel? Susan rang round the local
casualty departments, but he wasn't there.

The phone rang—it was the Methodist chaplain,
Peter Went, asking if Noel had got out. 'I don't
know,' was my reply. Peter told me, 'It was awful
in there—chaos reigned.' He was sure Noel was all
right, but it sounded hollow assurance. Father Peter

Smith rang, the Roman Catholic chaplain. 'Did Noel get out?' My answer was the same.

That afternoon the phone rang dozens of times with Christians assuring us of their love and prayers, but perhaps what meant more to me were the twenty or so calls from ex-inmates asking after Noel and assuring me, 'No one will hurt Noel.' I knew deep down that physically he would be fine, but emotionally he would be devastated. His prison; his chapel; his men; his friends; his colleagues. All the trust he had in them; all the long hard days he had worked for his Lord; the lives that had been changed by the power of God; the blessing God had poured on his ministry... why this? My Noel who has worked with the outcasts of society for more than twenty years and still managed to keep his naïve faith in human nature. What would this do to him?

I was never more aware of the prayers of God's people than I was that day. Each report on TV painted such an awful picture of sin and destruction. I was reminded by the Holy Spirit of the promise of God: 'Where sin abounds, grace does much more abound.'

The phone rang endlessly. I kept hoping it would be Noel, but still no word. I had calls from prison officers' wives, and we tried to comfort and reassure each other.

Becky had spent much of the afternoon in her bedroom. I went to her and loved her. This sophisticated seventeen-year-old, so often cool and detached, looked at me with tears in her eyes and then wept, 'It's my birthday, and I want my dad.'

At about 6pm John Hargreaves (the Assistant Chaplain General) rang to say, 'Noel is safe. He is in the prison with about 100 inmates who wanted

no part of the riot. When they can get these men
out to safety, Noel will be home.' Praise God for
the good news and praise God for a caring human
being like John Hargreaves.

John came to our home shortly afterwards and
took me to the prison officers' mess where I spoke
to Noel. 'Yes, love, I'm all right, and the lads are
OK, but we're very hungry—haven't eaten since
breakfast.'

John came back with me to our home. We had
some tea and prayed together.

Mark Smith, our young curate, came soon after
this. He was as bemused as we were at all the news.
Mark didn't say much, but he just stayed with us,
and his being there was a comfort.

Back at Strangeways Noel set himself to comforting the
sick and disturbed prisoners in the Remand Visits
section. Many were angry, many worried and tense.
He became aware that he was very hungry, as the
inmates were. But no one had, as yet, been able to get
any food to them. In his concern and shock it did not
occur to Noel that the riot would be reported on
television and that Norma would find out about it
and be desperately worried. Later he was to write:

I suppose at that time I didn't think of the fact that
this was going out on television and radio. I didn't
realise that Norma would be worrying herself sick.
And it wasn't until late in the afternoon when all the
lads who were in the Remand Visits were being taken
out that John Hargreaves, the Assistant Chaplain
General, arrived and said to me, 'Norma's worried
about you,' and I was led down to the Security Office
where I was able to get onto the telephone, ring
Norma, and let her know that I was all right. I

couldn't get away because there were so many things happening.

That night at 9.30pm, as the Governor said to me, 'It's time you were going home,' I realised I hadn't eaten since breakfast-time and I was hungry. Peter Wilkinson supported me as I got to the gate. I came out and it was dark in Southall Street. I'd left my old car over on the rough ground at the far side. It was always a quiet place over there, but that night, as I made my way across the road, suddenly I was surrounded by lights and reporters and cameras, and they wanted to know what had happened in the prison and what was happening at the moment; how it had all started. I couldn't give them very much, but they wanted answers. I spoke to them for a few moments. I didn't realise that it was going out on television—not only throughout this country, but in other parts of the world as well. In fact my brother in Canada said that there was a shot of me on Canadian television.

When I got home the house was surrounded by reporters wanting to talk. They had asked my wife for stories, and for photographs, and it was Becky's birthday. It was 1st April. And as I came in through the door, suddenly Becky came into the hall. I know she loves me, but that night she put her arms round me, and she sobbed and she sobbed, 'Oh Dad, I'm so glad you're all right.' That child was so worried about her dad, and as I tried to say to her, 'I'm all right, love. Don't be worrying,' her mum said to me, 'All day she's kept saying, "The only birthday present I want is my dad to come home. I want my dad home."'

Noel had not arrived home until 10 o'clock that night. Norma saw his face as he walked in through the front door: grey, drawn and with a black eye. He explained to her that the injury to his eye was self-inflicted in his struggle with the young man at the microphone. All the while, as they stood in the hall, Becky clung to him as if she never wanted to let go of her father again. Norma immediately ran Noel a hot bath. She had realised at once by looking at him that he was in shock. So when she offered him something to eat and he refused, she did not press any food on him.

'Come on,' she said. 'Let's get you upstairs into a nice warm bath. And then bed! I insist.' Noel allowed himself to be ushered upstairs. Bath and a bed were all he felt he could cope with. He found he could not even speak to them all much, he was so exhausted.

Norma put the answer-phone on and said, 'Now we'll get some peace.'

But at around 11pm the door-bell rang. Norma flew to open the front door only to be confronted by a reporter from the national press. 'Can I just have a picture of the reunited family?' he demanded.

'No,' said Norma, her eyes glinting. 'It's far too late.'

'But it's my brief.'

'No, certainly not!' she snapped.

'I'll camp outside the house all night then!'

Norma slammed the door shut. At that moment she couldn't have cared less how he was to spend his night. Her only concern was how her Noel was ever going to get through his.

Finally she eased her way into bed and lay beside him, knowing he was awake but with his eyes closed. She longed to talk to him; to help him by letting him share the agonies and frustrations of the day with her. But he lay quite still and unrelaxed, like a stranger. *I've shared his life for twenty-six years*, she thought, *and now in the hour of his greatest need he is withdrawn and uncommunicative*. She bit her lip and turned over.

It would be best, she knew both as a wife and an experienced nurse, to let him take his own time to recover sufficiently to be able to talk to her. But it hurt even so, and it was a long time before she slept.

Noel himself lay awake all night, longing for sleep; but sleep would not come. He found he could not speak about the experience yet—even to Norma. It was as if he were still steeling himself for further shocks. If he did let the barricades down, he did not know if there would be any Noel Proctor left to do anything at all in this world. As he lay quite rigid in their bed, he found the events of the day replayed through his mind. Over and over he saw the young man running towards him, snatching the microphone. He saw the officer unconscious on the floor, with a jeering crowd 'booting' him. He saw the chapel, his chapel, being wrecked and destroyed. He remembered with a shudder that the cross up on the chapel roof had been hurled down to the yard below. And he had lost his Bible, which Norma had given him on their twenty-third Wedding Anniversary.

Then the events of his past life began to replay themselves in his mind interminably, as his over-active imagination refused to relax. He remembered 1973 when he felt as if something had died within him: too late to see his father before he died, his mother's death, Norma's miscarriage and their lost baby, Norma's cancer. It had all been so hard, so very, very hard, to search for and rediscover faith. He shifted in the bed, aware now that Norma was asleep at last. It was true that in the past seventeen years they *had* rediscovered their faith in Jesus Christ and his power. Well, he had to admit to himself, *he* had. Norma's had never foundered in the way his had done.

But now? He tried to blank out his thoughts, and found it was no good. After eleven years of work at

Strangeways Prison, during which he and the team had seen many lives touched and transformed by the power of the gospel, everything was falling in around him. The great wall of faith and work he had built up was collapsing in a shower of slates, violence and obscenities. Why had it all happened? Was it his fault? Had he done anything wrong and was there anything he could have done to stop it? He had taken the mike from the lad who had grabbed it that morning. He had talked the lads down. He had encouraged them to sit down again in their seats. He had felt completely alone at the time but that he was needed to be there. And then when the prisoner ran down the aisle and attacked an officer, somehow he knew that was it and there was no way he could stop this thing getting completely out of hand.

By the time it was growing light on Monday 2nd April Noel was up. 'I'll have to go in, Norma,' he said on his way out. 'I'm sorry.' She nodded and kept calm. He kissed her goodbye.

Suddenly she grabbed his arm. 'I'll bet those reporters are still out there waiting for you.' She ran and peeped through the bedroom curtains. 'Yes,' she called. 'They are. There's two carloads of them outside.' She thought for a moment and then said, 'Can you get out at the back?'

Momentarily the ghost of a smile hovered on his face. 'You bet I can,' he said. He slipped out of the back door and through into the garage before any of the reporters were aware of the fact. Then he was out and away down the road before they managed to follow him. Becky did not fare so well. As she left the house to go to school, she found herself surrounded by them and their insistent questions. It took her some time to get away.

As Noel drove towards Manchester he was surprised to find all the traffic stopped and diverted by the police.

He managed to get through and made his way towards the main gate. As he did, the first thing to hit him was the noise of shouting and screaming from the prisoners on the roof. He rounded a corner and looked up at the bright April sky. There on the roof were groups of men. Most wore gags or bags on their heads. Some wore officers' peaked caps. They pranced, screamed and jeered. Fists waved. Slates hailed down. Many rafters were showing. Some prisoners were hunched astride the apex of the chapel roof; some sat nearer the parapets for security. Torsoes were bared. Verbal abuse hurled down, along with the rain of bricks and missiles. It was an ugly and dangerous sight. One had a megaphone and was shouting. After a moment, Noel realised that the prisoners were playing to the gallery of the press gathered outside in Southall Street.

*It makes me sick*, he thought and his hands clenched. A wave of anger shot over him—fury that the inmates were doing this. And underneath the anger was an emptiness. After all the blessing of the past years and months, all the hard work, seeing all the lives touched and changed by the power of God, this was happening. Indeed, where was God in all this?

Even as he dashed into the officers' club next to the main gate, slates continued to hurl down. There were torrents of hatred and abuse. And there was always the threat of fire, of an inferno developing. Someone gave Noel a cup of tea. As he drank it he looked around at the faces of staff in there and saw the looks of despair, anguish and hurt. It was a scene he was never to forget. Some asked how he was and he was able to chat a little.

Later on a tea-bar was set up in the mess for the twenty-five days of the siege. This became a God-sent area as everybody worked together: staff, firemen, policemen, education personnel, probation officers and others. The chaplaincy team manned the tea-bar, doing eight-hour shifts. They found they were often to play a counselling role—sometimes able to help staff families as well.

As the day progressed Martin Fielding, the Diocesan Press Officer, came to see Noel, took a statement from him and from all members of the team and handled the press on the chaplaincy's behalf. As the days went by Noel realised how helpful and supportive Martin was and he became more than grateful for his help, particularly as during those first few days the press hounded him and his family.

Towards lunchtime the Governor came to Noel and, realising he was in shock, said, 'I don't want you here today. Go on home. Get some sleep.' So Noel was persuaded to leave and was accompanied by Father Peter Wilkinson, the senior Roman Catholic chaplain, all the way home in the car. Once home they realised that Norma was on duty at Heathlands, so Peter waited with him until Noel was settled in bed. Noel and Peter knew each other well, had worked together in the past, and were like brothers to each other. 'Come on, Noel,' said Peter. 'You must get some rest.'

'Could I have done something to stop this terrible chaos?' asked Noel. 'Am I to blame?'

'No. No. No.'

'But all my work is ruined, isn't it?'

Then, even with the questioning still uppermost in his mind, Noel fell asleep at last. Peter quietly left the room.

# 10

## 'You Have Experienced Your Crucifixion'

Back at the prison smoke was drifting out of some of the cell windows, settling in a grey-yellow cloud above the building. A police helicopter hovered overhead, monitoring the whole situation. The rioters on the roof had tried raising clenched fists at it and hurling bricks towards it, but had given that up as pointless.

Down below, amid the noise of their jeers and sirens wailing, prisoners who wanted to get out were still running for the main gate. Officers in riot gear, helmeted with see-through visors, wielded their shields. Some ran with an injured inmate on a stretcher. Paramedics waited to put the man into an ambulance. Hospitals were standing by. Policemen were there too, truncheons in pockets or held in readiness. The Prison Officers' Association Branch Chairman gave a brief interview to the press, in which he indicated that he was saying very little about what was happening. 'The prisoners may be listening in now,' he explained. 'They will have radios and will be following everything.'

By the evening only 119 inmates were unaccounted for. Some of these had used the prison switchboard to telephone out to a local newspaper with their demands: these centred around better conditions inside the

103

prison, better conditions for visitors when they came, and improvements for remand prisoners.

There were confused eye-witness accounts from escaping prisoners, who spoke of wings blackened by fire; cell doors wrenched off their hinges, bed frames thrown into the wells between the landings which were piled up with mattresses, chairs, buckets and a mass of debris. Planks of wood had been ripped out, and there were holes in the walls where bricks had been torn out. Graffiti was painted on the dirtied grey walls in a jumble of black and grey capital letters. By evening, part of the building was ablaze, and the night sky was lit up by flames and smoke. The fire could be seen raging inside the prison through the cell windows, which glowed red against the silhouetted building.

It became known that the Governor had made contingency plans to storm the prison, using nearly 400 officers to regain control. However, the Deputy Director of the Prison Service decided this could run the risk of injury or even death to some officers, as the situation was so volatile. He decided that the plan to storm the jail should not go ahead. So began the twenty-five-day siege of Strangeways. In retrospect, it was seen that this was the worst riot in the history of the British Prison Service. One prisoner died in hospital afterwards from natural causes. One officer, Wally Scott, died on 5th April in Bury Hospital as a result of a heart attack on the Sunday night. Forty-seven prisoners were injured over all and 147 police and staff were injured too. Many staff suffered afterwards from stress and post-traumatic shock, which took a long time for full recovery. Many staff were sent on detached duty to prisons all over the country, which meant they were separated from family and friends. Prisoners too were sent all over England. As a result they too were not able to see family. Those involved with the chaplaincy and meetings were bussed away along with all the others, and this was not easy for them.

On 5th April the Home Secretary, David Waddington, announced a judicial enquiry, to be headed by Lord Justice Woolf. This was to become a turning point for all involved in the British Penal System: the Government, staff, inmates, the Prison Service, chaplaincy teams, all other professionals and lay visitors involved in prisons, and for those concerned with penal reform and the rehabilitation of offenders.

By 1.30pm on the afternoon of Monday 2nd April Norma was off duty at Heathlands Nursing Home where she worked as a Sister, and arrived home. She checked on Noel and found him sleeping peacefully at last and ran downstairs again. Moments later she saw Captain Ian Ferguson coming up the steps to the front door. She later wrote:

Ian, bless him, Noel's constant colleague in all his years at Strangeways. They were like brothers; not physically, for Ian's hefty fifteen stone was like Goliath to Noel's ten stone, but spiritually they were brothers in Christ.

Ian embraced Susan and me and we had a coffee together. I said, 'How was it, Ian?' and the emotional dam burst its banks. Ian cried and cried.

'Oh, Norma, Noel went into the middle of the rioters trying to calm them and I thought they would kill him. One man lifted a fire extinguisher to bring it down on Noel, and I just thought that was it.'

Noel was garrisoned by prayer and the hosts of God were protecting him. I knew this without a doubt.

I asked Noel about this incident much later and he

said, 'Yes, I told the lad to drop the extinguisher, and he did. I wasn't brave, Norma. I just had no sense of danger in the chapel.' Then he witnessed the attack on the prison officer, and also the courage of the prisoners who got him to safety.

During those weeks Noel spoke only of the wonderful professionalism of the Strangeways officers, and found in the weeks following the riot that the bond between chaplain and officers was strengthened.

We received hundreds of phone calls of love and reassurance. By this time we had received about 800 letters and cards from Christians and non-Christians. One that moved me to tears was from the Jewish Rabbi at the prison, who spoke of his love and respect for Noel and assured us of his prayers.

Noel threw himself into the shift rota, working round the clock with the chaplaincy team. The Governor described the riot as 'an explosion of evil' and we realised that because God's blessing had rested on Strangeways, Satan had attacked and tried to destroy it.

Jesus said, 'I will build my church and the gates of hell will not prevail against it.'

Still no tears from Noel; still withdrawn; still spiritually bruised and broken. Why, Lord?

Norma put down her pen, knowing that she would have to give Noel time before he would be able to talk about this experience and relate to her again. She bit her lip and found herself praying for the courage to carry on while he remained so locked up in himself.

Noel continued to work long hours at the prison. Everyone there began to be affected by feelings of tension, anxiety, fear and rejection. His own thoughts were confused and muddled. Everyone was hurt deeply, both emotionally and spiritually. Those in the chaplaincy team were no exception, but through it all they tried to support each other. All the letters and phone calls and prayer built up a solid wall of support, and this meant a great deal to Noel. He said later that they had no contingency plans for what to do as chaplains, yet the Governor wanted them to be involved, and so in the days that followed sometimes they got very little sleep.

The chaplaincy as a team looked after the tea-bar in the Officers' Club and went out to visit prisoners in police cells, not only in Manchester but on the outskirts of Manchester too. They went to the hospital to see those who had been hurt. When Wally Scott had his heart attack on the night of Sunday 1st April, Noel visited him in hospital and went on afterwards to see his wife.

The chaplains visited the homes of staff too. The Bishop of Manchester allowed the church hall at St Clements near Waterloo Road to be used for the families of prisoners who were on the roof; families who were worried about what was happening to some of their loved ones who were inside. And so it became a meeting place where the chaplains went each day to see the families there, to try to reassure them, to try to give them comfort. Each morning the chaplaincy team would meet in the Visitors' Centre in Caernarvon Street, which had now become the place of meeting for all the different organisations; for probation; for the chaplaincy; for all those who were involved in any way; for staff who needed comfort and counsel. The Bishop of Manchester came many mornings to pray with them, and then Garth Rogers, the Methodist chaplain, took over the job of speaking to the media, because he realised that it was too much for Noel. And

Noel found this a tremendous help throughout the whole period.

After the first few days they decided that they would work on an eight-hour shift each, so that a chaplain would be there round the clock. Noel often found himself walking round the prison at 2 o'clock in the morning, going down to the Officers' Mess where he could get something to eat, to give to the firemen, police or staff who were on standby; endeavouring to help, and to encourage them.

On Tuesday 3rd April Noel drove down early to the prison so that he could help man the tea-bar. But when he arrived he was asked to help in the negotiations with and counselling of some thirteen lads who wanted to come down from the roof. As he was standing waiting to go and talk to them he realised he could hear shouting from the roof. He stepped back and looked up. Nearby was a fireman with a hose trained onto the smouldering cells. Suddenly Noel shouted, 'Lend me your hose!'

The fireman looked at him, startled. 'What for?'

Noel cried, 'These blackguards!'

The fireman followed his gaze and the two of them watched helplessly as the rioters paraded up and down in vestments they had stolen from the chapel. Abuse floated down on the breeze from the roof.

'Give me that hose, I say!' shouted Noel. 'I'm going to baptise them! I'll not only baptise them, I'll wash them off the roof! I'll get them off the roof if it's the last thing I do!'

The fireman kept his hose firmly trained onto the flames and smoke that were flaring out of the cell windows. 'I never thought I'd hear a chaplain say that,' he said and shook his head.

Noel clenched his fists. 'But I'm so angry!' he cried. Yet the great surge of anger was soon to give way to the old feeling of emptiness inside him. He knew perfectly well that hoses were never used in such a way. As he trailed slowly back to the barricade in order to help with negotiating, he realised suddenly how tired he was; he was not thinking straight. As he made his way to the barricade and surrender point on F Wing, the full force of many negatives struck him: fear, horror, destruction—all were happening in a place where people had worked and given of themselves for years.

This particular day the thirteen inmates surrendered. Members of the Board of Visitors, chaplains, doctors and prison officers were all involved in the negotiations and in seeing the men as they came down. Over the twenty-five days of the siege Noel had witnessed no assaults on prisoners by any staff. There were, however, times when a few hard-core prisoners had come and chased away other prisoners from the barricades, who had wanted to get out.

Noel decided to go home for lunch and as he opened his front door he heard voices. He stepped into the front room and saw Norma sitting talking to Sister Dominic.

'Hello there,' he said.

Sister Mary Dominic lived at the convent on the Bury New Road. She was a little, elderly Roman Catholic nun, who often came in to the prison to take classes and pray in the prayer groups. On the table was a bouquet of flowers and Noel guessed she had brought them for Norma. He opened his mouth to say something, but Sister Dominic looked at him. She drew herself to her feet and embraced him.

'Oh, Noel,' she said in her Southern Irish accent. 'Noel. This is Passion Week and like our Lord, you feel alone. The men you have trusted have left you. Noel, you have experienced your crucifixion. You've had your tragedy, you've had your heartaches, you've had your tears. Your work seems to have fallen in around you. Like the Master as he saw his disciples scattered, you've seen your congregation scattered. Your flock has gone to prisons all over the country. Oh yes,' she said, 'you have been crucified, but God is going to give you a glorious resurrection. A resurrection that is far greater than you can ever imagine. Easter is ahead and you will know new life in Christ. New beginnings, a whole new ministry.'

With this word of discernment she stopped. Noel stared at her helplessly and burst into tears. A little while later he drove her back to the convent. Afterwards, when he came back out of the convent, he sat in his car and simply sobbed.

Later he realised that this was the turning point. He said:

I suppose it was then that I began to experience something of God's healing power in my life. Up until then I was in shock. I was in anger. I was in hurt. Now, as the tears flowed and as I sobbed, I could feel the love of God beginning to flow into my life. People prayed for me. People loved me. Even though the hurt was so great. In the days that followed I got phone call after phone call. On that Sunday when the tragedy happened, Norma said that the phone never stopped ringing. Many of the callers were ex-prisoners who reassured her and said, 'Nothing'll happen to Noel. They all love him.' She was frightened and those ex-prisoners reassured her.

And in the weeks that followed we received over a thousand letters from many people all over the country, and all over the world, assuring us of prayer, assuring us of God's love, saying that God had scattered the Christians who were in Strangeways Prison in order to bring blessing to others. And how true this was. We heard so many stories from different parts of the country, where prisoners had been witnessing to the power of Jesus Christ in their lives. But how it hurt. It hurt to think that the work that had been going on in Strangeways over those years had suddenly disintegrated. It was no longer happening. Oh it hurt, and the tears flowed.

Up until this point Noel had been unable to talk about his experience in the chapel. He could not share it with anyone. Norma grew in her understanding of this and wrote in her journal about Sister Dominic's visit:

So time passed and Noel went through varying changes. No public speaking, no TV or radio interviews. No newspaper reporter could entice him to agree to an interview. The healing process was beginning and the doubts, fears and suffering—yes and bitterness—were slowly fading; but today look into Noel's heart and note the scars left from the agony. Search his mind and you will find many of his questions unanswered. He is coping in God's strength and will know his Easter in God's timing.

# 11

## *Seeing Through a Darkened Glass*

One morning shortly after Sister Dominic's visit, and when Norma was off duty, she took out her journal and began to write. The house was very quiet and her pen flew across the page. Every now and again she paused, thought and wrote again. After an hour or so she stopped and put her pen down. She stared unseeingly out of the window. She looked around the room in the house which she and Noel had built up together. Then, slowly, she picked up the journal and read what she had written. She had begun with the day of the riot—Becky's birthday:

Sunday morning, 7.00am. Noel was already on his way to the prison. At home I was still in bed, but awake. Today was Sunday, but it was also Becky's seventeenth birthday. I looked back over those years with thankfulness to God, remembering when she was just months old and I was diagnosed as having cancer. I wondered if I would ever see her grown up. Now she is seventeen, beautiful, intelligent and like Susan and Helen very, very precious.

Thank you, God, for the blessing of life.

I have known for some months that I now have a secondary spread of the cancer. I knew when Noel went to Withington Hospital to have a rodent ulcer removed from his face. I couldn't tell him how I was when he needed me, and with God's help I would be there with him.

Christmas came and I thought that perhaps it was my last with the family. I could not feel depressed. God was in control of our lives and I knew only peace.

1990: This year Susan had her midwifery finals, Helen her degree finals and last teaching practice, and Becky her first year 'A' level exams.

The family come first, although watching the changes in my body I know there is no recession of the cancer. My strength and my peace I find daily in the assurance of Christ's love for me, and my faith in him is steadfast.

1st April was to be a happy day. Helen was working at college towards her finals, but Susan was off duty, and so I knew that when Noel came home to lunch we would celebrate Becky's special day.

Susan was taking charge of lunch preparations and the radio was on. The programme was interrupted to announce that there had been a riot at Strangeways. It had started in the chapel. We stood in disbelief. It couldn't be true—not the chapel!

There. It was written now and out in the open. Her cancer had come back after all those years. And she knew she could not tell Noel and the girls just yet. All her married life she had wanted to protect him and the girls from the knocks of the world. *Just a little while longer*, she thought, *and then I'll tell him*. She had in fact written him a letter explaining all about it, but the days had passed by and still she had not found the right moment to give it to him. Then, with the eruption of the riot, and his shocked response to it, she knew she could not devastate him further by telling him. It was a

secret she was going to have to have the courage to keep
for a little while longer. She leaned back in her seat,
tired and unwilling to admit it. She knew she ought to
be filled with fear for her future, but a wonderful and
supernatural peace had held her all along. This peace
was holding her, she knew. And it would continue to
hold her.

The phone rang. As she picked it up she heard Noel's
voice. He sounded tired. 'Wally Scott's died, love. You
know, the officer who had the heart attack on Sunday
night after he'd insisted on staying to help at the
prison.'

'Oh no,' said Norma. 'His poor wife.'

'I'm going to visit her,' said Noel. 'I'll phone you.
Actually. . . ' he paused, 'they may want me to take the
funeral.'

Norma stood quietly for a moment by the phone. She
felt very sad for Wally Scott's family, but a part of her
at least was glad that at last Noel was communicating
with her again. Very slowly things were coming out:
about staff who had been hurt; about hospitals he had
visited; about wives he had tried to comfort; about
prisoners' families camped out in St Clement's Church
who needed support; about staff involved in the negotiations who were sleeping in the hospital area and who
needed reassurance; about other members of staff who
came and supported him and prayed with him. She
knew that when he was ready he would share the
deeper hurt as well. Father Peter Smith and Captain
Ian Ferguson were also welcome visitors to their home
and they too began to share some of the burden of
tension and pressure. She raised her chin a little. She
was going to play her part and continue to support
them all for as long as she could.

One morning towards the end of the first week of the
siege, Noel made his way towards the Officers' Club.

He looked up at the roof and saw some of the prisoners holding banners with messages scrawled on them. A few days before one had said, 'No Dead.' Rumours were still rife in the region about the numbers of dead. No one really knew, but horrific stories had circulated and many inmates were in hospital with the injuries they had received during the first hours of the riot, or suffering from overdoses of drugs they had stolen from the dispensary.

To counteract the noise of the prisoners shouting their demands, the police who circled the perimeter walls were playing loud music and prison officers used a screaming siren. The police helicopter was to strafe the prison building that night with an hourly beam of light. The tactic was to deprive the prisoners who were still holding out of sleep. Peaceful negotiations had seen all but thirty-eight of 1,647 prisoners now accounted for. Tactics were now to include the use of noise as a psychological weapon.

As Noel continued wearily towards the Officers' Club he saw another banner unfurled on the roof. This one read, 'We are deeply sorry for the Scott family over the loss of their father. We are human.' Noel felt too tired to respond, even with a shrug. He passed on and went inside. He knew now what the inside of the prison looked like: everything that could be torn up, or thrown down, had been done so. Landing wells were piled high with smoke-blackened debris, later soaked in water by the firefighters. The gym was wrecked. Both the chapels were completely destroyed. Much was gutted by fire. Windows were smashed. Both the chaplains' library and the Remand Centre prison library were torn apart. It had been an explosion of evil, thought Noel, for the riot had started in one chapel and moved to another. These were the only buildings to be totally destroyed. Rioting prisoners used the chalice to drink cocoa from and paraded about in vestments, mocking. One of the first things the rioters did was to push the cross off the chapel roof, smashing it onto the yard below. Noel agreed with the Governor that this was a battle between the forces of good and evil.

There was a heavy weight around his heart that seemed to have lodged itself there. He could not understand it, but he knew he felt guilty all the time. Constantly he asked himself whether there was anything he could have done on that morning of 1st April which he had not done. Was it his fault that the riot blew up out of all control? Was he to blame? Sister Dominic's words had helped him considerably, but even so he found himself questioning his faith and, more particularly, his calling. People said that he was still suffering from shock. His thoughts tended to be confused. Always he felt empty, as if nothing could reach him. And the guilt was there all the time.

After a while he came out of the Officers' Club and saw an officer he knew quite well, called Dave. Dave was collecting for Wally Scott's family and had a box in his hand. 'Come here, you idiot!' called Dave. Startled, Noel stopped. 'Just look at you! What do you think you are doing, looking so grim?' Noel permitted his tensed facial muscles to relax a little.

'You know, you're taking this thing far too seriously. This was going to happen. All right, it happened in the chapel, but it could have happened anywhere. It had nothing to do with you. It was going to happen anyway.'

Noel opened his mouth. 'Look . . .' he began, but Dave waved the collecting box at him.

'Nothing to do with you!' he repeated, emphasising each word. 'Snap out of it, Noel. If you crack up, what's going to happen to us?'

Noel looked at Dave for some moments. His words were like a welcome glass of water in a desert.

'Do you know, Dave,' he replied, 'that's the best sermon I've ever heard!'

Dave grinned and Noel went on his way, feeling somewhat lighter in spirit than he had before. Perhaps his ministry did have something to offer after all.

One of the hardest things to bear for all the staff was that a few days before the riot HM Chief Inspector of Prisons, Judge Stephen Tumin, had published a report which praised the way conditions were improving in Strangeways. Noel wrote in the first prayer letter to be sent out after the riot:

Brendan O'Friel, the Governor, and all the staff had really moved Strangeways forward, and the improvements were felt throughout the whole establishment, giving us all a sense of fulfilment and a pride in our work of rehabilitation. The Education Department was providing opportunities for inmates to improve themselves. The work in physical education had to be seen to be believed as more men and boys were being allowed to use the facilities of the various gymnasiums. The probation workers were making great strides in preparing men for release and making sure of after-care.

All the chaplains have asked 'Why?' as we have seen our work torn to pieces before our eyes and we have all been damaged and hurt in ways which take a long time to heal. At first it was a real sense of hopelessness and frustration, as the work which had taken years to build was destroyed. Then came the bitterness and anger against those who had perpetrated such evil. This was followed by the feeling of rejection and emptiness.

Oh yes, Strangeways was a tough place. It had

been called a human warehouse. We had seen so
many things happening when men were packed in
like sardines. And the slopping out was something
of a degrading situation. But many good things had
been happening since Brendan O'Friel had taken
over. We were seeing more men in the workshops.
We were seeing more men employed. We were seeing
more people coming into the groups and classes for
education and probation, and the chaplaincy. We
were seeing more men taking part in the gym. And
we were seeing things happening that were good,
productive and positive.

Noel did take Wally Scott's funeral in North Manchester. The Chaplain General came up from London
to be present at the service, as was Bishop Stanley of
Manchester. This service was televised and made
national news. As Noel shared his thoughts and feelings in the sermon, he said, 'During these last days we've
all been hurt deeply. We have suffered two bereavements—Wally and also our prison. Every one of us
has been hurt emotionally and our feelings have been
confused, muddled, and we've also been hurt spiritually
as the attacks of evil have bombarded us, leaving scars
and wounds which will take a long time to heal. There
have been those of us hurt physically. Although Wally's
health had suffered over the years, I'm sure the events
of Sunday 1st April increased the pressures on him. Yet,
as Wally was a fighter who refused to accept defeat, he
refused to go home when he was ill that night. So the
message to us all, as we come to pay our respects and
condolences, is to press on to victory.'

As the days of the siege went by, Noel and the other
chaplains in the team slowly began to accept that all
their work had indeed *not* been a waste of time and
energy. The Assistant Chaplain General, John Har-

greaves, spoke at the Palm Sunday service, held in the Officers' Mess and quoted Romans 8:31: 'If God be for us, who can be against us?' Slowly they regained energy and, as Noel said, 'a desire to see the phoenix arising out of the ashes; the phoenix of God's blessing, where a new prison would come with new opportunities and future blessings'.

In spite of these stirrings of hope there were still inmates parading on the roof every day, in full view of the media who appeared to be permanently camped outside. By 10th April there were fewer than twenty prisoners holding out. The Governor still used the tactic of peaceful negotiation.

Between the 13th and 18th April more inmates surrendered and three were taken to hospital with suspected food poisoning. There were now only seven hard-core prisoners left unaccounted for. On 19th April the Governor announced that all 1,647 inmates who were in the prison when the riot began were accounted for. But still the prison had not yet been recaptured. As Easter approached, many people felt they were living out a personal Holy Week. The chalice was eventually found in the ruins of the prison, quite flattened. A prisoner called 'Big Donald' said, 'Give it here,' and beat it back into a more or less recognisable shape. Noel decided to keep it safe until he could think of a use for it.

Noel was never to forget the day the Control and Restraint team said to him, 'We've taken back your chapel. Will you come and see what you can get out of it?' So the Control and Restraint team formed up, with Ian Ferguson and Noel behind them, and marched forward into the chapel, singing as they went, 'Onward Christian Soldiers.' Momentarily Noel chuckled to himself. What a sight they must look with their helmets on! But it was a sign to him that they were marching to victory. They were not marching to defeat. And afterwards the staff who had marched with them said, 'That's a picture of the future. We're not going to give in. We're going to win.'

The chuckle almost immediately died away though. It shocked the chaplains to see the devastation in the chapel. The wooden statue of Christ on the cross was smashed. The organ was completely ruined. Everything was fire-blackened and soaked in water. Every stick of furniture was torn up and thrown down anywhere. Noel simply stared at it, stunned. Later he found his Bible, completely unusable and swollen up after the soaking it had received from the firefighters. It was the one Norma had given him on their twenty-third Wedding Anniversary. Could Strangeways ever open again, he wondered? And if it did, would there ever be a new chapel?

On 25th April, with all but five prisoners now recaptured, prison officers in riot gear stormed the prison, quickly regaining control of the upper wing floors. The five fled to the roof, hurling missiles as they went. They were then faced with the choice of surrender or spending the night on the roof, surrounded by officers. By 6.00pm they decided to give themselves up. The young man who had first run down the chapel stairs on 1st April to shout his protest was the last to leave the roof. The five were taken down on a hydraulic platform, which was lorry-operated. They came down to world media coverage, punching the air, waving, clenching fists in salute and giving the thumbs-up sign. When they reached the ground they were led away. Prison officers turned to each other and shook hands, smiled and gave three cheers for the Governor.

Afterwards they made a final sweep through the prison. No bodies were found. Perhaps the sources of the rumours of sightings of dead bodies came from the sight of men who had passed out in the uproar and frenzy, overcome by drugs they had stolen from the dispensary.

Questions were asked in Parliament about the handling of the siege, and about the way media coverage may have played into the hands of the rioters. Nevertheless, the then Home Secretary, David Waddington, was adamant that any storming of the prison could have resulted in deaths and serious injury to staff and inmates alike. The facts were that in spite of prisoners parading a homemade noose on the roof to the waiting cameras below, there had been no hostages taken, no killings, and no really serious injuries. There had been no escapees, and no risk to the general public's safety. The prison officers and the Governor had done magnificent work and David Waddington was proud of them. He said that a new prison would rise from the ashes of the old. There would be a new Strangeways. That was for certain.

# 12
## Aftermath

After the longest siege in British penal history, work began in May to sort out the mess that was Strangeways. Refurbishment started on the remand wings which had been relatively untouched by the rioters and the fire. There were to be new, bigger cell windows—a prisoner would at least be able to see through the window now, without having to stand on a chair to do so. There was a new ventilation and heating system, and new stainless steel cladding for the roof that would weather to look like the old slates. Slopping out was to be a thing of the past: each cell was to have a stainless steel washbasin and toilet. No more of a whole wing having to use eight toilets. It had only taken one man to stuff his socks down the toilet for the whole place to be flooded. Whatever a man had done, there should at least be decency. Security and the exercise area were also to be improved. All this would take at least a year to complete.

In the meanwhile, the only prisoners left in Strangeways were those working in the Officers' Mess and helpers in the kitchen. During the siege Noel had held services in the Officers' Club. The first United Service held in the prison was in May and took place in the hospital waiting room. Prison visitors, helpers, friends, chaplains, some staff and two prisoners all came and joined in: denominational barriers no longer divided anyone. It was not a particularly comfortable place to hold a service and the toilet next door kept flushing. Yet at the end of that service one of the prisoners asked how he could become a Christian. The following Sunday fourteen prisoners came. Little by little, as the time went by, Noel saw that God was blessing again. The convent where Sister Dominic lived offered room for the Wednesday night prayer group. This idea was taken up immediately. It was truly ecumenical in spirit. Noel loved going, as did Norma. Everyone met there as brothers and sisters in Christ. People from all the denominations met together and prayed in a unity that became greater and greater.

Suddenly, after the media explosion of those twenty-five days, there was no more interest in what was happening in the prison. Those on the ground were left to pick up the pieces. Perhaps the report of the surveyors after the riot went deeper than simply being a report on the actual prison buildings. It reflected how many of the staff and inmates felt: 'Strangeways prison is structurally sound, although inside it is a mess.' Prisoners, many of whom wanted nothing to do with the riot, were sent as far away as Bridgend and Swansea Prisons. The number of marriages and relationships which fell to pieces as a result was only one aspect of the inmates' suffering. The chaplaincy received many letters from prisoners, which shared how angry and bitter some of them were with the ring-leaders of the riot.

Noel was involved in the Care Team that was formed in the prison after the riot. This was available to help staff suffering from post-traumatic or post-incident stress. Many staff were having nightmares, involuntary recurring thoughts when they relived scenes from the uproar, drinking too much or taking their troubles home with them. Team members found a great source of support in each other, as indeed did the chaplains.

One day Noel received a letter from a former inmate who had been sent to Lincoln Prison. 'I wanted to tell you that I decided to be a Christian when I was at Strangeways. I don't understand what is happening to me, but I feel Jesus has given me a new purpose in life.' One ex-inmate wrote, 'The consequences of what happened will mean that many Christian prisoners from Strangeways will have been moved to prisons all over the country and thus the Light that was in Strangeways has now been spread much further.' These were just two of the many hundreds of letters of support and encouragement received from all over the world.

Ian Ferguson, Peter Smith and Noel became involved in working with the staff in the reorganising inside the prison. One job was to pull out sheets and blankets and take them to the laundry in trucks. They found themselves laughing over this one day. 'I've found muscles I never knew I had,' cried Noel.

'Me too!' said Ian with feeling.

'I'm surprised to see you lot doing a job like that,' said a voice from behind them. Noel turned round and saw a prison officer watching them quizzically.

'Oh yes,' laughed Peter. 'We know what's good for us.'

Soon they were to put on dungarees and begin painting K Wing, which had not been damaged very much. After painting their fifth cell, Noel and Ian decorated a room which they thought would make a good chapel. However, in the end they were given a bigger room for a chapel, which they shared with the Education Department.

In the middle of May Noel had to go down to London in order to attend the Woolf Enquiry. Noel presented his evidence and was interviewed by Lord

Justice Woolf for about an hour and a half. The Chaplain General of Prisons was also present. After Noel had given his eye-witness evidence he was asked what his aims were in the job.

'Well,' he replied, 'we normally had five services each Sunday, for Catholics, Anglicans and Methodists.' He cleared his throat. 'Our aim was—is—rehabilitative. We want to show that men can have a different life if Christ comes into their life. They can have a life outside crime; an alternative to crime. A life of responsibility and purpose; worthwhile, with peace and happiness in it.'

Lord Justice Woolf leaned forward. 'Go on.'

'We try to make the services attractive and provoke heart-searching so that prisoners can see there's a better way.'

'What happens after the services?'

Noel said, 'After the services many men ask for counsel, or to have a talk. We can talk to them about an alternative to a life of crime, about putting their faith in Jesus Christ. Sometimes we take them to the chapel. Sometimes we see them in their cell. You see, sir, it's one of a prisoner's few rights—the right to practise his religion—and I have to co-ordinate this.' He looked straight at Lord Justice Woolf. 'You see, large numbers of men have been coming to the services. It would be sad if they have to lose this opportunity in the future because of what has happened.' He paused and dropped his gaze. He said quietly, 'But of course I'll abide by whatever is recommended.'

Lord Justice Woolf sat on for a few moments. Then he rose to show Noel and the Chaplain General, Archdeacon Keith Pound, to the door. On their way out he said to them, 'I have got no brief for this, you know.' He stopped. 'I need your prayers. Will you pray for me?'

'Oh, surely we will,' said Noel. And afterwards, as he walked away, he thought, *What a very caring man. What a humble man in such a powerful position.*

Later Noel arrived home from the station in time to go with Norma for a walk with their Yorkshire terrier, Charlie. How Noel enjoyed these walks, today especially when he told her all about Lord Justice Woolf. They both shared what had been happening in their respective days, listened to each other, unwound and generally relaxed. 'Oh, it's good to talk to you!' he cried. 'How was Heathlands?' He knew her answer before she gave it to him.

'It was lovely,' she laughed. 'I know I need to be needed, but there are so many people to help there.'

They carried on in silence and companionship. She squeezed his hand. It was good to have the old Noel back, even if it were for only a while. She remembered the letter she had written him, now in her bedside drawer, which told him about the cancer. Could she share it with him now? She glanced at him. He was happy for once, and cracking a joke about fifty per cent of his congregation turning to Christ in the first service held in the hospital waiting room. 'Fifty per cent of the congregation of prisoners. That's a better proportion than even Billy Graham gets!' he chuckled.

She entered into the spirit of things: 'And how many prisoners were in this congregation?'

'Oh, er, well, actually, two.'

'Two!' She burst out laughing.

'If one turns to the Lord that's fifty per cent, isn't it!'

She smiled and they turned towards home. She knew she could not tell him now.

'By the way,' she said, 'I've got a present for you at home.'

'Oh? And what's that?'

'You know how upset you were when the Bible I'd given you was lost and ruined in the chapel that day?'

His face went less mobile and she felt him grow tense.

'Yes?'

'Well, I've got you another one.'

'Oh Norma. That's lovely. Thank you.'

'I've written you a message inside.'

When they got home he unwrapped the Bible and read her words at the front: 'This Bible replaces the one that I gave you on our twenty-third Wedding Anniversary, and which was destroyed in the riot in Strangeways in April 1990.' She had also written:

Our God of the past. Eleven years have done great and mighty things at the prison. We rejoiced in that. Satan has tried to destroy eleven years of faithful ministry, but Jesus has promised, 'I will build my church and the gates of hell shall not prevail against it.'

Our God of the present. God has noted our tears, our questioning and our brokenness. And his love is healing us by reminding us of his promise, 'Don't struggle, but be still and know that I am God.'

Our God of the future. God assures us that after the crucifixion comes the resurrection to new life, new beginnings and new miracles. In the chaos of Strangeways stands Jesus with his arms reaching out and saying, 'Don't despair. Behold I make all things new. Heaven and earth will pass away but the word of the Lord endures for ever.' Praise God. So hang in there. Romans 8:28 is still our verse. All my love, Norma.

He turned in the new Bible to the New Testament and found Romans 8:28. 'And we know,' he read, 'that in all things God works for the good of those who love him, who have been called according to his purpose.'

*What a verse*, he thought. *You could spend all your life trying to plumb its depths.* He turned and looked at Norma. 'Thank you,' he said simply. 'I shall treasure this for always.' Then he went over and kissed her.

In spite of all the support received from the other chaplains who felt a deeper comradeship and brother-hood between them than ever before, and in spite of the support of the Care Team and the encouragement of the increasing number of letters and phone calls flood-ing in, Noel still had to cope with waves of bitterness and emptiness that could be triggered off by the tiniest thing. One day he turned from the pile of letters and frowned. Yet another person had written, kindly inten-tioned he knew, saying that one good result from the riot was God scattering his children from Strangeways as missionaries. Noel's brow furrowed. He felt he could not accept this. And his heart was filled with doubt.

One evening as he went into their bedroom he noticed the plaque over the bed afresh: Romans 8:28 again. 'All things working together for good . . .' *How can this be?* he said to himself, shaken by a spurt of anger. *Eleven years of blessing have collapsed at work.* Despite the 1,200 letters he was to receive all told, he simply could not see how all the horrors of the riot and siege—all the ruin of his and everyone else's work—could really and truly work together for good. How could it? He sat on the edge of the bed and slumped for a moment. Norma was out, on duty at Heathlands. He knew she believed that verse all right. She had believed it even when she had had cancer back in 1973. She had clung to it all along. She was living proof that the Bible spoke truly. He gave himself a shake, saying, 'Oh, get on with you, you idiot,' and went back to Strangeways in a slightly better frame of mind.

Another morning, as he went about his statutory duties in the prison, he was met by a lad who had been sent back to Strangeways to finish his sentence. This lad had been in the choir on the morning of 1st April and had witnessed the full force of the riot in the chapel. 'This lad is asking for you,' said a prison officer.

'Hello there,' said Noel. 'How are you? I can see they've sent you back for another dose!'

The lad flung his arms round Noel and began to cry.

'Steady there. Steady,' said Noel, gently extricating himself. 'Come on now.'

The lad managed a smile. Then he said, 'I had to tell you. You see, before the 1st of April I was not a real Christian. I know I was in the choir and that, but I was still on the touch line. But now . . . well, now I am one of the team for Jesus.'

'That's great news!' cried Noel. 'Praise the Lord!'

The lad smiled. 'I want to go straight now.'

The prison officer turned to stare at them for a moment. Then he turned back and carried on with his work.

One chaplain was to tell Noel, 'I visited a police container unit and the officer there said that he had always questioned the work of chaplains in prison until these lads had arrived from Strangeways. A number of them read their Bibles, and their behaviour was different from that of the other prisoners, and quite openly they told of how they had accepted Jesus into their lives while at Strangeways and how his power had changed them.'

So, little by little, Noel gradually came to realise that the work was still going on. This encouraged him. The encouragement slowly built up over the summer until he began to feel a lot steadier and more at peace.

One day a policeman rang the chaplaincy from Leamington Spa and said, 'I've got a lad called Will Michaels here.'

'Oh yes,' said Noel. Will, a former drug pusher and burglar, had become a Christian in prison and stuck to his faith over some months. He had led the way on the morning of the riot in rescuing the prison officer from the gang of kicking prisoners. Later he was to receive a shortening of his sentence and a Queen's Pardon. For now he had obviously been shipped out to Leamington Spa in the general dispersal of the prisoners.

The policeman said, 'I can't make him out.'

'Why's that?' asked Noel.

'Well, he's asked for a bucket of water and soap and a scrubbing brush, and he's washed his cell down and completely got rid of all the graffiti and dirt!'

Noel scratched his head, unsure of how to react.

'Then he asked for paint. So we gave him some. When I asked him what he wanted it for, he said that just because he was a prisoner it didn't mean he liked to live in filth and dirt. Anyway, I pressed him a bit more and he's told me such a tale.'

'What tale?' asked Noel.

'Oh, that Jesus has come into his life and given him a new reason for living a different life!'

'Well, that's wonderful,' said Noel, his spirits lifting.

There was a pause on the phone. 'Er, the thing is,' said the policeman, 'I never thought a prisoner, of all people, would make me think seriously about my life.'

In the moments that followed, Noel had the privilege of praying with this police officer on the phone.

When he put the phone down he was filled with joy. So some of his work had not been in vain after all.

He could not wait to get home and tell Norma about it. She was off duty when he arrived and her voice sounded tired. He grabbed Charlie's lead and called, 'Come on. Let's go for a walk.'

There was a pause and she replied, 'I'd love to, only . . .'

'Only what? Have you got a meeting?'

'No. It's not that. It's that I feel . . .' She stopped.

He waited, anxious to make the most of the evening sunshine.

'I feel rather tired today.' Her voice was low.

He looked at her in surprise. It was true; she did look tired and there was something . . . he couldn't quite make it out. Her face looked weary somehow.

'Have you got a headache?'

'Er, no darling. I'll be all right.'

Noel put the lead away. 'Come on,' he said kindly. 'You put your feet up and I'll make you a cup of tea.'

Over the tea he tried to cheer her up and by the time he'd finished, some of her old sparkle was back.

He said, 'Haven't the gang of three done us proud? Susan's passed her midwifery finals and she's working at Bradford Royal Infirmary.'

Norma nodded, remembering all her own struggles to qualify.

'And Helen's done very well in her academic work at college and has only one more teaching practice to do. And Becky. . .'

'Becky,' interrupted Norma, 'has passed all her GCSE exams with flying colours! And her first-year Sixth Form exams.'

'How come we produced such brilliance?'

They both laughed.

Twilight drew on and still they sat in a companionable silence. Noel held Norma's hand. *I hope she's all right*, he thought quietly to himself and cast a questioning look at her. He remembered how she had been at the Christmas Eve service at Elmwood Church the previous December, as if she were labouring under some strong emotion. He had assumed that she was all right. But now he was not sure. He had been so involved with the riot and its aftermath that, as he suddenly realised, he had not really had the time or the opportunity to think about how Norma might be feeling. His hand tightened around hers. *From now on*, he thought, *I'm going to make sure she's all right.*

# 13

## Living with Cancer

The weeks went by. Soon it was high summer and then early autumn was looming. Noel continued to work daily in the prison. He found that in common with other chaplaincy team members, officers and inmates it was hard to come to any definite conclusions about anything as far as their emotions were concerned. Inmates were really suffering from overcrowding in the police cells in and around Manchester; parents and families of other prisoners sent away as far as the South of England had all the problems of travelling to visit them. Many people suffered for months with emotional and psychological hurt as a result of the trauma of the riot. Some staff were sent on detached duty around the area. Some were transferred to other jobs; their children had to be uprooted from school and their houses put up for sale. This affected families deeply. The chaplaincy did all it could to support others. Ian Ferguson was moved to Stafford Prison. Everyone missed him, especially Noel, as they had worked together for so many years.

By early autumn there were just under fifty inmates, housed in the hospital and employed as cleaners and workers in the kitchen and the mess. These prisoners were allowed some free association and videos, so it gave Noel a lot of encouragement that a fair number chose to come to the Bible classes, discussion groups or fellowship groups. Once over half the inmates came to a meeting; two lads made a commitment to Christ. Then K Wing was almost ready to take about 150 inmates and Noel knew that this would ease the pressure in police cells around Manchester. He had a chapel made out of six cells knocked into one; people sent gifts of hymn books, other books and money. He knew that there was still a work to be done in Strangeways. In the middle of all this, after the Woolf Enquiry was over, they were told that Manchester Prison was coming up for 'market testing'. Everything was up in the air, pointing towards a new era. No one knew if he or she would still have a job in the months or years to come. It did not help to ease the pressure, tension and heartache of life inside.

At home Noel was quieter than usual. He and Norma carried on with all their normal activities. Norma greatly enjoyed her local church, St Paul's. She had a good group of friends there, who had all prayed and worked together, especially after the church was burned down a few years before. They met in the school while the church was being rebuilt. The new vicar, Stephen Fletcher, began house groups and slowly the church grew. One evening, at the Wednesday prayer meeting, Norma had a vision. She tried to explain it to the others there. 'There's a boat. A big stately galleon with bright colours and it's very strong. There are people hanging out of all the windows, and over the decks, with hands out-stretched. Oh!' She paused. 'And the water is full of other people, desperate to be rescued, some swimming and some sinking. The people on the boat are pulling them in, rescuing them. Oh! It's wonderful. Everything is so brilliantly coloured.' There was a long silence. Finally she said, 'I believe that the boat is us, at St Paul's. We mustn't give up, whatever we do, because we have such a ministry of helping and rescuing people.'

Noel was still up when she came back at one o'clock in the morning, her face completely lit up. He listened and rejoiced with her. *I haven't got what she has got in the way of spiritual gifts*, he thought. But his heart lifted and he was thrilled on her behalf. Then he watched as she set off upstairs to go to bed. She stopped halfway up, pausing for breath. She coughed again. He knew she had been coughing a lot lately. He ran up the stairs and gave her his arm. Later, when she was asleep, he still lay awake. She looked so tired lately. He turned over. Perhaps their planned weekend away at Barnard Castle, visiting old friends from their County Durham days, would help. Yet in his heart, deep down, without him naming it to himself, Noel was beginning to realise what was wrong with Norma. He knew too that he would wait until she was ready to tell him about it.

In retrospect, this weekend was a turning point in their lives. There was no going back as far as the cancer was concerned and in the end Noel did ask her what was the matter, as she spent so much time coughing and having trouble catching her breath as she went upstairs.

Afterwards Norma wrote about their experience in her journal:

Now it's September. Please God, let me live until December for Helen's graduation. I am living for Helen's graduation, and with that over, I would be at peace. Oh, I would love to be around for Becky's graduation, for their weddings, for my grandchildren, but I don't ask for that.

I have had a dry irritating cough for some weeks now and I am breathless when I climb stairs or go up an incline. I know my condition is worsening, but I want to keep it hidden from my family for just a while longer. When Helen finishes her teaching practice, then I will tell them how ill I am.

Noel and I have had a few days' holiday in Co. Durham, visiting old haunts and old friends from parish days. My cough has been particularly troublesome and I know I haven't looked well. Noel, I so want to tell you I am ill, but you have been through so much, how can I heap more sorrow on you?

Then one evening Noel said, 'Norma, is this cough worrying you?' and I told him as gently as I could of the secondary spread. I am amazed, as he looked at me and said, 'Yes, I know. I just wondered when you would tell me.' I explained to Noel that the only treatment on offer to me was chemotherapy, and I know about cytotoxic (anti-cancer) drugs and their awful side-effects. I have always said that I want quality in my life, not quantity.

We loved and cuddled each other and we wept together and committed it to the Lord. Noel knows I'm no quitter. I shall fight in God's strength for a while longer. When the time is right, we shall tell the girls.

No bitterness, no struggling, no more rebellion. At times I feel weary, at times exhilarated, but always grateful to God for today—tomorrow I must trust him for.

How I thank God for my work at Heathlands, for my colleagues, for the fellowship we enjoy together. Heathlands helps me to forget about myself, as there are so many patients and staff who need me. Inherent in me is the need to be needed; to reach out and touch somebody else.

I try not to think that I'm dying with cancer, rather that I'm living with cancer. God's grace is available to me each day and I'm taking it one day at a time.

It's wonderful to have Noel's loving support and to be able to be open with him. Please God, I ask again that you will spare me to see Helen's graduation!

As I look back on my life, I have had so much: loving parents, grandparents, family relatives, a good marriage, a loving and devoted husband, three beautiful and talented daughters. I have been totally fulfilled.

On the way home from Barnard Castle they called in to see Susan in Leeds. As soon as Susan saw her mother looking so shocking, she became suspicious about her mother's health. She managed to take Noel on one side and asked him outright what was the matter. He sat down suddenly at the table and tears flowed down his cheeks. Susan guessed straightaway that Norma must have a secondary spread of cancer. 'And the only thing that's keeping her going is Helen's graduation,' said Noel. He shook his head. 'Why didn't she tell us?'

Susan put her arms around him. 'Because she wanted to spare us,' she said, wiping the tears away from her own eyes. 'I'd better pretend I don't know yet,' she said after a while. 'Perhaps next time I'm home for the weekend, she'll tell me then.' She looked at her father. 'Look, Dad, I think you'll have to carry on at work. She won't want you brooding at home, will she?'

He looked at his hands. 'No, she won't. No, I'll carry on as long as possible.'

On 30th September Noel drove to the Lake District to spend the night at Newby Bridge. The next day he was to watch Barry Cuttle (a Manchester solicitor) and his son and daughter do a sponsored relay swim from Newby Bridge to Appleton on Lake Windermere, which was to raise £10,000 for the work of the chaplaincy. Noel smiled momentarily to himself as he drove up the motorway with the POA Chairman and Secretary, remembering clearly one night near the beginning of the siege of Strangeways. He had been negotiating with prisoners to get them to come down off the roof and surrender. Barry Cuttle had been in the team of negotiators. In a lull Barry had suddenly said quietly to Noel: 'What's happened to your organ in the chapel?'

Noel replied, 'Well, if the prisoners didn't destroy it, the Fire Brigade certainly have because they've poured so much water in!'

Barry looked him straight in the eye. 'I'll get you a new one,' he said.

Noel laughed. He knew people *thought* they meant what they said at 2 o'clock in the morning, but he always took such things with a pinch of salt. Tomorrow would be another day.

Barry said, 'No, I mean it. I'll do a sponsored swim for you.'

Barry had been as good as his word, and now Noel was on his way to watch him.

Noel booked into the hotel for all three of them. He and Ivor Serle had to share a room and by 10.00pm Ivor had settled down and was ready for a good night's rest. But something was strange in the room. Ivor lay still and tried to work out what it was. All at once he realised it was the quietness that was so intense. In fact it was so quiet that he could not get to sleep. Ivor turned over and saw Noel kneeling by his bed, praying he guessed. Noel was so quiet; he never made a sound. Ivor turned back again, but sleep eluded him.

In the end he took another look at Noel, who had now got into bed and was reading his Bible. By this time the sense of quiet was unbelievable, and with it came something else. There was a peace too in the room. And in that hotel room near Lake Windermere something said to him, 'Ivor, you've got to have some of that peace. You talk to Noel about it in the morning.' Later Noel was to write about this time in Ivor's life:

That morning, as we were making our way down to the place where the swim was to take off, Ivor said to me, 'I'd like to be baptised, Noel.' And I looked at him and I said, 'Ivor, for an adult to be baptised you've got to commit your life to Jesus. Are you ready to do that?' And he said to me, 'I think so.'

Nothing more was said. I had no chapel. We were having our services in the Officers' Club, surrounded by bottles of whisky and beer, so it was 'real thirst after righteousness'! But a few days later Ivor said to me, 'Have you done anything about arranging my baptism?'

I said, 'No, I want to talk to you first,' and so we went down to the Christian World Centre and had our dinner one day.

I said to him, 'Why do you want to be baptised?' At that time Norma was very ill, and Ivor said to me, 'I have watched you through the riot and before the riot. I've watched you as you've looked after the staff and the prisoners through these difficult times. I've seen you with your dungarees on painting cells and doing jobs that I never expected from you.' And he added, 'Now you've got a wife who's ill. If your faith can give you that courage and that strength to cope the way you have done, I want that faith.'

I felt really humbled by what Ivor said. We went into the little studio at Christian World and I explained to him step by step what it meant to commit your life to Jesus, and that day Ivor knelt with me in the little studio and he asked the Lord Jesus to come into his life.

A few weeks later we borrowed a church at Blackley and his friends came and we had the baptism, and Ivor shared with the people before he was baptised why he was being baptised. Yes, perhaps if the riot meant nothing else but that Ivor Serle should come to a place in his life where he wanted to put Jesus first, well that was worthwhile.

Meanwhile life had to carry on at home. Norma continued to write her journal, glad that she had been able to be open with Noel at last. There was a peace, she found, in knowing that he knew and that he loved her. She felt a sense of calling in the writing and did not really know how to explain it. But she knew that she almost had a duty and a purpose in the writing. She guessed that somehow some of it might get into print one day, and that as she had something to say, she really had to take out the old-fashioned yellow-cornered and hard-backed journal and put herself into it. So she sat up in bed many evenings during the autumn and wrote it all down:

So much has happened in the last few weeks. Susan came home for the weekend and it was wonderful to see her, but she notices the change. Becky has told her, 'Mum is always tired these days.' So Sue asked Noel and he told her—she is devastated. At bedtime Noel told me that Susan knows and so I went into her room and embraced my first born and we sobbed together.

'Mum, I don't understand God's dealings with you and Dad. Strangeways' riot has crushed you both, but why this? Dad will be torn apart.' I expect all our lives we will keep asking why, especially in the dark areas of our experiences . . . so many questions unanswered. What is faith if it is not reaching out into the darkness of doubt and despair, crying,

'Lord, I don't understand, but hold on to me for I trust you, Lord'?

Sue wrote to Alan and Flo, two more people who have befriended us all these past eleven years. They surrounded us with their prayers.

Stephen Fletcher, our Rector, called and we shared with him what we were going through. Stephen was so sensitive and caring.

I asked for a healing service in our home on the Wednesday and asked to be anointed with oil, according to the Scriptures. Noel asked that he be anointed with oil also. Wednesday came and my closest friends Annie, Alan and Flo, Stephen, Noel and I met in our lounge. God's peace was already filling my heart and mind. We had a time of praise and worship, then three readings from Scripture; a time of confession and waiting upon God followed, then they each in turn anointed Noel and me with oil, and the sign of the cross was made on our foreheads.

Stephen asked me to sit for this, but I felt compelled to kneel, for after all I was in the very presence of the King of kings.

It was a wonderful time and I felt so blessed. I was surrounded by those who loved me and longed for my healing.

Jesus, we all must face our Gethsemane in life and even in the midst of the sadness, like you I caught a glimpse of your glory. Praise God!

## Note

[1] Since Norma was first diagnosed in 1973 the treatments and options available to cancer patients have come on in leaps and bounds. The options and side-effects of cytotoxic (anti-cancer) treatment in the 1990s offer much more hope

and promise than they ever did. The choice of the management of cancer is an individual choice; many complexities have to be taken into account, based on a spectrum of factors. Not to have chemotherapy the second time round was Norma's individual choice. Her objection was not to drugs or medical treatment as such (which can include surgery, antibiotics, iron), but to the anti-cancer drugs and their side-effects. Keeping her dignity right to the very end was very important to her. She did not have anti-cancer drugs, but she did receive some other types of drug treatment towards the end.

*Susan Proctor MSc, RGN, RM*

# 14

## Norma's Journal

How I thank God for my friends. How kind and caring they are—and how discreet. Today Annie called with some home baking; such practical Christianity.

Yesterday I felt really off colour. So tired and weary. 'Oh God, give me some energy. I want to live fully whatever time is left. Thank you, Jesus.'

Noel, bless him, so warm and loving, keeps his thoughts and feelings hidden. He is so grateful to God for each day we have. 'Lord, in my anxiety, I plead that you will spare my life for a little longer. Please don't crush Noel.' Then I realise I see things with only limited sight. I see only my situation. I need to pray for wider vision, knowing that God sees the whole panorama of our lives. He is the Alpha and the Omega. 'Lord, I surrender to you. You are in control of my situation. Thank you, Lord.'

Helen phoned. Her teaching practice is going well. She is happy. Thank God.

Becky is busy sorting out her choice of university. God, guide them all. I remember my grandmother's philosophy from many years ago: 'Those whom God guides are well guided.'

Today I told Bridget Salmon, my colleague for eleven years. She and I are like chalk and cheese, but we have a good relationship. Today we wept together, we embraced and held onto each other. Bridget reminded me: 'Norma, God is love and he loves you. Fight on in his name.' How I thank God for my friend. Over our working years we have laughed together and remained loyal to each other in the nursing profession. Bridget tried to impart some of her strength to me, but most of all she promised to pray for me.

Today I feel so weary. I look around the home that I love and I want to do so much, but my energy is spent. I had a phone call from a Jewish friend to tell me her husband is suffering from lung cancer and is now very poorly indeed and is on a morphine drip. Poor man, not long retired and now this. Is it wrong to ask what life is all about?

Someone has said: 'Faith is trusting when we can't understand,' but at times it's almost impossible. 'Oh God, help me to hold onto you!'

My heart aches for Noel. He tries to be cheerful, going about his duties. Yesterday, he took the funeral of a fifty-three-year-old prison officer who died very suddenly from a massive heart attack. He visited the family, trying to impart some comfort to them—it can't have been easy.

Noel, you know how much I love you and how precious these twenty-six years have been. I have a husband who is very special and I treasure him. 'A marriage made in heaven.' Thank God that over our relationship is the stamp of his approval.

It's good to reach out in the night and hear words of comfort and reassurance; to feel Noel take hold of my hand and squeeze it, just to let me know he cares.

'Lord, minister to Noel. Impart your strength and grace to him. He gives himself unsparingly to all.

Anoint us both in your Holy Spirit. Jesus, I'm tired, but I rest in you. Thank you for your peace.'

I told Bill Sheehan, the nursing officer at Heathlands, how ill I am. He was shocked, but practical and supportive. Susan is home for the weekend and, bless her, she takes over in the kitchen. She has told Becky about me. She says that she modified it for her. So now only Helen needs to be told, and if God spares me I will wait until the end of her teaching practice.

I went with Susan and Becky to a craft fair at the school today. Normally I would stay for ages looking at the stalls, but I felt too weary to look around.

So many people are praying for me. How I thank God for the power of prayer.

I am going by coach to Margie my sister in Hampshire for a few days. I'm not looking forward to the long coach journey, but I know it will be worth it just to be together and put the world to rights. Margie phoned to say that a girl who works with her, after being told about me, had given her a vial of Holy Water from Lourdes for my use. However different our theology might be I was really touched by the kindness of this woman reaching out to me in love. God can only be exalted by such action.

Susan is on leave and will be home for a few days to look after Noel and Becky.

The few days I spent with Margie were wonderful. I was treated like royalty. Everyone was so kind and attentive. It was good just to be with my sister, who, bless her, put on a brave face and tried so hard to be positive. I never realised how much she loved me, and I hid my tears from her. She said, 'Noel and you are such a special team. No one thinks of one without the other. So I cannot believe that God will split the two of you. You have so much more to do for him.'

She was so sincere in what she said that I wanted so much to believe it—but life isn't that simple. We parted at the coach station and her reserve crumbled and she wept openly. I hated being the cause of her grief.

Noel told me he had had a visit from Bridget, my colleague, who wanted to talk to him about me, and they'd finished off praying together. Such warmth and depth of feeling. People are so kind.

Helen is home from teaching practice for just a few days. I must try to be strong and keep up the pretence of all being well. I will tell her when the time is right.

I feel so weak. I wish my appetite would improve. It seems strange to me, for however poorly I have been in the past I could always eat. I don't want to burden my family and friends. I long for healing; to be stronger. And even if I don't ask 'why?' with my lips, my heart is continually questioning.

'O Lord, I don't pretend to understand and I hate how I feel, so in this darkness, Lord, I reach out my hand to you. Just hold me tight. I love you, Jesus, but I don't understand your dealings with me.'

Tonight our friends are meeting in our home to pray with Noel and me, and to minister to us. The rector has brought bread and wine so we can celebrate the Holy Communion service.

It was a wonderful evening. Noel and I shared how we felt. My own feelings were quite mixed. A few days previously we had been to town, my first visit for weeks, and in walking along Market Street we had to stop three times so I might rest. It was discouraging for me and I felt so low. As usual I voiced what I felt before my God (I never see the need for pretence before him, for his word tells me that he knows what I'm thinking) and in my frustration I cried, 'Lord, if this is living, please let me die. I don't want to feel perpetually weary. I want to live.' On the Wednesday of the meeting I felt really good. Emotional, but at peace. Before we parted, we sang 'In the name of Jesus, we have the victory'!

Next day I felt poorly and vomited twice, in spite of having eaten next to nothing. Noel read to me Psalm 103 from the Living Bible and I was comforted.

Helen has an interview at a school in Barnsley on Monday 5th November. The references from her present teaching practice are glowing. God *is* in control of our lives.

I thank God for Noel—so patient and caring, and for darling Becky who is at home and sees me at my worst. How I wish I could spare them.

Noel visited the Isle of Man yesterday to speak at two meetings on the invitation of the Chief Constable, Robin Oakes. He enjoyed his time there and spoke of the friendliness and warmth of the people. At last evening's meeting, an elderly gentleman asked him where I was, said he had read *The Cross Behind Bars* three times and that I had inspired him. I felt quite humbled that I should inspire anyone, but God uses us all and I felt encouraged that somehow I had been of help to this man. Noel said I had been prayed for most earnestly. I knew it, for I slept so well and felt so at peace.

When Noel returned home at about 8.00am this morning, the first thing he did was to offer thanks to God that we were together again. No wonder I love him so much!

This morning I am off duty and from my bedroom I hear the happy noise of children on their way to school. I have been talking with the Lord and listening to him. I was reading Psalm 34 in the night.

Verses 8–9 are beautiful with the promises of God. I have asked him to touch my cancerous body. I so long to be healed; to waken to vitality.

What is it about us that when people ask us how we feel we say 'fine'? This morning my defences were down and when Noel asked, I wanted to drop the façade and say, 'I feel rotten, weary and despondent,' but why add to his burdens?

I don't need a façade with the Lord. He sees right into my heart. He doesn't see me as a wife and mother, or as a ward sister. He sees me as his weak and vulnerable child, and he cuddles me in his love. 'Lord, I need your strength. Just hold me and let me know you are with me always.'

My dear colleague Bridget and my wonderful friend Judy convince me to see a specialist. I saw a very human and compassionate man, who, when he examined me, confirmed all I already knew. He referred me to Christie Hospital. My first visit is to be in early December.

Norma left her job at Heathlands by the end of November. Her cough was worse, and fluid in her stomach made her feel uncomfortable, even causing her to vomit at times. Finally she plucked up the courage to speak to Helen:

I told Helen as gently as I could and tried not to alarm her. She was naturally anxious.

I was apprehensive about going to Christie's and yet I need not have been. Dr Stewart, the consultant, was positive and so easy to talk to. I discovered later that he was a committed Christian. He had several X-rays taken and said that there was fluid on my left lung that would need draining, after which he would start hormone treatment.

So I was admitted for a few days for scanning, X-rays and chest aspiration. The drug I was prescribed was new, and I was to be a 'guinea pig'. *Please God*, I thought, *let it work for me*. It didn't—I was so sick constantly that I was becoming dehydrated. My appetite was non-existent, for whatever I ate just wouldn't stay down. The drug was changed and thankfully I began to eat a little.

Becky and Susan went on several long walks and finally Susan said as gently as she could, 'Mum won't be around for my birthday next June. That's what we've got to face. Together.'

'I've known really,' said Becky and thrust her hands into her pockets. 'And I know how serious it is.'

'Yes.' Susan thought about her mother and how uncomfortable she must be: the cough affected her at night and the nausea all day. The fluid affected her stomach and the rest of her was wasting away. 'Come on, Becky. Let's go home.'

December came, and with it all the Christmas preparations. First, however, there was Helen's graduation at Leeds University. Norma had been literally living for this day and took trouble with her hair, her make-up and her clothes. Noel became anxious when Helen explained to him about the vast flight of stairs up to the main hall where the ceremony was to take place. When they arrived and looked up the stairs, Noel knew that Norma would never make it. He rushed round to see if there was a lift, but could find nothing. 'I *will* get up there,' said Norma with the old, determined glint in her eye.

Eventually, while Helen went off to robe, a couple of strangers came along and between them half-carried and half-supported Norma in a fireman's lift until she was in the Great Hall, and seated more or less comfortably.

Helen graduated on 18th December at Leeds University. I felt so ill that day, but nothing was stopping me from going to the proud event. Helen looked lovely. So young, so full of life. I was a proud mother and so thankful to God that I had been spared to see this day.

Christmas was almost upon us. Susan took over the Christmas shopping. Helen cleaned and decorated the house and everywhere looked lovely.

Susan was working until 2.00pm on Christmas Day, so Helen and Becky cooked the dinner. It was lovely to be together as a family.

In January I began to feel poorly again and noticed my abdomen was swollen. I was taken into Christie's again and 1.5 gallons of fluid were aspirated from my tummy. I felt so weak. I couldn't stand and became very despondent. I was inundated with cards and flowers and the assurance of hundreds praying for me. Yet in the darkness I cried out, 'Lord, have you forgotten me?' Immediately his words came: 'A mother may forget the child she bears, but I will never forget you. I have carved you on the palms of my hands.'

Susan and Noel knew how much it meant to Norma to keep her dignity, particularly while she was in hospital. Everyone in the family respected her decision as far as the chemotherapy was concerned. It was hard for Norma to accept that part of the treatment for removing the fluid from her stomach was to take water tablets, which meant she had to keep asking for bed pans or the commode. It mortified her to sit on the commode with only screens around her bed.

Once Norma came home again she was very weak. She had to be turned constantly, and although she never complained of pain she was in a lot of discomfort.

Often Becky came home early from college, anxious to help. She knew she would not be able to move Norma on her own, so she would ring their friend Flo Eccles, from the corner, who would come round and help. The most difficult thing Becky found was that her mother kept apologising to her for interrupting her 'A' level studies. *I don't mind. I want to help you*, thought Becky. *My 'A' levels will be all right. Please don't keep saying you are sorry.* But poor Norma did not realise and Becky did not know how to tell her.

Noel too got himself into the new routine. He knew that Norma wanted him to keep on working and not to brood, so he arrived at Strangeways for 7.30am. By 9 o'clock he was back home, giving Norma her breakfast and settling her down for the morning. He drove back to work, and then returned for lunch so that they could eat it together. It was a punishing schedule and one day he nearly fainted at work. However, he decided to keep going. What else was he to do?

Many afternoons Flo or Annie, Norma's two close friends nicknamed 'the golden girls', came round to see her. She had the phone by her bed if she needed help and Becky was always home late afternoon, if not before.

The staff of Heathlands were also a great support, not only to Norma, but to the whole family. They often brought gifts of food and flowers. A wheelchair and oxygen, bedding and food supplements were all provided by the nursing home.

Norma herself always made an effort to see visitors when they called. Her faith was unshakeable, although she always kept her feet firmly planted on the ground. Susan says, 'She still had her doubts and fears, the anguishes and the physical horrors that go along with cancer, but that love she had for the Lord just sustained her. Her faith was incredibly strong. She felt she had been given eighteen Christian years that she did not deserve. Each of those years was a gift and a blessing in her eyes.'

Noel says, 'She often spoke about the eighteen years we had had together to see the girls grow up. This was what we had asked for initially. Those eighteen years were very precious to her.'

Noel was ashamed of his own reactions to Norma's cancer back in 1973 when he had not really felt able to confide in anyone. This time he did not make the same mistake. Staff and prisoners knew, and he found that this helped. There was always someone to call on if he felt he could not cope: friends, hospital, prison staff, church, Heathlands, the girls. They were all there when he needed them.

Norma continued to write, although often she felt too weak to put down much. It became a struggle for her to write in this journal, so she did it in fits and starts, always determined to finish:

Discharged from Christie's again, thankfully eating and it's staying down—moving around slowly but surely, and ready for my next check-up in two weeks' time.

People have been so kind, offering help in so many ways. The feeling of being dependent, however, is awful. I have good days and bad days. Someone was discussing with me from Romans 12, knowing what is 'that good acceptable and perfect will of God'. I confessed that God's will had not been acceptable to me. I questioned his dealings, then I was reminded again of Jesus on the night before his crucifixion saying, 'Father, if it be possible, let this cup pass from me. Nevertheless, not my will but yours be done.' If Jesus found the acceptability of his Father's will difficult, then who was Norma Proctor to find it otherwise?

Helen has got her teaching post in Barnsley. Susan has a new boyfriend. Becky hopes to go to Edinburgh University if her 'A' level results are favourable.

I take one day at a time. There is some improvement, but I'm holding onto Jesus with all I have.

Noel struggled on through that winter of 1991. Even when spring began to show signs of new growth he felt as if he were in the dark; in a prison in his own mind. One day he said:

I remember when Norma was very ill in February 1991. It was a Sunday morning and Becky rang just after the services were over to say that Norma couldn't get her breath—could I get home? I rushed home, and sure enough the fluid was gathering in her lungs and she couldn't breathe. I rang up Christie Hospital and they said they would send an ambulance out. Within three-quarters of an hour the ambulance was there. The ambulancemen came in and they wrapped her in a blanket. They put her in the carrying-chair, and then perhaps this was the point that really hurt most of all. They put the blanket round her head to carry her out to the ambulance because of the snow and the sleet.

Norma had always said that she wanted dignity when she died—one of the reasons why she wouldn't have chemotherapy. That day, as they carried her out, something seemed to go inside me. Suddenly I was really angry. Angry with a God who I knew loved me and cared for me. I knew he had brought me through all these experiences down the years, but I was angry because Norma seemed to be losing her dignity, when the one thing she wanted was that. As I followed the ambulance in the car to Christie Hospital the Lord and myself had a real row. I couldn't help but argue with him. 'What are you doing? What are you playing at? She wants a little bit of dignity in her death, in her last days. Why can't you give it to her? What kind of God are you?' And so I went on. Perhaps I needed some of my anti-swearing tablets, because there were some terrible words coming out as the tears were running down my face in the car that day. The hurt that was inside me was bubbling out and I couldn't take it out on anyone else except the God I worshipped.

We got Norma settled into the ward and I never said anything to her about what was happening. She knew deep down that I was hurting very much. I left her that night and when I came home Becky was there in the house, but I was tired. I went to bed, but I couldn't sleep. I couldn't say my prayers. I knew that between me and God there was a barrier. Something was wrong in our relationship, and I knew that I was the one who had caused it. He wasn't a God of hardness, he wasn't a God of cruelty, he wasn't a God of discipline. He was a God who was trying to teach me, and I found it hard to learn.

That night, as I lay in my bed, there was no sleep. I tossed and I turned. Oh, I was hurting so much. In the early hours of the morning I was very conscious of a presence in the bedroom. Becky was in her own bedroom, but in our bedroom there was a presence. Not a presence of awe and holiness, not a presence of hardness or discipline or pressure, but a presence of care, a presence of love, a presence that was reaching out to me, a presence that was so close I could feel it. And as clear as crystal I heard a voice saying, 'Stop your fighting, stop your struggling. She's mine and I love her. Give her to me. I'll look after her.'

When I got up in the morning I was at peace. I couldn't explain why. I'd had no rest, yet I was at peace. I got myself sorted out and went off to

Christie Hospital to see Norma. By then they had taken fluid off her lungs and she was feeling better. I told her what had happened. I told her of the fight and the argument and the row that I had had with the Lord. Perhaps I was a bit like Job of old. I had to come to dust and ashes before I realised his presence and his power.

And when I'd told her the story she started to laugh at me. She said, 'I knew you were fighting with the Lord, but there's no point. Jesus has given us these eighteen years to see our girls grow up; to see our girls give their lives to Jesus; to give us great blessing in our ministry. We have seen so many wonderful things happening and we have known his presence and his blessing. Now we have always known that he could call us home. We have always known that this sword of Damocles has been hanging over us. I am ready to go. And God has got a new ministry for you,' she said. 'Why don't you let him give it to you?' I have thought of these words often.

Yet it was strange in the weeks that followed. I clutched at every straw. One night I returned from the convent after being at a prayer meeting. Susan, Helen and Becky were with their mum, and little Sister Anne had talked about a man over in Dublin who was a healer, who could even pray with people on the telephone and these people had been healed. And that night when I came home we got on the telephone to Dublin. He wasn't in. He had gone out to a prayer meeting, but he would be in at 9 o'clock the following morning. The amazing thing was that where Norma was concerned she was content. As she said, she had no pain—she had discomfort, but no pain—and she was ready to go to the Lord. But I was fighting, I was struggling.

The following morning, just after 9 o'clock, we rang Dublin again and this brother came on the phone and he talked to Norma and he talked to me. And he prayed with us both. I suppose I was expecting too much. Norma wasn't. She knew. She had accepted the fact that she was going to be with the Lord Jesus and she was ready to go. And in many ways she wanted to go. She prepared her own funeral service and the rector of our parish came regularly to bring us communion. She even prepared the talk that he gave and the hymns that were sung. It was all as if she knew it was coming and it was all going down in this book that she was writing since the day of the riot—her memoirs, or her journal as she called it, which she continued to write until three weeks before she died.

# 15
## Norma Goes Home

*Nothing can ever separate us from his love.*
*Death can't, and life can't . . . (Rom*
*8:37—Living Bible).*

For their twenty-seventh Wedding Anniversary in March Susan bought her parents a baby alarm. This was set up near Norma, who was sleeping downstairs by now so that she could indicate if she needed help. Noel found he could hardly sleep because he could hear her as she coughed throughout most nights and her breathing was loud and laboured.

She struggled over her last few journal entries:

Time has passed and now it is April. Many visits to Christie Hospital to have fluid drained from my lungs and abdomen. Dr Stewart is always helpful and honest—he pulls no punches and raises no false hopes.

The initial weeks were dreadful, the treatment made me so ill. I lost three stone and looked awful.

Today the 20th April. I have good days and bad ones. I know hundreds are still praying for my healing and I am comforted.

As a family we have talked quite openly about death, for healing is not only physical but spiritual. When I came home from my last stay at Christie's, the dining room had been made into a bedroom for me. No more climbing stairs. It's a haven and I feel God's presence with me at all times.

Noel said he has stopped struggling with the Lord over my healing. He had wept so often seeing my weakness and then one night he told the Lord, 'I hand Norma over to you, Lord. No more pleading and struggling. You are in control of our situation and I leave her with you.' He told me of an indescribable peace filling his heart and the very presence of God filling his room.

I awakened the other night to hear the words of St Paul echoing in my bedroom. 'I have fought a good fight. I have finished the course. I have kept the faith, henceforth there is laid up for me a crown of righteousness which the Lord, the righteous judge, will give me and not to me only, but to all who love his appearing.'

I know I am dying, as my family know it too, but I am in his hands. I am not struggling, only resting in him.

Does this mean I understand his dealings with me? No! Does it mean I no longer want to live? No! But I trust my God. Many of my questions are not going to be answered this side of eternity. We see only through a darkened glass, but one day we shall see Jesus and the darkness will pass away.

'The Son of God who loved me and gave himself for me' (Galations 2:20).

I have lived a fulfilled life—as a woman, a nurse, a wife, a mother, and above all as a follower of Jesus Christ since I was thirteen years old.

No one has been more loved. No one has been made to feel so complete.

Noel Proctor is the only man I have ever loved and I could not begin to describe his devotion to me.

Noel is and has been God's precious gift to me. Our relationship has the stamp of God's approval all over it.

This is what I pray my girls will find—fulfilment in life and completeness in their Saviour.

Norma's journal was to end here.

On the early May Spring Bank Holiday Monday Norma was able to go to the opening of the 'new' St Paul's Church, Kersal Moor, finally rebuilt after fire had destroyed it four years previously. With Noel's help and the aid of a wheelchair she gazed up at the building and her face filled with delight and memories. She recalled how long they had been going to this their parish church; how the congregation had had to meet in the school after the fire; how a new young vicar and his wife and children had come and had guided the church into meeting in house groups; how a new unity had sprung up between them all and the church had really grown.

Inside, the church was resplendent with its new interior, the flowers and the happiness of the people who had worked, given and prayed for its arising from the ashes of the fire and despair. 'Take me to see the new window of the Holy Spirit,' Norma asked, and Noel pushed her over. She sat and gazed at it for some time.

Afterwards, as they were leaving, she said, 'I want my ashes buried just outside the church door.' Noel nodded and squeezed her hand.

By this time Norma was too weak to continue writing, so Noel and Susan contrived writing on her behalf:

Norma is now too weak to walk the short distance from her bed in the dining room to the settee in the lounge, so Heathlands have loaned us a wheelchair, which means to get her moved she puts her arms around my neck and waist and I lift her onto the chair. As long as her knees don't buckle, we can manage, but her legs are swollen up with fluid and are very heavy.

Bridget, her colleague from Heathlands, has had to go to Trinidad as her mother is seriously ill. Norma is missing her visits, but Bridget has rung a couple of times and these calls have given Norma real encouragement.

We had a long talk one evening after our prayers about the subject of death. Norma has no fear of it, only of the process of dying, and all its indignities. She was anxious to talk to the girls about it, especially Helen and Becky. She spoke to Helen on the Saturday and it resulted in them both experiencing a closer bond of union than they already had.

Becky and I talked about death and how that as Mum is drawing near to it we must keep our eyes on Jesus. I knew Becky's mind was full of questions . . . mine was as well.

It was Saturday evening and Norma was in bed in the dining room, surrounded by her family photos and her antiques gathered over the years. We had our own prayer time together and suddenly she said, 'I haven't heard you singing round the house lately.' My reply was that there hadn't been much to sing about. She said, 'Sing "Great is thy faithfulness".' I did try, but after a couple of lines I broke down in tears. Suddenly her weak voice took over and encouraged me to sing on. Helen came in and played the piano. It was nearly 11.30pm when we finished praising and worshipping the Lord Jesus. As I climbed the stairs I could not help but admire her strength and faith.

Norma was never in any pain, for which we thank God, but she had a lot of discomfort from the fluid gathering in her tummy, legs and lungs. Her continual coughing was sapping what little strength she had left. On Sunday 19th May I was supposed to preach at Lymm, but rang to make my excuses and stayed with Norma.

Susan was with me to help care for Norma and on Monday, as her cough had become so distressing, Sue called for Dr Smith, the GP, to visit. Sue mentioned to Norma and me that he may suggest she be admitted for professional care, in a hospice. When he came he did discuss this option with us and appropriate arrangements were made. We had a phone call from St Ann's Hospice in Heald Green to say they would have a bed on Tuesday morning.

Monday night was difficult. Sue and I were up with Norma for most of the night. She was distressed because of her cough, uncomfortable because of the fluid and so very, very tired and weak. At one point when we came to her she was saying, 'I want my mummy.' I got really worried, but Sue reassured me that this often happens when people are seriously ill.

Perhaps the humour of the situation came through when at 7.45am Norma called for me. She wanted to know why I was not getting her ready for the ambulancemen who were due at 10.00am. I found Sue asleep in the lounge—she hadn't even managed to get back up the stairs to her own bed after being up with Norma all night! Together we bed-bathed Norma and got her ready for her journey.

Sue went with her in the ambulance and I followed on later. At St Ann's Hospice the love and genuine concern were beautiful and Norma was clearly at ease and had peace of mind.

I collected Becky from college at 3.00pm and we went out to see Norma. She was very weary and drowsy and after a time asked us to leave. She made us promise to ring her when we got news of Helen's interview for a new teaching post in Sowerby Bridge near Halifax. This must have been playing on Norma's mind, for she asked Pat McEvoy (a friend) to ring later that evening for some news.

Helen rang at 9.00pm to say that she had got the job and I at once rang the hospice. The chap on the switchboard said he would go and tell Norma.

At 10.30pm the night sister rang to say that Norma's breathing was difficult, but an injection had been given and she was settling down. I asked to be kept informed and I would come if she felt it necessary.

At 11.10pm the phone rang again and I was asked to come. I reassured Becky and told her to go to bed and that I would be back soon.

When I arrived there, Norma had already passed away in her sleep. I sat at the bedside and read aloud to her, her favourite passage, Romans 8, sobbing as I moved from promise to promise in those wonderful verses. I looked at Norma and perhaps it was the light or the fact that I had just kissed her on the lips, but she appeared to be smiling—she was in the presence of the Lord Jesus whom she loved so much.

Norma was the first person to be buried at the 'new' St Paul's. Her funeral took place on Wednesday 29th May 1991. Stephen Fletcher took it, working from Norma's own plans, which Noel had written down. The church was packed; there was standing room only at the back. The road outside was clogged with the parked cars and coaches of the mourners. Yet Norma would not have wanted anyone to grieve when she herself had passed into the presence of her Lord and Saviour. Although there was deep sadness and sorrow during the service, by the end came a surge of uplifting as the final hymn was sung. As the organ thundered 'Thine be the glory' round the church, people's hearts were uplifted. Yes indeed, where was the sting of death? Where was the victory of the grave? For as the prison officers who shouldered her coffin walked steadily down the aisle towards the open church door, a sense of resurrection and the Christian's eternal hope meant that many sad hearts were raised, catching the sense of purpose and faith with which Norma had viewed her own death.

Later Noel wrote about her funeral in the prison prayer letter:

As I write this letter so many memories are filling my mind, of years that I have shared a ministry with my wife Norma, and although she is now with the Lord she loved and served, I feel that in writing this letter, she is sharing it with me.

Thank you for the beautiful cards and letters of loving concern which many of you sent, and for the prayer support which helped me and my daughters realise that we were not alone at this time of grief. Your love has given us the impetus to pick up the pieces again. One letter from a prayer partner's dream diary read as follows: 'I saw a lovely lady dressed as a bride entering the kingdom of heaven. I was told she was Norma. And as the gates of the Beautiful City opened wide—so she went in singing, and that is where she is now—singing in praise to her Lord.'

What a wonderful encouraging vision! It reminded me of the moment when the six prison officers carried Norma's coffin out of St Paul's Church, to a full congregation singing 'Majesty'. Yes, she would have been singing the Lord's praise as she entered heaven's gate. Was it any wonder that our Governor Bill Ginn said that normally funerals depressed him, but he experienced a great uplift as he shared with the crowded church at Norma's farewell?

Over the years God has blessed Norma and myself in our ministry for his kingdom. She was the incentive and the encouragement to me in all that we did, and I miss her very much.

As a final tribute, the Rabbi from Heathlands Nursing Home led a Memorial Service for Norma on 9th July. This was very moving. Although she and he had come from differing backgrounds of faith, they had had a great respect for each other. Norma had respected the Jewish faith and was interested in it.

So a chapter was closed for the Proctor family. Noel tried to prepare himself for the future. The challenge would be great, he knew, both in living a life on his own now, and in still working at the prison with dedication. How difficult was that going to be, he wondered, now he was on his own?

# Part Three
## *New Beginnings*

*Our God of the future*. God assures us that after the crucifixion comes the resurrection to new life, new beginnings and new miracles. In the chaos of Strangeways stands Jesus with his arms reaching out as he says: 'Don't despair. Behold I make all things new. Heaven and earth will pass away, but the word of the Lord endures for ever.'

Praise God. So hang in there, Noel. Romans 8:28 is still *our verse*.

From Norma's note in Noel's new Bible, 1990.

# 16

## Coming to Terms

Noel awoke and lay quietly for some moments in the double bed upstairs at home. He still went to sleep on the same side of the bed as he had always done and woke up on the same side. He did not need to reach out to the other side to feel its uncreased emptiness. In any case, he had slept there on his own for some weeks before Norma had died, when he and Susan had made her a bed-sitting room downstairs. Yet he could never get used to it: the being on his own in bed, the quietness in the house, the way everything remained exactly as he had left it the night before in the bedroom.

Oh yes, he was all right. He was warm and comfortable. His fridge was stocked with food, much of it from kind friends and neighbours. He knew he had to be thankful—there were so many visitors and phone calls and invitations that he did not have much time to be lonely. The girls were a great help and Becky was still based at home, which made a lot of difference. He sighed and turned over and looked at his watch. It said 6.45am. It was too early to get up, although soon Charlie would be whining to be let out. Then he would hear Becky begin to move as she got ready to go out to her job as a care assistant at Heathlands. It had been hard for Becky—coping with leaving college, her revision and 'A' levels as Norma was dying, and then

167

Norma's death and further 'A' levels to be taken. He turned over and looked at his watch again. At least Becky was not left in the house on her own all day while he was at work. She had the holiday job at Heathlands to occupy her mind and give a framework to her days before she went off to Edinburgh University in the autumn.

The minutes ticked on and Noel knew he ought to get up. So far Charlie had not whined, but Noel knew he would soon be making a fuss to go out into the garden. Somehow Noel was finding it harder and harder each morning to get up and face the day. He simply did not want to get out of bed in the mornings. It was hard to understand himself at times. He had always had boundless energy and a love for his work. Getting up in the morning had always been the least of his problems. Now, however, he found himself thinking of the day ahead with something akin to dread. How was he going to cope with the incessant demands at work? With always having to have a word of encouragement? With planning, looking ahead—the person who was paid to be the official believer in hope?

'Oh stop it, you idiot,' he said to himself and flung the covers back. The sun was shining round the curtains into the room, but he felt no inclination to get out of bed and draw them back. If Norma had been there, she would have welcomed such a day.

'Dad,' came Becky's voice from down the landing, and simultaneously Charlie barked.

Noel sat up and swung his legs out. He dragged himself up and reached for his dressing-gown and slippers. 'Hello,' he called to Becky as he set off downstairs. He patted Charlie, taking some comfort from the Yorkshire terrier's hairy licks and weavings round his feet. He waited in the doorway while the dog trotted round the garden, sniffing everything. The day ahead of him stretched out as a blank. There was nothing to look forward to, he thought; nothing nice could ever happen again. Everything was dreary without Norma. Charlie shot back, scattering hair as he went. Noel sighed. He knew he must not let himself think like this. He had peace in one way, because he knew that Norma was with the Lord. He knew that one day he and she would be together again. It was just the living now that was so hard. Everything in their home spoke to him about her: her clothes, her antiques, even her friends who brought round cakes and offered their help. It all underlined how terribly he missed her, how terribly empty the house was, how empty his life was.

He raised his chin a fraction. Well, Becky would be down soon and it was up to him to be a father to her and have a cup of tea with her before she went to work. As ever, her arrival in the kitchen in a frantic last-minute rush raised his spirits and even brought a smile to his face. He was late himself now and he rushed through breakfast and getting dressed. Just as he was leaving the phone rang. He grabbed it. 'Dad, it's me— Helen. Are you all right?'

'Yes, darling.' He paused a fraction. 'I'm all right. Are you?'

She said, 'Yes, not too bad.'

'I'll ring you tonight, darling.'

'OK.' Her voice sounded happier. 'Bye, Dad.'

He put the phone down. How kind his daughters were. How they were trying to mother him. Sue had been on the phone last night, planning to come over for the following weekend. He was wrong, he thought, to allow himself to imagine that there was nothing to look forward to; because the truth was that he would *always* have them to look forward to, no matter what.

He backed his car out and drove off to the prison. The lightening of his mood, however, did not last. He found himself getting tense over the wheel, and sitting hunched in the driver's seat. Why on earth was he forcing himself to go into work anyway? *I've got far more troubles than these characters I'm going to help with their problems and difficulties and family squabbles*, he thought. He drove too fast into a parking space and had to jam his foot on the brakes. *My problems are far greater.*

The day passed as he knew it would. He was fine while he was at the prison, but once at home again all he wanted to do was bury himself in a corner and fend off the world. When he was at home he felt as if he could not face inmates or staff the next day. Yet when he was at work such thoughts seemed unrealistic. He pulled himself up from his chair and looked at the vacuum cleaner. Suddenly, even the energy required to plug it in seemed too much. Norma had always kept the place so neat and welcoming, so, reluctantly, he changed his mind and ended up by hoovering the entire downstairs. Later he ate his tea, talked to Becky, spoke to Helen on the phone and wrote a note to Susan. Then he sat back exhausted. He had never really realised before how much Norma did, both in running the house and in mothering the girls. She had always talked to them about their futures and their careers, as well as any problems they might have. Now there was only him, and although he was more than willing to try and enter into Norma's role with them, he found it a new experience and one which required him to learn how to be the most helpful.

That night, although he felt drained and tired out, he found it hard to get to sleep. Getting up the following morning was even more difficult than the day before. *Why do I have to bother?* he thought. *My problems are overwhelming me. I'm so lonely, so tired, so fed-up.* The bedroom was empty and still and, of course, there was no Norma. There never would be any Norma again, this side of eternity. *Why on earth do I need to go and help the prisoners, when most of them have far fewer problems than I've got?* he thought again, frowning.

He went, however, just the same. He backed his car out of the drive and drove doggedly down the same old road, while his heart was entirely drained and he felt completely lonely.

Most of the men in the prison at the time were remand prisoners. There were usually under 400 of them and a lot of them were making court appearances. This meant that Noel had little opportunity to invite them to his classes, as they did not get back in time. So once he had checked who might be available for groups and classes later on in the day, he was a bit freer to visit men who were serving their sentences.

This particular morning he went to see a man called John, who had asked for a copy of the Good News Bible the week before. Noel opened his cell door and said 'hello' to John, who was sitting on the bed. The hard-backed Good News Bible lay on the bed beside him. John looked up and said straight out, 'Noel, I was praying for you last night.'

Noel's expression did not alter. He leaned his head slightly. 'Thank you,' he said.

John said, 'I know you're going through a difficult time.'

Noel looked at him properly and saw the concern on the younger man's face, the blond crew-cut, the frown marks between his eyebrows. He sighed. 'Go on, lad.' He knew John meant well.

John leaned forward. 'I asked God. I said, "God, I want you to give me a message for Noel."' He pointed to the Bible. 'But I didn't know where to look.'

Noel came and sat on the bed next to John. He

waited to hear the inevitable platitude or verse that somehow would not speak to him any more. John was busy searching through the Bible and Noel felt like saying, 'Look, if you use the Bible as a lucky dip, hunting for guidance, and you let a hard-backed version "fall open", it will nearly always fall open in the middle at Isaiah or the Psalms. It's no good treating the Bible like that. It's not a magic book. We've got to get to know our Bible and study it and learn from it in the normal way.' A joke rose to his lips about a man who asked for a message from God and opened his Bible at random three times. The first time he read, 'Judas went out and hanged himself.' The second time he read, 'Go thou and do likewise.' And the third time he read, 'What thou doest do quickly!' But somehow Noel did not feel in a jokey mood, and in any case it would only deflate John if he were to get a quick laugh, when the lad was so in earnest.

'Go on then, John,' he said at last. 'I'm listening.'

John took a deep breath and with his finger on the small print read carefully. 'Isaiah 43 verse 2.' He stopped and looked at Noel. 'I've put my own words into it, like. It seems . . . right somehow.'

Noel was silent, rebuked by John's concern. *He's only had a Bible for one week*, thought Noel. *Who am I to say God cannot give him a message when his Bible falls open?*

John read, '"When you pass through the waters of affliction I will be with you; and when you pass through the rivers of tragedy they will not overflow you. When you go through the fire of bereavement you will not be burned, neither will heat kindle upon you, for I am with you," says the Lord.'

Noel bowed his head and sat in silence. John closed the Bible and was quiet. In a few moments Noel found he could not hold back his tears. They flowed down his cheeks. John put his arm round Noel. Together they sat for some minutes in the cell and Noel felt comforted. At last he got up and blew his nose. 'I'll come and see you later,' he managed to say and then slipped away.

When he got the chance to sort out his feelings, Noel realised that God's ways of dealing with people were truly amazing. A young inmate, not even professing to be a Christian, had helped him and ministered to him with what certainly was a direct message from God. In a strange way he felt less lonely, as if he belonged more to the human race. He no longer felt as if he were estranged from God by his grief.

In the afternoon Noel went to see John. He shook him by the hand and said simply, 'Thank you.' In the minutes that followed John talked at length and asked how he too could become a Christian. Noel found himself overjoyed to be able to lead him to a personal faith in the Lord Jesus Christ.

As they talked further John shared some of the problems and hardships of his own life and Noel tried to help him. Really, they were just like an older and a younger brother struggling amid the problems and frailties of this life to cling onto a belief in Jesus. In spite of everything, God was still there. Noel turned and looked back at John before he locked the cell door behind him, and his grin was genuine this time.

Noel clung onto this verse from Isaiah and repeated it many times to himself as the days and weeks slipped by. Yet it was a deeply difficult time and each day was a passage of time to be endured.

He found himself feeling that he too was in a prison. Whereas the men he dealt with were behind actual bars, he was in a prison within himself. He had seen this many times in other people, and now became aware that he felt the same. He realised that prisons of the mind are greater and more powerful than prisons of bricks and mortar. They need dealing with, these prisons we make for ourselves within our own personality and character. Perhaps that was why David, in the Psalms, wrote, 'Bring my soul out of prison that I may praise thy name.' Noel was comforted as he meditated on these words. He had walked with God for many years and knew that he could not give up on his faith easily or lightly. But when was he going to feel that peace and freedom within himself and so experience real freedom and joy in Jesus Christ? It was strange how he could still preach about it and mean it, in his public position, and yet all that seemed to remain for him privately was a blankness and dreariness that stretched endlessly ahead of him into the future without Norma.

Noel was to look back at this time in his life and accept that God does not make mistakes. The realisation came to him that God had, in his severe loss, been breaking Noel. Perhaps Noel needed to rediscover the faith he had had in his early Belfast days when he had learned from Billy Johnson's practical example what being a real Christian was all about. Perhaps Noel needed to get back to his roots and had to rediscover the power of the Holy Spirit in his ways of dealing with him. He was not sure, but he clung to the core of his faith, and, like Job of old, tried to trust God in the storm, in the turmoil, in the blank, in the emptiness, in the apparent lack of meaning.

One evening, as he took Charlie for his nightly stroll, Noel found himself remembering a beautiful four-year-old girl called Maria, who was the daughter of one of the young remand prisoners. Her father was in prison and her mother was a drug addict. In spite of all this the child was a delight when she came to visit her father, trotting around the visiting room in her innocence and pleasure at seeing him. The staff too were touched by her and made a fuss of her.

One day when she was at home with her mother the drug supplier called. Soon he and Maria's mother were arguing, shouting and fighting. Maria ran between them, perhaps trying to bring about peace. No one knew. As she did so the argument became ugly, and the drug supplier lashed out at the mother in a vicious kick. Maria took the full force of the blow, staggered and fell. Later she died from this attack.

Noel walked on and on until it was getting quite dark and Charlie was trailing along, having exhausted all his energy. Why was life so bitter? And yet when the prison population heard about this incident a wave of conscience had swept over them. With the father in prison and the mother in hospital, the only people left to make the funeral arrangements were Maria's grandfather and grandmother. The prisoners asked Noel to arrange a collection, which he did. Noel remembered his own amazement when many men gave their entire weekly canteen allowance, which they received to buy cigarettes, jam, sugar, sweets or whatever they liked. In the end Noel was able to take £400 to the grandparents, which paid for little Maria's funeral. What was this power of conscience that swept over them, unless it was the voice of God calling to them? It was remarkable to be a witness of this; to see how many prisoners gave and gave again, many to the Laura Davies appeal. It was rarely spoken about in society, but Noel felt it was a beautiful thing to behold the power of conscience as it stirred men. If God could speak to such men at such times, then surely he could be trusted to speak to Noel in his present loneliness?

One night Noel had a dream. He was not one to dream very much, and this made the resonance of the dream all the more powerful. In the dream he heard

Norma calling him by the familiar name she had always used for him. 'Noely,' she called. 'Noely.' When he awoke during the night her voice was still so real. There was no anguish in the dream and no sorrow, so what did it mean? As he sat up, fully awake, and thought about it, he realised that she had been trying to tell him that she was all right. Everything was well with her. He need not worry. He leaned back against the pillows, suddenly exhausted. *I can trust the Lord for her*, he thought. *It is good. All is well*. And he fell into a dreamless and refreshing sleep.

# 17

## The Experience of Suffering

In the weeks and months following Norma's death Noel found himself questioning the faith that he had followed all his adult life. It was not that he set out to question in an intellectual way; but more, when he least expected, the questions raised themselves with powerful insistence in his mind. He could not ignore them, for they would not go away. Did God make mistakes? What was the purpose of the struggle, heartache, tears, pain, anguish, bewilderment and confusion which people experienced in this life? Was there life after death? What did life mean anyway? Had he been kidding himself all these years about the very existence of God? What was the point of preaching the gospel to others, when he was no longer sure what truth was anyway?

Noel's professionalism at work held him to his task; and also the habits of a lifetime meant he did not neglect to attend church, to meet with other believers and to read the Bible. Yet he knew something of cataclysmic proportions was shaking him to his roots and he no longer knew how to go on with God.

He still found it difficult to get up in the mornings and face the day. Often he would find himself wondering what had happened to Norma and where she had gone. He remembered how he had seen her suffer, how he had seen her flesh shrink off her so that she no longer looked like the girl he had known and the woman he had loved. He had sat at her side in the funeral parlour and looked at her, and watched her and prayed with her. Doubts had come into his mind then. Was there something on the other side? What was it all about? Where was she now?

Such thoughts gnawed away at him and he still felt as if he were in another prison—a prison within himself and a prison that was hurting him very deeply. *Who can I go to?* he thought. Everyone looked upon him as the clergyman, the preacher, the man who knew all the answers. He had to tell the men in prison that there was a better way of life, that Christians could see their loved ones on the other side, that we would have a new body, that the old things would pass away, and that there would be no more tears, pain, suffering, or death! He buried his head in his hands momentarily, then raised it and shook it as if to clear his mind. Here he was, questioning it all. What had happened to him? What on earth was going on? And how would it all end?

One day in the prison, Noel was told that a man called James had had a sudden heart attack and had been rushed to North Manchester General Hospital. He was only in the hospital for about half an hour when he had another heart attack and died. However, the medical staff were able to resuscitate him and save him. So two days later Noel went up to the hospital in order to see him. Driving over in the car Noel wondered what he would find when he got there. James had been very insistent all the time Noel had known him that the Bible was 'Hans Christian Andersen'. According to James everything in the Bible was a fairy tale; there was no point to life. You lived and you died, and that was the end of it.

Noel walked into the Coronary Care Unit and was told that James was unconscious. So Noel simply went to his bedside, took his hand and prayed for him out loud. Just as he was finishing praying, a male nurse came in and said to Noel, 'Do you think that works?'

Noel looked at him with a grin and said, 'Well, you ask him in a couple of days' time and James'll tell you!' Then Noel left.

Two more days passed by and Noel visited again. This time James was sitting up in bed, smiling all over his face. His first words were, 'Thank you, Noel, for praying for me. I heard you!'

Noel was amazed. 'You heard me?'

'Yes.'

'Well, that's incredible.' And it flashed through Noel's mind how many times people go into the presence of someone who is unconscious and assume they cannot hear. People could say tactless things like, 'She doesn't look a bit well,' or, 'I don't think he's going to make it,' and be completely unaware that the patient may be able to hear, even though they cannot respond. Hearing is apparently one of the last faculties to disappear.

'Thank you for praying for me,' said James again.

Noel was silent. Here was a man who believed the Bible was a fairy story now thanking him for praying for him!

'It's a bit like old Paddy,' said Noel, trying to make a joke out of the situation to give himself time to come to terms with it. 'When the doctor came in and examined him, he said to Paddy's wife, "I'm afraid you're not going to have him for very long," and Paddy opened his eyes and said, "I'm all right!" His wife tapped him on the arm and said, "Be quiet! The doctor knows better than you do!" '

James smiled briefly and then stared at Noel. 'Listen,

Noel,' he said. 'When I went into this experience of death I was in a place where it was so dark that it was a darkness you could feel. Everything was pressing in upon me. Away in the distance I could see a light and something within me was urging me to get to that light—to get there as quickly as I could. And so,' he continued, 'I started my journey to get to the light. I stumbled and fell in the pitch darkness. I couldn't see where I was going, but eventually I got to the light. Just as I was about to step through the doorway into the place where the light was, the door slammed in my face. And that's when they brought me back. They brought me back to life in Intensive Care.'

James looked at Noel intently, and he said, 'Noel, you know what my attitude has been in the past. But I'll tell you this. Nobody can tell me now that there's not something on the other side.'

So Noel sat and talked to James about the Lord, and about God's power. Noel knew that James did not know anything about the questioning he himself was going through at the time. James knew nothing of the doubts penetrating Noel's personality and shaking the very roots of his faith.

As Noel left the ward that day, after talking at length with James, he could not help but reflect that somehow God was deeply involved. If it was not so serious, it would be funny. Noel thought, *God, you've used that man to minister to me and he didn't even know he was doing it.* He got into his car in the hospital car park and sat there for a little while, thinking about what James had said; thinking about his own doubts, his own fears, his own misapprehensions; thinking about his own weaknesses and failings. And suddenly he just burst into tears. 'Oh Lord, you're so gracious, you're so loving. How is it that you use the things that are so outside our thoughts and imaginations to speak to us, to teach us, to bring us back to the place where we ought to be?' James' near death experience was to give Noel a new hope.

In the weeks that followed, some of the pieces of the jigsaw that had so troubled Noel's mind and heart began to settle into place. He began to understand a little of the meaning of all the sufferings he had endured over the past eighteen months. And it was not only him, but inmates, staff and family alike. Everything he had worked for in the prison had seemingly been swept away in the riot. Everything he had built his life around at home had seemingly died with Norma.

And yet . . . and yet he was beginning to realise there was a purpose in it all. It was not an easy or quick realisation, but slowly the ideas came together. He thought about a story he had read where a scientist told how he had watched insects emerging from their cocoon. Each time, a piece of horny shell appeared to hinder the insects' progress, but when the scientist tried to help one creature by removing the shell with tweezers, it curled up and died a few moments later. Then the scientist realised that the shell had a purpose: it caused the insect to develop muscles so that it could survive in the big world it was joining. Noel wondered whether perhaps human beings needed the struggle as well. Perhaps God allowed the struggle, heartache and confusion to enable them to develop those spiritual muscles so necessary if they were going to be any use for the kingdom of God. Perhaps the experience of pain and suffering drives humans back to the cross and makes them sort out their priorities in life. And if that is true, then obviously God does not make mistakes.

As Noel reflected on these things—and as he looked back over the time of the riot and its aftermath; over Norma's illness and death—he finally saw that God was breaking him, stripping away all the props in his life, making him rediscover his faith afresh. He was rediscovering the power of the Holy Spirit and his ways of dealing with people; rediscovering his own message and calling; relearning that simplest and most profound of all lessons: what it means to trust the Lord, in everything and all the time. God had been by his side all the time, even though Noel had not realised it. God had known Noel's needs and, as the old poem says so clearly, 'When there is only one set of footprints, it is then that he's carrying you.'

James' testimony to life and light 'on the other side' brought Noel back to rediscover, as it were, the Lord Jesus Christ. In turn Noel now saw that there was an urgency in his ministry and his message; that he had been helped to see that men needed to change, to be ready for that day when they were going to meet the Lord. *And I'm learning,* thought Noel, *by the experiences that God is bringing me through, by the things he is teaching me and by the way he is ministering to me, that my best is not good enough. It has to be what God wants.*

He found himself remembering a story he had read once about a man called Sir John Thornhill. He was an artist and he was asked to paint a mural in a church. The scaffolding went up and the planks on top of the scaffolding, and Sir John and his apprentice began work on the mural. When they had it completed Sir John stood back to look at his handiwork. He was so engrossed in the detail of what he had done in the painting that he forgot where he was on top of the scaffolding, and he was going further and further back. The young apprentice suddenly realised that he was near the edge of the scaffolding. If he shouted he would maybe make Sir John fall, so he did the only thing he could think of. He grabbed one of the paintbrushes, ran forward, and slapped it down the mural. Sir John dived at him. 'What are you doing,' he said, 'destroying my painting?' Then suddenly he realised that by destroying the painting, which could be repaired, the apprentice had saved his life.

Noel considered how sometimes God takes the thing that is precious to us in order to give us his best. Our own preciousness, our own belongings, our own family, our own loved ones—perhaps they become so precious to us that his best is left to one side. Sometimes it is a hard lesson to learn, and yet it is only by learning it that we can experience God's blessing.

On 9th November 1991, just over five months after Norma's death, the prison chaplaincy team organised a Prison Fellowship Rally in the Methodist Central Hall, Manchester. When the evening arrived the hall was full, many having brought coachloads from all around the North-West to hear about the chaplaincy's work in prison. Ex-prisoners and wives came, prison visitors came, ordinary churchgoers who received the prayer letter and prayed for the work came too. Folk who were simply interested to find out more came along and waited expectantly to hear what Noel was going to say.

First, however, Ross Peart, the Methodist chaplain, got up and welcomed everyone to the hall, which had been lent by his church for the occasion. He announced, to general clapping, that Noel had been made an Honorary Canon of Manchester Cathedral. So Noel got up, thanked him and stood in front of the crowd. He was wearing his dog collar as usual, and a poppy for Remembrance Sunday. 'I don't know why they've made me a canon,' he said with a grin. 'Maybe no one else would do the job! And there again,' his grin broadened, 'maybe they'll want to fire me!'

After the laughter had died down he spoke seriously for a few minutes about what had been happening in his life since Norma had died. 'I thank God for the eighteen years he gave Norma and myself to see our girls grow up and find careers. Those were eighteen bonus years.' He talked with pride about his daughters for a moment and then he paused. 'Norma used to say that as long as she had a job to do for the Lord, then she would be alive to do it. She used to wonder why others died, and she was still alive; but that was the reason. She still had a job to do. About three weeks before she died, she told me she was quite ready to go, because she knew she had completed the work on earth that God had given her to do. "I have fulfilled my job," she said, "and I am ready to go home."'

Noel leaned forward on the lectern, his face intent. The green curtains on the stage behind him were closed, hanging in folds. Only the illuminated cross stood out against them, quite stark and bright. 'How good it was in those last three weeks that we were able to talk about Norma's approaching death as a family. We tried to prepare the girls. It is so important. So important to talk and share and tell your loved ones that you love them. One night, as we shared, with Helen playing the piano, we sang "Great is thy faithfulness" and I'd like us to sing that hymn tonight.'

Noel led the singing, conducting the audience with his face alight. He radiated strength and energy and purpose. And, although he did not say it, it was apparent to some watching that God had indeed brought him very low, like Job; but now, knowing so much about heartache, hurt, loneliness and struggle, Noel was still with God, and being gently restored to that new life and phase of ministry that Norma had prophesied would happen back in February when she had been in Christie Hospital. He was like a man who has had all the stuffing completely knocked out of him; and then, ever so gently, been reassembled again. The marks of his sufferings would always be with him. But the joy and quietness of the Lord were also with him, and in a new way. He was like a man whom suffering has rinsed in mighty waters and then placed, with a surprising peace, back on the river bank.

'Since the riot,' said Noel, 'we've lost Garth Rogers, the Methodist minister, and Peter Smith, the RC priest, to other prisons. Ian Ferguson, from the Church Army, has gone to Stafford Prison. We have been joined by Brendan Curley, from the RC cathedral in Salford and he would like to share a few words about how he has settled down to a life behind bars!'

Brendan got up, looked at the audience and told them, quite simply, how he had conducted his first interview in Strangeways. 'I had to interview a man who had been remanded for committing a murder. I expected to meet a big man who was full of aggression; instead of which I met a man full of fear and insecurity. He was the father of several children and he was haunted day and night by what he had done. He could never get away from himself and had to face himself and the consequences of his action every moment of every day. I longed to say something significant to this man, something helpful. But somehow it was hard to find the words.' He paused. 'I found the whole experience quite overwhelming.

'The way the media present crime and criminals is to make the people who haven't committed crimes feel good and very self-righteous. Us and them; the good guys and the bad guys. But when I'd been at Strangeways for a few months,' said Brendan, 'I realised that many of the prisoners can be generous and thoughtful and caring. It's not a case of us and them really. I've thought a lot about the word "redemption" in these weeks and what it means; for God was in the world reconciling it to himself. Inside Strangeways is a lot of broken and suffering humanity. But,' he stopped for a few moments and looked out into the hall, 'it is frightening how some men have given themselves to violence. The violent action and reaction. Nevertheless, God has called all of us to turn to face him and to be reconciled with him and be at peace with him. All of us have done wrong of one kind or another. We all need forgiveness. We all need to be reconciled to God.'

Amid applause he sat down and Noel took over again, singing the old favourite 'Take my life and let it be, consecrated, Lord, to thee'. Again, as he sang, the strength of his renewed dedication was apparent. Even though he was unaware of it, there was a new singleness of mind, determination and purposefulness about him.

'Let me introduce Alan to you,' cried Noel and beckoned forward a very tall young man, who had to have the microphone adjusted to a new height. People settled down in their seats and waited to hear him. Alan spoke quietly and seriously. 'I was on remand for committing a serious crime. It was going to be my second sentence. Anyway, I asked if I could go to the church service one Sunday so as I could have a chat to my mate who was also on remand. During the service I wasn't really listening because I was too busy talking to my mate, but I did hear a bit. It was about a real rose and some artificial roses, and a bee coming in and finding the real rose. At the time I thought, "What on earth is Noel Proctor on about?"' He grinned and the audience responded.

'When I got back to my cell I found that I couldn't stop thinking about it all. What did Noel's talk mean? What did it mean to be real, like the real flower? I knew I could get three, five, seven years in prison. It came over me that I had wasted my life and that my life was false and artificial. People used to see me walking down the street looking smart and say, "Alan, you must be doing well." But I knew really that there was nothing behind it and that I'd perhaps only have 10p in my pocket. I asked my cell mate what he thought and he thought I was mental. He said, "Are you after Noel Proctor getting you a phone call?" Anyway,' Alan laughed, 'I said I wanted to see Noel and he came along. I said I wasn't happy in my life and he said, "Do you want the Lord Jesus in your life?" So I said, "Who is the Lord Jesus?" We talked more and I decided to say that yes I did want Jesus in my life. We prayed and nothing happened. Anyway, Noel gave me a Bible and I read a bit about Jesus Christ and I got interested, so I delved into the Bible a bit more and started going to Noel's groups. It was funny, but gradually I realised that things were changing and I wanted them to change. The pictures on the cell walls came down, and the way I dressed and made up my bed roll changed. When I was at the meetings there began to be a warmth in me and I started being happy.' He shrugged his shoulders. 'Happy in Strangeways! Then if I read about a victim of a crime in the paper sometimes I cried about them, whereas before I would think, "Good on yer, mate," about the criminal. So I told Mum and Dad.' The audience waited in anticipation. 'I think they thought I was after religion so that I could get my sentenced shortened. But at the trial they gave me three years, which was what I expected, and nothing was mentioned about my Christianity.

'I've been free for a year now. It's true that temptations do come after release and they came to me. I've failed Jesus Christ many times, but he has never failed me. Six months ago I got a job.' He paused. 'Jesus is a great man and I love him.'

He went and sat down to a round of applause. The people who were listening acknowledged his seriousness of purpose and intent. Noel stood up and said, 'When Alan came out of prison I had a phone call from a policeman who was going into schools and he said, "Is there anyone you know of who could come into schools with me and talk to the youngsters?" And I immediately thought of Alan. I gave him Alan's name. He got in touch with him and Alan was thrilled with this idea. He began to go into the schools and talk to the youngsters and tell them how he had been a bully, how he had been a tough character and how God had changed him into a new creation in Christ. The policeman rang me up about two weeks afterwards and he said, "I have taken him to three different schools, and his experience of what God has done in his life and how God has changed him is remarkable. This lad is really helping these young people." Alan has shared with us tonight and as well as that he's joined up with a church and he's going forward with Jesus.'

Noel smiled at Alan and then everyone began to sing again. The meeting was nearly over.

# 18

## Changes of Heart

In April 1992 Noel drove to the Methodist church, Bury, to attend a wedding blessing. As he sat listening to music playing and waiting for the bride to arrive, Noel could see the back of the bridegroom's head at the front of the church. Noel got up and went over to shake him by the hand. 'Hello, young man!' he said and Will turned round, his face lighting up. 'Hello, Noel!' The two men grasped each other's hands fervently and Noel slipped back to his seat. It was inevitable that his thoughts should turn to Norma and his own wedding in 1964 and there was an element of sadness in his memories. Yet, resolutely, Noel put this on one side. Today was Will and Margaret's day; she was remarrying and now being blessed in that marriage to a man she had divorced four years previously.

Noel remembered Will on the day of the riot in Strangeways' chapel. He had helped to rescue the prison officer and, as a result, had had his sentence shortened eventually. He was also the inmate who had later cleaned up his cell to the amazement of the policeman on duty in Leamington Spa.

Now, as the moments ticked by and the guests in the church waited for Will's bride to arrive, Noel thought about the transforming power of Jesus Christ.

Will had been a £1,000-a-week drug addict. He had

189

been a notorious thug in the town, needing to get the money by any means to pay for his heroin addiction. He was so addicted and difficult to live with that in the end his wife Margaret divorced him, and he was left without her and his son and daughter. He was caught out trying to get away with a serious fraud and was remanded in custody at Strangeways.

Noel remembered clearly how Will used to speak about this time in his life, and he smiled to himself. 'I kept noticing this singing and whistling nutter who used to walk round the landings. I asked my cell mate who it was and he said, "Oh, that's Noel Proctor. If you want a phone call, he's a soft touch. He'll get you one."' So Will thought about this and decided to ask Noel to ring his wife for him and find out why she had not been to see him. When Noel returned from making the call his face was serious and he tackled Will about it straight away.

'You are separated,' he said.

'Er, yes.'

'I've found out from your wife that you've done a lot to hurt her. You've broken into her home twice to get money to pay for your addiction. And you've burgled your brother as well!' Noel's voice had risen with amazement.

Will bit his lip. He knew in his heart how low he had sunk and hated himself for it. He waited for Noel to tell him off, but instead Noel said, 'I think I can give you a Bible if you'd like one.'

Will frowned. He did not want to offend Noel and so he replied, 'Yes. Thank you,' even though he knew he would not be bothered to read it.

Noel said, 'You have hurt your ex-wife a lot and you are going to have to give her time to get over this burglary.'

'I know,' muttered Will.

After Noel had gone Will looked at the Bible in his hands. As a boy in Bury he had gone to church, been in the Sunday school and the choir, but now it meant nothing to him. He got up, the Bible still in his hands. He looked around for somewhere to put it. There was nowhere, so casually he chucked it into the corner of the cell. There it lay, title upwards, behind a chair.

When his cell mate noticed the Bible he said to Will, 'Hey, have you read Noel Proctor's book?'

'What?'

'It's called *The Cross Behind Bars*. It's supposed to be all right.'

Will shook his head. But the following Monday, when he was allowed to go on his weekly visit to the library for some Westerns, the first thing he saw was *The Cross Behind Bars* on the shelf. It seemed to jump out of the shelf at him, so, with a quick glance around, he took it down and hid it in his pocket. Then he got his allocation of paperbacks about cowboys and strolled back to his cell, untroubled by the fact that he had stolen a book.

As he read Noel's story, Will became gripped. He read it three times in all, and the only part of it he was to recall afterwards was the incident when a lifer at Dartmoor asked the local bishop if there was a sin God could not forgive. The bishop replied, 'The only sin God cannot forgive is the unconfessed sin.' This thought would not leave Will alone. He started to borrow all the books he could find from the chaplains' library and read them carefully. In the end he got tired of reading about how men and women in prison found this guy they called Jesus. Will had no intention of giving up his macho image during the day, especially in front of his cell mate, but at night, as he lay trying to get to sleep on his bunk, all the pressures

and the guilt crowded in on him. He knew how deeply
he had hurt Margaret and his children. And what about
his parents? And his brother? All the things he knew he
had done wrong, and all the people he had wronged,
crowded into his mind.

He enjoyed reading and so asked another prisoner if
he had any books to lend him. The prisoner handed
him a book with its back cover ripped off. The front
cover was entitled *Holes in Time*. It was the autobio-
graphy of a gangster. Will grinned. Now this looked all
right. It would be a good read, pass the time, and
obviously would not be religious. So he settled down
on his bunk to read. Halfway through he was startled
to read that the author, Frank Constantino, had given
his life to Jesus Christ and decided to become a modern
disciple.

Will put the book down and stared at the ceiling in
the cell. Was there nowhere, and no book, where he
could get away from this guy, Jesus Christ? He waited
all day, but there was no opportunity to be alone. At
night he somehow found he could not pray in front of
his cell mate.

Next morning Will asked his mate to slop out. 'I did
it yesterday!' said the cell mate. 'It's you today.'

'Oh, go on. Please. I'll do it tomorrow.'

'Oh, OK,' said the cell mate, grumbling a little.

Will waited until he had gone with the bucket. As
soon as the cell door banged shut, he buried his head in
his hands. Could he do it? All he remembered from
Frank Constantino's book was he had written that for
good or bad he could not undo what he had done in the
past. All there was left was for him to go forward and
start a new life. But could Will do this? Could he start a
new life? Three times he had tried to come off drugs
and each time was bitter. *I can't face that again*, he
thought. Even though he was free of them now, he

guessed he'd go straight back onto them again once he got out of prison. He picked up the Bible from the corner and looked at it. His cell mate would be coming back soon. *All right*, he decided suddenly, *I'll do it. I'll ask Jesus Christ into my life as well*. After a few moments he opened his eyes. For a second he wondered where he was. Then of course, where else could he be but in a cell at Strangeways, on remand? Did he expect Jesus to wave a magic wand? He got up and looked at his face in the mirror—but it was still the same, the same old Will Michaels, who looked no different now that he had asked Jesus into his life. The memory of all his past behaviour swept into his mind and he cried out, 'Oh, forgive me. Forgive me. Please forgive me.' There was a clattering outside the cell door and a laugh. His cell mate was back, empty bucket swinging. Will sat on his bunk again and composed his face. 'Hiya, mate,' he said as the other man walked into the cell.

When he awoke the following morning Will found he felt a lot better. He could only describe it to himself as feeling free.

'Hey!' he called out to his mate. 'Hey, I'm free! I'm a new creation in Christ, even though I don't deserve it!'

'Oh, shut it!' said the other man. 'I don't want to know!'

For the next fortnight Will immersed himself in the Bible. He joined some of Noel's groups, and told as many inmates as he could about his new-found faith. He got a lot of taunts for this, but quite a few other lads began to take notice of him and listen to him. He began to find it difficult to cope with all the different things people were saying to him and as he prayed he realised that he needed a sign. He needed God to indicate to him one way or the other that he was doing the right thing in becoming a Christian and witnessing to his newly found faith. It just seemed to come into his mind that he should write a letter to the author of *Holes in Time* and maybe in the reply the author would say something that would be a part of that sign.

One evening, about midnight, he decided he would write to Frank Constantino and tell him what had happened. So next morning he asked his cell mate to help him write the letter. 'Can I write abroad from prison?' he asked.

'It's fourteen years since I was in before, and I can't remember the rules,' his mate groaned. 'Are you a nutter or something?' he asked.

However, he did try to help Will work out the best way to write the letter. It so happened that Noel called in later to see how he was, so Will asked him straight out if he would help them with the letter. Noel stood quite still and stared at the two of them. 'You don't know what God is doing for you, do you?' he said. 'I'll have to pray for you. Come here, the both of you!'

Will never took in the prayer. He was too busy trying to pray his own. When Noel had finished, Will opened his eyes and noticed his mate trying to conceal the fact that he was brushing away a tear from his eye. *It's no good worrying about your macho image when you're really getting to grips with Jesus*, thought Will kindly.

Noel interrupted his thoughts. 'Didn't you hear what I was praying, man?'

Will stared at him blankly. 'Er, sorry. I, er, wasn't listening.'

Noel sighed in exasperation. 'You don't need to send that letter!'

Will's face fell. Perhaps he and his mate had got it wrong, had . . .

'Because Frank Constantino is coming in person, in three weeks' time, to this prison, all the way from America. So you can hand it to him personally!'

At Will's trial he was given four years for fraud. After becoming a Christian he decided to confess to the police the three further crimes of burgling Margaret twice and his brother once, and he was given a further six months for these crimes.

After he had been released some time, the police in Bury asked him to accompany them into schools and tell the young teenagers how and why he had kicked the habit and warn them against a life of crime. Eventually his changed lifestyle won back the heart of his former wife, in spite of everything she had gone through in the past, and she agreed to marry him again. In the autumn he was going to leave his job as a lorry driver and breakdown truck driver on the motorway and do some training in the Scriptures and evangelism at Cliff College.

As Noel waited in the Methodist church that morning, he bowed his head and marvelled at the grace of God. True, it would not necessarily be easy for Will and Margaret. But with the love and power of God to help them, they would have every opportunity to make a good and stable marriage. Noel knew that the many prayer partners and churches they represented would help to pay Will's fees at college. People might knock the church—and sometimes they were right to do so—but where else in society would a man like Will find help and acceptance in his struggle to rehabilitate himself?

There was a bustle at the church door and Margaret appeared, looking radiant and carrying a bouquet. Their six-year-old daughter Patricia was a bridesmaid and their nine-year-old son Paul was an usher. Noel smiled at her and then looked over to Will; he had moved into position to greet his bride.

And to crown it all, he had chosen a former policeman to be his best man! As Will often said, the worst prisons were those you made yourself. Prisons of bricks and mortar were not as bad as those. And here was a wonderful moment in his life, when all prisons both inside and outside were being left behind.

As the year wore on Noel began to see new problems emerging in the prison. There were many changes now being implemented after the Woolf Enquiry, but the shock waves of the riot and siege still lingered on. A human price among inmates and staff alike, in terms of stress and uncertainty, was still being paid. One officer had a heart attack two years after the riot and this was put down to the stress and strain resulting from the riot. There was much uncertainty about the future as the prison had to be submitted for market testing. No one quite knew what the future would hold in terms of jobs and opportunities.

Noel and the chaplaincy team had found that being Christians did not in any way exempt them from trouble, tragedy and hurt. The general lack of certainty about the future hit them as much as it did anyone else. Noel realised, as he looked back, that he had had to learn to adapt to frequent changes as he moved through crisis, tragedy and bereavement. It wasn't easy, especially when some days he still felt like packing it all in and Norma, who had always encouraged him to keep going, was no longer at his side. Yet as he weathered these storms Noel realised that even as he had questioned the fundamentals, he had rediscovered his faith in Jesus Christ as Lord and had, as a result, an even clearer focus on what he wanted to do.

The chaplaincy team had become even more ecumenical. It was running sixteen classes a week now, with fewer than 400 prisoners in the prison. This meant that as the classes were all wing-based, they were bringing in helpers to run them, and the team was touching far more men's lives than it had ever done before. The team got a lot of help from Prison Fellowship members, from church people who had become interested through reading the prayer letter and from prison visitors who found they no longer had the number of inmates to visit (because the prison population was so much lower at that time in the smaller, refurbished building) and so wanted to come in and help with running the groups.

The prison now prepared to put in a bid under the new government rules about market testing. This was based on the continuation of the implementation of recommendations in the Woolf Report. From the chaplaincy point of view Noel felt all these were healthy developments. The chaplains would still be needed; they had the time to go and sit with prisoners who had heard bad news from home. Drugs and alcohol were the main addictions manifested by the prisoners and so teamwork was built up in counselling and group therapy skills.

A group of staff were now allocated to run each wing. This meant that staff had the opportunity to build up relationships with the inmates. Whereas in the past an officer could be on 'A' wing one day, at court the next day, and on another wing the following day, now he was able to get to know inmates on his particular wing. This relaxing of the regime, which included the fact that hats were no longer worn by the officers, meant that a real communication could grow between staff and prisoners, and in time confrontations and 'scenes' were less likely to occur.

More organisations were also offering help for rehabilitation of offenders after they left prison: Lydia House, the Adullam Homes, the New Life Centre in Stockport and the Langley House Trust. Joe Whelan is a field officer for the Langley House Trust. He comes into Strangeways each week and talks regularly to the men about what they are going to do when they get out, particularly if they have had problems with drugs or alcohol. The trust has hostels and homes for rehabilitation and also places for men with nowhere to go. Joe often waits for a man outside the prison on the day of his release and becomes a 'bridge' for the ex-offender. Instead of the discharge grant going straight to the man's old drug supplier or local pub, Joe helps the man and accompanies him to a hostel or a home.

Joe too served a long sentence in prison. However, he became a committed Christian during his imprisonment and since his release over ten years ago, has not reoffended. He is now welcomed by the authorities, not only in Strangeways, but also in other North-West prisons. He has proved himself to be a reliable, caring and effective field officer.

Noel found himself developing a bond with Joe, who was a great support to him after Norma died. Like a brother, Joe would insist on Noel sharing how he felt during his bereavement. This helped Noel considerably as he readjusted to life without her.

Noel began to receive more and more invitations to speak to outside organisations: many schools around Manchester, and in Cumbria; Harrow School; Magistrates groups; theological lectures in colleges; the Development Course for chaplains, and annual meetings of the Prison Service Christian Fellowship. Students from theological colleges also came into the prison to learn from the work of the chaplaincy team.

After working for over twenty years in British prisons and longing to see change, Noel felt that one positive result from the riot was that the Woolf Report recommended changes, and Strangeways was determined to put these into practice. Hope in the future era was at last rekindled.

As he thought back to 1st April 1990 when the riot had broken out in the chapel, Noel remembered that no one had ever thought that the siege would go as far as it did. Manchester had had problems, but had always contained them in the past.

The Woolf Report had brought about changes, with better sanitation, better food, more time spent out of cells, and the introduction of personal officers. Yet prison will never be an easy place. Society will make sure of that. For some prisoners being away from their families is a punishment in itself. For others, it is sadly a blessing, when they can at last get on their own, face themselves and try to make themselves a future.

# 19

## *Righteousness Delivers from Death*

As Noel sat in his office one day the phone rang. When he picked it up he heard the voice of Wilfred, an ex-inmate who had recently been discharged. 'Hello there,' said Noel. 'How are you?'

'I'm fine.'

'What can I do for you?'

There was a pause. Then Wilfred said, 'Look, I've got a flat in Blackley.'

'Oh, I thought you had paid a lease on a house.'

'Well,' said Wilfred, 'what a mess that was. It's frightening what can happen once you leave prison, Noel.'

Noel agreed. He knew from hard experience with the men over the years how vulnerable they were when they first got outside.

'I'd paid my lease all through my sentence,' said Wilfred, 'just so that I *would* have somewhere to go when I got out. As soon as I arrived there the bailiff arrived and asked me to leave. When I asked him why, he said the owner had not paid the mortgage and it was going to be repossessed! So I got this flat in Blackley, but . . .'

'Go on,' said Noel.

'But somehow, Noel, I can't find a church. I can't

settle down and frankly I don't know what I am going to do if I don't find somewhere soon and settle down.'

'Have you tried your local Church of England?'

There was a pause. 'Where is it?'

'In Crab Lane. Look, I think you'll find you'll be accepted there straight away.'

'Do you think so?'

Noel laughed. 'I'm sure so,' he said and put the phone down. He sat back in his chair and thought about Wilfred.

It had still been the old Strangeways when Wilfred arrived in Reception, over six feet tall, a Forces background, divorced and very articulate. He was also cynical and not always easy to get along with. Noel grinned to himself as he recalled Wilfred's story. There he was, in Reception, over fifty years old and wondering what he had come to. All at once a rather smelly youth wandered in and sat down and put his feet up on the table. Wilfred noticed he had holes in both soles. The youth, who seemed to think he owned the place, said, 'What are you in for?'

Wilfred replied: 'Well, we won't go into that now, but what are you in for?'

The feet jigged about a bit and the youth smirked. 'I robbed a bank of £56,000!'

Wilfred could not help replying, 'Well, it's a pity you didn't buy yourself a new pair of shoes!' However, his humour was short-lived. He was given some food but the door was locked, and it seemed to Wilfred that he had to eat his dinner in a cage.

Later, he was interviewed by a member of the chaplaincy team. He answered all the questions readily enough until the minister said to him, 'Will today's decision make any difference to you 100 years from now?'

Wilfred stared. 'Are you mad? I'll be dead then anyway.'

The minister smiled and got up to go. 'You think about it,' he said.

Wilfred was put in a cell, eight by ten, on his own. It was dingy and dismal. After the door had been clanked shut and the key turned, he sat quite still on the bunk, and quite alone. He tried the door, but of course it was useless. He realised that he felt afraid, given up by everyone, and no one was left who wanted to know him. *I've led a bad life*, he thought, *since leaving the Forces when I was thirty. I was fine until then. But since* . . . He shook his head. He knew no one would accept him now or in the future, and he could hardly blame them. He got up, stretched and paced up and down. He was frightened to death, big as he was. He thought, *What am I doing here? What's my life all about anyway? I was brought up decently, and now look at me! Here I am, over fifty years old, and stuck in a cell in Strangeways.* He slumped down on the bed. He had been a good con man, he knew that. He had cheated people and robbed banks, not with a gun, but with a pen. He had found it easy, enjoyable even, to rip people off. There were people, he knew, who would never trust him again in his home town. Yet now he felt his own inadequacy and loneliness keenly.

His domestic life was a mess. He knew only too well that no one would visit him or write to him, and that there was no one else to blame but himself. And so Wilfred sat on, in the bitterness of his spirit, facing up to some very unpleasant realities while his whole world fell apart around him. What was he going to do?

As he sat on he became aware of some singing. The music was rich and stirring and reminded him of his youth in church and Sunday school. Whoever would be singing in a place like this? The music ebbed and flowed and Wilfred's heart lifted as he heard it. *It's beautiful*, he thought, and wondered what it all meant. Later he realised that the central rotunda in the prison, topped by a dome, had excellent acoustics and that was why the music had sounded so wonderful as it floated down the wings.

Next morning he said to the man in the cell next door as they queued to slop out, 'What was all that going on upstairs last night?'

'What?'

'The singing.'

The man chuckled. 'Oh! That's the God squad. It's the Jesus freaks, Noel's army!'

Wilfred was nonplussed. 'What do you mean? Who is this Noel?'

'Oh, he's the little bloke who runs round the landings at high speed, handing out anti-swearing tablets.'

Wilfred laughed. 'Go on!'

'You'll bump into him sooner or later. He carries packets of peppermints and calls them anti-swearing tablets!'

*Mmm*, thought Wilfred. *What a good idea. If your mouth gets refreshed by a mint you might not feel so inclined to give out a mouthful.* 'How do I meet this Noel?' he asked.

The man moved towards the toilets with his bucket at his side. He thought for a moment. 'Well, he plays the trumpet on Christmas Day.'

'Christmas Day! It's only June now. I can't wait til then!'

'Well, when they serve out tea you'll sometimes see him in a corner, near the centre stage where they serve out the food.'

'Right,' said Wilfred, determined to speak to Noel as soon as he could.

Later on, at tea time, Wilfred saw a clergyman

standing in the background, near the food. 'Is that him?' he asked his mate from the morning. The man nodded. So Wilfred approached Noel, wondering quite what to say. 'Er, excuse me. This singing lark, this song squad you have on a Friday—is there a chance for me?'

Noel stared straight at Wilfred and raised his eyebrows slightly. 'I don't know about that, Wilfred.'

Wilfred opened his mouth and then closed it again. He was shaken to realise that Noel knew his name. He had hardly been in the place five minutes, so how did Noel know?

'What are the chances of me joining one of your groups?' he asked, looking down at Noel from his greater height. This seemed to make no difference whatsoever to Noel, who stood his ground quite calmly.

'I don't think so at the moment. You are cynical and you'll be a disruptive element in my class.' And with that, Noel turned and walked away.

Wilfred was not happy over the next couple of days. His conscience kept bothering him and he could not get away from it, or from himself. One night he dreamed he had died and gone to hell. There were red-hot coals and he had bare feet and was afraid, and all around him hung dead rats and snakes. It was so vivid and so horrible that he woke up in a sweat and it took some time to calm himself down. He decided he must get a better life, but what could he do? He buried his head in his hands. *Just look at me*, he thought. *I am awful. And whatever is going to happen to me if I die in here?* He knew he had to do something to change himself; to be honest and decent; to get away from his conscience which was killing him. He never ever wanted to live the way he used to before he came to prison. He knew he could go back to earning his living dishonestly, but every part of him revolted against going back to that kind of life again when he was eventually released.

Two days later his cell door was flung open and Noel handed Wilfred a Bible and said, 'Read the Gospel of St John!' Then he turned and walked out again, locking the door behind him. Wilfred had hardly managed to get to his feet before the door slammed and Noel was gone. He turned the Bible over in his hand, looked at the cover carefully and then placed it by his bed.

Wilfred was not approached by Noel again until a week later. During that week Wilfred found himself wrestling day and night with the questions that haunted him: What did his life mean? And how could he ensure he would be able to live a decent and honest life when he finally got out?

On Friday evening, the following week, there was an unexpected jangle of a key turning in his cell door. The cell door flung open and a big officer was standing on the threshold. 'Jones!'

Wilfred stood up and nodded.

The officer jerked his thumb in the direction of the landing behind him. 'God squad!'

Wilfred stood a moment and then said, 'Where do I go?'

The officer nodded in the direction and said, 'Go down there and report to the lad waiting there.'

So Wilfred went along to the class, enjoyed singing and joined in the discussion. However, halfway through he caught Noel's eye and then turned away. He had started to get cynical again during the discussion and knew he should not have made that obnoxious remark that had risen, unbidden, to his lips. Afterwards he apologised to Noel.

Once back in his cell Wilfred could not settle down. Why was it so typical of him to be nasty and cynical when he really liked and admired what Noel and the other lads were doing in the meeting? He simply did not know. But he realised with a fresh force that he had to change. He must change. He must become decent again. There must be something better in life than this cell.

Finally he got undressed and settled himself to sleep, feeling terrible all the while, trapped, useless and nasty. He awoke in the middle of the night, and found that tears were falling down his cheeks. He remembered his dream of hell and was deeply disturbed. He clambered out of his bunk and walked up and down. He picked up a book he had been reading, but one glance was sufficient to tell him that for the moment it would not satisfy him in the turmoil he was in. Then his eye fell on the Bible, still closed and lying neatly where he had placed it when Noel had given it to him. With a sudden decisiveness he took two paces across the floor, picked it up and let it fall open in his hands. Then he sat on the bunk and began to read. 'Book of Proverbs' said the title, so Wilfred flipped back the pages until he found the beginning. Then he settled down to read it.

He read the entire book, all thirty-one chapters, right through. Finally he finished reading, and with the Bible still open on his knee, sat and stared unseeingly at the cell wall opposite. Every inch of his body was shaken by what he had read. Over and over and over again he could see himself in the pages. It was almost frightening, but this was a different fear from the fear he had felt when he was first locked in his cell. Slowly he turned the pages back to chapter 10 and reread the words in verse 2 that had so jumped out of the page at him when he first took them in:

> Ill-gotten treasures are of no value
> But righteousness delivers from death.

He read these words until he knew them by heart. In their stark simplicity they spoke to him, told him what he was and gave him the answers to all his questions.

Had he not spent twenty years getting 'ill-gotten treasures' by fraud and deception, only to find now that all that money was of no value to you when your world fell apart? And was he not so terrified of death that he was desperate to do anything to find an answer? And was the answer not written here in black and white, that righteousness was the key? He nodded and thought. The last thing he was was righteous, and he wanted to be righteous; to live a life doing right, saying right, following what was right. But how was he to get righteousness? He fell asleep again with this thought uppermost in his mind, and the dream and his tears were forgotten.

Next day he asked to see Noel and explained his dilemma. Noel smiled at him and said quite forcefully, 'Look at you. Don't you realise? It's God talking to you through these proverbs.'

Wilfred felt quite surprised. 'But how can God talk to me? My conscience is killing me.'

'Man is a trinity, like God is,' said Noel. 'You are spirit, soul and body.' He gestured to the cell window. 'People out there might not forgive you, but God will and can and does.'

'How?' asked Wilfred.

'Have you asked him? Have you read John's Gospel? Have you met Jesus in the gospel?'

'Er . . . no, not yet,' said Wilfred anxiously.

'Well, you get stuck into it and I'll come and see you again,' said Noel.

Wilfred read and read again. Finally, on his own, he thought to himself, *I don't follow all of it, but surely the answer must be Jesus Christ. I must accept him and his ways.* And quite quietly and soberly, he did.

It was only after he made this decision that Wilfred suddenly realised something had happened, as if somewhere deep inside him had been released. Emotions he had not experienced for years, and which he later realised were joy and happiness, began to bubble up inside him. He felt free. In the days that followed he was fully aware of the paradox of his situation. He knew he was free and released inwardly, even though outwardly he was locked in a cell, had no freedom and certainly would not be released for some time.

The curious thing was that, as Wilfred said later, he actually enjoyed being in Strangeways for all the time he served there. He had such inner peace. All his guilt went, and the loneliness which had so frightened him, no longer troubled him. He knew that if he had God, he could never be lonely. He was no longer separated from him, so he could never be lonely.

After his initial problems on release Wilfred settled happily at the church in Crab Lane and made several friends. He has kept clear of all trouble ever since. He was thrilled to be accepted by this church and became friendly with a seventeen-year-old boy there who had injured his knee. Wilfred visited the family and tried to help them. Some two years later he married the boy's widowed mother and eventually they led a church house group together, where Wilfred's practical knowledge of the Bible was put to good use.

In November 1992 he shared a platform with Noel at the Prison Fellowship Rally. Jokingly Noel introduced him. 'Wilfred used to work in the prison kitchen and dished out the sugar for the tea line. One day I said to him, "Wouldn't it be wonderful if we shared a platform together sometime?" And this is exactly what we have done many times.' Wilfred told the audience how shocked he had been to hear about the Strangeways riot when he switched on his radio one day in his flat. He had felt quite sure Noel would be all right, because, as he said, 'Noel was well loved.' Strangeways had a reputation in Manchester for being a hard place.

But nothing like the riot had ever happened before. Strangeways had never been like that. 'It was shocking,' said Wilfred, 'that Noel was treated the way he was in the riot.' He smiled at the audience and talked to them and then ended up by saying, 'Noel told me I only needed to find the right girl. I'd been a terrible husband before, but now here he was encouraging me. Anyway, I did meet the right girl and we got married. She's sitting here in the audience tonight.' The audience clapped and Wilfred said, 'I'm a difficult man to live with. But I'm not so pompous or bombastic now, although my wife might disagree!' Everyone laughed. 'We've both been ill, and I've had a stroke and I know that the Lord is saying to slow down. But I am happy. I've got a home, and a wife, and our pets; and I am happy. My present life is so good!' And amid clapping he went and sat down.

# 20
## Looking to the Future

Life continued for everyone in the prison. Strangeways put in a bid to the Prison Department at the Home Office, to continue running the prison as they were already doing. Eventually, after a lot of uncertainty and stress about the future, this bid was accepted. The building continued to be renewed: cream paint was everywhere, the place was cleaner and lighter, the landings, stairs and wings were all made with grills or bars and this meant a physically clearer vision for everyone concerned with the running of the prison. There was a new gym, a new hospital, a new chapel and a whole new entrance area, done in red brick and toning in well with the old building. The remand section had never really closed. By March 1994 the newly refurbished Manchester prison was reopened, the five wings occupied and the number of inmates slowly built up at the rate of fifty prisoners a week, until the total of just under 900 men was reached. Sanitation was much improved: each man now has his own cell, with a toilet and washbasin either inside or adjacent to the cell. Slopping out, with all its indignities, is a thing of the past. The new kitchen facilities have also brought improvements: food is now served hot, is on the whole improved in variety and quality, and served at normal times when people outside would also be eating. The old routine of lunch at 11.30am and tea at 4.30pm has gone. Now men can make their own drinks as well.

This new element of dignity for the prisoners in their daily routine has become an incentive to them to enter into the new *compact* being requested of them by the prison authorities. In this the authorities promise to give them a purpose while they are in prison, will endeavour to help them with their problems while in prison, and will prepare them for release after prison. In return, the prisoners promise to behave themselves, go to work, and begin to look at their own lives through discussion and acceptance of help. Both parties then sign the compact, which undergirds the whole building up of the new era in the prison. Relationships between all concerned are now seen as playing a key role in the new Manchester prison.

A *personal officer* is appointed for each eight to ten inmates. He can get to know them as individuals and take an interest in them. The prisoner can choose to go to him if he needs help with any problem. In certain cases this has given great encouragement. There are still some problems, but these are becoming fewer.

Then there is *sentence planning*: during his sentence a man is given some education, he can work in the packing workshops, and if possible he is given an opportunity to learn a trade. Prisoners can learn computer skills, refurbish NHS wheelchairs, be trained and then make three-piece suites. New ideas include a hairdressing salon in the prison and special courses in painting, decorating and plastering. All this is useful employment.

There is now *pre-release* preparation. Some inmates are able to go out into one of the Christian after-care homes. If a man suffers from a drink or drug addiction, help is given both in treatment inside and also after he is released, when he can go to a special home where training and help are given to overcome his addiction. A *Job Club* has opened in prison, so men can write out to firms and industries, trying to find employment upon release. So far the results have been encouraging. Many men who have come to the Job Club have been interviewed by firms, and some have been successful and have been offered a job upon release.

The personal officer can also bring in a trained *listener* to get alongside any of his men who are finding life hard-going. These listeners are other inmates, trained to listen and absorb emotional and verbal outpourings. They can often offer support as they too will have experienced many of the same anxieties and feelings.

*Telephones* are now available and men can keep in touch with their wives and families, or girlfriends. This is important as it allows for continuity and openness in family relationships. In the past all this had to be done by letter. Visiting facilities have also improved. There are crèches, and inmates can have weekly rather than, as in the past, monthly visits. Men on remand can receive daily visits. This all helps to keep family relationships sound during a sentence and, hopefully, upon release.

The compact does put some demands and restrictions on the prisoners. They have to be prepared to take the right attitude towards it, learn more about themselves and their motivations. They have to want to improve. Some men have signed the compact and then thought they could stay in bed in the mornings. This is not acceptable. If they do not bother to come out to work they do not receive any pay and they are locked up again. They must accept the fact that they are to make an effort to help themselves and enter into the activities laid on by the Education Department, physical training instructors, Probation Service and chaplaincy team; all of whom are endeavouring to make structured activities available.

The chaplaincy offers Bible and confirmation classes, prayer and fellowship groups, as well as services on Sundays and a Sunday afternoon concert. Noel is finding that men come to these concerts now, not simply to get out of their cells as in the old days, but because they want to come. Such men are often very interested to find out more about an alternative to a life of crime. Noel wrote in his prayer letter:

> We have a group of inmates who have accepted Jesus, and they meet with us each morning to pray for the prison (those who live in it, and those who work in it). This is a real source of strength. David Palmer, our new assistant chaplain, who has been working for three years already with the Board of Social Responsibility regarding drug addiction in the Diocese of Manchester, has begun a drug rehabilitation group in the prison, which is being used to help men leave an addiction which will destroy them and shows them how to get really 'high' on Jesus! There is a new wave of optimism in the prison and everyone concerned is looking forward to a future, when conditions are so much improved.

When Manchester Prison came through the 1990 tragedy, Noel and his colleagues often wondered what would happen in the years that lay ahead. Now they know they are seeing developments which are useful, practical and fruitful. Naturally, it has not been easy for prison staff to readjust to the new prison and yet they are doing it. *Care teams* have now been started in every prison so that if there is any incident, such as violence or the discovery of someone who has committed suicide or whatever it may be, a team member is available to draw alongside their colleague and offer support and encouragement. Everyone knows how difficult it is to cope with the aftermath of emotions and reactions caused by such incidents; it has an effect upon staff and their families.

As Noel looks at the new Manchester Prison now he can see, as was said after the tragedies of 1990, that the phoenix is beginning to rise again from the ashes of the past. In many ways Manchester is a flagship for other big, local prisons, where men can be treated with some dignity and, above all, where men can find some sort of purpose in life. They do not have to live in the shadowland of drugs and drink. The desire of the new Manchester is to show men that there is indeed light through prison bars.

The Governor, Robin Halward, sees this as a challenge:

> It is almost inevitable from time to time that you get disorder in prisons, so you construct buildings that reduce the effect of disorder as much as possible. Now we have buildings which are much stronger and much better controlled, where it will be easier to prevent any disturbance from spreading than it was in the old Strangeways.
>
> The physical treatment of prisoners is very important. Every cell now has a toilet and a washbasin, and therefore we no longer have the degrading process of slopping out. But in the end behaviour is more about relationships than about buildings, important though they are. With the new Strangeways the emphasis is on the relationships between staff and prisoners, prisoners and prisoners, and staff and staff. This has the potential to create a community that does not have within it the seeds of destruction that existed previously.

Noel agreed with the Governor. He stood in the new chapel, so beautifully replacing the old, and was deeply thankful for all that gave hope in the new Strangeways. The chapel is smaller, of course, and men are now frisked before attending a service or group as a matter of common practice. But it is a place filled with peace and a sense of the presence of the Holy Spirit. The area is multi-purpose. The communion rail and altar dais can be curtained off, the chairs turned and the room used for films, lectures, concerts or education. But as a chapel it is as lovely as any church in the land.

Noel crossed over the blue carpet and looked at the statue of the risen Christ hanging on the wall above the communion table. The arms were outstretched towards the people, the robes flowing. The old statue and cross had been destroyed in the fire during the riot. Norma and her friends from St Paul's Church, Kersal Moor in Salford, had given money to a fund they had begun and raised the £700 needed to replace it. Then they had gone out and bought this new one and donated it to the prison chapel. Noel looked at it now, with the tiny plaque underneath in memory of his beloved Norma.

In spite of Norma's early death Noel still believes in God's healing power today. He knows that even while Norma led meetings with him and talked and demonstrated God's healing power to others she was aware that she was dying slowly of the recurrence of cancer. But she had done this out of conviction that not only was God calling her to do it, but also that in the end the healing, wholeness and salvation of the inner man were even more important than the body's physical healing. To free people from the prisons of fear, insecurity, hurt, grief and guilt was the reason why Christ himself came to the world and bore the sins of the world on his shoulders by hanging on a tree and then rising from the dead on Easter Day.

At home Noel can see Norma's vision for their parish church gradually being fulfilled. Her picture of St Paul's, Kersal Moor, being like a 'stately and colourful galleon filled with church members pulling in people sinking beneath the waves all around them' is evident both in the church's present experiences and future plans. After his retirement in the winter of 1995 ideas are being shared for Noel to base himself at this church and, with a team of church members, become involved with helping parishes in need.

Now in the chapel he bowed his head for a few moments and remained quite still in front of the statue of the risen Christ. He remembered the previous spring when he had travelled to Buckingham Palace to receive the MBE. It was on the way home in the train that he had settled down in his seat, relaxed and begun to reflect upon all the turbulent events in these last few years of his life. Gradually everything had settled into a pattern in his mind. He had come to a new understanding, an acceptance, a sense of peace. He lingered on in the chapel for a few moments; then he turned, walked quietly back across the carpet, out through the door and away into the prison.

# *Epilogue*

## Buckingham Palace—9th March 1993

Noel walked up the steps into Buckingham Palace on this special day with Helen and Becky beside him. When they reached the top of the steps Noel had to go in through one door and his daughters went inside by a different entrance. They would be shown to the visitors' seats, while he was taken to a different room and shown, along with all the other people who were to receive Honours, what he had to do, and how to do it; when to step forward, what to say, and when to step back. It was like a rehearsal, all very professional and very well done. Once inside he found himself looking around at the wonderful portraits and pictures in the corridors. It seemed quite awesome to be in such surroundings, in among such people. Noel raised his chin slightly. *What am I doing here?* he thought, as he glanced at all the others gleaming in their best clothes. He looked down at his own suit which he had hired for the day. *It's not really me*, he thought, *to be dressed up like this and in with a crowd like this. One day I'll be going to see the King of kings, and I won't need to hire a suit then, and when I do see him my beloved partner Norma will be beside me. Only we'll no longer be man and wife but brother and sister in Christ.* He sat down and let his eyes scan the beautiful room. The pictures and furniture were glorious and he was proud to be there and to accept the MBE, not only for himself, but also on behalf of all those at Manchester Prison. There had been many heroes during the riot, and many were unsung. The staff and chaplaincy team had been marvellous—and a lot of the inmates had also shown tremendous courage in helping the prison staff. Yes, he was accepting this Honour on behalf of all those who had shown such courage.

As he looked round quietly he could not help thinking back to all the experiences that had brought him to Buckingham Palace. He could see now in his mind's eye the smoke and flames billowing out of the old Strangeways roof and through the tiny cell windows. He could remember the taunts, cat calls and slates hurled down from the roof as staff and prisoners ran the gauntlet to escape. He could remember the total devastation in the chapel, everything smashed, his Bible soaked and ruined. He remembered that first Tuesday where he was hurting so bitterly inside that he couldn't even talk to Norma about it. He had driven home for lunch and found Norma and Sister Dominic in the lounge; Sister Dominic, the little Roman Catholic nun who came in to take classes in the prison. She had brought some flowers for Norma and as soon as he arrived her first words were, 'Noel, you have experienced your crucifixion. You have seen your flock scattered all over the place, to all the prisons throughout the country. Your work seems to have fallen in around you. You have had your tears, and your heartache, and your anguish, and you are suffering. But Noel, God has got a glorious resurrection for you—a resurrection that is greater than you can ever imagine.' And with that he had burst into tears. Perhaps it was then that he had begun to experience something of the healing power of tears. When he had taken her back down to the convent in the car, he came out of the convent, sat in the car and just sobbed. Perhaps that was when God really began to deal with him. Her words had comforted him and stayed with him in the years since the riot.

He remembered the months after the riot, when he had first realised how ill Norma was and how he had guessed and understood why she did not tell him. He had been so angry with God, not for taking Norma so much sooner than he had expected, because he knew everyone had to die and they had been given the wonderful eighteen bonus years to see their daughters grow up; but because of her suffering and the indignities of her illness when he had known how much it meant to her to keep her dignity. How he had shouted at God as he drove to Christie Hospital and how Norma had known and loved him and teased him ever so gently. 'God has a new ministry for you. Why don't you let him give it to you?'

Noel sat very quietly in the ante-room at Buckingham Palace. All around him was subdued laughter and well-bred voices and best suits. He only thought of Norma; she would have loved being with him today. He realised now that in her death God had been bringing him through the valley, through the darkness, through the experience where everything was falling in around him. He knew now what grief was about, and why people can be angry when they lose a loved one. Now he could understand about prisons within the personality and within people's own characters. He knew because he had been in a prison like that. And slowly, slowly God had let him realise that the prison door was unlocked and he had stepped out into a new freedom, a new discovery of faith.

Soon it was time for him to be led forward to take his place in the sedate queue of people who waited with suppressed excitement for their turn to be presented to

Her Majesty. When Noel caught a glimpse of her and then went forward, he saw that she was a little woman and that she had a flowery dress on. He found himself thinking that she was somehow not quite what he had expected her to be. He had imagined her in the grandeur and glitter of a state occasion, but now he realised that she was a human being, just the same as he was, as everybody was; that human nature is the same the world over.

He stepped forward and bowed. The Queen shook his hand and said, 'Chaplain of Strangeways, that must be a difficult job.'

Noel looked at her and said, 'We have our moments, Ma'am.'

Then she pinned his decoration to his lapel and shook his hand again. And that was the end of the interview. Noel backed away from her and heard the orchestra on the balcony playing 'Moon River'. That was one of the songs Norma had enjoyed listening to; she had always associated its romance with their relationship.

As he went to his plush gilt chair to watch the others, Noel could not help remembering the officer, James, whom he had visited in hospital. How he had sat on by the man's bedside and found himself wondering if there was life after death at all.

As he had listened in silence to that life-after-death story, somehow his own faith had been rekindled. James had done something for him that day in hospital that the Queen, in all the pomp and ceremony of royalty, could never do for him. He would have to think about these things again. It was almost too much to take in at the present. He turned round, caught Helen's eye and smiled.

On the way back in the train that day Noel was thinking how Her Majesty the Queen in her generosity had welcomed him to Buckingham Palace and given him a memento that was very precious to him. He was a Canon of Manchester Cathedral, now an MBE and had also received a commendation for bravery from the Home Secretary. He was proud, pleased and humbled to have received these Honours from his country and to have met the Queen. But he had to admit that none of these things meant as much to him as Jesus Christ did. They meant nothing in comparison to the preciousness of being able to lead one person to the Lord and see their life transformed.

None of it meant anything in comparison to his rediscovery of the Lord Jesus Christ in a way that he had never known him before. Jesus had taught him how to weep, how to smile and laugh again; he had taught him how to be lonely, and how to adjust to loneliness; he had taught him how to return to him and cry out to him.

God was teaching him in his mercy and by the ruthlessness of his love, that all things did indeed work together for good to those who were called according to his purpose, and that the reason for God's sometimes inexplicable way was that Noel was being conformed into the image of God's Son, Jesus Christ. He leaned back in his seat as the train travelled on towards Manchester and closed his eyes for a moment. 'Thank you, Lord,' he said. And he knew himself to be a man at peace.

Noel retires as a prison chaplain at Strangeways on 31st December 1995. However, he is not anticipating a quieter life. He has been granted by the Bishop a licence within the diocese of Manchester, and will be working with the Director of Evangelism, Canon Wilfred Gash. As a Canon of Manchester Cathedral he will also be working with the Cathedral in a pastoral role. His services have been accepted as a weekly voluntary chaplain at the North Manchester Hospital. And of course he will continue to be a member of his local church, St Paul's, Kersal Moor.

# Sources

1. Noel's typed evidence as submitted and presented to the Woolf Enquiry (14th May 1990).
2. *The Observer* (8th April 1990).
3. *Church Times* (11th May 1990).
4. Many local papers from April–July 1990—useful mainly for pictures.
5. Noel's own recollections.
6. Video *Out of Darkness into Light*—John Whatmore/Media Services.
7. *Gatelodge*, Prison Officers' Magazine (June 1990).
8. Prison Service News (May 1990).
9. Norma's private journal.

# Special Edition Update

## Retirement – and a New Ministry

'God has got a new ministry to give you. Let him
give it to you.' (Norma's words to Noel.)

Noel woke up on the morning of the 31st December
1995. He stretched and then slowly pulled himself out
of bed. He had often wondered what he would feel like
on his very last day at work. Well now he knew. It was
a sad, flat feeling compounded by a twinge of anxiety
somewhere in the background. He caught sight of his
bedside clock. 'Better get moving,' he thought. It
wouldn't do to be late on his last morning at work.

So the daily routine took over: first the short drive
down the Bury New Road to Strangeways, then going
through security, and finally preparing for his last services in the prison chapel that morning. There was quite
a crowd of lads at the services and Noel spoke to each
one afterwards. He accompanied them back to their
cells and then went out of his way to visit several more
in their cells to say goodbye. After that he went round

1

and said goodbye to many of the staff he had worked with over the years. He managed it all with a cheery grin, a joke cracked and an anti-swearing tablet offered with a laugh. But when it was all over he decided to go back to the chapel and sit there on his own in the quietness for a while.

He stayed on for some time, head bowed and arms gently resting on the chair in front. Memories came flooding back, one mixing with another. Foremost was the memory of the riot, that terrible day when the whole place seemed to go up in flames. All the work he and the other chaplains and numerous helpers had done was just smashed to bits. While he had been trapped in the vestry with ten or so prisoners, other inmates with masks hiding jeering faces had pranced up on the roof, hurling down slates. The police in riot gear used their shields to shelter prisoners and staff alike as they hurried to run the gauntlet and escape to the waiting buses outside the gates. It had been awful. Later he had gone back into the chapel with the fire crew singing . . . until they had seen the blackened devastation in there and the song had died on their lips.

He remembered too the hundreds of men over the years who had come to services, the many who had asked for counselling, who had come to his Bible study and training groups, and those who had made a stand for Christianity both inside and outside prison. God's blessing had indeed touched and changed many lives.

Then there had been his slow and grievous realisation that Norma had entered her last illness. When eventually she told him, he realised he had already known it in his heart. After her death what he now recognised as a form of depression had set in, as he had struggled to learn how to live on his own and cope with himself in his loneliness.

As all these memories washed over him in the silence

of the chapel that last morning, Noel found himself being thankful to God for all that had taken place, even the very worst things. For in the end darkness had not overcome light, and the Faith had triumphed.

But how was he going to manage? All at once the doubt and anxiety he had recognised earlier on that morning surfaced in his mind. Yes indeed the past had seen victory, but what about the future? What was going to happen? How would he fill the long days? In a moment of revelation he saw how he had used the prison as a form of 'escape' in the years following Norma's death. The friendship and camaraderie of the staff and lads alike had kept him going, giving meaning and shape to his days. Now there would be none of that. Oh, he could pop in and see them, but it would not be the same. Not the same at all. He had joked often enough in recent weeks about being launched into the era of the bus pass and old-age pension, but now the old jokes did not seem quite so funny any more. What was he going to do?

Not only was he being assailed by doubts but fear was there too. He allowed himself to face this. A very real fear was pricking round the edges, as he stared at the reality of a lonely retirement. He slipped to his knees and buried his head in his hands. 'Oh, Lord, have mercy on me!' he cried. 'Oh, please, help me. I'm scared and vulnerable and getting older. And I don't know what I'm going to do! Please, help me. Please.'

In the days that followed he endeavoured to settle into the new way of life. He found himself constantly being tempted to look back in a not very helpful way. It was so easy to realise how much he missed the fellowship of the chaplain's team, and the friendship of staff, helpers and prison visitors. Most of all he missed the inmates and his early morning times of prayer with a few of them in the chapel. How they had prayed for him during the most difficult times. And he had prayed for them. It was easy to recall all this and compare it with his present rather aimless days.

One day as he was vacuuming the front room, always trying to keep it nice as Norma would have liked, he had a sudden flashback to when Norma had been in hospital. He had been sitting with her and holding her hand. Just before he left she had said, 'I'm ready to go home to the Lord, and God has got a new ministry to give you. Just *let* him give it to you.'

He turned off the Hoover automatically and gazed unseeing out of the window. He admired her courage and faith so much. But never until now had he really thought about this 'new ministry' that she had said God was going to give him. What did she mean, '*Let* God give it to you'? There wasn't very much new ministry about his life at present, he thought as he put the vacuum cleaner away and began to clear up his few dishes. But maybe that was because he was too busy looking back to his old ministry!

Unwillingly he recalled a favourite story he liked to use in sermons when he was preaching on the famous passage in Paul's letter to the Philippians: 'Forgetting those things which are behind and reaching forward to those things that are ahead, I press toward the goal for the prize of the upward call of God in Christ Jesus.'

He walked to the shelf and took down his old sermon notes. After a few moments he found the place:

In May 1954 Roger Bannister became the first man in history to run a mile in less than four minutes. Within two months John Landy beat his record by a second or two. Later that year the two met together for an historic race. As they moved into the last lap Landy held the lead. It really looked as if he might win. As they neared the finishing line he was haunted by the question,

'Where's Bannister?' And as he looked back to see where Bannister was, Bannister flashed past him and took the lead. Later on Landy said, 'If I hadn't looked back I would have won.'

Now Noel realised that perhaps this was the way God was answering his urgent cry for help from that morning of the 31st December. He had to learn how to understand himself and how to prepare for the future. He needed time to remember and think about those precious words of Norma's: *'Let him give you your new ministry.'* It was important for him to have this time to adjust and be willing to look forward again, trusting that God would lead him on. 'I'll try, Lord,' he said as he prayed quietly. 'I'll try to keep my eyes on Jesus and not look back in an unhelpful way. I'll try to keep going forward.' Perhaps that was going to be the way to live a successful retirement, he thought. So why not give it a go!

So it was that in January 1996, when the North Manchester Hospital invited him to become a part-time voluntary chaplain on Mondays and Thursdays and do ward visiting, he accepted at once. Noel found he quickly fitted into the team of full-time chaplains there and really enjoyed working with them. But when he was invited to join the staff permanently he decided to stay as a volunteer. 'When you get to my age,' he joked, 'you don't necessarily want to be on call at night!' However, he found himself being drawn into the tragedies and heartaches of the patients, as he sat beside different beds and talked and listened. He remembered a woman who had tried to make a joke about her crippling arthritis, and a young doctor who told Noel that he did the patients more good than the doctor did!

One day as he was visiting in a ward he heard a voice calling out, 'Noel! Noel!' Instantly he guessed this must be someone who had been in Strangeways. It was a sad story he heard. 'You see when I got out I got drunk one day and then I got knocked down by a car. And I admitted to myself that I could have been killed, entirely by my own fault.' He clung to Noel's arm and stared at him with agonised eyes. 'I could have been killed, but I know I'm not ready to die.' In the conversation that followed Noel explained to him how to accept Jesus as his Saviour.

Noel was encouraged by this and began to feel that God was putting his seal of approval on this hospital ministry. One day as he sat beside a woman who was facing an operation the following day, she asked him to pray with her. Afterwards she said, 'What does Jesus want of me?' Noel said to her, 'He wants you to give him your life.'

'But what does that mean?'

He replied, 'It means he's knocking at the door of your life at the moment. He said, "Behold I stand at the door and knock and if anyone will hear my voice and open the door I will come in."'

So she prayed with Noel again and asked the Lord Jesus to come into her life. She had her operation and made a good recovery. Once she had gone out of hospital she joined up with a church.

As Noel reflected on this encounter he began to see more clearly that God was giving him his new ministry. Yet even the 'high' moments of seeing people becoming Christians in hospital, and being welcomed onto the chaplaincy team, did not fill up the other five days of the week. Noel still missed the fellowship with the lads from the prison. He was still lonely.

It was around this time that he had a phone call from Keith Heywood of the Radcliffe Male Voice Choir, inviting him to join the second tenor group. 'I believe you're retired now and we're looking for some more tenors,'

Keith explained. It became a highlight on a Wednesday evening to go along to the rehearsals, join in the concerts, meet in the different churches and be involved with all the people through the music. It was a hobby, an interest and fun. Noel really enjoyed it. He had also made friends with Ron and Beryl Pipes, through Beryl's work as a lay reader in the prison. He was touched when Beryl told him that she had heard Norma giving a talk back in the 1980s and, as a result of that, Beryl had rededicated her life to the Lord. Many times Beryl and Ron invited Noel to join them on their caravan holidays, and after he had retired Noel felt able to accept and go all the way down to Christchurch in Dorset and stay a week at a time with them in the static caravan. The interest and their company and care meant a lot to him and all helped him to adjust to his new way of life in retirement. Then as Ron had an operation and a tumour removed from his brain, Noel felt he could in his turn help them at a difficult time in their lives.

As he reflected on the different ways his life was opening up, how Noel thanked God for the choir, for good friends like Ron and Beryl, and also for all the friends and acquaintances at St Paul's church. This had been Norma's local church and Noel was a worshipper there whenever he was at home on Sundays.

Suddenly he found himself in demand. *Light Through Prison Bars* was published late in 1995, and Noel found himself being invited to speak at services, meetings, dinners and Christian Viewpoint events, as he promoted this book. He travelled to Tonbridge, Walton-on-the-Naze and Grendon Prisons, up to Durham and then down to Devon and Somerset. 'Certainly the Senior Citizens Railcard is being fully used!' he joked to Beryl one day. 'Have Bible, will travel!' she laughed back.

Before, while he was working at Strangeways, he had not been able to accept many such invitations. He was always too busy and committed to running his classes and groups in the evenings. But now he was a free agent and beginning to find another part of this new ministry that Norma had spoken about. He was put in the *Manchester Who's Who* as an after-dinner speaker, and this led to so many invitations that in one year he had 246 speaking engagements.

One morning the phone rang in the hall. On the way to answer it he kicked a ball gently in the direction of Goldie, Ron and Beryl's little dog that he was looking after while they went out for the day. 'Come on Goldie!' he cried as he picked up the receiver. 'Fetch!' Then he said 'Hello' into the silence on the other end.

'Oh, good morning,' came the reply. 'I'm the secretary of the Association of Surveyors and Auctioneers and we wondered if you'd be free to come and speak to us at our annual dinner.'

For once Noel was nonplussed. 'Er . . . well, I know nothing about auctioneers and surveyors!'

'One of our members heard you speaking at a breakfast meeting recently and he's recommended you. So we'd like you to come along and share your story with us on the night. It's going to be at the Piccadilly Hotel.'

So Noel agreed, wondering even as he did so what he had let himself in for. He knew Piccadilly Gardens in the square at the top end of Market Street in Manchester. It was quite near the main railway station for the London trains. The hotel was a big concrete building of several storeys that towered above the square. It was expensive to stay there and Noel had never visited it before.

Eventually the evening of the dinner arrived. A friend dropped him by car outside, and Noel, in his dog collar, made his way through the main doors. Once inside he was shown to a big ballroom. There were about 300 people there, mostly men. Noel was invited to sit at the top table with the mayor and mayoress. He gazed around the room: all the men were in tuxedos and bow ties. 'My goodness,' he thought, 'I'm really out of my league in this place!' There was a toastmaster who introduced a harpist and then a flautist, who played while the meal progressed. Noel ate sparingly and, while appearing relaxed and confident, he found himself quelling worrying thoughts. Would his normal approach work with these sophisticated men? Whatever would they think of him singing them a song like he usually did? Noel's mind went blank. Then he made up his mind: he would have to carry on and say what he had prepared, and trust that everything would be all right.

As the dinner drew to a close the first speaker stood up. He was the captain of the Royal Yacht *Britannia* and he talked about his work on the boat, all the different people he had met over the years and all the ports and countries he had sailed to. Then the president of the society rose to his feet. He described the twelve months of his presidency, the cities he had visited, the people he had met, the money he had made and the property he had bought. Applause greeted this. Noel shifted in his seat. He felt more and more out of his depth.

Finally it was his turn. The toastmaster invited him to speak, and while the ballroom hushed Noel got to his feet. He opened his mouth and said, 'I've been listening to your president talking about all the money he's made and all the property he's got and I don't think I'm in that league!' There was polite laughter.

'But you know while he was talking I kept thinking of a chorus I heard years ago. It goes like this,' and he began to sing.

> *My home is in heaven just waiting for me*
> *And when I get there how happy I'll be.*
> *My home's in heaven, the rent is free*
> *For Jesus paid it on Calvary.*

Noel never got any further with his chorus. For as he sang, 'the rent is free . . .' all the men suddenly erupted with shouts and laughs. 'Never! Never! Never!' they cried, banging the tables, rocking on their chairs and roaring with laughter. 'No one ever gets a free rent from us!' Noel joined in the general merriment, while his mind raced along. Of course! These were auctioneers who sold property and who also rented it out. The idea of free rent was a huge joke to them.

At last the room calmed down and Noel, more relaxed now, spoke into the buzz of conversation and chuckles that were still simmering. This was the breakthrough and he knew they would listen now. So gradually silence spread as Noel told them about his experiences as a prison chaplain and about the riot. Eventually he got to the point when he knew he could speak to their hearts, asking: 'What is the priority in your life?' As an aside he joked, 'You know, with all the money your president's got, has nobody ever told him there's no pockets in the shroud? Maybe he ought to make a donation to the Chaplains' Fund!' A big cheer greeted this.

At last he had finished what he had to say and sat down. He knew he had tried to get across the message of God's love to these people and that was all anyone could do. To his surprise there was a scraping of chairs as the people in the audience got to their feet and gave him a standing ovation. It had never happened to him before and Noel grew quite pink with surprise, pleasure and embarrassment. Later the mayoress came and spoke to him privately and Noel had the privilege of being invited to pray with her.

Finally the evening drew to an end. The suitcase, which he had brought full of books to sell, was now empty. He chuckled to himself as he sped down the stairs to the foyer and the taxi home. It had been a wonderful experience and so worthwhile in more ways than one! And the money he had taken in book sales would be ploughed back into buying more to give away. Thrilled, delighted and thankful he relaxed in the black cab back home.

## New opportunities

The Bishop of Manchester had given Noel a licence to work as an evangelist in the diocese. The first mission he took after his retirement was at Middleton in north Manchester during the school holiday week at the end of May. This was a DIY effort with the congregations of St Leonard's, St Margaret's and St John's Thornham all sharing in the activities. Noel was the only visiting missioner. There were three holiday clubs for children and door-to-door visiting after prayer in the rectory.

One evening it was raining. Noel was partnered with a woman called Jane and together they knocked on the doors. At one house a lady opened the door and invited them in. The words and tears spilled out: 'This year,' she said, 'I've lost four loved ones and the grief has been so tremendous I've not known where to turn or what to do.'

They listened and talked. From his own experience of bereavements Noel empathised with what she was going through and eventually prayed earnestly with this woman that God would help and guide her. The following Sunday she and her daughter came to the service and afterwards she asked for counselling and then gave her life to Christ. Noel felt overwhelmed. This was something precious that was happening in the woman's life. And at the same time God was graciously blessing his own 'new ministry'.

The mission continued with music groups, a meeting at the local pub, a ladies' luncheon where 17 asked for counselling, and a dinner for 80 on the Friday evening.

So many wanted to talk about spiritual things, about the meaning of life and about God, that no one wanted to go home! It was after midnight when the owner of the hotel came and asked if they would mind leaving. The mission ended with an open-air meeting in Jubilee Park. Over 200 people came, many who had been contacted through visiting. At the end nine people committed their lives to the Lord.

After that Noel took missions in several places in the North West, including a weekend at Capernwray. At Bacup there was a special service for all those who had lost loved ones over the previous five years. Noel shared how God had brought him through the darkness of bereavement and how little by little he was regaining strength. One man who had lost his wife wept with Noel afterwards as they talked together about the hurt they had gone through over the loss of their loved ones. At the end of the service there was communion. Nineteen people who had been challenged by the service stayed afterwards for prayer in the side chapel.

Noel also travelled to various prisons and did missions there, sometimes with Alpha course teams: Gartree Prison, then to Grendon, Liverpool, Leeds, Hindley, Borstal at Buckley Hall and even back to Strangeways at Christmas 1998 to play the trumpet on Christmas morning. He was invited to Perth by Franklin Graham, son of Billy Graham, and shared in a festival there, visiting several prisons in the area and enjoying working alongside the Prison Fellowship Group.

One day Noel spotted an advertisement asking for chaplains to help with the police in Greater Manchester. He was immediately interested in applying, although doubtful at the same time. It would mean he had joined the 'opposition' so to speak, but he made enquiries anyway. Eventually he was interviewed and accepted as chaplain to the Greater Manchester Police Service. It was explained to him that the main area of his ministry would be to get to know the policemen and women and all that they were involved in. This would be particularly to support younger police officers who had to bring bad news to people's homes. If members of the public were killed in car accidents and other tragedies, a police officer could well need the support of someone like a chaplain who was not immediately involved. Noel was to work in the Bury division and the area was shared out between himself and the Roman Catholic priest.

'So now I "loiter with intent" at three police stations,' he liked to joke when giving talks.

One Friday, as he set out to visit his police stations, he found himself praying, 'Lord, give me some assurance that I'm doing the right thing here. I don't want to be in a place where I'm not doing what you would have me do.' When he arrived he went round and had a word with as many officers as he could, and then talked to the inspector. An officer who was on reception asked if he could have a talk to Noel. 'Surely,' said Noel and drew up a chair alongside him. Ross told Noel that in the past he had been a committed Christian, but that when his wife had died nine years before he had been angry and embittered, and had lost his faith. He stopped going to church, did not read his Bible and no longer prayed.

He stared blankly across the room. 'Spiritually I'm dead now,' he said. 'And anyway I remarried in the end and my new wife had no interest in spiritual things.'

Noel listened and then opened his mouth to speak. But each sentence was punctuated by interruptions. Ross had to break off each time to answer people's enquiries at the counter. So before Noel left him he said, 'Let me give you a book,' and he gave Ross a copy of *Light Through Prison Bars*. Noel looked at him straight in the eyes and said, 'There are some parts in this book that talk about how I dealt with my wife's death. I believe it'll help you.'

Ross took the book and turned it over in his hands. 'Thank you,' he said.

Later the following week, as Noel returned from Perth, there was a message on the answerphone from Ross. It was clear and to the point. 'I've read your book. I've been challenged, and for the first time in nine years I feel I've been set free from my own personal prison. I've committed my life to the Lord Jesus again. My wife and I have talked and she's taken a step of commitment too and we're both going to church again.'

Noel was filled with joy. How wonderful it was for Ross to find his way again; how wonderful that his wife was with him and keen to know more. And what a wonderful answer to his own prayer asking for assurance. He picked up the phone there and then and rang Ross. 'I'd like to come and see you, and talk and pray with you,' he said, and Ross agreed.

So the following Friday, Noel went to meet Ross. As he drove up the motorway he began to pray again, 'Lord, how am I going to get a chance to talk to him? There's always so many people about and inevitably so many interruptions.' When he arrived there was a different officer on the counter.

'I've just called in to see one of the staff,' said Noel.

'Oh well,' said the officer on duty, 'there's been a robbery down at the Halifax in Prestwich and most of the staff are out dealing with it.'

'Oh,' said Noel. 'Is Ross about by any chance?'

'Oh, yes, he's upstairs waiting for you.'

And so it was that Noel and Ross were able to talk for a good hour with no one disturbing them. With a twinkle in his eye, Noel said afterwards, 'Do you think the Lord allowed that robbery to take place just so the station would be really quiet and we could talk without any interruptions?' He chuckled and shook his head. He did not know at all, but one thing he did know was that it had all worked out perfectly and that he and Ross had been given the opportunity to share and pray together at just the right moment. Noel was so thankful. God was putting his seal of approval on the fact that he was in the right place and at the right time.

Another ongoing joy for Noel was his three daughters: Susan, Helen and Becky. Susan had a PhD and was now working as Senior Nursing Officer. Helen worked as a teacher and had just accepted a post as Deputy Head. Becky had finished her PhD and was now working in clinical psychology. He often saw them and even more frequently spoke to them on the phone.

After Christmas one year Helen and Becky came over on a Saturday in January to spend the day with him. 'We're just off into town to see if there's anything in the sales,' called Becky, 'but first I've got to go up to Grimshaw's [the garage] to get a new aerial for my car. Would you like to come along Dad?'

So the three of them set off and were soon crossing the garage forecourt. As they passed a row of cars parked there Noel noticed a red Corsa.

Helen said, 'Do you like that little Corsa, Dad?'

Noel looked at it briefly, 'Yes,' he said. 'It's very nice.'

Straight-faced, Helen said, 'Well, it's yours!'

Noel stopped dead. 'Mine! What do you mean, it's mine!'

The two girls began to grin. 'Well, we've all clubbed together and bought it for you!'

'Bought it! For me?'

'Yes, Dad. For you.'

'But what about my old Renault, the old banger with 120,000 miles on the clock?'

Helen laughed. 'That old thing! I got £700 for it!'

Noel was so overwhelmed that he could not speak for

a minute. His three daughters had decided to buy their old dad a nearly new car. He could hardly believe it. 'So I won't have to go around doing my preaching in a car that breaks down from time to time!'

'No, Dad, you won't,' said Helen.

'Exactly,' said Becky.

When they got into the reception area in the garage the man behind the counter began to do their paperwork. When he had finished he looked up at Noel and said, 'You know I've had husbands buying cars for their wives. I've had parents buying cars for their children. But this is the first time I've ever heard of children buying a car for their dad. They must love you!'

Later that evening when Helen and Becky had left in a whirl of laughter and carriers full of bargains they had bought at the sales in Manchester, Noel sat up late in the front room. The casual words of the garage man lingered in his mind. How he thanked God for the love of family and friends and of those who had stood by him over the years and encouraged him in the work he had endeavoured to do. He was now approaching his seventieth year and so far had had excellent health. The books had been a blessing to many people and he thanked God for that too. He thought about becoming 70 the following year and began to pray that God would still use him in his old age. Suddenly he started to chuckle as a joke slipped into the seriousness of his prayers. He had read it recently in a magazine. 'A man in his sixties is like a well-worn tyre. He's balding, he's bulging and he's losing his grip!'

'Well, Lord,' thought Noel, 'help me to hold on to my grip even though the other two things may apply!'

## The potential in everybody's life

Noel thought back to the day when he had been thrilled to be invited by Salford University to receive an honorary MA degree. After the students had received theirs, he had then received his. Afterwards he was given the opportunity to move forward and speak to over 400 students. 'An MA,' he joked, 'means that I am Marvellously Altered, although I haven't worked for it like you all have. Nevertheless I have worked for God for many, many years and I've been marvellously altered by the power of the Lord Jesus Christ. If God can take a lad like I was from the backstreets of Belfast, a lad who'd got nothing going for him, and use him, then he can use every one of you too. There's a potential in everyone's life. If only you can see and believe in that potential, then God will use you and bless you.'

They had listened to him as the hall went quiet and still.

This idea of the potential in everyone's life began to live with Noel and take a hold of him. One Christmas he was invited to Trinity School to give a talk. He had realised that today's young people did not have much faith in organised religion but still needed to find the purpose and meaning of their lives. They were hungry for that. So he decided to 'give it to them straight'. He arrived and was shown to the gym where 200 kids stared back at him.

'Did you know that statistics say 6 out of every 100 young people, both boys and girls, end up in jail!' he cried. 'So you'd better put your hands up, the 15 of you sitting here now who'll land up there. And I'll see you afterwards!'

There was total silence and a complete 200 per cent concentration.

'You'll need a power to help with the peer pressure

through drugs and drink,' he said. 'I was a kid from the tough streets of Belfast, selling newspapers for a few pence and getting into bad company with other young lads. Some of them ended up in trouble, borstal or prison. But somebody took the trouble to tell me about that power to change me and give even me the dynamic to live a useful and purposeful life.'

At the end of his talk five black boys, two white boys and two white girls came out and took a booklet.

'That took some courage,' Noel said to them. 'But God can use the potential in *your* lives.'

In May 2000 he went to Manchester Grammar School and took the Friday Christian Assembly. There were 200 plus boys waiting to hear him. He had planned a careful talk, but during the night before he had unexpectedly woken up and known immediately that he should simply give his testimony and talk about his experiences. Next morning he abandoned his prepared talk with a shrug, and as he stood before the boys he said, 'You know girls are showing boys up these days. Boys seem to have lost their confidence and self-esteem. But God can transform your lives and give you back your confidence . . .' And so he told them his story, so well known to him, yet fresh to them in the new millennium. Afterwards 32 boys came forward and took a booklet.

Noel wrote in the *Prison Service Journal* (114):

'As a prison chaplain for 25 years I met many men whose lives were barren and empty. Their situation appeared to give no hope either for the present or for the future. Yet in many cases, underneath that existence of chaos, crime and uselessness, there was a potential that needed to be awakened and developed.

My ministry to those empty lives, men who so often felt that there was no purpose in their living, was to say that if God could make something of my life then he could do the same in theirs.

The privilege and responsibility of prison chaplains is to find ways of penetrating the hard exterior of lives that have been blighted by heredity, environment and downright selfishness, in order to discover the untapped riches. We are not able to break through these barriers with argument or even psychoanalysis. Only the power of the Holy Spirit can reach into the deep recesses of damaged lives, bringing healing, forgiveness, peace, purpose and fulfilment.'

Now Noel is established in his 'new ministry', about which Norma had prophesied as she lay in her hospital bed, dying but at peace. And this ministry is ongoing.

One Saturday morning in the early summer of 2000, Noel got on the train at Piccadilly bound for London Euston. He was due to give a talk at three o'clock that afternoon to a group of volunteers who worked for an organisation called Christmas Letters to Prisoners. As he boarded the train he realised that it was crammed full and he was not going to be able to find a seat. 'What a crowd,' he thought and soon discovered they were all heading to watch Brazil playing England. He stood for a while but then decided to try another second-class compartment. There was one seat left and he sat down quickly and thankfully. The train sped on but at Watford was unaccountably held up. The passengers began to get restive. Noel looked at his watch. There was still time to spare but he wished the train would move.

Suddenly the woman next to him burst out with, 'I'm a Buddhist and I want to talk to someone about it!' Embarrassment rippled among the passengers. Everyone looked away, except Noel of course.

'Well, I'm a Christian!' he shouted back at her. 'And I want to talk about it!'

If anything the other passengers settled even more

rigidly in their seats and stared fixedly into their newspapers and books. But the woman concerned clutched Noel's arm.

'I'm an ordained priest in the Church of England,' he said clearly. 'Can I help you?'

She was a retired teacher and the words poured out: her father had died in Australia, she had not been able to go and see him before his death, and now how could she carry on? What could she do about her guilt?

Quietly Noel began to talk to her. He shared his experiences and his own bereavement. As she listened he glanced up. Just about everybody in the carriage was looking at him, newspapers forgotten, faces interested and relaxed. He smiled to himself, gave the lady a copy of his book and shook her hand.

At last the train pulled up into Euston. By now Noel knew he had no chance of getting to his meeting on time. As he dashed along down the escalator to the underground he chuckled. What a talk he now had to give to the volunteers! That was if they had waited to hear him of course!

Yet he need not have worried. They were all there when he arrived 40 minutes late, eager to hear what he had to tell them, laughing as he explained about his impromptu sermon on the train. Then they were quiet as he shared with them about the great and wonderful love of God: 'As he opens the doors of opportunities for us and allows us to share his message of love and power we can realise again and again that he is able to do exceedingly abundantly above all that we can ever ask or think.'

And so the day came to an end. He settled down for the night calmly and thankfully, glad about all his memories, at peace with Norma's prophecy to him about his 'new ministry' and looking forward to his future with his Lord and Saviour, Jesus Christ.